PORTRAIT OF MR. JUSTICE HOLMES BY CHARLES HOPKINSON

This portrait was completed shortly before Mr. Justice Holmes's retirement from the bench, and is reproduced through the courtesy of the artist

JUSTICE
OLIVER WENDELL HOLMES

A BIOGRAPHY BY

SILAS BENT

Garden City Publishing Company, Inc.

Garden City, New York

MANUFACTURED IN THE UNITED STATES OF AMERICA

To

JUDGE PORTER SIMS

and in memory of his father

JUDGE JAMES C. SIMS

Acknowledgments

To NUMEROUS former secretaries of Mr. Justice Holmes, to newspaper men in Washington, Boston and New York, I must express a sort of blanket appreciation. Each name would lose its significance were I to catalogue them all. To Mark Lauter, who assisted me in preparing for the chapters about the work of Judge Holmes on the Massachusetts bench, I am indebted. This work could not have been done without the sympathy and encouragement of James Henle, president of the Vanguard Press, or without the unfailing help of Elizabeth Sims Bent.

Introduction

TAINE MAINTAINED that the literature of a people expressed its social and political circumstance. The dogma of the French historian, philosopher and critic, now generally accepted, may be extended, with all its implications, to the life and opinions of Justice Oliver Wendell Holmes. That a span of more than ninety years, crowded with physical and intellectual adventure, rich in personal associations and friendships, registering and reacting upon a changing scene and a national economy which was revolutionized during that span, should be adequately described with all its adumbrations in a single volume, certainly is not to be expected; the most that has been done here is an attempt to reflect the environment and to some extent the inner life of a man already recognized as one of the very greatest this country has produced and nourished.

Mr. Justice Holmes once said, when questioned about certain details of his life: "Since 1865 there hasn't been any biographical detail." This was the sort of humorous overstatement which he would never have permitted to creep into the written word; but his admirers may well feel that even a smattering of biographical detail is superfluous in dealing with a mentality so opulently stored. To them no better reply is likely to be found than was written by the father of the Justice to Ellen Emerson, when the elder Oliver Wendell Holmes was completing a memorial sketch of Ralph Waldo Emerson. "Everybody," he told her, "wishes to know from the original sources of intimate knowledge those conditions of an extraordinary life which it shares with ordinary lives—with their own. Dr. Johnson's cups of tea and his hoarded orange-peel make him real to us, and we are thankful to Boswell for telling us about them. In a generation or two your father will be an ideal, tending to become as mystical as Buddha but for these human circumstances, which remind us that he was a man 'subject to like passions as we are,' as well as Elias, of whom the Apostle speaks. It will delight so many people to know these lesser circumstances of a great life that I can hardly bear to lose sight of any of them, except the infirmities which time brought with it; and even these were very much less painful to tell of than such as have fallen to the lot of many famous men."

From the infirmities which befell Emerson, Mr. Justice Holmes has been happily exempt. Although he lived much the longer, his mind, even after his ninetieth birthday, remains retentive, flashing and powerful. One is tempted to say that he goes back in lineal ascent to the "uninjurable man" of his beloved Plato, whom in his youth he had discussed with Emerson. His Civil War wounds and his unremitting toil afterward have left him unwearied and unimpaired.

Abraham Lincoln, complaining that biographies were false and misleading, wrote that the life of Burke he was reading "paints him as a perfect man, magnifies his perfections and suppresses his imperfections, describes the success of his hero in glowing term, never once hinting of his failures and blunders." Although diligent search has failed to uncover noteworthy "failures and blunders" in the career of Holmes, no attempt has been made here to magnify his perfections. This is not, praise be, an "authorized" biography. There is no need for its publishers to give heed to Lincoln's sardonic query: "Why do not book merchants and sellers have blank biographies on their shelves always ready for sale, so that when a man dies, if his heirs, children and friends wish to perpetuate the memory of the dead, they can purchase one already written, but with blanks, which they can fill up eloquently and grandly at pleasure?"

Mr. Justice Holmes, unassuming and by preference unadvertised, although he has had the just pride of a noble intellect, steered clear from the first, whenever he could, from contemporaneous encomiums or the prospect of posthumous applause. He has not feared to be made "the victim of a biographer", nor has he asked to be made a beneficiary. His strong sense of personal privacy and his dislike of publicity led him to feel that letters should remain the sole property of those who wrote them and those to whom they were addressed; very few of his letters, therefore, are incorporated in this book, and those only with his consent, reluctantly granted. A few of them had been published.

To lawyers, the philosophy of Oliver Wendell Holmes, his gift of clothing the law with romance and beauty, his splendid projection of a rational legal science, his poised and passionless justice, must always remain his monument. To those who consider also "those conditions of an extraordinary life which it shares with ordinary lives" the spiritual integrity of the man, his courage and courtesy and knightliness, and his relentless industry in the pursuit of his mental aspirations, will be the legends most clearly visible.

S. B.

Barnstable, Mass.
November 10, 1931.

Contents

Book I

YOUTH AND WARRIOR

Book II

JURIST AND THINKER

Book III

STATESMAN AND PHILOSOPHER

BOOK I

Youth and Warrior

CHAPTER 1

Facets of a Personality

NOT UNTIL Justice Oliver Wendell Holmes was nearing his ninety-first milestone did he find time to rest on his oars. He had spoken more than once with tolerant derision of man's impulse to repose, and he had even considered it for himself. At the age of eighty he had observed: "I always thought that when I got to be fourscore I could wrap up my life in a scroll, tie a pink ribbon around it, put it away in a drawer and go around doing the things I wanted to do. But I learned that when you have taken one trench there is always a new firing line beyond."

Thereafter, with ideas as his targets, he remained on the firing line, an active and relentless marksman. Although he was doing more work than any of his associates in the Supreme Court of the United States, rumors recurred that he would retire on account of age. These he repudiated periodically; he would quit work only when work ceased to be fun.

The father of the Justice, Doctor Oliver Wendell Holmes, affectionately known to his country as "The Autocrat of the Breakfast Table", had written in 1889 to John G. Whittier: "Here I am at your side among the octogenarians. At seventy we are objects of veneration, at eighty of curiosity, at ninety of wonder."[1] When the son reached ninety he was an object of wonder chiefly because of his preeminence here and abroad as a jurist, his profound influence on legal thought, and the brilliance of his retentive, flexible and richly caparisoned mind. His qualities as a statesman and philosopher, his lucidity and verbal power as a literary stylist, his tolerance and a wit "above the law", were widely acclaimed. Yet a certain tang and debonair vigor of the man escapes the public within whose ken he strides, quite without design. He does not seek attention. He dislikes publicity, does not read newspapers, and cannot be interviewed.

Herbert Spencer, a favorite author of the Justice in his young manhood and later, was one of thousands to propound the question, How to live? "Not how to live in the material sense only, but in the widest sense." The Justice, believing in "the joy of life become an end in itself",[2] may seem to the thoughtless recklessly pagan in his standards. The truth is that he has learned not to live in the material sense only. This was clear enough, if in no other way, from a comparison of his pictured face with the photographs of John D. Rockefeller which filled the rotogravure sections of the newspapers when the multimillionaire was ninety-two years old. Whatever Mr. Rockefeller's benefactions as a philanthropist in later years, he lived only in the material sense during his active career. The Justice has led a more adventurous life than the oil multimillionaire, but he has been heard to say that since 1865, when his services as a warrior were terminated, it had yielded no biographical detail, for after that his adventures were in the mental realm. "An Admirable Crichton in war as well as in jurisprudence",[3] he was called; and indeed he shares many of the qualities of that Scottish scholar and adventurer whose exploits with the sword and in letters won him an informal title subsequently picked up by Barrie as the title of a play. The snowy hair and mustachios of the Justice, his forehead and clean-cut cheeks and lean, aristocratic nose, his sparkling eyes and unquenchable spirit, bespeak the triumph of intellectual enterprise over the merely material.

The Justice has achieved a wisdom wider than the market place, deeper than any oil well. Perhaps he took early lessons in that first of all universites. Plato's *Academy*; for in his boyhood he became a critic and admirer of the Greek philosopher.[4] One is reminded of Walter Pater's envy of those who matriculated in this school. "For us in the modern world," he wrote, "with its conflicting claims, its entangled interests, distracted by so many sorrows, with so many preoccupations, so bewildering an experience, the problem of unity with ourselves, in blitheness and repose, is far harder than it was for the Greek within the simple terms of antique life."

MR. JUSTICE HOLMES

This is probably the most widely known picture of the great jurist

CAPTAIN OLIVER WENDELL HOLMES

This picture, taken in 1862, is reproduced through the courtesy of the
"Massachusetts Law Quarterly"

Yet Pater did not live to see the Twentieth Century. Life in his day compares with the complexities confronting Mr. Justice Holmes as algebra compares with calculus. Despite that difference, and despite the wistfulness of Pater's plaint, one senses that the Justice has managed to arrive at a unity within himself, "in blitheness and repose". In the common acceptance of the term he is not often in repose, but he has the repose Pater meant, which has its springs in self-mastery.

Stuart P. Sherman attributed to the professorial profession the vices of "pedantry, indolence, timidity and intellectual quietism, which is a euphemism for the sluggish tolerance of men without philosophic conviction or intellectual purpose." The observation is worth recalling because it sets forth with precision what Mr. Justice Holmes has escaped. Pedantry? Laziness? Fear? One smiles at the thought. Nor is there ever about him a trace of sluggishness, mental or physical.

In the field of jurisprudence, Mr. Justice Holmes is to be classified, if he can be classified, in the sociological rather than in the historical or the analytical school.[5] Yet he has been a profound student of the history of law, especially the common law, and of our Constitution. He attempted to harmonize established codes with current conditions; unwilling to concede that the nerveless hand of the past can shape the present, he regarded the law as an organic, growing institution, molded by—and not shaping—the social emergencies of the moment.[6] He adjusted law to life. Accepting the empirical character of life and thought, he held that intelligence is the causative and directive force of life, and that intelligence must be free, both in its operation and in its expression, if it is to enjoy to the full its creative powers. A passage of his, frequently quoted, comes to mind:

"When men have realized that time has upset many fighting faiths, they may come to believe even more than they believe the very foundations of their own conduct that the ultimate good desired is better

[5]

reached by free trade in ideas—that the best test of
truth is the power of the thought to get itself accepted
in the competition of the market, and that truth is the
only ground upon which their wishes safely can be
carried out. That, at any rate, is the theory of our
Constitution. It is an experiment, as all life is an experiment."[7]

In a letter to the Harvard Liberal Club, seldom quoted, the
Justice set forth in another metaphor his adherence to the principle of freedom in ideas and their expression. "With efferves-
cing opinions," he wrote, "the quickest way to let them get flat,
as with the not yet forgotten champagnes, is to let them get exposed to the air."[8] Presumably ideas animated by life and truth
would not prove flat, stale and unprofitable. But the Justice
manifests a scientific caution in approaching truth, or discussing
its approximation. "The truth to me," he said once, "is what I
can't help but believe; but I do not suppose that my can't-helps
are compulsory for the universe."

So far as "what lawyers call law" is concerned, Mr. Justice
Holmes accepts the conception of Austin, that law is a command
of a political superior—in Austin's day a monarch—to an inferior; in this United States it is the command of the politically
superior State or Federal Government to each of the units who
make up its organization of control, as well as to those who have
not the right to vote. As a legal philosopher, however, the Justice has evinced time and again a reluctance to accept the Austinian definition; he thinks it too constricted and limited.
Austin, for example, held that the decisions and rules laid down
by courts were representative of the monarch, the political superior, and so were law; but that the mores of a people were not
law until the courts approved and affirmed them officially. Mr.
Justice Holmes accepted custom and convention as a sort of law
in themselves, and so treated them in his decisions. When he
was lecturing at Harvard, some six years after his graduation
from the law school there in 1866, he set forth in the *American*

Law Review, of which he was editor, a criticism of the Austinian theory in these words:

"Austin said, following Heineccius (Recitationes, 72), that custom only became law by tacit consent of the sovereign manifested by its adoption by the courts; and that before its adoption it was only a motive for decision, as a doctrine of political economy, or the political aspirations of the judge, or his gout, or the blandishments of the emperor's wife might have been. But it is clear that in many cases custom and mercantile usage have had as much compulsory power as law could have, in spite of prohibitory statutes; and as for their being only motives for decision until adopted, what more is the decision which adopts them as to any future decision? What more indeed is a statute; and in what other sense law, than that we believe that the motive which we think that it offers to the judges will prevail, and will induce them to decide a certain case in a certain way, and so shape our conduct on that anticipation? A precedent may not be followed; a statute may be emptied of its contents by construction; or may be repealed without a saving clause after we have acted on it; but we expect the reverse, and if our expectations come true, we say that we have been subject to law in the matter in hand. It must be remembered, as is clear from numerous instances of judicial interpretation of statutes in England and of constitutions in this country, that in a civilized state it is not the will of the sovereign that makes lawyers' law, even when that is its source, but what a body of subjects, namely, the judges, by whom it is enforced, *say* is his will. The judges have other motives for decision, outside their own arbitrary will, beside the commands of their sovereign. And whether those other motives are, or are not, equally compulsory, is immaterial if they are sufficiently likely to prevail to afford a ground for prediction. The only question for the lawyer is, how will the judges act? Any motive for their action, be it constitution, statute, custom or precedent, which can be relied upon as likely in the generality of cases to prevail, is worthy of consideration as one of the sources of law, in a treatise of jurisprudence."[9]

Even at the age of thirty-one the future Justice was striking out for himself and was saying things, as in the passage quoted, calculated to shock those of his contemporaries—and this included practically all of his contemporaries—who dealt with the law as a rigid and formalized institution. He gave due weight to precedent, but he did not regard it as sacred. All the motives influencing a court's decision he regarded as more than mere factors in the law, for he accepted them as law.

And the Justice does not accept the theory, conspicuously advocated by Rousseau, that there are "natural rights" which mankind enjoys.[10] We have only such rights as we can enforce; that, although the Justice has never put it in those words, appears to be his attitude. In all society, he says, rights arise from the obvious need of forbearance and tolerance, since mankind lives in communities. But man has no natural or residuary right to live in a community. He is enabled to live there only by conforming to the tacit rules formulated for deportment. Writing for the *Harvard Law Review,* the Justice admitted a "transcendental basis" in beliefs and wishes, because they are adopted arbitrarily. But if men live together, that is, in communities or in a society, further conditions are imposed. We can live only on the terms imposed by those conditions. These he regards as compulsions, against which no "natural" right can prevail.

Regarded by some as an aged "survivor" of another era, the Justice in truth keeps aggressively abreast of the times. His approach to the law is thus better than the approach or attitude of judges who have let themselves live in the past and get out of tune with the present, or who fail to note the straws in the wind which indicate the future. Although he would object vigorously to being called a reformer, he has been a reformer of the established postures of lawyers and jurists. "Law is the business to which my life is devoted," he has said, "and I should show less than devotion if I did not do what in me lies to improve it, and when I perceive what seems to me the ideal of its future, if I hesitated to point it out and press toward it with all my heart." He has pressed toward that goal by adapting the rules of law to the practical necessities of life. He likes to say·that he practices, toward such rules, an "enlightened skepticism". In the first chapter of his first book, *The Common Law,* he noted that "the life of the law has not been logic; it has been experience."

In some quarters there is a disposition to regard the Supreme Court as a sacrosanct tribunal exempt from mortal comment or criticism. It is the only institution in the United States which commands such respect and admiration that to speak of it with levity or contumely is to subject oneself, in almost any company, to reproof and ridicule. And it is the only institution, probably, in which each member may exercise to the full his personal powers. Mr. Justice Holmes achieved his eminence in the legal world, here and abroad, by the unhampered exercise of his personal powers. Yet it is difficult to see why the notion should prevail that the Court is beyond criticism. Few sound lawyers think so; and one would think that Justice David J. Brewer, in his speech on "Government by Injunction", on Lincoln's Birthday in 1898, would have dispelled that illusion when he said:

> "It is a mistake to suppose that the Supreme Court is either honored or helped by being spoken of as beyond criticism. On the contrary, the life and character of its Justices should be the object of constant watchfulness by all, and its judgments subject to the freest criticism. The time is past in the history of the world when any living man or body of men can be set on a pedestal and decorated with a halo. True, many criti-

[9]

cisms may be, like their authors, devoid of taste, but
better all sorts of criticism than no criticism at all.
The moving waters are full of life and health; only in
the stagnant waters is stagnation and death."

Mr. Justice Holmes himself might have written the last few
lines of that paragraph; let us say the last two sentences. He was
not yet a member of the Court when the words were spoken,
but doubtless concurred heartily in them. His own character,
achievements and intellect combine to shield him from malicious invective, but there were times when his attitudes and his
pronouncements met with ill-favor here or there. Thus in the
Massachusetts Law Quarterly,[11] Frank W. Grinnell, secretary of
the State Bar Association, and managing editor of the publication, good-naturedly reproved the aptitude of the Justice in
epigram, and took him to task on the score of the fact, now accepted commonly enough, that Judges themselves often make
law rather than merely "finding" it. (It is a fact which Mr. Justice Holmes has stated on his own account more than once.) Mr.
Grinnell quoted an "epigram" of the Justice in the case of the
Southern Pacific Company against Jensen: "I recognize without hesitation that Judges must and do legislate, but they do so
interstitially; they are confined from molar to molecular mo-
tions."[12] Mr. Grinnell thought this "really somewhat out of
place",[13] and made the point that the community as a whole,
and lawyers themselves, as advisers and in settling cases out of
court, both found and made law. The phrase, "judicial legislation", he regarded as somewhat misleading slang.

In the same issue of the quarterly was published "A Study of
the Judicial Approach to Constitutional Questions", in particular the police power, by Forney Johnston, who observed that
Mr. Justice Holmes had excluded his personal reactions to certain legislation by "substituting that of a composite citizen of
his own manufacture—a sort of hypothetical man-in-the-street".

Mr. Johnston wanted to know whether the judgments being
rendered by the Supreme Court were "the individual judg-

ments of the learned justices or judgments of a *poltergeist* like
the good demon who kept Socrates advised". He thought the
method disconcerting, uncharted and unsatisfactory. Avowing
a sincere admiration for the intellect and nobility of character
of the Justice, Mr. Johnston expressed a fear that the Court had
"been drifting toward the philosophy of Mr. Justice Holmes,
which is in no sense juristic".[14] The Justice he described as "a
veteran and distinguished Crusader"; and if the Justice saw the
article, which doubtless he did see, that phrase probably an-
noyed him more than any other in it, for certainly he has never
set himself up in that capacity. Mr. Johnston did indeed say that
the Holmes "thoughts, nobly and subtly stated, advanced by
one of the foremost jurists of the age, of necessity have exerted
a profound impression."

It has seemed worth while to sketch these criticisms, in part
because of the character and locale of the periodical in which
they appeared, in part because they raise certain questions
which must be considered. Far from being a veteran crusader,
is Mr. Justice Holmes even to be considered a Liberal, and if so,
of what stripe? Has he exerted a profound influence? Is the
Court "drifting" to his view?

More than once the barbed wit of Mr. Justice Holmes has
punctured the reformer posture. Bred and reared in a hotbed
of reformers, where were initiated, among other "blue-nose"
movements, those for emancipation of the Negro, for woman's
suffrage and for prohibition; surrounded by those attitudes, disciplines and moral fervors commonly associated with Puritanism, the humor of the Justice has served him as a buckler, and
his philosophy (much as Aristotle, at Philip's direction, served
Alexander) has been a guide and preceptor. Surely his objection
to being called a crusader is well taken.

The case for liberalism is a little better. Scores of his written
opinions, both in dissent and for the majority, might be cited
in support of his staunch stand for freedom of opinion and of
speech, in many cases for the right of States to meet their own

legislative problems in their own way, even though sometimes he thought the statute itself ill-advised—a stand which would have delighted any Jeffersonian heart. He has been the outspoken champion again and again of the rights of labor as against predatory exploitation; but he has been just as liberal toward capital and property rights, as we shall see. It would be precarious to class him as a State's rights man. He has been candid in rebuking socialism, and equally candid in rebuking those who are afraid of socialists. He is not to be corseted, indeed, within the formula of any economic, political or social sect. In economics, for that matter, he is conventional, and in apparent accord with the main tenets of Ricardo, Adam Smith and the Justice's friend, John Stuart Mill.

The Justice has no abracadabra of relief or reform. Openminded, acutely aware of changing social conditions, he thinks of the law as a loom, and he is ready, like a weaver, to adapt ancient legalisms to the warp and woof of "moderns". Hear his own words:

> "When I think thus of the law, I see a princess mightier than she who once wrought at Bayeux, eternally weaving into her web dim figures of the everlengthening past—figures too dim to be noticed by the idle, too symbolic to be interpreted except by her pupils, but to the discerning eye disclosing every painful step and every world-shaking contest by which mankind has fought and worked its way from savage isolation to organic social life."[15]

Mr. Justice Holmes does not regard the law as the place for an artist or a poet, although he himself has exhibited attributes compatible with either of these creative activities. "The law," he says, "is the calling of thinkers."[16]

A professor of law once spoke of the Justice as "a master of dialectics".[17] This may have been a little irritating to those who thought of the word "dialectician" as a term of reproach. Perhaps it was not so construed by the professor; but there sprang instantly into the minds of admirers, in all likelihood, sayings of the Justice which served to refute the imputation. Prevailing moral and political theories, the necessities of the moment, even the personal prejudices which judges share with their fellows, he has said, "have a good deal more to do than the syllogism in determining the rules by which men should be governed." And again, in that very paragraph: "Historic continuity with the past is not a duty, it is only a necessity."[18]

Only a necessity!

In that phrase may lie the deep-rooted liberalism of Mr. Justice Holmes, which refuses to accept a mere necessity as a compulsory guide, whether it appear in day-to-day life or in the law. It is a little difficult, indeed, to classify him as a liberal, in the common sense of that term; certainly he is no professional liberal. His tolerance does not stop with labor, for example, nor is he the champion of the underdog. In his attitude toward capital and toward property rights he is as fair-minded as in his attitude toward workers.[19] If labor has the right to combine in unions, then Mr. Justice Holmes thinks capital should have a right to form combinations, so long as the combinations do not violate the kind of evils—not the specific evils—which the Founding Fathers intended to avert or cure through the Constitution. He said, after ascending the Supreme Bench, that property rights would be secure "so long as this Court is here".

The professional liberal, who is notoriously illiberal at certain points of the compass, denies to capital and to property practically all rights; and the professional liberal has found occasion more than once to berate the Justice for his far-spreading tolerance.

Often Mr. Justice Holmes has been an innovator. He is credited with having originated the present practice of treating torts as a separate branch; his book, *The Common Law*, published in 1881, is still regarded after half a century as a classic; eight years earlier he had edited the twelfth edition of Kent's *Commentaries*, with many voluminous notes, and that edition is even now preferred by many lawyers; he has warred always for a greater flexibility both of the law and of the Constitution; he has said that he knows of no Constitutional principle to prevent the Supreme Court from reversing itself; he has added new areas for the exercise of the police power,[20] and he has attempted to reorganize the method of interpreting the Constitution rather than seeking to change the instrument itself.

There can be no quantitative audit of such an influence. It is too pervasive and subtle to be measured with a yardstick. It is more apparent among young attorneys and students in law colleges than among elderly practitioners of the law, and will affect the bench of the next generation even more than the Judges of this.

Although Mr. Justice Holmes knew Emerson personally and profited from the acquaintance, not this but the Civil War was his greatest moral experience. There was a job to be done, and at first it was disconcerting to this young blade of a patrician New England family, an intimate of the top-loftiest members of that close corporation which was Back Bay society, to find that some fellow from the woods around Cambridge, of whom no one had ever heard, could do the job better than he. It put him in his place. It chastened him. Although spiritually he had never accepted transcendentalism, and had never been the heir of his Puritan forefathers, he recognized the value of this deflating moral discipline. More, he wrested from it the faith of the soldier, the faith which sent him back again and again to face the artillery of the enemy.

Five times the young volunteer was wounded, thrice gravely. A bullet went through his breast at Ball's Bluff, a bullet through his neck at Antietam, and a ball shattered a heel at Fredericksburg. The Twentieth Massachusetts, to which he was assigned, known as "the Harvard Regiment", was fifth in all the Army of the Potomac in its percentage of losses. Nothing else in life so marked the younger Oliver Wendell Holmes as those years. They convinced him beyond peradventure that struggle is the destiny of man on earth, and bred in him a conviction that the dangerous life is the best. "Men carry their signatures upon their persons,"[21] he said; he did not mean it so, but his signature is writ large in his battle scars.

Of heroic proportions, physically and intellectually and spiritually, Mr. Justice Holmes came, partly as a result of his war experience, to say that "the deepest cause we have to love our country" is "that instinct, that spark, that makes the American unable to meet his fellow-man otherwise than simply as a man, eye to eye, hand to hand, and foot to foot, wrestling naked on the sand".[22] Never was aristocrat less class-conscious. But a flash of his blue-gray eyes, a touch of skepticism and of gentle malice, an aloofness, prompted the saying that he was in lineal descent from the Stoic philosophers.

Even so, no one ever found in the Justice quite that sternness, that austerity nor that arrogant pride which Zeno taught his disciples on the "Painted Porch" in the Agora at Athens. Nor, despite his unshaken loyalty to the rocks and barberry bushes of his New England, did one sense in him that city-state pride which characterized the ancient Greeks. Yet Mr. Justice Holmes is more American than most of his contemporaries, even though he declined in his young manhood to read newspapers and has stuck to that resolution. He once gave that abstinence as an explanation of the fact that he had never been carried away in any of the recurrent political and social and emotional tides which have swept periodically across the United States since the Civil War. He has kept his head clear, but he has not always escaped the impact of these forces. Out for a walk in the spring of 1919, for example, he saw with a little intake of breath that the flowers were in bloom. In a moment he knew—the World War was over. For years, although he had read no communiqués, no battle stories, no casualty lists, the wells of that naïve wonder and delight, that response to the simple beauties of nature, had dried up in him.

An omnivorous reader, Mr. Justice Holmes nowhere displays the catholicity of his mental life more clearly than on the high-roads and in the byways of literature. For years, certainly through 1904, he listed all the books he read. He entertained a notion that no book was quite finished until he had set down the title and author, perhaps with a marginal notation. It was as though a marksman were notching his gun. No notion can be given here of the range of these adventurings; but it may as well be said now as later that he has enjoyed vastly such books as *Nize Baby, Gentlemen Prefer Blondes, Poems in Praise of Practically Nothing*, detective stories and French novels. His weakness for detective stories is such that he has had to ration himself. His fondness for French fiction is such that once, when he told a portrait painter that he could have but an hour for a sitting, Mrs. Holmes interrupted with: "Take as much time as you need; he only wants to get away to one of those naughty French novels."

On another occasion, while a Judge of the Supreme Judicial Court of Massachusetts, when he found the long-winded speeches of the lawyers especially trying, he advised them gravely to take a course of reading risqué books, that they might learn to say things by innuendo.

And to the Justice there is significance in Samuel Hoffenstein's jingling comment on red-blooded men and their opposite; that although the latter might have chests hairless and flat,

> "There's something underneath the hat
> Of such a man—a kind of demon
> That lets him boss ten thousand he-men."

No more need be said of the lighter literary diet of one who is acclaimed the chief ornament of the Supreme Court. Nor can much be told of his more weighty fare, so vast is the menu. As the Justice approached ninety he re-read Horace and the Greek classics; he had been inflamed in his youth by Ruskin, and re-read him, too, only to find that Ruskin had worn thin while Emerson was still full-bodied. He admires Proust, Gabriel Tarde and Jean Henri Fabre; he is the intellectual familiar of Herbert Spencer (whose "social statics" he once said in an opinion "should not be written into the Fourteenth Amendment of the Constitution"), of Darwin, Pepys, De Quincey, Wordsworth, Walpole. Of Hemingway he wrote to Owen Wister:

> "There is something quite remarkable about the author. . . . It is singular. An account of eating and drinking with a lot of fornication accompanied by conversation on the lowest level, with some slight intelligence but no ideas, and nothing else—and yet it seems a slice of life, and you are not bored with details of an ordinary day.
>
> "It reminds me of a reflection that I often make on how large a part of the time and thoughts of even the best of us are taken up by animal wants. . . . And I sometimes say that if a man contributes neither thought nor beauty to life—as is the case with the majority—I would let Malthus loose on him. But then this lad could write this book, and it must be a work of art. It can't be an accident and naiveté. So let him survive—but as you promised he would, let him leave his garbage."[23]

The allusion to Malthus reminds me parenthetically that Holmes in his college days was so stricken with the Malthusian theory that he thought it should be written in letters of fire on the heavens. "This fellow," he said to himself, "has stuck a sword into the very bowels of the principle of population." But he told a visitor, nearly three-quarters of a century later, that he observed the principle of population still walking jauntily about, apparently not at all discommoded by the sword in its vitals.

At seventy the Justice wrote to Wister, as recorded in *Roosevelt: The Story of a Friendship,* that he was having very little literature that winter. "One of my favorite paradoxes," he noted, "is that everything is dead in twenty-five (or fifty) years. The author no longer says to you what he means to say. If he is original his new truths have been developed in improved form —his errors exploded. If he is not a philosopher but an artist the emotional emphasis has changed. But for all that a great man is discernible as great. And the bottom feelings don't change even if the objects of them do. I found the intensity of Dante's spiritual rapture so thrilling and absorbing that I could think of little else, and the song of his words is divine. Shakespeare will say a few words now and then that seem the beginning of the road to Paradise ('In Belmont lives a Lady' and so forth). But Dante does it every twenty lines, and he carries you there, too. . . . He weeps for he is still in Purgatory, but he is a poet and a troubadour and he goes singing through his tears. . . . However, I must leave a little room for Rabelais. . . . I read the last two books. What temperament, what gusto! Everything beginning to hum, like culture in Chicago.—And what a seed book, how many germs of Swift, Sterne, perhaps even Thackeray. . . ."[24]

This allusion to Rabelais inevitably brings to mind a review Judge Learned Hand of the United States District Court wrote of the Holmes *Collected Legal Papers* for the *Political Science Quarterly*. After praising the speeches and essays generously—and deservedly—Judge Hand wrote:

"Life must be viewed *sub specie Puritanica*. Man is born to strive, perhaps to lose, but the wages of the great-hearted are secure, and they know it. Let them be at peace, if they will only fight manfully. These speeches do indeed teach the strenuous life. Am I only a weakling, or will others too miss in this the note of something more precious than 'the cold passion of the Puritan'? They say the soul of Rabelais roams the earth gathering spirits for the Abbey of Theleme, those who are gay, nimble, courteous, feat, witty, amorous, simple, courtly, kind, pleasing, happy, genial, wise, humble, tolerant, joyous. Now the initiated tell us that among these there is none he has more certainly chosen than the Captain of Antietam, young then and young now. Rabelais was indeed not a presentable person at a bar association or commencement exercises, but suppose he had rudely shouldered himself in once or twice. They would have been scandalized, and properly, too, and yet, and yet—"[25]

The Rabelaisian attributes which Judge Hand smilingly holds Mr. Justice Holmes to manifest might be thought to have cropped out in certain of his dramatic predilections. He used to attend a burlesque house in Washington; and one evening, when the show was a little rawer than usual, which is saying a great deal, he turned to the man on his right, a stranger, and ejaculated: "I thank God I am a man of low tastes."

On another occasion he said that Judges were given to naiveté, and needed a touch of Mephistopheles. Possibly he perceived just that touch in Justice John Marshall Harlan—who died in 1911—of whom Mr. Justice Holmes was fond when they were associated on the Supreme Bench. "I do not venture to hope," he once confided to a friend, "that Harlan and I will ever agree in an opinion, but he has a place in my heart. He is the last of the tobacco-spittin' judges."

Holmes himself is no tobacco chewer. During the Civil War he took pride in blackening a short clay pipe, but afterward he found this a bit too strong for his palate. For a while he smoked cigarettes. "I thought they made me cough," he said, "and I still think they are frivolous." So he turned to cigars.

As for intoxicants, the Justice in his later years has congratulated himself that he has "a rational constitution." He says that when he was young and could absorb liquor, he liked it, but that when he grew old and couldn't stand it, he really didn't care for it. His youthful preference, however, was not for "hard" liquors, but for champagnes.

That touch of Mephistopheles, or, if one prefers, of Rabelais, is sometimes in evidence when the Justice is reading his opinions in the Supreme Court. Occasionally he deviates from the printed page upon which the Court has agreed, to interject witty or ironic epigrams of his own. No stenographic record is made on "decision days", so there is no authority to cite on what he has said. A Washington correspondent,[26] who has "covered" the Court for years for a press association, heard the Justice give the majority opinion in the Nixon case from Texas, involving a statute excluding Negroes from Democratic primaries. The Court nullified the law, and the correspondent, who was listening from a distance of perhaps ten feet, was sure the opinion contained some sweeping commentaries on the conduct of primaries, virtually reversing the earlier Newberry decision that primaries could not be regulated by the Federal Government. But when he got a copy of the Court's decision a few minutes later he found to his mortification that the broad remarks of Mr. Justice Holmes were not there.

This was an experience to which the Court reporters became accustomed in time; for the Justice often interlarded his opinions with conversational asides—to the whole courtroom. Others on the bench seldom, if ever, did so. Sometimes a certain elfin gaiety has its way with Mr. Justice Holmes.

There are those who say that Mr. Justice Holmes was in his proper sphere for other than legal reasons when he went to the Supreme Court; that he is an American aristocrat, and the Court is an aristocratic institution superimposed upon a country which professes to be democratic.[27] There are moments when the members of the Court do exercise statesmanlike and legislative functions, so that in the strict etymological sense of the word we have a thinly operating super-government of the few; but this is not true in its essence. Presidents are sent to the White House on action of the whole electorate, Senators by their States, Representatives by their Congressional districts; but members of the Court represent the whole country, protecting minorities against majorities, executives against legislators, and lawmakers against executive tyranny. In a deep sense the Supreme Court is regarded by some as the most democratic body we have.

It may be well here to dispel another illusion, somewhat widely entertained, that Mr. Justice Holmes was "The Great

Dissenter". In part this fallacy gained ground because of the striking nature and phrasing of his dissents, which can be read and understood with ease by laymen. One need only turn to the record of Justice Samuel Freeman Miller, a Kentuckian appointed by Lincoln, who had served twenty-eight years when he died in 1890.[28] In that time he dissented about one time in five. Mr. Justice Holmes, in a similar period, dissented about one time in ten. As a dissonant voice in the Court he was not half so loud as Mr. Justice Miller. In concord and agreement he was twice as consistent.[29] Other examples of dissenters, though not so striking, could be cited.

The last decision Mr. Justice Holmes read in the Supreme Court was not in dissent, but expressed the opinion of the majority. On Monday, January 11, 1932, it was noted by spectators that the Chief Justice assisted his associate to his seat behind the bench, and that the venerable Justice seemed somewhat feebler than usual. But his voice was clear, and the opinion he read was as luminous and as cogent as was his wont. On the following afternoon, as a court attendant was helping him with his overcoat, he said casually: "I won't be in tomorrow."

The attendant supposed that the Justice intended to rest for a day or two. He did not guess that a resignation was already in the hands of President Herbert Hoover. It was characteristic of Mr. Justice Holmes that he should be thus oblique and matter-of-fact about his retirement; he disliked having a "fuss" made over him, and he practiced a New England reticence in regard to personal emotion. He had told the President in his letter that "the time has come and I bow to the inevitable." That was a concession to the weight of years and a confession of his failing health.

"I know of no American retiring from public service," said the President, "with such a sense of affection and devotion of the whole people."

Chief Justice Charles Evans Hughes and the other members of the Court united in a letter expressing to their associate their sense of loss at his resignation, terminating a judicial service of "unique distinction in uninterrupted effectiveness and exceptional quality".

"Your profound learning and philosophic outlook," they said, "have found expression in opinions which have become classics, enriching the literature of the law, as well as its substance. . . . While we are losing the privilege of daily companionship, the most precious memories of your unfailing kindliness and generous nature abide with us, and these memories will ever be one of the choicest traditions of the court."

"For such little time as may be left to me," Mr. Justice Holmes replied to this glowing letter, "I shall treasure it as adding gold to the sunset."

So indelibly had the Justice impressed his thought and character on American jurisprudence that his figure, it was widely felt and said, must continue to exercise its influence on the Bench he was quitting. "This is how to stop," said Walter Lippmann in the *Herald Tribune,* "with every power used to the full, like an army resting, its powder gone but with all its flags flying. Here is the heroic life complete. . . ."

These brief glimpses of a diverse and richly endowed personality do all too little justice, it is to be feared, to the Holmes prestige in this and other countries; and they may have been inadequate in depicting a nature which delighted as vigorously in scaling the Swiss Alps as in mounting intellectual peaks. Let them serve for the time as a bowing acquaintance with the only American jurist whose name is commonly associated in eminence with the name of Chief Justice John Marshall.

CHAPTER 2

His Father

A CERTAIN IRONY attaches now to a playful letter written to a good friend by Dr. Oliver Wendell Holmes, then a fairly successful young physician in Boston, about his first-born. He confided that there was "a second edition of your old acquaintance, an o. w. h.", making the initials very small. Dr. Holmes was then thirty-three, for this was in December of 1842, and the infant was twenty months old. The father vowed that he was "gradually depositing the turbid particles of juvenility—not sitting up quite so late—drinking, singing, smoking in a more subdued vein, but on the whole cheerful and comfortable".

In the following year the young physician became a benefactor of mankind by publishing, somewhat obscurely, his essay on "The Contagiousness of Puerperal Fever", an original and valuable contribution to medical lore. It was irritating to the profession because it was logical, and logic was neither taught nor practiced in the medical schools of that day. The two leading obstetricians of this country took the upstart abusively to task. Undismayed and unruffled, Dr. Holmes republished the essay with an introductory note in which he said: "There is no epithet in the vocabulary of slight and sarcasm that can reach my personal sensibilities in such a controversy."[1] And it was not long before his revolutionary findings were saving the lives of thousands of mothers and infants.

Possibly this was the greatest contribution the elder Holmes ever made to his world; but the fact has been obscured by his later literary fame as an essayist, novelist and poet. The author of *The Autocrat of the Breakfast Table,* of *Elsie Venner* and of *The Chambered Nautilus* became the Petronius of an intellectual New England aristocracy never since then, as an indigenous group, approached in the United States. The asthmatic little gentleman was the arbiter of wit as well as manners and of elegance in letters.

So has his fame descended to us. He himself thought *The Chambered Nautilus* his greatest verse, and declared that in writing it he reached "the highest state of mental exaltation and the most crystalline clairvoyance, as it seemed to me, that has ever been granted to me"; yet Edgar Allan Poe transcribed reverently another verse, *The Last Leaf;* Lincoln knew it by rote, and hundreds rejoiced to recite it.[2] It may be, as John T. Morse, Jr., says in the *Life and Letters of Oliver Wendell Holmes,* that "these facts mean much." He concedes, however, that Dr. Holmes did not achieve a very giddy height of Parnassus, and quotes appropriately Sainte-Beuve's saying: "The greatest poet is not he who has done the best; it is he who suggests the most; he, not all of whose meaning is at first obvious, and who leaves you much to desire, to explain, to study; much to complete in your turn." Measured by that standard, or by Oscar Wilde's saying that the poet is one in whom the verse-form *"releases* power", the good doctor fares ill. He had facility and wit and at times a goodly satire, but by and large his collected verses have somewhat the troubadour tinkle. Not only as poet but as essayist and novelist his figure has shrunk during the last half century; to the dimensions of that figure in its heyday we shall return a little later in an effort to clarify its influence in the life of the son.

Dr. Holmes wrote to his sister on March 9, 1841, that between eight and nine o'clock of the evening before there had appeared at No. 8 Montgomery Place, now Bosworth Street, a small individual who might be addressed in the future this way or that, the highest of his fancied titles being President. Well, he had heard that immortal chorus, "For unto thee a child is given," and none will withhold in such circumstances a touch of sentimental sympathy with any parental phantasy. The dear soul, as a fact, had not quite quit his touch with actuality; for the present, he said, the youngster was "content with scratching his face and sucking his right forefinger".[3] This, he may have supposed, was the royal road to the White House.

Years afterward, when the son had ascended to the Supreme Judicial Court of Massachusetts—"a position more honorable than any of these merely political forecastings", as the biographer of Dr. Holmes observes—the father exclaimed: "To *think* of it!—my little boy a Judge, and able to send me to jail if I don't behave myself!" Although he lived to the good age of eighty-five, he died while his son was still in the highest court of his native State, before he ascended still higher, not only to the world's greatest tribunal but to a recognized status as one of the world's greatest jurists.

Therein is the irony of those tiny initials, so written probably because the father thought his offspring but an infinitesimal mite of humanity, and even in the pride of his paternity could foresee for him no greater future than the Presidency. One thinks of the father now, not as an innovator in the practice of medicine nor as an author, but as a sire. Time the leveller has dealt in sarcasm with the elder Oliver Wendell Holmes. Seldom in this country does a son overshadow a conspicuous parent; our ruthless practice is to submerge and scrap the offspring of our noteworthy men, in a sort of reckless prodigality. The tendency of the family strain is to thin out, rather than to wax fuller and stronger.

That the younger Holmes should even have approached his father's stature in the Boston of that day was in itself sufficiently remarkable. His senior was to the New England manor born, son of Abiel Holmes, a Congregational clergyman and historian. The Reverend Abiel was born in 1763 in Woodstock, Connecticut, and died in Cambridge, where he had established the first parish of his faith, in 1837.[4] The family stretched back past Thomas Holmes, a lawyer of Gray's Inn in London during the sixteenth century, and there is in Westminster Abbey a statue of Sir Robert Holmes. To this country there came John Holmes, to settle at Woodstock in 1686, not as an original grantee of the township, Mr. Morse reminds us, but "taken in on the way by the company of 'Goers' because he was 'the kind of man they wanted'," since "he knew something of surveying". He set up a sawmill and a fulling-mill, probably under a Colonial subsidy, for government was in business in this country even in that day. John Holmes gave to Woodstock, too, the land which is now its South Common. One of his sons, David, is noted contemporaneously merely as "Deacon Holmes", a title of dignity and power when the place of worship was the town hall. Connecticut, it may be said in passing, adopted half a century before John Holmes settled there a written Constitution, the first in the history of mankind. Neither the Virginia House of Burgesses nor Faneuil Hall was the cradle of American democracy; it was born at Hartford.

The son of "Deacon Holmes", named David, too, was a Captain in the "Old French War" and a surgeon in the Revolution. (The younger Oliver Wendell Holmes comes honestly by fighting blood.) And the son of Captain-Doctor David Holmes was Abiel Holmes, the clergyman who sired Dr. Oliver Wendell Holmes. Abiel was a Yale man, and his first wife was the daughter of the Reverend Doctor Ezra Stiles, president of that college. Abiel's second wife, whom he married while a pastor at Cambridge, was Sarah Wendell, only daughter of Judge Oliver Wendell of Boston, who gave his name to Dr. Holmes and to his great-grandson, the Justice.

The Wendell family preceded the Holmes family to this country. Evert Jansen Wendell came to Albany about 1640 from Emden, East Friesland, Holland.[5] It was on that side of the house that the Holmeses were kin to Wendell Phillips, abolitionist orator, advocate of woman suffrage and campaigner for prison reform; to the Richard Henry Danas, father and son, lawyers, poets, essayists, and politicians; and to William Ellery Channing, theologian. Wendell Phillips, as a contemporary of Dr. Holmes, but of somewhat different caliber and fiber, merits a little attention here.

Wendell Phillips expressed better than most of his contemporaries a liberalizing influence then fermenting in the intellect of Massachusetts.[6] He was one of that group—Emerson, Thoreau, Channing, Theodore Parker, Margaret Fuller, Lowell, Whittier

—with which, as we shall see, Dr. Oliver Wendell Holmes had but little in common save an active intelligence. He alone among that group—for Parker had died by then—joined Horace Greeley in his concern about the welfare of the working class in the United States. This was in the seventh decade of the nineteenth century; and William Lloyd Garrison, one of the most arrogant and intolerant of Bostonese, refused to take part in a proletarian crusade with Greeley and Phillips, denying indignantly that there was in the United States any such thing as wage slavery.[7] Against slavery black or white Wendell Phillips was a tower of strength.

Despite this disregard for the certitudes and securities of the "genteel tradition", Wendell Phillips was of the true aristocracy, and the son of that John Phillips who was Boston's first Mayor. Related to the Hutchinsons, the Brattles, the Schuylers, the Bradfords and the Livingstons, he was enmeshed in gentility. He was a great-grandson of John Wendell, and of that Jacob Wendell who married Sarah Wendell, daughter of Dr. James Oliver, famed in his day as a physician, who was graduated from Harvard in 1680. The youngest child of Jacob and Sarah Oliver Wendell, born in 1734, was Oliver Wendell, who married Mary, daughter of Edward Jackson; it was their daughter, Sarah, who married the Rev. Abiel Holmes. Oliver Wendell, graduated from Harvard at nineteen, became a merchant and the founder of the Massachusetts Bank, the first in New England: He was a Representative and selectman, and a delegate to the Provincial Congresses of 1775-6 with such men as John Hancock, General Joseph Warren, and Samuel Adams.

On that side of the house versifying began early; for Sarah Wendell was descended from Anne Bradstreet, daughter of Governor Thomas Dudley of Massachusetts Bay, whose husband, Simon Bradstreet, was himself twice governor of the province. In 1650 there was published in London a volume of her poems, *The Tenth Muse, Lately Sprung up in America;* but there seems no indication that she was on close terms with any of the nine established muses. Her granddaughter, Mercy Bradstreet, married Dr. James Oliver, and their daughter, Sarah, married Jacob Wendell.[8]

Henry (Brooks) Adams, reflecting in the autobiographical *Education* on his own part in this intertexture of settler families, and his descent from two Presidents, mused:

> "Had he been born in Jerusalem under the shadow of the Temple and circumcised in the Synagogue by his uncle the high priest, under the name of Israel Cohen, he would scarcely have been more distinctly branded, and not much more heavily handicapped in the races of the coming century, in running for such stakes as the century was to offer; but, on the other hand, the ordinary traveller, who does not enter the field of racing, finds advantages in being, so to speak, ticketed through life, with the safeguards of an old, established traffic. Safeguards are often irksome, but sometimes convenient, and if one needs them at all, one is apt to need them badly."[9]

Adams wondered whether the mere accident of such a birth, whether "starting from a nest so colonial—so troglodytic—crowding on ten pounds of unconscious babyhood" was in his case an advantage. He never got to the point of playing the game, he said, but lost himself "in studying it, and watching the errors of the players". The late William Marion Reedy thought differently; he thought family was a bit too much for Henry Adams. It did not prove too much for Dr. Oliver Wendell Holmes, but was a delight; he invented for New England the phrase, "the Brahmin caste".

Dr. Holmes was born in Cambridge, in an old wooden gambrel-roofed house which had once been the Law College of Harvard. It had served as the headquarters of General Artemas Ward and his Committee of Safety; there, plans were laid for fortifying Bunker Hill.

Emerson, heir of eight generations of Puritan divines, was of "the best New England stock", in the opinion of Dr. Holmes. Of the Doctor, Emerson said in his *Journal* that he "resembles Fontenelle, and Galiani, and Moore, though richer than either of them". (Philosophers and poets, please, but not crusaders.) "He is an Illustrated Magazine with 20,000 accurate engravings." We may be sure the Doctor would have hoped that some of these engravings might be reproductions of family portraits, for he had a certain contempt of the man with a daguerreotype. He did not bother a lot about his ancestry but he was consciously a patrician.

Dr. Oliver Wendell Holmes had no such fervor for social justice as his cousin Wendell Phillips. If Garrison shut his eyes to wage slavery it was because recognition of it would be to mitigate the horrors of black slavery; Dr. Holmes shut his eyes to it because, as an aristocrat and a Brahmin, he accepted economic inequalities as the foundation of class rule, and he was acutely class-conscious. He did not like the proletarianism of Phillips because he thought it not a "wholesome moral entertainment for the dangerous classes". In the second volume of *Main Currents in American Thought*, Vernon Louis Parrington incorporates an understanding chapter on Dr. Holmes as "The Authentic Brahmin", and to illustrate the point that he regarded the social agitator as little better than a firebrand quotes this passage from *The Poet at the Breakfast Table*:

> "You can't keep a dead level long, if you burn everything down flat to make it. Why, bless your soul, if all the cities of the world were reduced to ashes, you'd have a new set of millionaires in a couple of years or so, out of the trade in potash. In the meantime, what is the use of setting the man with the silver watch against the man with the gold watch, and the man without any against them both? . . . Here we are travelling through the desert together like the children of Israel. Some pick up more manna and catch more quails than others, and ought to help their hungry neighbors more than they do; . . . but we don't want the incendiary's pillar of cloud by day and a pillar of fire by night to lead us in the march to civilization, and we don't want

a Moses who will smite the rock, not to bring out water for our thirst, but petroleum to burn us all up with."[10]

Mr. Parrington notes that Dr. Holmes revealed his social bias by praising Everett, Webster, Bryant, Wilkie Collins, the Grand Duke Alexis and their spiritual kinsmen, rather than such men as Phillips and Parker and Thoreau and Greeley. "His heroes were respectable souls rather than militant." But the son of the Doctor developed a soul which, while eminently respectable according to conventional social standards, was yet incorrigibly militant.

Father and son were genteel New Englanders. In his chapter on *The Reign of the Genteel,* dealing not with the Holmeses in particular but with the New England of that day, Mr. Parrington observes: "Like Edith Wharton's contemporary Knickerbockers, the Brahmins conceived the great business of life to be the erection of barriers against the intrusions of the unpleasant. . . . The immediate consequence of this concern for defensive breastworks was the reign of the genteel in life and letters, a reign that set up a court of critical jurisdiction over the domain of American letters. The essence of the genteel tradition was a refined estheticism, that professed to discover the highest virtue in shutting one's eyes to a disagreeable fact, and the highest law in the law of convention. Gone were the franker days of Robert Treat Paine when a wit might find his choicest *bon mots* in the bottom of his cups. Coarseness had given way to refinement. It was the romanticism of Brahmin culture, with all Falstaffian vulgarity deleted, and every smutch of the natural man bleached out in the pure sunshine of manners. It was the Victorianism of a more maidenly purity than the English strain, so carefully filtered by passing through the Puritan mesh that the smallest impurities were removed."[11]

"The genteel tradition" is George Santayana's phrase, but Mr. Parrington employs it in the passage I have quoted somewhat differently from its coiner. The sense in which he employs it makes it applicable to the younger Oliver Wendell Holmes; in

Santayana's philosophic meaning the phrase was inapplicable to the son, although still quite in drawing with the character of the father. The elder Holmes was committed to a life preestablished by tradition, by private habit and by social mores; his son preferred above that sort of security the hazards of intellectual adventure and lonely pioneer thought. This predilection for treading out new paths even at the risk of censure and peril had flared up, as we have seen, in the young physician's essay on puerperal fever, but in his later life the flame burned down to embers; he became what Randolph Bourne stigmatized as the "tired radical". He still had a free-ranging mind, but not in truth a liberal mind.

It would be interesting to know how great was the influence, in effecting this change, of what Mr. Parrington regards as a sort of super-refined Victorianism in the Boston literary set; for when studying medicine in Paris, back in 1833, Dr. Holmes assimilated that inquiring habit of mind which produced his researches into puerperal fever. He wrote his parents that "merely to have breathed a concentrated scientific atmosphere like that of Paris must have an effect on any one who has lived where stupidity is tolerated, where mediocrity is applauded, and where excellence is deified. . . . I have more fully learned at least three principles since I have been in Paris: not to take authority when I can have facts; not to guess when I can know; not to think a man must take physic because he is sick."

As a successful writer, Dr. Holmes was willing to guess when he might have known better. He summed up the spiritual standards of different classes as "the comfortably rich, the decently comfortable, the very rich, who are apt to be irreligious, the very poor, who are apt to be immoral." Personally he opposed all the radical currents of his time; and Charles A. Beard and Mary R. Beard remind us that until the eve of the Civil War—in which his son was to be thrice wounded—he put off abolitionist appeals by saying that "we must reach the welfare of the blacks through the dominant race."[12] That sentence might have set the key for Henry

W. Grady, editor of the Atlanta *Constitution* and for years the South's most eloquent post-bellum defender of the "superior" race's dominance.

This alienation of Dr. Holmes from disturbing social problems, and preoccupation with conventional guaranties, must not be permitted to obscure the fact that he was in the forefront of the Boston revolt against the tyrannies of Calvinism which had lain for two centuries like a wet blanket on New England. The revolt did not take on the rowdy characteristics of the "Boston tea-party", but was waged over polite tea cups. An English essayist once spoke of Dr. Holmes as a "heresiarch". At home he was regarded by the orthodox, even when mildly inclined, as a heretic; and his *Elsie Venner* aroused storms of protest. He had the courage of his convictions in letters if not in humanitarianism, and he had the courage of his convictions in matters of metaphysics. His biographer tells us that the solemn "whey-faced" preachers who called on the Rev. Abiel Holmes were so repugnant to the preacher's young son as to fan into fire a spirit of religious secession; certainly some of his smartest satire in verse was directed at the fruits of Puritanism, and certainly he imparted to his own son the impulses of that "enlightened skepticism" of which, as a Judge, he sometimes spoke.

The heresy of *Elsie Venner* was that the author dared imagine an alien element introduced into the blood of a human being during the prenatal period, and portrayed this being as developing in conflict with certain ophidian characteristics and instincts. Dr. Holmes said his purpose in writing the novel was to suggest the limitations of human responsibilities under certain conditions. He wrote the story in 1860, and followed it later with another, *The Guardian Angel*, which he called its "natural sequence". In this he "attempted to show the successive evolution of some inherited qualities in the character of *Myrtle Hazard*"; these stories might be called, he suggested, "Studies in the Reflex Function in its Higher Sphere", but he thought this would frighten away all but the professors and the learned ladies. "If I should proclaim," he added, "that they were protests against the scholastic tendency to shift the total responsibility of all human action from the Infinite to the finite, I might alarm the jealousy of the cabinet-keepers of our doctrinal museums."[13]

One may fancy that this was a sly dig not only at the religious dogmatists but at those romantic liberals, such as Wendell Phillips, who based their faith upon the perfectibility of man. The good doctor said he expected the supernatural to be "at least as convincing as the natural".

William Dean Howells had been United States consul at Venice for six years, and subsequently had written his *Venetian Life* and *Italian Journeys,* before he went to Boston in 1871. He was there at the invitation of James Russell Lowell, which was auspicious; but the young man hailed from Ohio, and Brahmin Boston required double certification for any mere mid-westerner. Therefore Lowell took him to call upon Dr. Holmes,[14] and a little later the doctor, with Mrs. Holmes, climbed the steps to the newcomer's apartment as a social recognition. Thereafter, having heard that Howells had said the smell of the Back Bay salt water reminded him of Venice, Boston quite relaxed; while living there he wrote *The Rise of Silas Lapham*. He met Dr. Holmes often at the homes of Henry Wadsworth Longfellow and of James T. Fields in Boston. To the latter, *The Guardian Angel* was dedicated, "a token of kind regard from one of many writers who have found him a wise, faithful, and generous friend."

Howells saw at once, and subsequently duly recorded in his *Literary Friends and Acquaintances,* that literature in Boston was in the hands of "the people who were and who had been socially first in the city since the self-exile of the Tories at the time of the Revolution." To name her literary lights was to say patrician, "in the truest and often the best sense, if not the largest. Boston was small, but these were her first citizens, and their primacy in its way was of the same quality as that, say, of the chief families of Venice." Yet Longfellow, the most famous of them "if not the greatest of all the literary men of Boston", was an outlander like himself, for Longfellow hailed from Portland, Maine. Dr. Oliver Wendell Holmes was first, Howells thought, in "the suggestion of social qualities in the humanities. Holmes was one of the brahminical caste which his humorous recognition invited from its subjectivity in the New England consciousness into the light where all could know and own it." He was "allied to the patriciate of Boston by the most intimate ties of life".

Dr. Holmes himself once said of Bostonians that "we all carry the Common in our heads as the unit of space, the State House as the standard of architecture, and we measure off men in Edward Everetts as with a yardstick." This, too, Howells perceived, as might have been expected of so sensitive and penetrating a visitor; and, harking back again to his Italian experience, he observed: "To value aright the affection which the old Bostonian had for Boston, one must conceive of something like the patriotism of men in the times when a man's city was a man's country, something Athenian, something Florentine."

Dr. Holmes had that feeling for Boston, although he always protested that he loved his place in the country, first at Pittsfield and then at Beverly Farms, as though he felt that to be too strongly urban were somehow a reproach; and his son, even in the Machine Age, which tends strongly to smother local loyalties, shared it with him.

The son shared with his father, too, membership in the famous Saturday Club, which dined monthly at the Parker House. Dr. Holmes indeed was a founder, and participated in those informal meetings before 1857, when the club had no officers. The seed from which it sprouted was a quartette of Emerson and his admirers, who fell to dining together at "Parker's", which the doctor dubbed the "Will's Coffee-House of Boston". Around the original nucleus gathered others, so that "it grew into a club as Rome grew into a city, almost without knowing it." Emerson, Holmes, Motley, Hawthorne, Whittier, Lowell and Longfellow might be called charter members. In addition there were Whipple, Professors Agassiz and Peirce, Richard H. Dana, Jr., and Charles Sumner.[15] Subsequently there were taken into the august fold such men as President Charles W. Eliot of Harvard, Professors Felton, Norton and Goodwin; William H. Prescott,

J. Elliot Cabot, Henry James and William James, William Dean
Howells, T. B. Aldrich, Charles Francis Adams, Henry Adams,
Francis Parkman, Judge Hoar, George Frisbie Hoar—a co-mem-
ber with the younger Oliver Wendell Holmes—and many another light.

Of them all, it is safe to say, Dr. Holmes was the wittiest talker
and the most eagerly heard. He sat at the head of the table; but
there were times when he was glad to yield—not that he ever
monopolized attention, but that he was required by a tacit conspiracy to wield the baton—as when Asa Gray, who taught natural
history at Harvard for two score years, returned from London
with the astonishing tale that Darwin had confided to him, prior
to publication, his theory of evolution. Agassiz and Jeffries Wy-
man debated the theory for the club, with what result is not recorded; and in 1876 Gray's *Darwiniana* was published.

Into such a galaxy as this swam the ascendant star of the
younger Holmes. To such a galaxy Longfellow had read parts of
his translation of *The Divine Comedy;* and the younger Holmes,
who had a weakness for reading the classics in the original, satisfied himself that the original was not much better than the superb
translation.

It may be said in passing that in later life Mr. Justice Holmes
was fond of uttering a dissent when reminded that he had the
reputation of reading the classics in the original: Latin and
Greek, as a matter of course, and French and German almost as
much as a matter of course; but Italian and Spanish and even
Portuguese also. With a "pony", he vowed, it was not so difficult.
"But," he once added solemnly, "I always qualify that against the
Day of Judgment; for I read in the original only the purple
patches. Suppose on the Judgment Day *le Bon Dieu* were to call
me up and say, 'Now tell us, Holmes, very briefly, what you got
out of Socrates in the original that you would not have got out of
a translation?' And then I would have to say: 'But, Milord—' "

This whimsicality was emitted on the eve of the Justice's ninetieth birthday anniversary, when he had been rereading Thucy-
dides in the original, apparently just to improve his mind, per-

haps to refresh his recollection about the Peloponnesian War. For it was not birth alone that made the younger Holmes in his boyhood a favorite of Emerson, in his young manhood the intimate of William James and men of that caliber; it was a quality of mind and thought. His father could introduce him into an intellectual aristocracy, but the son must make good his place there. In those years he became, or began to be, an artist in words. Those years of companionship with his alert and sprightly father, and with the brilliant figures who delighted to associate with the father, help to explain how he learned to strip legal documents of their dismal verbiage, and how he came to invest them with limpid beauty. They help explain how it was that he learned to write with Addison and Swift.

CHAPTER 3

The Boston of His Boyhood

MODERN BOSTON is a far-flung Irish city of more than two millions population, corrupt politically and discontented socially, a metropolitan ganglion of skyscrapers, markets, banks, apartment houses, crawling traffic and congested wharves. Very different it is from the Boston of less than one hundred thousand people in which the baby Oliver Wendell Holmes sucked his right forefinger; for it was more than a provincial capital, such as New York or Philadelphia or Richmond, or even St. Louis on the western frontier. Chicago was a village of less than five thousand; New York, however, was already the overshadowing metropolis, with half a million population in the area now called the greater city. Yet despite the disparity in size, Boston was culturally and commercially a national capital, the Hub around which the New World turned.

When more than a quarter of the Twentieth Century had gone its way the London *Spectator* observed: "It is unlikely that changing America will ever again provide the opportunity for the rise of such a personality as that of Charles W. Eliot." The *Spectator* reckoned without its Holmes, who was seven years the junior of Dr. Eliot; for changing Boston and the changing New World provided opportunities for the development in him of a personality even more distinguished than Harvard's "Grand Old Man". Changing? Within the span of Justice Holmes's life the United States was to grow from a rural country, with some twenty million people, into a fabulous industrial imperialism. Its population during that time multiplied more than six-fold, its exports forty-fold, its railway mileage and the value of its manufactured products sixty-fold, its national wealth fifty-fold.

When the Justice was born William Henry Harrison, doomed to occupy the White House but one month, was President, and the first bath-tub was not to be installed there until ten years later. The canary-colored coaches of the Concord stage, averaging six miles an hour, took two days for the journey from Boston to New York. The postage on a letter between the cities was eighteen and three-fourths cents, provided the letter was a single sheet; if a check or paper money were enclosed, the postage was doubled, and travellers usually acted as unofficial carriers for their friends. Fearful and wonderful, from the standard of today, was the paper money of that day, decorated, according to the fancy of the issuing bankers, with pictures of sheep, pretty girls, oxen, loads of hay, Virginia tobacco plants, Georgia cotton or Kentucky mares. In Boston Spanish coins still circulated, and the dollar was six shillings. Farmers thereabout harvested their barley with the scythe and their wheat with the sickle of Boaz. Sometimes they wore silk hats and stocks to church. Texas was still an independent republic, the friction match was but eight years old, the quill was in use as the honorable predecessor of the fountain pen, and the sewing machine was yet to come.

Three generations of the Holmes family span the history of this country from the Revolution through the World War. Sarah Wendell, only daughter of the Honorable Oliver Wendell of Boston, was six years old when she saw the British enter the town and quarter a regiment of cavalry in the Old South Church—to Washington's great wrath. She was hurried off to Newburyport, and heard people around her saying that "the redcoats were coming, killing and murdering everybody as they went along".[1] She was the second wife of the Rev. Abiel Holmes (his first wife, as noted before, was Mary, daughter of the Rev. Dr. Ezra Stiles, president of Yale College, where Abiel was educated), and the mother of the elder Oliver Wendell Holmes.

The elder Oliver Wendell Holmes married, on June 15, 1840, Amelia Lee Jackson, the third daughter of the Hon. Charles Jackson of Boston, who was an Associate Justice of the Supreme Judicial Court, where later her eldest son was to sit for twenty years.[2] Like Sarah Wendell, she was descended from Edward

Jackson and Dorothy Quincy, the "Dorothy Q." celebrated in verses familiar to New Englanders of that day.

After the death of Amelia Holmes in 1888, the Doctor wrote to Elizabeth Stuart Phelps Ward, in reply to a letter of condolence, that to the last his wife had been "comely in aspect, gracious in manner, cheerful, easily pleased, until within a few days of the end, when she grew weaker very rapidly, and presently left us with that sweet smile on her face which the parting soul sometimes leaves on the features. To the few who looked upon it, it was like a celestial vision. Forty-five years we lived most happily together."[3] To their happiness their eldest son, who was devoted to his mother, contributed a large share.

In New England, textiles were then on their way to replace whaling as the section's chief industry; but it had not been long since the nine children who first worked in Almy and Brown's cotton mill—every day save the Sabbath for fourteen hours—had received for their labors from thirty-three to sixty-seven cents a week. This was the New England in which William Lloyd Garrison declared there was no wage slavery. As a fact, it was the section in which wage regulation and wage slavery, as well as black slavery, had their historic origins. It regulated wages on the basis, not of a minimum but of a *maximum,* a contingency belatedly suggested in a majority opinion of the United States Supreme Court three centuries later. Let us turn to the *Records of the Colony of the Massachusetts Bay in New England* under the date of October 3, 1633, and read:

"It is ordered, that maister carpenters, sawers, masons, clapboard-ryvers, bricklayers, tylars, joyners, wheelwrights, mowers, etc., shall not take aboue [above] 2s [two shillings] a day findeing themselues dyett & not aboue 14d [pence] a day if they haue dyett found them, vnder the penalty of vs [five shillings] both to giuer and receav, for euy [every] day that there is more giuen & received. Also that all other inferior workemen of the said occupacons shall haue such wages as the constable of the said place, & 2 other inhabitants, that hee shall shuse, shall appoynct.

"Also, it is agreed, that the best sorte of labourers shall not take aboue 18d a day if they dyett themselves & not aboue 8d a day if they haue dyett found them, vnder the aforesaid penalty, both to giuer and receaver. . . .

"Further, it is ordered, that all workemen shall worke the whole day, alloweing convenient tyme for foode and rest."

On November 8, following, price-fixing was established, wages having been "reduced to a certainety, in regard to the greate extorcon vsed by dyvers psons [persons] of little conscience, & the greate disorder wch grewe herevpon, by vaine and idle wast of much precious tyme, & expense of those imoderate gaynes of wyne, stronge water, & other supfluities." In view of the wage reduction, it was thought "very just & equall" to prevent excessive prices for the food the workman must buy; and so it was ordered that no provisions, nor even clothing, should be sold for more than four pence in a shilling above the wholesale cost, or its cost "for ready money in England". Dealers were watched to prevent their violating this order, and neighbors were urged to spy upon one another. Not only was religion compulsory in the province, but wages and prices. Later, most Boston merchants owned slaves.

From such roots grew the New England which nourished Mr. Justice Holmes, whose labor decisions, Theodore Roosevelt was to note, "have been criticized by some of the big railroad men and other members of large corporations."[4] "Big railroad men" were influential in Boston, although it was not until five years after the first steam locomotive waddled along ten miles of track in Maryland that Massachusetts adopted the ungainly contraption. After that Massachusetts' dollars went plentifully into the new enterprises, and State Street, whose offices were dominated by residents of Beacon Hill, waxed fat on them for a time.

They waxed fat, and they encouraged the nine Muses. A State Street banker, to give but one example, endowed the Boston Symphony Orchestra. "A peculiar and perplexing amalgam Boston always was," Henry Adams noted; and "one heard of Bostonians worth five millions or more as something not incredible." This was in his young manhood; he was three years the senior of Oliver Wendell Holmes. Adams would have liked to help build railways, "but had no education. He was not fit."

What, then, of the religious, recreational and social life of the young Holmes? Orthodox Boston looked askance upon his father, Dr. Holmes, because he spoke light-mindedly about doctrinal dogma;[5] yet in his Montgomery Place library, where the young Holmes read and studied, there was a trace of sanctity, if not its actual odor. The lively countenance of a Revolutionary preacher, the Rev. Samuel Cooper, as painted by Copley (born in Boston, this pre-Revolutionary artist was of Irish parentage), smiled from the wall. On the Doctor's desk was a hand lens imported by the Rev. John Prince of Salem (where twenty "witches" were hanged). The Rev. Mr. Prince was an early student of the sciences. On a bookcase was Jeremy Belknap's *History of New Hampshire,* containing a chapter contributed by the Rev. Manasseh Cutler; and the Rev. Mr. Cutler was not only a clergyman but a lawyer, physician, astronomer, botanist, entomologist, explorer, colonist, State and national legislator, who declined to ascend the Supreme Bench of one of the territories when Washington offered the honor. He had a pastorate at Hamilton, a village in Essex County, Massachusetts.

On a lower shelf of that bookcase was a volume of Plato bearing the inscription: "Ezra Stiles, 1766. *Olim e libris,* Rev. Jaredis, Eliot de Killingworth." Both men were scholars and philosophers. One may fancy that young Wendell Holmes fingered this book when he began, at sixteen, to read Plato as part of his course in Greek.

By that time Emerson had succeeded Theodore Parker as a lecturer at the old Music Hall in Boston. Parker, whom Emerson called one of the four great men of the time, had gone abroad for his health, and was to die in Florence, Italy. One of his biographers called him "the best working plan of an American yet produced", and a fellow clergyman said that he had "a conscience since Luther unsurpassed". He was an incendiary gospeller, and may well have influenced Oliver Wendell Holmes as a small boy; for Dr. Parker, the son of New England yeomanry, whose father was a Captain of the Minute Men on Lexington Common, was a militant abolitionist, and said he wrote his sermons with a pistol on his desk and a drawn sword within easy reach. He had cast aside the Calvinistic tenets of predestination, total depravity and a God of vengeance; and he had established in Boston a "rationalistic society" which hoped for man's perfectability and his "progressive development" under an evolutionary theism. Not all his discourses were metaphysical, however; he talked politics and named names. He thought the Constitution "a provisional compromise between the ideal political principles of the Declaration, and the actual selfishness of the people North and South". This country was not a democracy, he held; it had thrown off theocracy, aristocracy, monarchy, and had enthroned "the institution of money, the master of all the rest". And he excoriated gentlemen of the Back Bay as often as he chose, and as freely.

Strong meat for a youthful stomach! And Emerson, when he ascended the platform, delivered messages which, if less militant, still were stirring enough, both religiously and politically; for his transcendentalism kept step with Jeffersonian principles in the governmental field.

Oliver Wendell Holmes, after hearing an Emersonian discourse, often ran out of the hall in the hope of a walk home with the sage; and on such an occasion he confided that he had begun to study Plato.

"You should hold Plato at arm's length," Emerson advised. "Say to him: 'You have been pleasing the world for two thousand years; see whether you can please me'."

It was a year later, perhaps, that the youth wrote an essay on Plato, an essay primarily intended to be critical, and laid it respectfully on the knees of the master. Emerson read it attentively.

"Yes," he mused, "you have done very well, but you haven't killed Plato. When you shoot at a king you must kill him."

Often in later years Oliver Wendell Holmes meditated this reproof.

The reproof seemed more significant as time went on because Emerson's philosophy was so often compared with Platonism. It was the philosophic lecturer and not the transcendentalist who impressed and to some extent guided the inquiring mind of Oliver Wendell Holmes, the student and thinker. Yet he could not but wonder at the change which had come about in the very nature of the pulpit, and perceived in Emerson a protagonist of that change. His father before him had noted it. "The history of the Congregationalists in New England," said Dr. Holmes, "would show us how this change has gone on, until we have seen the church become a hall open to all sorts of purposes, the pulpit come down to the level of the rostrum, the clergyman take on the character of a popular lecturer who deals with every kind of subject, including religion."

Emerson dealt with every kind of subject, and although he mingled with the life around him he thought of the things of the world as incomplete images of unchangeable ideas. He thought that buildings, customs, rituals, institutions, were perishable and ephemeral, that thoughts were things, were realities and causes. We find Oliver Wendell Holmes in later life urging his associates to "think things". He was skeptical of verbalisms. "A word is not a crystal, transparent and unchanged," he exclaimed; "it is the skin of human thought."[6] Every opinion, he asserted, tends to become a law. "Man is born a predestined idealist," he said, "for he is born to act. To act is to affirm the worth of an end, and to persist in affirming the worth of an end is to make an ideal. The stern experience of our youth [the Civil War] helped to accomplish the destiny of fate. It left us feeling through life that pleasures do not make happiness and that the root of joy as of duty is to put out all one's powers toward some great end."[7]

In that same speech, delivered June 28, 1911, at the fiftieth anniversary of the Harvard class of 1861, Mr. Justice Holmes admitted that "I am apt to wonder whether I do not dream that I have lived, and may not wake to find that all that I thought done is still to be accomplished and that life is all ahead." Years afterward he told a visitor that he no longer supposed he had dreamed the universe. "I recognize in you," he said, "a separate entity, which is an act of faith."

It was an act of faith, not of knowledge; the Justice said he could write all he knew on half a sheet of note paper, but that he would want to reserve the other half so he could write in it: "I'm not sure!"

Emerson, a penetrating social and political commentator, committed himself to no party and no cult. He was accused of holding aloof from "the daily dust of life". There is good reason for saying that he kept his feet on the ground most of the time, and that young Holmes lent the closer attention when the speaker was solidly planted. His celebrated saying that "a foolish consistency is the hobgoblin of little minds, adored by little statesmen and philosophers and divines," might almost have been the text from which Oliver Wendell Holmes, in *The Common Law*, asserted: "The truth is, that the law is always approaching and never reaching, consistency. It is forever adopting new principles from life at one end, and it always retains old ones from history at the other, which have not yet been absorbed or sloughed off. It will become entirely consistent only when it ceases to grow."[8] He would not prescribe for the law "a foolish consistency"; nor in later years was he to hold that the Supreme Court must be too consistent to reverse itself.

Even before the boy began studying Plato, he had a notion that he would like to study art, and bought a set of etching tools. It does not appear that he wanted to devote his life to this pursuit; it interested him, and he thought he might become proficient in it. As a fact, art was a continuing pleasure to him, and his feeling for it cropped out again and again in his writings;[9] few lawyers are on such friendly terms with the classics and the moderns. But he abandoned presently the hope that he might express this feeling with competence in anything but words. Such etchings as he produced were a disappointment because he thought them of no merit whatsoever. But he never embraced the delusion, somewhat widely tolerated, that mere proficiency makes an artist. "That thing at the end of the mantel there," he once said, "is a Whistler. Now, a fellow who is proficient may come along, and study that for a while, and say to himself, 'This fellow has got a new wrinkle; why, I can do that!' And he goes away and does it, to his own satisfaction; but it lacks that final wiggle which is genius."

Hours in the Holmes study in Montgomery Place, lessons at the feet of Theodore Parker and Ralph Waldo Emerson, a novitiate with etching tools, did their part toward the enrichment of the youthful Holmes and the widening of his horizons. Not many healthful diversions were open to him. The Boston of his middle teens made the bar and the billiard-table more accessible than many Back Bay parents suspected. There were skating and swimming and a dancing school; there were baseball and football and hockey all in embryonic form. There was the Charles River, really an estuary, on which to sail a boat. But the greatest fun was sleighing, here and there over the three hills upon which Boston is seated, or into the countryside beyond.

Every Boston youth in those days, as most youths do now, fell in love, or thought he was in love, once in every so often. As a rule these were strictly chaperoned affairs, for Boston was still prudish in her deportment and her notions. As young men approached "full age" they were certain, sooner or later, to learn something of the seamier side of the city, and to observe if not to share vice in its uglier forms.[10] It had the meretricious attraction of freedom from culture and superiority to prudishness. Social life was still much what it had been when Boston was the capital of a British province; that is to say, it was provincial and colonial.

To a lad of Oliver Wendell Holmes' vigorous physique an annual event of great excitement and splendor was the snowball

fight on Boston Common between what I may term the polite
and the rowdy elements of the town. It was embryo warfare, in
truth, with stones not infrequently encased in the snowballs, and
sometimes with sticks coming into play in the dusk. Often the
battle brought bloodshed. It was a boisterous fun, but fun it was
to a youth who, though as thin as a rail in those days, was a head
taller than most of his fellows and could throw a snowball farther. To go home to a late supper panting and hot and tired but
victorious brought a high sense of achievement. Ten years
later, on the battlefields of the Civil War, Oliver Wendell
Holmes recalled the lessons he had learned on Boston Common.

For eighteen years the Holmes family lived in Montgomery
Place, afterward Bosworth Street, and there a sister and brother
were born to Oliver Wendell, Jr.: Amelia, who became Mrs.
Turner Sargent, and Edward Jackson Holmes. Both were to
precede their father in death, but Edward left a son, who sur-
vives and is director of the Boston Museum of Fine Arts. Meanwhile, in the winter of 1887, the Doctor's wife had followed his
younger son. All these losses came after the Doctor had moved,
in more prosperous days, to Beacon Street, on the river side.

At the very end of 1884 the Doctor happened through Montgomery Place and saw workmen tearing down the modest house
where, in the distant past, he and his wife and children had spent
so many happy years.[11] As for the house in Cambridge where he
himself was born, not a vestige of it was left. "We Americans live
in tents," he complained. He recalled that when he left Montgomery Place he had moved for a time to Charles Street, near
the Cambridge bridge, where his study looked across the river to
a range of hills on the western horizon; then he had been "improved" (as he put it) out of that home into the Beacon Hill
house he built, where he pegged down his tent-stakes for the last
time.

It was a site he had coveted since his boyhood.[12] Long before
the waters of the estuary were filled for building purposes he had
seen a patch of land out there and had hoped that some day he

might have a house on the tiny island. By the time his ambition was fulfilled it was no longer an island, but the artificial site had the advantages he coveted: a view over the waters to Bunker Hill and the spires of Cambridge. In his later years Oliver Wendell Holmes and his wife moved in to care for the aging author. "Mrs. Judge knows how to make me comfortable," said the Doctor, "and does it remarkably well." She and Judge Holmes—for the son was now in the Supreme Judicial Court of the State—accompanied the old gentleman to Symphony concerts and rehearsals, to teas, and once in every so often to dinner at "Young's" or "Parker's". A cataract threatened the Doctor's sight, and he grew restive under enforced idleness. In the Beacon Street house, asleep in an armchair in his beloved library, he died October 7, 1894.

Until summoned to the Supreme Court in Washington in December, 1902, Judge Holmes lived in the dignified four-story brick house his father had built; then his nephew, Edward J. Holmes, took over the place.

Not all the time of the Holmes family was spent amid the slush and murk of a wintry Boston. From the standpoint of the children the gay and delightful months were those in the country. When Wendell was eight years old, in 1849, the Doctor built a summer home on the Lenox road near Pittsfield, on land which had been in the family for generations. It embraced 280 acres, and was part of a section bought from the Province in 1738 by the boys' great-great-grandfather, Jacob Wendell. In that day the name of the place was Canoe Meadows.[13] It was a pleasant land, with the masses of Greylock in the distance, with the waters of the Housatonic for variety, with a stately maple at the gate and a huge old pine near the house. Hills and green fields and woodlands made a splendid amphitheater for the children's play, and some of their most vivid memories clung about it. There seven summers were spent, until the place threatened to become too great a drain upon the family purse.

From the windows of the house at Canoe Meadows, according

to the Doctor's lively fancy, the children could see all summer a lion rampant, a Shanghai chicken, and General Andrew Jackson on horseback, "done by nature in green leaves, each with a single tree". Most of the trees on the tract itself were planted by the Doctor, assisted by a tenant; some were slips from English nurseries, not more than a foot high when set out. The two small boys helped with these tasks, and played among the pine woods on the hilly slopes around, or among the clover and hay, once patches began to be cultivated. They rolled in the grass and waded in the streams. It was a healthful, rollicking life. Wendell throve upon it; his brother, who had inherited the father's asthmatic weaknesses, did not fare quite so well. Yet the land lay more than a thousand feet above sea level, in Berkshire County, a rolling plain between the Hoosacs and the Taconics, east and west. The village of Pittsfield, christened in honor of the Earl of Chatham, was not incorporated until 1861, five years after the Holmes family, whose place was two miles south of the village, had moved from the neighborhood. Until the incorporation, the community was known as Boston Plantation, and the name was reminiscent.

Even in the boyhood of Oliver Wendell Holmes, slaves had vanished as household servants in his Boston. They did not thrive amid the rigors of New England winters, and the descendants of men who had bought and sold them like any other chattel began to perceive the moral implications of the traffic. And although the political background of the gentlemen and yeomanry who settled Massachusetts were not greatly different from the experience of the so-called Cavaliers in Virginia, the climatic and geographic conditions of the one made for small farms and compact communities, while the plantation—which was the feudalistic aim of the colonizing companies—was readily possible in the other. In colonial Boston mantels were adorned with images of the sacred—and profitable—cod; nor were New Englanders ashamed of dealing in rum, grindstones and fishing tackle. Virginians would have blushed to acknowledge such occupations. These facts, as legend and tradition, infiltrated into the consciousness of Oliver Wendell Holmes, and often came uppermost in later years. When he was approaching ninety he told a visitor from south of the Mason and Dixon line that he had always thought Southerners "put on a lot of side".

"Perhaps," the caller suggested—himself unmindful that slavery had once been the order of the day in New England—"that is because of an inherited feeling due to the institution of slavery; perhaps the presence years ago of a servile class in the population has left this relic." The Justice looked a little doubtful, but assented.

Returning on the following day, the visitor told the Justice he had been taken severely to task by his wife for his explanation of that "side" to which jesting reference had been made. "She says," he explained, "that slavery had nothing to do with it. No, after the Civil War and Reconstruction, so she says, the South had nothing left but a social attitude."

"Yes," said the Justice, "several years ago a Southern woman said that very thing to me at a dinner table. It made me feel pretty bad."

It is pleasant to think that the social and economic conditions in New England, stripped of feudalistic trappings, encouraged the democratic spirit, and that Puritanism was the parent of what Elihu Root has called organized self-control. Indeed, church membership was a condition for sixty years of the suffrage in Massachusetts, and for a century thereafter property qualifications for the vote were maintained. John Adams feared the masses as much as he feared any monarch, and said so. The New England aristocracy which produced Oliver Wendell Holmes the elder was dedicated to caste. The good Doctor himself, however, was no snob, and had a high faith in democratic processes. "Not by aggression," he exclaimed, "but by the naked fact of existence we are an eternal danger and an unsleeping threat to every government that founds itself on anything but the will of the governed."

How sanguine were the prospects of that day! "One cannot

look upon the freedom of this country," cried Emerson, "without a presentiment that here shall laws and institutions exist in some proportion to the majesty of nature. . . . It is a country of beginnings, of projects, of vast designs and expectations. It has no past; it has an onward and prospective look."

From New York Herman Melville, in the year before his *Moby Dick* was published, echoed as high a hope for the land. "God has predestinated, man expects, great things from our race," he vowed; "and great things we feel in our souls. The rest of the nations must soon be in our rear. We are the pioneers of the world; the advance guard, sent on through the wilderness of untried things, to break a new path in the New World that is ours. In our youth is our strength; in our inexperience, our wisdom."

The steam engine, the telephone and the telegraph, which seemed to some the justification of this lofty optimism, were in fact, so far as the Boston of the Holmes children was concerned, to sever it abruptly from its past, throw the old Calvinistic universe into the junkpile, and create a new New World. Many winds of doctrine, political, economic and religious, were to blow about the boy and the man Wendell Holmes, and many tides of mass emotion were to sweep across the land. To a certain extent Boston was an enclave amid this excitement and confusion. For nearly two centuries after the city was founded, in 1630, it had stuck loyally to its old form of government, and had debated its municipal problems in town meetings. Thus, until a city charter was granted in 1822, the community was distinctly homogeneous. It had a color and a character of its own, which persisted well into the life of Wendell Holmes. Every man who walked Tremont Street, so it was said, had under his hat his own theory of the cosmos. Elsewhere, half a century earlier, the Founding Fathers had supplanted the Church Fathers as venerated oracles; in New England, despite its weighty delegation of Founders, and despite the fact that politics was still regarded as a career, metaphysics was a thing apart.

Spiritual monitors were not necessarily apart. The Rev. Abiel

Holmes, grandfather of Wendell Holmes, who had once been pastor of the First Church of Cambridge, had taken to college an equipment supplied by his mother, which included a Dutch liquor-case containing six large bottles filled with strong waters such as brandy, rum, gin, and whiskey; "doubtless enough," Doctor Holmes thought, "to craze a whole class of young bacchanalians."

Nor was the Doctor himself by any means an abstainer. When Wendell was ten years old the Doctor began composing annual odes for Harvard's "famous class of '29", of which he had been a member, and which made much ado about its gatherings. He was a member, too, of the Porcellian Club and the Knights of the Square Table (subsequently merged), of whose meetings he spoke with gusto after Wendell was well past his majority.

> "It was a great change [he wrote] from the sober habits of a quiet clergyman's family to the festive indulgences and gay license of a convivial club. The Goddess of Wisdom did not always preside at the meetings, but undoubtedly there was refreshment, and possibly a disguised use in the unrestrained freedom of these occasions; sooner or later there was a chance that a young man, who had to face the temptations of the wine that was red in the cup, or sparkled in the tall wineglass, would be betrayed into some degree of excess which might lay the foundation of evil habits, but more probably would pass away like the bubbles on the beaker's brim. Fortunately, there were no reporters at these meetings, for many tongues forgot the lessons they had been taught at the sober family board, and indulged in wit, or what passed for it, which would have borne chastening to advantage.
>
> "Oh, this was the period of illusions! The suppertable and the theater seemed lively as compared with the Assembly's Catechism and Saurin's sermons, which I remember my father placing in my hand with

commendation. Wine was very freely drunk in those days, without fear and without reproach from the pulpit or the platform. I remember, on the occasion of my having an 'Exhibition', that, with the consent of my parents, I laid in a considerable stock, and that my room was for several days the seat of continuous revelry; but we must remember what an immense change opinion has undergone since my time in regard to the use of alcoholic stimulants."[14]

By this time women had been emancipated from the graver thralldom and compulsions of Calvinistic Boston. Elizabeth Cady Stanton has told vividly what that thralldom was. Women could not hold property, whether they earned it or inherited it; if unmarried, they must put it into the hands of trustees, and if married, they were required to give up all title to it. They were not citizens, of course, could hold no office, and were not "a factor in the human family". A wife occupied much the same legal position as a domestic servant, and her husband could punish her "with a stick no bigger than his thumb". She did not even own her clothes, and "had no personal rights".

Boston standards were high for the male, fortunately for the youthful Holmes. He was not born wealthy, but he was born into a society which even European capitals might envy. In any country the writers of that day would have merited distinction, although here, to be sure, sex barriers were not erected as in the home and in the courts and at the polls: Harriet Beecher Stowe and Margaret Fuller and Elizabeth Stuart Phelps held their places unchallenged. As for Boston's place in the sciences and in medicine—certainly no science then—there was no need to be ashamed; and it was felt with good reason that any young American privileged to sit at the feet of the Harvard faculty need ask nothing more. There was a saying that if one were born in Boston there was no need to be born again; it remained for Irvin Cobb to modify this irreverently by averring that a man born in Boston and educated at Harvard was like a twice-laid egg.

And in any community the clergy of that day would have been noteworthy. The Rev. Drs. Channing, Palfrey, Frothingham, Everett, were shining vice-regents of the Lord, to say nothing of Parker and Emerson. Parker, disregarding the dictum of Saul of Tarsus, actually vowed there was a *maternal* element in the Divine Being; but Boston as a whole could not quite go that.

No one seems to know just what the Puritan was, or is, if there are any of the simon-pure type remaining. That is, no one seems able to frame a definite and certain description or analysis to which large numbers of persons will agree. This much is sure: that the religious revolutionists who dominated English politics during the Commonwealth, and whose children were the early settlers of New England, did repudiate the theory of a divinity in kingly coercions, and did stand for freedom of conscience of a certain sort. The settlers of Jamestown, who preceded the Puritans to this country, accepted the Church of England and it became the State Church of Virginia, as of other Southern States. Yet it does not appear that the South was less severe than New England in its disciplines. Benjamin Franklin proved clearly enough that even the Massachusetts of his day could produce an independent soul, as unconventional socially as a Greenwich Villager pretends to be and an authentic free-thinker to boot. The Puritan came, moreover, to associate God pragmatically with go-getting; and under the impact of evolution and the Machine Age he surrendered his harshest postures toward original sin, predestination and such-like. He even came to approve divorce, in cases of desertion and cruelty.*

*Samuel Eliot Morison, in *The Maritime History of Massachusetts, 1783-1860*, on page 22, gives this description of the "Yankees" as a new people: "A tough but nervous, tenacious but restless race; materially ambitious, yet prone to introspection, and subject to waves of religious emotion. . . . A people with few social graces, yet capable of deep friendships and abiding loyalties; law-abiding yet individualistic, and impatient of restraint by government or regulation in business; ever attempting to repress certain traits of human nature, but finding an outlet in broad, crude humor and deep-sea voyages. A race whose typical member is torn between a passion for righteousness and a desire to get on in the world." Frank W. Grinnell quoted this passage in his paper, *John Winthrop and the Constitutional*

Undoubtedly the Puritan has been made a popular scapegoat, and the word has become a catch-basin for undeserved reproaches. Some of these animadversions were deflected to the Fundamentalists of the South during the period when Dayton, Tennessee, was a news cynosure, but there does not seem to have been much inclination to admit that the Fundamentalists were but continuing the Puritan tradition and practices.

Let us see for a moment what Mr. Justice Holmes thinks of the Puritan. One might expect him, in view of the upbringing which I have attempted to describe, to be a bit impatient of the sect. Not so: he thanks God that the Puritan still lives in New England and will live there "so long as New England lives and keeps her old renown."[15] Acknowledging the austerity of the Puritan, he praises Puritan virtues. He spoke February 12, 1866, at the two hundred and fiftieth anniversary of the First Church in Cambridge, where his grandfather had held a pastorate, of "the august figure of the Puritan"; and he proclaimed himself a political heir of Thomas Shepard, founder of the church, while denying spiritual kinship. "Even if our mode of expressing our wonder, our awful fear, our abiding trust in face of life and death and the unfathomable world has changed," he said, "yet at this day, even now, we New Englanders are still leavened with the old Puritan ferment. Our doctrines may have changed, but the cold Puritan passion is still here."[16]

Judge Holmes, then on the Supreme Bench of his State, was forty-five when he made that speech. Never a hot-headed man, the tides of passion had for years run high in him, and it had been a cold passion; yet one fancies that the Puritanism of it was fairly

Thinking of John Adams, for the Massachusetts Historical Society, which has incorporated it in Volume 63, February, 1930; and he quoted even more fully in his lecture on "The Government of Massachusetts Prior to the Federal Constitution," delivered at William and Mary College and incorporated in *The Genesis and Birth of the Federal Constitution,* published by the Macmillan Company. Mr. Grinnell is impressed with the statement of the historian that "The Yankee race, in fact, had never been all English". It was "a new Nordic amalgam on an English Puritan base; already in 1750 as different in its character and its dialect from the English as the Australians are today".

well diluted. "The Puritan had his ancestors like the rest of us," said Judge Learned Hand in a speech about the Justice, "spiritually as well as biologically, and he was perhaps especially liable to sports and throw-backs."[17]

The Boyhood of Mr. Boyhood

well dinned." The Puritan had our ancestors like the rest of us,"
said Judge Learned Hand in a speech about the Justice, "spiritually as well as biologically, and he was perhaps especially their
to worries and mrreux.

CHAPTER 4

At Harvard

B Y BIRTH, environment and tradition it was foreordained that
young Oliver Wendell Holmes should become a Harvard
man. His father had been the Class Poet in 1829; the son was to be
Class Poet in 1861. The father, after studying law somewhat
lackadaisically for a year, had turned to medicine, and had taught
anatomy in the university; there the son, after turning aside from
philosophy as a life pursuit, was to teach law. Practically all the
boys the son knew had attended Mr. Dixwell's Latin school;
nearly all of them were to become fellow students at Harvard.

So that when the youth walked down the steps of Mr. Dixwell's
school in Boylston Place, Cambridge, one day in June, 1857, having finished his course there, he knew he had got a good deal more
than a smattering of Latin and Greek; he could see ahead of him
the gracious architecture and spacious campus of Harvard College, and he might have foreseen, if he had bothered to ponder it,
that Harvard would be the last rallying point, among great
American universities, of the "dead" languages and other classics.
What he did not quite foresee was that Miss Fanny Dixwell,
daughter of Epes S. Dixwell, principal of the school he was leaving, was to become his bride some sixteen years later.

In the Class of 1861 were Henry Pickering Bowditch and
Frank Emmons, the one a celebrated physiologist, the other, for
thirty years with the United States Geological Survey, a world-
famous geologist. The roster is studded with names associated
with New England's part in the intellectual and social history of
this country: Leonard Case Alden, Charles Cotesworth Beaman,
John Bigelow, Elihu Chauncey, Stephen Goodhue Emerson,
Joseph Emery Fiske, Wendell Phillips Garrison (third son of William Lloyd Garrison), Albert Hale, Alpheus Holmes Hardy,
John Prentiss Hopkinson, Henry Pickering, Albert Stetson,

James Kent Stone, Flavel Coolidge Stratton, Franklin Weld, Edward Wigglesworth, Henry Wadsworth Longfellow and Robert Singleton Peabody; of this slight list, the last-named two did not go through to graduation. Scollay Parker, although a Georgian by birth, had a New England ancestry which went back to 1670, and his mother was a granddaughter of William Scollay of Boston, for whom Scollay Square was named.[1] Closer personally to Holmes than these men was Norwood P. Hallowell, a Philadelphian of Quaker parentage, who became Class Orator, served with Holmes in the Twentieth Massachusetts, and was wounded with him at Antietam. His death in 1914 evoked from the Justice a stately sonnet.

Other students at Harvard in those days were to become warm friends of Holmes, if they had not been warm friends even before that association. William James was a boon companion, not a fellow-student; although they drifted somewhat apart later, chiefly because James was so much abroad before he began teaching in the university. James was a son, George Santayana noted, of "one of those somewhat obscure sages whom early America produced: mystics of independent mind, hermits in the deserts of business and heretics in the churches". Between Holmes and James there was a close mental kinship, and both became eminent as philosophers; as for James, "his excursions into philosophy," said Santayana, "were accordingly in the nature of raids," and he noted that "on points of art or medicine [for James studied medicine] he retained a professional touch and an unconscious ease which he hardly acquired in metaphysics."

James and Holmes were continually, during their college days, "twisting the tail of the cosmos", and in later years sometimes wrote to each other about "our dilapidated old friend the Kosmos". James, a year the elder, urged Holmes to join the Society for Psychical Research.

"Why don't you study Mohammedism?" Holmes retorted. "Hundreds of millions of men and women think you will be eternally damned without it. We go through life staking our salvation on incomplete and imperfect knowledge. [Subsequently he

put this thought into a dissenting opinion.[2]] Life is like an artichoke; you pull out a leaf, but only the tip is edible. You pull out
a day; only an hour or two is available for spiritual thoughts."

The warmth of affection James felt for Holmes cropped out in
letters addressing him, in some obscure spirit of fun, as "Wen-
dle". From Berlin, on September 17, 1867, he wrote, in part:

> "I was put in possession this morning, by a graceful
> and unusual attention on the part of the postman, of a
> letter from home containing, amongst other valuable
> matter, a precious specimen of manuscript signed
> 'O. W. H. Jr.' covering just one small page of note
> paper belonging to a letter written by Minny Tem-
> ple! ! ! ! Now I myself am not proud—poverty, mis-
> ery and philosophy have together brought me to a
> pass where there are few actions so shabby that I would
> not commit them if thereby I could relieve in any
> measure my estate, or lighten the trouble of living—
> but, by Jove, Sir! there *is* a point *sunt carti denique
> fines,* down to which it seems to me hardly worth while
> to condescend—better give up altogether.—I do not
> intend any personal application. Men differ, thank
> Heaven! and there may be some constituted in such a
> fearful and wonderful manner, that to write to a friend
> after six months in another person's letter, hail him as
> 'one of the pillars on which life rests,' and after twelve
> lines stop short, seems to them an action replete with
> beauty and credit. To me it is otherwise. And if per-
> chance, O Wendy boy, there lurked in any cranny of
> *thy* breast a spark of consciousness, a germ of shame at
> the paltriness of thy procedure as thou inditedst that
> pitiful apology for a letter, I would fain fan it, nourish
> it, till thy whole being should become one incarnate
> blush, one crater of humiliation. Mind, I should not
> have found fault with you if you had not written at all.
> There would have been a fine brutality about that

which would have commanded respect rather than otherwise—certainly not *pity*. 'Tis that, *writing*, THAT should be the result. Bah!

"But I will change the subject, as I do not wish to provoke you to recrimination in your next letter. Let it be as substantial and succulent as the last, with its hollow hyperbolic expression of esteem, was the opposite, and I assure you that the past shall be forgotten."[3]

James reported that he was "a mere wreck" bodily, and had slipped away from Boston without telling anyone; he had refrained from telling Holmes in confidence "partly from a morbid pride, mostly because of the habit of secrecy that had grown on me in six months." His physical condition, indeed, plunged him later into a mental despair such that for a long time he resisted with difficulty an impulse to destroy himself. His external life, he told Holmes, "resembles that of a sea anemone; and the internal, notwithstanding the stimulus of a new language and country, has contracted the same hue of stagnation."

"I wish I could communicate to you," he continued, "some startling discoveries regarding our dilapidated old friend the Kosmos, made since I have been here. But I actually haven't had a fresh idea." He went on to tell what he had been reading in German and French, and his tone became more hopeful. "You had better believe," he said, "that I have thought of you with affection since I have been away, and prized your qualities of head, heart and person, and my priceless luck in possessing your confidence and friendship in a way I never did at home; and cursed myself that I didn't make more of you while I was by you, but, like the base Indian, threw evening after evening away which I might have spent in your bosom, sitting in your whitely-lit-up room, drinking in your profound wisdom, your golden gibes, your costly imagery, listening to your shuddering laughter, baptizing myself afresh, in short, in your friendship—the thought of all this makes me even now forget your epistolary peculiarities." He wanted to know about "girls fallen in love with," about what Holmes was reading and what stories he had heard. In a postscript he inquired about "the result of your study of this *vis viva* question."[4]

A little more than three months later James, still in Berlin, wrote:

"The ghosts of the past all start from their unquiet graves and keep dancing a senseless whirligig around me so that, after trying in vain to read three books, to sleep, or to think, I clutch the pen and ink and resolve to work off the fit by a few lines to one of the most obtrusive ghosts of all—namely the tall and lank one of Charles Street. Good golly! how I would prefer to have about twenty-four hours' talk with you up in that whitely lit-up room—without the sun rising or the firmament revolving so as to put the gas out, without sleep, food, clothing or shelter except your whiskey bottle, of which, or the like of which, I have not partaken since I have been in these longitudes! I should like to have you opposite me in any mood, whether the facetiously excursive, the metaphysically discursive, the personally confidential, or the jadedly *cursive* and argumentative—so that the oyster shells which enclose my being might slowly turn open on their rigid hinges under the radiation, and the critter within loll out his dried-up gills into the circumfused ichor of life, till they grew so fat as not to know themselves again. I feel as if a talk with you of any kind could not fail to set me on my legs again for three weeks at least. I have been chewing on two or three dried-up old cuds of ideas I brought from America with me, till they have disappeared, and the nudity of the Kosmos has got beyond anything I have as yet experienced. I have not succeeded in finding any companion yet, and I feel the want of some outward stimulus to my Soul. . . ."[5]

Begging for news, James said he supposed Holmes was sinking ever deeper "into the sloughs of the law—yet I ween the Eternal Mystery still from time to time gives her goad another turn in the raw she once established between your ribs." He found in Berlin life "a certain flatness to the high-tuned American taste", and apologized for writing "when in the dismalest of dumps". Holmes, he thought, was "the one emergent peak, to which I cling when all the rest of the world has sunk beneath the wave".

After returning to the United States, James expressed the fear, quite common in that day among the whole group, that Holmes worked too hard.[6] He sometimes spoke fondly of having "wrangled" with Wendell for an hour; to Holmes his friend was "Bill" James. In no one did James "find a more sympathetic philosophic companionship at this period,"in the opinion of his son, Henry James, who edited the letters.

That the future Justice of the United States Supreme Court and the future founder of Pragmatism were exceptions in the personnel of nearly any university is obvious; yet it is to be noted that there were differences of mental posture between the Harvard men of that day and of this, and that there were certain differences between the university then and now. It is worth our while, without invidious intention, to clarify somewhat the dimensions of these discrepancies.

Not until after the Civil War did industrialism become dominant in New England; prior to that politics and the "learned professions" were the careers open to well-bred and intelligent young men. If Webster and the Adamses had been born three-quarters of a century later, probably they would have developed into Captains of Industry, although it is a little difficult to fancy Webster in that capacity. Quite the same thing would have been true (had they been born, say, a century later), of Clay and Calhoun, Washington and Jefferson and Marshall and Madison in the South. As late as the middle of the Nineteenth Century, however, the philosophy of Jeremy Bentham largely colored the political and social thought of the whole United States; and although New England was in favor of a protective tariff, the belief prevailed generally that it was injudicious to interfere otherwise with the operation of economic and social forces. The principles of *laissez-faire* were ascendant.

That school of philosophy was abandoned by Daniel Webster, it is true, after he was hard-bitten during the forties by the Presidential bee, but his apostasy did not carry with him the majority of those who had been his followers; his political shiftiness brought him but disappointment and regret. The intellectual element of New England, deeply influenced by English thought, sought economic, political and religious freedom. The Puritan no longer exercised rigid authority over deportment or opinion, and the community practiced a large tolerance, albeit seldom a friendly or cordial tolerance. There were exceptions, of course, mostly individual, and the heightening bitterness between the North and South increased the number of exceptions. John C. Gray, a good friend of both James and Holmes, wrote to another friend: "In some men this attempt to abolish slavery has taken an extraordinary and perfect development to the exclusion of all patriotism, as in Charles Sumner."[7] But it is safe to say that in the Boston of that day it would not have been necessary, before inspecting a rare edition of Casanova's memoirs at the public library, to sign a document vowing that one's interest was purely typographical, and to promise to look only at the pictures, not once at the text. Nor would the Boston of that day have insisted that the nude cherubim beside the city seal on the granite facade of a public library be draped with stony ribbons.

It must not be supposed from this that either Boston or its famous university was of conspicuously loose morals. The motto of the university in 1643 was *Veritas,* but around 1700, probably during the presidency of Increase Mather, it was changed to *Christo et Ecclesiae;* and the elder Oliver Wendell Holmes stirred up something of a tempest when he proposed light-mindedly that Harvard return to the earlier seal. The Harvard Club of New York invited Dr. Holmes to speak at its annual dinner on February 21, 1878; this he had to refuse to do, because he dreaded travel at that season, and he regretted it because, so he said, New York "de-oxydizes and de-Bostonizes me". He did write two sonnets, however, to be read at the dinner;[8] and in justifying their contents he asserted that "the Harvard College of today wants no narrower, no more exclusive motto than Truth —truth, which embraces all that is highest and purest in the precepts of all teachers, human or divine; all that is best in the creeds of all churches, whatever their name; but allows no lines of circumvallation to be drawn around its sacred citadel under the alleged authority of any record or of any organization."[9]

Already *Veritas* had been inscribed above the door of Memorial Hall at Harvard, and the good Doctor evidently did not suspect that his sonnets would cause such a stir as they did. "It seems to me," he wrote to John O. Sargent, then president of the New York club, "that my bouquet was like the one I saw Modjeska smell the other evening in *Adrienne Lecouvreur*—had some subtle poison in it—at least for certain idiosyncracies." He thought it should do no harm; "there is a good deal to be said in favor of truth, although it poisons some people who have lived too long upon the opposite kind of diet."

The College seal was not changed, and Charles W. Eliot, who had become president, did no more than mention to Dr. Holmes, casually, that he had received a letter about the sonnets. "They have invented a new mode of torture—readings from one's poems, by Dr. Holmes and me," grumbled James Russell Lowell. "We bow our necks to the yoke, like patient oxen, and leaning away from each other as oxen will, strive to retrace our ancient furrows, which somehow will not gleam along the edges as when the turf was first broken."[10] The storm which the Harvard sonnets had blown up was not serious enough to cause Dr. Holmes further torture.

The ferment in New England was intellectual rather than moral; "Wendy" Holmes and "Bill" James felt the ferment and were part of it. Dr. Eliot, the first president of Harvard who was not a clergyman, had not yet reached that post during Holmes's undergraduate days, and his slogan of "power and service" as the road to success had not been heard. The Graduate School of Business Administration, the last act of his official career, was still unborn by nearly half a century. Education erects a caste system, founded primarily upon taste and intelligence; and Harvard still educated young men on the caste basis. It was then and it still is the leading and the oldest American college, and in a sense a national institution.

Dr. Abraham Flexner's strictures upon American universities, and upon the Harvard business school in particular, even if fully justified when published in 1930, could not apply to the Harvard which Holmes attended.[11] Nor could it affect the loyalty which Holmes felt for his alma mater. He himself has uttered as good a reply, perhaps, as any other to Dr. Flexner's criticisms:

> "It has been one merit of Harvard College that it has never quite sunk to believing that its only function was to carry a body of specialists through the first stage of their preparation. About these halls there has always been an aroma of high feeling, not to be found or lost in science or Greek—not to be fixed, yet all-pervading, and the warrant of Harvard College for writing the names of its dead graduates upon its tablets is not in the mathematics, the chemistry, the political economy, which it taught them, but that in ways not to be discovered, by traditions not to be written down, it helped men of lofty natures to make good their faculties. I hope and I believe that it long will give such help to its children."[12]

That was said in 1884, and has been repeated in substance more than once since then. On the two hundred and fiftieth anniversary of the College we find Holmes telling the law school:

> "At Harvard College is realized in some degree the palpitating manifoldness of truly civilized life. Its aspi-

rations are concealed because they are chastened and instructed; but I believe in my soul that they are not the less noble that they are silent. The golden light of the University is not confined to the undergraduate department; it is shed over all the schools. He who has once seen it becomes other than he was, forever-more."[13]

Holmes and James and other Harvard men formed in 1870 a dinner club, which had no name. Among the early members were William Dean Howells—in a sense an outsider—John Fiske, Henry James (the novelist), John C. Gray, Henry Adams, T. S. Perry, John C. Ropes, A. G. Sedgwick and Francis Parkman; among later members were Henry L. Higginson, Sturgis Bigelow, John T. Morse, Jr. (who wrote the *Life and Letters of Oliver Wendell Holmes*), Charles Grinnell, James Ford Rhodes, Moorfield Storey, James W. Crafts and H. P. Walcott.[14] The organization was not unlike the Saturday Club to which the elder Holmes belonged, and was hardly less noteworthy in its membership, although it was less celebrated. Even after William James had discontinued accepting other invitations to dine, he would join "the club", knowing he could go there "without any sense of responsibility and knowing that he would find congenial company and old friends".

Here the young men discussed, without special preparation, current as well as past and future questions. They had no hesitation among these boon companions in revealing what Holmes afterward called "the passionate curiosity as well as the passionate awe which we feel in face of the mystery of the universe". Here he and James could "wrangle" as they had done when Holmes was in college.

It was in 1859, while Holmes was in college, that Darwin's *Origin of Species* was published, with all its implications for the social sciences and, in the case of Holmes at least, for metaphysics.[15] Asa Gray was then teaching natural history at Harvard, and Darwin freely acknowledged his indebtedness to the

Harvard professor. Dr. Charles A. Beard now says that Darwinism was a product of "the age of early capitalism, materialism and sharp social conflicts"; and he reminds us that Darwin said in a letter to Haeckel that, after reading the *Essay on Population* by Malthus, "the idea of natural selection through the struggle for existence at once occurred to me."[16] This essay, Dr. Beard notes, was "a political and social tract to combat the 'dangerous' social doctrines of [William] Godwin", author of such tracts as the *Inquiry Concerning Political Justice*.

Darwinism, a subject of eager debate during college days, was still fresh and novel as a dinner-club topic. At the session of the British Association for the Advancement of Science, in 1931, the Darwinians were regarded somewhat as are the Fundamentalists in the religious field; and in the religious field there was an attempt to explain away Darwin's use of the word "fortuitous" in connection with variations, an effort to exorcise the bogy of chance in the evolutionary philosophy. But it is safe to say that the possible economic basis of the theory, when Holmes and James and Henry Adams were at Harvard, was no more a cause of excitement among them than was the theory of Sir William Ashley, that Calvin's letter sanctioning interest—and, by indirection, usury—marked the turn of European thought to capitalism; or even the later theory of Max Weber that Benjamin Franklin, a good Bostonian, expressed the inner "spirit of capitalism" in his "Advice to a Young Tradesman".[17] Those young men were more concerned with the destiny of man than with the approaching shadow of industrialism; but they were concerned, also, in the social and economic world around them, with the mounting feeling against slavery in the South.

Henry Adams, a student at Harvard when Wendell Holmes was there and a member of the dinner club, was somewhat too acutely conscious of being an Adams and a little too priggish ever to win a large place in the heart of Holmes. It is probable that the future professor of law exercised a greater influence on the future professor of history at Harvard than Adams exercised on him. Toward the close of 1862, while Holmes was recovering from a wound received at Antietam, Adams, secretary to his father at the Court of St. James, attended a houseparty given by Richard Monckton Milnes (Lord Houghton) at Fryston, and there met Swinburne, at the time an unknown. "The idea that one has actually met a real genius," he said afterward, "dawns slowly on a Boston mind, but it made entry at last." Listening to "the rush of Swinburne's talk", eccentric and gifted, Adams "felt the horror of Longfellow and Emerson, the doubts of Lowell and the humor of Holmes, at the wild Walpurgis night."[18] One may be sure that Holmes would have punctured that monologue with a shaft of mordant sarcasm.

At Harvard Henry Brooks Adams was a member of the Class of 1858, "a typical collection of young New Englanders, quietly penetrating and aggressively commonplace; free from mean-nesses, jealousies, intrigues, enthusiasms and passions; not ex-ceptionally quick; not consciously skeptical; singularly indiffer-ent to display, artifice, florid expression, but not hostile to it when it amused them; distrustful of themselves, but little dis-posed to trust anyone else; with not much humor of their own, but full of readiness to enjoy the humor of others; negative to a degree that in the long run became positive and triumphant. Not harsh in manners or judgment, rather liberal and open-minded, they were still as a body the most formidable critics one would care to meet, in a long life exposed to criticism. They never flattered, seldom praised; free from vanity, they were not intolerant of it; they were objectiveness itself; their attitude was a law of nature; their judgment beyond appeal, not an act either of intellect or emotion or of will, but a sort of gravitation."[19]

"Harvard College incarnate," Henry Adams called his class, and then admitted that it was "somewhat extreme". At any rate, it was very New England. Most New England boys, Adams thought, were "born too old" for college, like himself; and there is a legend that a seventeen-year-old graduate of Harvard began his Commencement paper with the words, "I am past the age of forming friendships."[20] Adams, who says that "no one took Har-

vard College seriously," may have been past that age when he
was graduated; certainly Oliver Wendell Holmes was not. Having set down something of what Holmes has said about Harvard,
it may not be amiss to note that the other undergraduate
thought the College "sent young men into the world with all
they needed to make respectable citizens, and something of what
they wanted to make useful ones." Adams thus differed essentially from Holmes in his attitude. "Leaders of men it [the College] never tried to make," he said. "Its ideals were altogether
different." The school "created a type but not a will"; four
years there resulted "in an autobiographical blank, a mind on
which only a water-mark had been stamped." And Adams vowed
he "got less than nothing" from his schoolmates.[21]

Bostonians and the New England atmosphere were not the
only influences encountered by Holmes in his life at Harvard.
He met there also, as undergraduates, excellent examples of that
Southern aristocracy with which the Northern aristocracy was
soon to be locked in lethal embrace. There was William Henry
Fitzhugh (Rooney) Lee, for example, a son of Robert E. Lee
(then Colonel of the Second United States Cavalry), and grandson of "Lighthorse Harry". Henry Adams thought this young
Virginian had changed little from the type of the grandfather.
Protesting that he liked the young man, Adams asserted that he
"was simple beyond analysis", ignorant and childlike, "helpless
before the relative complexity of a school". He and his fellow
Virginians at Harvard knew enough, however, to know "how
thin an edge of friendship" separated them from their college
companions. Strictly, Adams said with acidity, "the Southerner
had no mind; he had temperament". Neither the Virginian nor
the Bostonian was "a master of crime", but neither was of impeccable habits, both of them drank hard, and the Virginian,
Adams observed, seemed to suffer rather the more. "Commonly
the Bostonian could take some care of himself even in his worst
stages, while the Virginian became quarrelsome and dangerous.
When a Virginian had brooded a few days over an imaginary
grief and substantial whiskey, none of his northern friends could

be sure that he might not be waiting, round the corner, with a knife or pistol, to revenge insult by the dry light of *delirium tremens;* and when things reached this condition, Lee had to exhaust his authority over his own staff. Lee was a gentleman of the old school, and, as everyone knows, gentlemen of the old school drank almost as much as gentlemen of the new school; but this was not his trouble. He was sober even in the excessive violence of political opinion in those years; he kept his temper and his friends under control."[22]

At the moment the relative endurance and stamina of the North and South was of paramount interest, and Adams thought this contact with the Virginian, this opportunity to study Southern character, was "a sort of education for its own sake". But he doubted whether these slave-owning Southerners were any less fit to survive in the modern struggle for existence than were well-bred New Englanders like himself. "He [Adams] was little more fit than the Virginians to deal with a future America which showed no fancy for the past." In that sentence Adams drew sharply a line between himself and Oliver Wendell Holmes, who proved he had a fancy for the past, in so far as it might illuminate the present, and who was not afraid of the "future America", but managed to keep step precisely with it.

An emphatic and upbuilding force in the life of Holmes, Harvard was "a negative force" to Adams. He got next to nothing from the ancient languages, which Holmes continued to read in the original for years after Adams was dead; the two writers of that day who most influenced the world's thought, Adams complained, he couldn't remember having heard mentioned at Harvard: Karl Marx and Auguste Comte. The only teaching that appealed to him—and this was characteristic—was a course of lectures by Louis Agassiz on the Glacial Period and Palaeontology, "which had more influence on his curiosity than the rest of the college instruction altogether."

Adams, vexed that any Britisher could sympathize with the Confederate States of America, and piqued that some London noblemen were disposed to ignore the diplomatic representatives of the United States of America, watched the progress of the Civil War from the Court of St. James; Holmes and the majority of his class saw it amid the sweat and blood of camp and battlefield. The warmest friend Adams made at Harvard was H. H. Richardson, who hailed from New Orleans, and he attached himself to Richardson, he admitted, "as he attached himself to John La Farge or Augustus St. Gaudens or Clarence King or John Hay, none of whom were at Harvard College." Holmes cemented many college friendships in heart-breaking marches and shared dangers. Adams was amazed that he was chosen Class Orator, and had only the Class Poet as a rival on Commencement Day; it was foregone almost from the outset that Holmes should be Class Poet.

An elderly gentleman congratulated Adams, when he had delivered his class oration, on his "perfect self-possession"; he took no credit to himself for that. "Three-fourths of the graduates," he said, "would rather have addressed the Council of Trent or the British Parliament than have acted *Sir Anthony Absolute* or *Dr. Ollapod* before a gala audience of the Hasty Pudding." Self-possession "was the strongest part of Harvard College". Holmes learned new lessons in self-possession and self-control under battle-fire.

Of the eighty-one men in the Class of 1861 at Harvard, forty-seven fought for the Union, three for the Confederacy; of the non-graduates, twelve for the Union, two for the Confederacy. Eight were killed or died of their wounds; two died of disease contracted in the service. One served on the United States Coast Survey ship *Bibb*.[23]

At the first class dinner, held at "Young's" in Boston on July 20, 1864, Holmes read these verses composed for the occasion:

> How fought our brothers, and how died, the story
> You bid me tell, who shared with them the praise,
> Who sought with them the martyr's crown of glory,
> The bloody birthright of heroic days.

But, all untuned amid the din of battle,
    Not to our lyrics the inspiring strains belong;
The cannon's roar, the musket's deadly rattle
    Have drowned the music, and have stilled the song.

Let others celebrate our high endeavor
    When peace once more her starry flag shall fling
Wide o'er the land our arms made free forever;
    We do in silence what the world shall sing.

At the fiftieth anniversary dinner of the class, held at the Union Club in Boston, June 27, 1911, seventeen of the twenty-five living members were present, and Mr. Justice Holmes told them that, descending the western slope, he had found that middle life was better than youth, the later years better than middle life. On the following day, at the meeting of the Alumni Association, he delivered a more formal address.

"It has been my fortune," he said, "to belong to two bodies that seem to me somewhat alike—the Twentieth Massachusetts Regiment and the Class of '61. The Twentieth never wrote about itself to the newspapers, but for its killed and wounded in battle it stood in the first half-dozen of all the regiments of the North. This little Class never talked about itself, but, graduating just as the War of Secession was beginning, out of its eighty-one members it had fifty-one under arms, the largest proportion that any class sent to that war.

"We learn from time an amiable latitude with regard to beliefs and tastes. Life is painting a picture, not doing a sum. As twenty men of genius, looking out of the same window, will paint twenty canvases, each different from all the rest, and every one correct, so am I apt to think men may be allowed the defects of their qualities if they have the qualities of their defects. We all of us have our notions of what is best. I learned in the regiment and in the class the conclusion at least of the conduct that I believe best for the country and for ourselves—to see as far as one may the great forces that are behind every detail, and to feel them, for that makes all the difference between philosophy and gossip, between great action and small.

"It was a good thing for us in our college days, as Moorfield Storey pointed out a few years ago in an excellent address, that we were all poor. at least that we lived as if we were. I think that [sort of] training is much fitter to make a man than for a youth to have at twenty all the luxuries of life poured into a trough for him.

"Man is born a predestined idealist, for he is born to act. To act is to affirm the worth of an end; to persist in affirming the worth of an end is to make an ideal. The stern experience of our youth confirmed the destiny of fate; it left us feeling through life that pleasures do not make happiness, and that the root at once of joy and beauy is to put out all one's powers to a great end—the least wave of the Atlantic Ocean is mightier than one of Buzzard's Bay—to hammer out as compact and solid a piece of work as one can, to try to make it first-rate, and to leave it unadvertised."[24]

Harvard College and the Civil War were the twin training grounds of Oliver Wendell Holmes; amid the clash of ideas and the clash of arms his mind and character were forged. Although he freed himself from the group loyalties and prejudices and passions which are a heritage of those reared in the security of the genteel tradition, he remained faithful to Class and Regiment, to College and Cause.

Let us follow him into the war.

CHAPTER 5

Under Arms: Ball's Bluff

HALF WAY up the steep slope of Ball's Bluff, with the placid Potomac murmuring below, a thin skirmish line in blue held at bay temporarily a victorious force of Confederates on the crest.[1] Virginians and Mississippians, those rebels, hot-headed and gallant.[2] Beside the Colonel of the Twentieth Massachusetts Volunteers, in front of the blue line, stood Lieutenant Oliver Wendell Holmes, Jr., twenty years old and now being immersed, thanks to an official blunder, in his first baptism of fire.[3] A spent ball on its rebound caught him smartly on the stomach, knocked him flat and left him breathless.

"To the rear!" commanded Colonel William Raymond Lee.

The young officer made shift to crawl back. As he began to recover his wits and his wind, he thought he was not so much hurt after all. He could have remained back of the line in comparative safety, but at his urging a sergeant lent a hand to help him to his feet, and Holmes found his way back to the front. There, his sword upraised, he was a fair target for the enemy; and in less than three minutes another missile struck him, this time not a spent bullet but a conical minie ball, which tore off his shirt, entered the left breast just above the heart, and emerged on the right side.

The ball missed the heart, perhaps by a quarter of an inch, but it appeared to have perforated the lung. A surgeon who made a quick examination felt sure the wound was mortal.[4]

"Try to get him across the river," he directed; and comrades struggled down the cliff with the unconscious figure.

One hundred and fifty yards away lay the flat wooded surface of Harrison's Island, two miles long and some three hundred yards wide. To this haven the defeated Union forces were trying, amid showers of bullets, to transport their dead and wounded in frail skiffs, a scow, and a small metallic lifeboat. Hundreds were struggling for their lives to reach the island shore; some were drowning, some were slain as they escaped. It was one of the "most tragic and thrilling events of the war", and Massachusetts lost more of her sons there than in many more notable engagements.

Lieutenant Holmes recovered consciousness as he lay in a boat. Some of its occupants were dead, and he supposed, as the surgeon had supposed, that he was dying. Next to him a man groaned in agony.

"I suppose Sir Philip Sidney would say," the Lieutenant thought to himself, " 'Put that man ashore first.' I think I will let events take their course."[5]

Hustled ashore, the young man proved the next day to be somewhat better, and on the second day wrote his father a letter. The ball had passed outside the cavities containing the heart and lungs. The patient was moved presently to a Philadelphia hospital for a week, and there his father picked him up, had him put on a stretcher, and took him home on a bed in the railroad cars.

"Wendell's experience was pretty well for a youngster of twenty," the elder Holmes wrote to John Lothrop Motley. . . "You know how well all our boys behaved. In fact, the defeat at Ball's Bluff, disgraceful as it was to the planners of the stupid sacrifice, is one as much to be remembered and to be proud of as Bunker Hill. They did all that men could be expected to do."[6]

Young Holmes had experienced "a most narrow escape from instant death", but when this letter was written he was able to walk, despite an open wound. His father noted that he was "a great pet in his character of young hero with wounds in the heart, and receives visits *en grand seigneur*. I envy my white Othello, with a semicircle of young Desdemonas about him listening to the often-told story which they will have again."

United States Senator Edward D. Baker of Oregon, then Colonel in command of a California regiment, lost his life at Ball's

Bluff, with nearly a thousand of lower rank.[7] The engagement gravely involved the reputation of the commander-in-chief of the Union forces, and caused the imprisonment of General Charles P. Stone, although the precise nature of the charges against him remain a military mystery.[8] The only amplified story of the battle I have been able to find is in *The Twentieth Regiment of Massachusetts Volunteer Infantry,* prepared by Brevet Lieutenant-Colonel George A. Bruce for the Officers' Association of the regiment and privately printed.

The Twentieth stands fifth on the roll of northern regiments that suffered the heaviest losses during the war, according to this historian.[9] Officered largely by Harvard men, it was known popularly as "the Harvard regiment". The "exceptional ability and character" of the men is attested, in the view of Colonel Bruce, by the high rank many of them achieved in the service; and he appends this list:

> Brevet Major-General William F. Bartlett
> Brevet Major-General George N. Macy
> Brevet Brigadier-General William Raymond Lee
> Brevet Brigadier-General Francis W. Palfrey
> Brevet Brigadier-General Paul J. Revere
> Brevet Brigadier-General Charles Lawrence Peirson
> Brevet Brigadier-General Charles A. Whittier
> Brevet Brigadier-General Caspar Crowninshield
> Brevet Brigadier-General Edward N. Hallowell
> Brevet Brigadier-General Arthur R. Curtis
> Brevet Brigadier-General Henry L. Patten

Colonel Lee, a civil engineer who had been a classmate of Jefferson Davis at West Point and then had served in the Florida War, was appointed by Governor John A. Andrew of Massachusetts on June 27, 1861, to command the Twentieth. He chose his field and staff officers, with Paul Revere as Major, and less than a week later ordered the regiment into camp at Sprague Plain, eight miles from Boston at Readville Station. Here, with gently sloping sandy soil which dried quickly after rains, with the hills of Milton in the distance and with a pond of clear cool water nearby, the men drilled, bathed, and occasionally made sorties for drinks nearby. Tents were pitched the afternoon of July 10, and the place was named Camp Massasoit, in honor of that chief of the Wampanoag Indians who had been in alliance with the Plymouth settlers some two centuries earlier.

Recruiting was slow, because earlier regiments had exhausted the enthusiasm and to a large extent the young manhood of the community. It was not until July 18 that the regiment could be mustered into the United States Army; and even then the mustering officer reported the men as so deficient in stamina and capability that not more than one-third of them measured up to the average of his previous experience.[10] Nevertheless the company cooks got into action, a refrigerator was sunk, and presently the Twentieth was feeding not only itself but the Eighteenth Massachusetts, which occupied an adjacent field. There was battalion drill every afternoon, and the men rapidly improved in discipline, although some of them found it difficult to learn that they couldn't take part whenever they chose in excursions to Klemm's, up at Mill Village, for a glass or two of beer or liquor.

There was indeed a good deal of drunkenness among those who were fond of hard liquors; so that finally Major Revere with a small detail raided the bar and dumped into the street the whiskies, brandies and gins.

"On whose authority," the proprietor demanded, "are you doing this?"

Major Revere laid across the bar a large horse pistol.

"This," he said gently, "is my authority."[11]

Even this period of preparation was not without its mishaps. A recruit who was bathing with some comrades in the Neponsit River, close to the camp, was drowned. On the evening of August 12, when the regiment boasted but 468 enlisted men, Sergeant Buguey left the camp with a squad of fourteen of Company C, and encountered an agent of the New York Irish Brigade, who induced him and eleven of his men to desert. The twelve were followed and caught while awaiting a train transfer at Mansfield, and were jailed with the agent.

One week later orders were received from Washington to forward the regiment immediately. Colonel Lee was thus required to send along a complete roster of his officers; and young Oliver Wendell Holmes, walking down Beacon Hill with a copy in his hand of *Leviathan, or the Matter, Form and Power of a Commonwealth, Ecclesiastical and Civil,* by Thomas Hobbes (philosopher of English Puritanism), got the glad tidings that he had a commission as First Lieutenant.[12]

The impatient young man had enlisted four months earlier in the Fourth Battalion of Infantry, under Major Thomas G. Stevenson, and had gone into training at Fort Independence, in Boston Harbor; there, as Class Poet of Harvard, 1861, he had written an ode for delivery at the exercises on July 10. His commission was for Company A of the Twentieth, but he was transferred, before he went into battle, to Company G.

Colonel Lee reported to Washington his "ability and readiness to march on a few hours' notice with three days' rations, cooked in camp, with about five hundred officers and men, somewhat drilled, and with the few wagons that were ready". As a fact, the aggregate strength of the regiment was 538, but 250 additional men were transferred from other Massachusetts forces. Full ranks were never attained. Boston ladies sent a silk standard to the regiment, and the Governor presented it. The smoothbore muskets with which the men had been training were exchanged for Enfield rifles, bought in England by a Massachusetts agent just after Fort Sumter was fired on.[13] September 4 the regiment struck its tents and set out for the scene of war, with a formidable train of baggage wagons, ambulances and hospital wagons.

Unlike most of the Massachusetts regiments, the Twentieth did not parade on Boston Common amid the cheers and tears of onlookers. Although officered almost entirely from that city, the regiment never appeared there as an organization, during or after the war. Lieutenant Holmes was transferred with others to strengthen Company G, under Captain Henry J. Sweeny.

In New York there was a parade. The Sons of Massachusetts in that city gave the regiment a reception and dinner, at which there was much speech-making, and the men marched up Broadway to the ferry before moving on to Philadelphia. The next morning this city expressed its hospitality in a breakfast at the old "Cooper Shop". Thence to Baltimore, and thence in cattle cars to Washington, the regiment made its way, before being hurried to the front with its ranks but three-quarters filled. It had spent fifty-seven hours moving by trains and boats from camp to the capital.

After marching in review along Pennsylvania Avenue before Lieutenant-General Scott, the regiment moved out to Georgetown Heights. It was dusty and hot, and the camps were full of hubbub and confusion as the tired men pitched their tents at evenfall. There were no cheers save scattered shouts from other Massachusetts troops, and some of the newcomers thought this "cold and strange" after the enthusiasm that had greeted them along the way.[14] Not much time was vouchsafed to contemplate this circumstance; the men were speedily moved to another camp, then to a plain near Leesburg, Virginia. It was the first long march for the men, and the day was hot; but the next day they made fifteen miles and reached Poolesville, their objective, on September 14. Ball's Bluff was not to be fought until October 21. Until that encounter the regiment went through a steady gruelling of drills, dress parades and reviews. Their pickets on the towpath between the Chesapeake & Ohio Railroad's canal and the Potomac occasionally exchanged shots with rebel pickets across the river, and occasionally, in somewhat different temper, exchanged gossip or raillery.

"When you goin' to Richmond?" a rebel asked, thumb to nose.

"The day before you go to Washington," the Twentieth's picket replied.

Although the regiment, posted as it was on the front line, was so burdened with picket and guard duty that the men spent an average of five nights a week under arms, certain compensations were in evidence. No other troops were better equipped. When the Commander-in-Chief asked whether there was a supply of arms, uniforms and accouterments, Colonel Lee responded: "My regiment, Sir, is from Massachusetts."[15]

Ovens were constructed, and the men experienced the luxury of soft bread instead of hard tack. No other Massachusetts regiment, so it was said, enjoyed this distinction. Colonel Lee boasted that he could march "at sight order" with five days' rations, to say nothing of 650 rifles and sixty rounds of ammunition; and as a fact, when ordered to move forward for the fatal engagement at Ball's Bluff, he did have his men in motion within thirty minutes.

On Sunday, October 20, came the call to arms. Begun as a reconnaissance, the encounter was dignified by the name of battle only because of the heavy losses suffered. General Stone, examining a Negro deserter from the Thirteenth Mississippi the day before, had been told that the rebels in Leesburg were expecting him to attack, and had sent back their heavy baggage, because they anticipated being driven out. Colonel Bruce gives the force defending Leesburg and vicinity as the Seventh Brigade, commanded by General N. G. Evans, of Beauregard's First Corps, comprising the Eighth Virginia and three regiments of Mississippi infantry, with three companies of cavalry and six guns, in all about four thousand effectives.

Against this force, according to the historian of the Twentieth Regiment, General Stone actually employed, of eighty-four hundred present for duty, only twenty-two companies, less than two thousand men, "all without experience, having been in the field only one month, never having been in battle, and unacquainted with each other or their commanders."

About these figures, as often happens, there is some dispute. The *Century Cyclopedia* gives the number of Union men engaged as 1900, their losses as 894, the rebel losses, 302. In a letter written two years after the battle by John C. Ropes, Jr., to John C. Gray, Jr. (both Union soldiers), he tells of a visit to a military hospital near Baltimore, and says that the Adjutant of the Eighteenth Mississippi, who had lost his right arm at the shoulder joint, asserted that the Confederates had in all about two thousand men at Ball's Bluff, "only about 1500 of whom, however, were actually engaged. (The reserve, however, enabled the whole 1500 to fight.)"[16]

Both Union and Confederate wounded were under treatment in the hospital, and what Ropes has to say in this letter, as coming from an observant and candid Bostonian while the war was still in progress, is of interest.

"I must say the privates we talked with were far superior to the average of our privates. I do not mean that I have the materials for forming an estimate of our privates, for I have seen but comparatively few, and these chiefly Irish, but let the opinion go for what it is worth. Especially on military matters were these rebels well-informed and accurate, or desirous to be accurate. In manners they were exceedingly affable, and had the ease of manner which in the North we never see except among the upper classes.

"I saw men from South Carolina, Georgia, Virginia and Mississippi. It strikes me as very probable that one would notice the same difference between the English and French private soldiers. Certainly there is much the same difference between the English and French peasantry and lower classes. It is in short the difference between South and North, and is not, in my judgment, attributable to the influence of Slavery, except very indirectly, as most of these men probably never owned a slave. I imagine it to result from the much greater sociability produced by a mild and genial climate; and perhaps also from the greater equality of the white race produced by the laboring class being a distinct caste. Whatever the reason, such seemed to me to be the fact. [George Nelson] Macy [subsequently a Brevet

General] also told me he had always noticed the same thing; and he has had abundant opportunity for judging."

Not even young Oliver Wendell Holmes, a generous foe if ever there was one, could have spoken more kindly of enemies. Generosity of that sort, indeed, was characteristic of well-bred New Englanders. Macy, for example, who hailed from Nantucket, found an officer who had been in Barksdale's Brigade, which had often opposed his own brigade, and they compared with avidity notes of Ball's Bluff and the two Fredericksburg engagements, where they had fought each other. "Not an unkind word was dropped by either party," although the war had dragged at that time but half its crimson length across the land.

It may not be amiss, since reference has been made to the Holmes attitude toward the enemy, to quote from a speech he delivered on May 30, 1884, at Keene, New Hampshire, before the John Sedgwick Post of the Grand Army of the Republic: "The soldiers who were doing their best to kill one another felt less of personal hostility, I am very certain, than some who were not imperilled by their mutual endeavors. I have heard more than one of those who had been gallant and distinguished officers on the Confederate side say that they had no such feeling. I know that I and those whom I knew best had not. We believed that it was most desirable that the North should win; we believed in the principle that the Union is indissoluble; we, or many of us at least, also believed that the conflict was inevitable, and that slavery had lasted long enough. But we equally believed that those who stood against us held just as sacred convictions that were the opposite of ours, and we respected them as every man with a heart must respect those who give all for their belief.

"The experience of battle soon taught its lesson even to those who came into the field more bitterly disposed. You could not stand up day after day in those indecisive contests where overwhelming victory was impossible because neither side would run as they ought when beaten, without getting at last something of

[81]

the same brotherhood for the enemy that the north pole of a magnet has for the south—each working in an opposite sense to the other, but each unable to get along without the other. As it was then, it is now. The soldiers of the war need no explanations; they can join in commemorating a soldier's death with feelings not different in kind, whether he fell toward them or by their side."[17]

Let us return from this digression, by way of another Holmes quotation, to Ball's Bluff. In that same Memorial Day speech he said: "I remember, as I awoke from my first long stupor after the battle of Ball's Bluff, I heard the doctor say, 'He was a beautiful boy,' and I knew that one of those two speakers was no more. The other, after passing harmless through all the previous battles, went into Fredericksburg with strange premonition of the end, and there met his fate."

Friends fell to right and left of the young Lieutenant in his first engagement, which involved seven companies of the Twentieth. General Stone sent a battalion of the regiment to the towpath opposite Harrison's Island, and reported to General McClellan that he had "started a reconnoitering party towards Leesburg". The Twentieth dozed supperless on the towpath while another detachment crossed to the island and sent a scouting party on to the Virginia shore without finding rebel pickets. As to the misunderstandings between Union commanders we need not go into detail here; it is enough for our purposes, since Lieutenant Holmes was attached to the Twentieth, to know that Colonel Lee sent two companies of this regiment quickly to the Virginia shore and ordered the remaining five to the island. Lieutenant Holmes was among the latter. Around noon the next morning these began following their comrades across to the Virginia side; only twenty-five could make the journey at a time, so inadequate was the equipment. The narrow strip of river on that side was not covered by enemy sharp-shooters, and the landing was sheltered by a strip of woodland at the foot of the bluff. The cliff, nearly one hundred feet high, was too steep to climb in a straight line, and the men, in single file, ascended along a winding sheep-path. Lieutenant Macy (as he was then) guarded the rear with twenty-five men. There were minor casualties in scouting and skirmishing during the early morning, but the real fighting did not begin until the afternoon of the twenty-first.

Colonel Baker crossed to the bluff at two o'clock, and approved the position of the Fifteenth and Twentieth Massachusetts. He had spent two hours in getting his Californians from the Maryland to the Virginia side, and had scarcely half an hour to arrange his forces before the enemy opened the battle. After the lines were formed he said to Colonel Lee: "I congratulate you, Sir, on the prospect of a battle"; and, to the men of the Twentieth: "Boys, you want to fight, don't you?", which evoked a hearty cheer. Captain John C. Putnam of Company H was soon wounded (he lost his right arm, and was the second man of the Twentieth to be hit), and was sent over to the island. Posted in the open, the Twentieth suffered heavily during the three and one-half hours' fighting which followed.[18]

Even as late as five o'clock the Union forces seemed to have some prospect of victory, and the death of Colonel Baker about that time did not demoralize them. Colonel Lee of the Twentieth succeeded to the command, until Colonel Cogswell of the Forty-second New York claimed that post by reason of seniority. Finding that he could not break through the enemy line, Colonel Cogswell ordered a retreat to the river, and directed his subordinate officers to save as many men as they could. The movement down the cliff broke up all formation, but by six o'clock the survivors were beside the bank, save for the skirmishers half way up the bluff.

Dusk was gathering. The Confederates on the crest of the bluff could not descend without breaking up their formation; they remained at bay because of the skirmish line and the shots of scattered groups of Union soldiers, but they fired steadily at the men among the trees, on the shore, in the boats or swimming.

The scow, returning for its second load of wounded, was overloaded by a rush of uninjured men, and set out with her gunwales almost flush with the water. Midstream, one of the men poling her was shot and fell to one side, capsizing her. As the men, wounded or unhurt, rose to the surface, they struggled in a huge animate ball, entangled, rolling over and over as men tried to break apart and get their arms free for swimming. Only one was known to have escaped with his life from that fateful boat-load. The scow floated downstream and was lost.[19] Soon after, the metallic lifeboat, riddled with bullets, sank also. The frail skiffs disappeared. Within an hour there was no craft of any sort at hand, and those remaining on the Virginia shore who could not swim had no prospect of relief.

Colonel Lee, who had refused to leave the shore so long as wounded men had not been taken to the island, started with some subordinates up the river, attempted in vain to make a raft of fence rails, bribed a Negro to show them a boat, which proved to be water-logged, and finally was captured by a squad of Confederates.

Captain William F. Bartlett, in command of the men who remained, told all who could swim to plunge into the river and escape if they could. Many of the men threw their guns and other equipment into the stream to prevent the Confederates from getting them, and some disrobed. Although the distance was not great, the water was cold and the current strong; good swimmers sometimes found the effort too great after their exhausting afternoon. The water was like a lather where the rebel bullets struck, and many were either killed or disabled. Caspar Crowninshield, a junior Captain, swam across with his watch in his mouth and his sword in his hand, but forgot and left the watch beneath a haystack where he took shelter for the night. Lieutenant Norwood P. Hallowell swam across with his sword dangling from his neck. On the Maryland side of the island he found a skiff, which was utilized to save some of the wounded on several trips. Lieutenant Macy volunteered to swim to the island to look for other boats, and started out nude with his sword in his hand and wearing his cap, in which there was a picture of his *fiancée*.

He had to drop the sword, but he kept that cap. He was unable to find another boat.[20]

A Confederate detachment descended the bluff about ten o'clock that evening and took prisoner those left on that side of the river.

The dead and wounded were collected in an old house on the island, and the next day were ferried across to the Maryland shore. Second Lieutenant William Lowell Putnam, a kinsman of Lieutenant Holmes, died that day, and his body was sent to Boston.

At dress parade, a week later, a general order by Lieutenant Colonel F. W. Palfrey was read:

> "His Excellency John A. Andrew, Governor of Massachusetts, desires to express through the proper channel his sincere thanks to the officers and privates of the Twentieth Regiment of Massachusetts Volunteers for the bravery which they displayed at the recent battle at Ball's Bluff, and for the admirable discipline which their behavior there so strongly bears evidence of. He regrets the severe loss sustained by the regiment, and deeply sympathizes with the wounded and the suffering relatives of the dead and wounded, but will assure the regiment they have earned and own a name brilliant and glorious, and that the Bay State is proud to recognize them as sons, and as sons worthy of the Commonwealth and worthy to share past glories of the Commonwealth."[21]

Colonel Lee, Major Revere and some of their subordinates, who were captured, were confined in Libby Prison and then in almost intolerable quarters in the Henrico County jail, before they were paroled and subsequently exchanged. Brigadier General Lander, on hearing that Confederates had said "fewer of the Massachusetts officers would have been killed had they not been too proud to surrender," wrote some verses, of which the last two read:

Pride, 'tis our watchword: "clear the boats,
  "Holmes, Putnam, Bartlett, Peirson—Here!"
And while this crazy wherry floats
  "Let's save our wounded," cries Revere.

Old State—some souls are rudely sped—
  This record for thy Twentieth Corps—
Imprisoned, wounded, dying, dead,
  It only asks, "Has Sparta more?"[22]

So serious had been the losses of the Twentieth that further recruiting was necessary, and commissioned officers who had acquitted themselves well at Ball's Bluff were sent to Boston for that purpose. They opened an office at 7 Howard Street, and during the fall and winter were successful in filling some of the gaps in the ranks.

A silk memorial flag, a gift from the sisters of Lieutenants Lowell and Putnam, the former wounded, the latter killed, at Ball's Bluff, was presented to the regiment the following Christmas afternoon, and a letter was read from Charles Eliot Norton, who had not at that time begun his distinguished service at Harvard, in which he said in part:

> "The twenty-first of October is inscribed by Massachusetts in her calendar of days made memorable by the virtue of her sons. She will never forget your hard, faithful, glorious though defeated services on that day —when you baptized, not in vain, the soil of Virginia with your blood. These colors bear that date upon them, and while they revive the memories of your valor, they revive also the memory of your loss—of those brave dead who gave their lives for the cause for which Massachusetts had sent them out to do battle. Their memory is dear and sacred in our hearts forever. . . .
>
> "Take, then, this flag. Stand by it in the evil day. Bring it back when the sword has done its work, and

let the stains of smoke and blood upon it, and the rents in its folds, tell us the story of your deeds. And may He who is the God of Battles, as he is the God of Peace, give you honorable death, or bring you back safe from war, according as by death or by life you can best serve his cause."[23]

The silken flag bore on one side the words "Ball's Bluff" and the pine tree of the State, with a motto below: "Stand in the Evil Day." On the other side was the State motto with an arm and sword.

Lieutenant Holmes missed the stirring exercises at which the banner was presented. He was not able to rejoin his regiment until early the following spring, and moped at home, despite his "semicircle of young Desdemonas", until his wound healed and he was hale again. He was to become a Captain before he was struck down again, this time at Antietam.

CHAPTER 6

Antietam

TWO BULLETS, as at Ball's Bluff, hit Captain Holmes at Antietam. The first shattered his knapsack buckle, the second perforated his neck. But before this happened he had gone unscathed, after he had recovered from the first injuries, through the engagement at White Oaks and the Seven Days' battles of the Peninsula campaign, during McClellan's disastrous effort to take Richmond.

Illness he knew, and hardships. With the others of his command he went ten days and nights, sleeping unsheltered in the mud and on duty, often during driving rains, without removing his uniform or equipment, even his boots; but although he spoke often in after years of the strain and tenseness of danger, which set the pattern of his philosophy and taught him that "life is a profound and passionate thing",[1] never once did he allude, in public at any rate, to the adversities and discomforts of those days. His illness took the form of dysentery, and his father said with pride that it "did not keep him from being on duty until the last of the battles—Malvern Hill—had been fought".[2] This is not to say that he took part in all seven battles, for the Twentieth Volunteers, although it lost more than one-third of its men, was not invariably in the thick of the fighting.

While young Holmes was in Boston, the Twentieth had a breathing spell in winter quarters at Camp Benton. He could not reproach himself that he was missing his share of the fighting, but he did miss one joyful occasion: on November 12 the Twentieth received its first pay since leaving Massachusetts, and the money was in "good gold dollars", a custom which did not persist long thereafter. The men sent home collectively some $8,000.

New officers and new recruits were broken in, and the older men—older in service, not always in years—were trained further in company, battalion and brigade drill, in guard duty, skirmishing and bayonet exercise. Not until February of 1862 was a bathhouse completed in an old log structure which has been taken over for stores.[3] Thirty half-barrels were converted into washtubs; nails on which to hang clothes during ablutions were driven into the walls, a barber-shop was partitioned off in one corner, and in squads of twenty or more, from ten in the morning until seven in the evening, the men scrubbed themselves in high glee, then plied clothes brushes arduously.

Major-General John Sedgwick (who was to be slain at Spottsylvania a little more than a year later), took command on February 22 of the division embracing the Twentieth, and General N. J. T. Dana of the brigade. A few days later camp was broken, and after various stops along the way the men paraded on March 12 through Harper's Ferry, to the tune of *Dixie,* past the prison where John Brown had been confined.[4] The objective of this maneuver was Winchester, Virginia, but the Confederates had abandoned the town ere the Twentieth and the other forces in the move got near, and steps were retraced.

At Bolivar Heights the regiment encamped until March 24. Captain J. C. Putnam and Lieutenant William R. Riddle, each of whom had lost an arm at Ball's Bluff, returned hopefully to duty, but each found it impossible to stand the strain of active campaigning. Lieutenant Holmes, who returned about the same time, appeared to be of tougher fiber. On the twenty-third he was commissioned Captain.[5]

From Bolivar the regiment marched again through Harper's Ferry to Sandy Hook, took train for Washington and then boats to Fortress Monroe and Hampton. Disembarking, the men marched a mile out on the road toward Big Bethel and bivouacked, within plain view of the *Monitor.* It was difficult to believe that this insignificant craft, with her squat nine-foot iron-clad turret, had defeated, in an encounter some three weeks before which was to revolutionize warfare at sea, the formidable armored *Merrimac,* rechristened the *Virginia.* Trees were already budding in the warm bright air of the next morning, April 1, and the regi-

ment remained on the spot three days before setting out for Big
Bethel, where the men found earthworks and barracks abandoned by the enemy the day before. Heavy guns could be heard
the next morning, April 5, far in front, and presently brisker musketry. Trudging on through mud, the regiment encamped within
five miles of Yorktown, a little more than a mile from a semicircle
of Confederate forces.

Reconnaissance and picketing, enlivened occasionally by
enemy shells and musketry fire, filled the days until the sixteenth,
when four companies of the regiment moved forward with the re-
mainder of the division. They were now quite near the Confederate lines, with picket posts only an eighth of a mile apart. No
music nor calls were permitted; the men were aroused every
morning at three o'clock and kept standing under arms until full
sunlight. When not picketing the men supplied working parties,
night or day, on roads, fortifications and trenches. Sometimes
even the sound of enemy conversation could be heard.

On Easter Sunday, April 20, the whole brigade turned out under arms, formed in line of battle, and stood until after dusk, and
again until past midnight; but the routine of watching and working, skirmishing and digging, with the rattle of firearms in front
and almost incessant rain overhead, varied but little, although
with some casualties. Colonel Lee, Major Revere and Assistant
Surgeon Revere, who had been captured at Ball's Bluff, returned
to their posts on May 2, their exchange finally having been arranged. The very next morning the Twentieth moved forward
through a woodland, waded through a swamp, and without battle mounted its regimental flag as the first United States insignia
on the Confederate works at Yorktown.[6]

Jubilant at this easy distinction so soon after their Colonel's
return, the men were downcast the next day at being held near
Yorktown during the Battle of Williamsburg, and at spending
nearly eleven hours in covering about half a mile of ground
soaked with a steady downpour. All that night the regiment was
exposed to the cold rain, amid the deep mud. The next day it was
moved by boat up the York River and the Pamunkey, where it

disembarked into an immense open flat on the southerly bank. There were rumors that the Confederates, retreating up the Peninsula, were about to surrender, or at least abandon Richmond; but even on the twenty-third, after many hard marches through mud and rain, the rumors remained but thin comfort. During the next week there was a chance to rest for a while at Camp Tyler, so named in honor of the late President Tyler, whose magnificent estate was nearby. April 30 was severely hot, and the day was followed by a tempest of rain; at midnight heavy cannonading began in the direction of Richmond. Certainly the enemy was not giving up the capital without a struggle.

Fair Oaks (sometimes called the battle of Seven Pines) was a two-day engagement, fought on Saturday, May 31, and Sunday, June 1, 1862. The forces on either side numbered close to twenty thousand. On the first day General Joseph E. Johnston, commanding the Confederates, was wounded, and he was succeeded on the second day by Robert E. Lee himself. General George B. McClellan's main army lay north of the Chickahominy, a treacherous stream, "of which it was hard to say at the best of times where its banks were, and of which no man could say where its banks would be tomorrow".[7]

The engagement began in the early afternoon, and the Twentieth fell in without knapsacks, but with sixty rounds of ammunition and a day's rations. It waited impatiently at the Grapevine Bridge for orders to cross the river, and at 2:30 P. M. received them. The flimsy structure bore the weight of the men, but not all the artillery of the brigade could be got across. Only the Seventh Michigan and the Twentieth, of that division, got a share in the first day's fighting, and the Twentieth was the last regiment to get up into the battle. When it got within sight of the field, seven guns and the infantry were firing rapidly, and it went at quick-step to form on the top of a ridge near the Adams house, about equidistant west of Fair Oaks and north of Seven Pines. The hostile fire, from a woodland some 250 yards away, became hot, and the enemy made an attempt to capture the guns by assault, but fell back when within fifteen yards of them. In reprisal the whole line charged, and the Twentieth with the others moved forward at double-quick with fixed bayonets, tore down the fences on both sides of an intervening road, and plunged into the woods. The men of the regiment had to move over a muddy plowed field, and some of them sank to their knees at every step.

The enemy retreated, although in that part of the battle the Confederates used five brigades against three and one-half of Union forces; the total loss of the five brigades is given as 1,273, with General Hatton killed and General Pettigrew wounded and captured by the Twentieth. The Union losses in that part of the field were not half so great; and the Twentieth added to its laurels by capturing two Lieutenant-Colonels, as well as prisoners from North Carolina, Virginia, Georgia, Alabama, Tennessee, Mississippi and Texas regiments. The regiment itself lost a lieutenant and eight men, in addition to many wounded.[8]

The bridge on which the Twentieth had crossed the Chickahominy was carried away in the heavy rainfall of the morning of June 1, isolating the whole division from the left bank, and a lower bridge was also found impracticable. On the following night there was another heavy rain, succeeded by an extremely hot day and another storm that evening. Through all this weather the regiment remained in the advance line, occasionally moving forward a bit, and finally got within four miles of Richmond. Colonel Bruce, historian of the regiment, says that from May 31 to June 11 it was in such proximity to the enemy that the men were not permitted to take off their clothes; until the bridges were rebuilt they were on short rations, with no tents or blankets, so that they stood in the mud and rain by day and lay unsheltered in it by night.[9]

The Twentieth was relieved in the front line on June 20, and was sent a mile back to high ground, where the men had an opportunity to take off their clothes, "perform respectable toilets and put on clean clothes once more". Some cases of scurvy developed from the steady rations of salt provisions, and a ration of whiskey was given to each man every morning, "and did much good". Shelter tents were pitched on stilts, and under them beds were fashioned of poles on stakes some two feet high, to the great satisfaction of the troopers, who regarded these quarters as "dry, sheltered and airy" after their previous experiences. With a few lemons and raw potatoes mashed in vinegar the scurvy was subdued.

Twice the regiment was turned out under arms in expectation of an attack, and more than once slept in full accouterments, but there was no fighting, and for a fortnight there was a rest in preparation for the Seven Days' battles, now ahead of the forces.

General Lee moved on June 26 to crush the isolated right wing of the Union forces, which included the Twentieth Massachusetts, and to cut it off from its base of supplies on the York River. He detached forces from his center and right wing—which he daringly left in greatly attenuated form—and moved them behind this screen without the knowledge of the Union commanders, save for a report, obtained from a deserter the night before the attack was made. "Stonewall" Jackson began that morning a flanking movement with "Jeb" Stuart's cavalry on his left. The Twentieth fell back slowly to a selected strong position on the steep easterly bank of the Beaver Dam creek, near Mechanicsville, and retired the next morning to the Gaines Mill, four miles down the Chickahominy, where was fought one of the most stubborn battles of the war. Lee lost there 10,239 in killed and wounded, the Union forces 4,257 killed and wounded, with 2,941 missing. "At such cost the victory was dearly bought", in the opinion of Colonel Bruce.[10]

In the engagements at Garnett's and Golding's, the Twentieth sent out detachments as working parties, and was repeatedly under fire the morning of June 28 and the next day, but saw little close fighting. It lost no men on those days, although one or two were slightly wounded by fragments of shell. It was very hot, and during the marching some of the men were sun-struck, while nearly all of them threw away their blankets and knapsacks. At

Savage's Station the men witnessed the blowing up of a train of cars filled with ammunition; a huge white balloon of smoke rose from the intentional explosion, and the men thought it a grand spectacle. At Allen's Farm the Twentieth advanced beyond the front line and was credited with winning the engagement.

As the Twentieth marched toward White Oak bridge that evening a heavy squall drenched the men with rain. The cars which had contained the ammunition were still burning, and lit parts of the field, but a woodland beyond was dark, and seemed to be filled with dead and wounded South Carolinians, many of them groaning in pain. The men of the Twentieth helped as many of them as possible, and pickets reported, so close were the opposing forces, that they could hear the enemy taking the disabled off.

After crossing White Oak bridge the Twentieth's division marched on Glendale, where it halted on the Quaker road. (The bridge was destroyed a few hours later.) Colonel Lee took command of the brigade when it was sent at double quick to support another in distress, but it was held for two hours in the rear. This was a minor duel, but in the main fight, which was fierce and costly to both sides, the Twentieth took part in the late afternoon, and lost heavily. The men advanced through dead and wounded of both armies, and at one point found themselves entirely alone, in the open, in front of their own lines. They had got into a strange place under orders to connect two ends of the Union forces, but neither end was in sight. For nearly half an hour they held their ground, delivering and withstanding a heavy fire, until the danger of a wholesale capture became imminent and Lieutenant-Colonel Palfrey gave the order to about-face, withdrew the remnants of the regiment to a woods in the rear and reformed the line.

The fighting lasted until sunset, and the muskets became so heated that sometimes the men forced charges into them by bracing their ramrods against the trees. At midnight, the Confederate attempt to break through the line having been defeated, the Twentieth marched back down the Quaker road, toward Malvern Hill.

The battle of Malvern Hill was fought on July 1, and the Twentieth was stationed in a clover field, at the edge of an elevated plateau, overlooking a wide space of open country, with some fine woodlands nearby and handsome houses here and there. The men·were bedraggled and weary, but food and a five-hour rest somewhat refreshed them. Then, under a galling artillery fire, the position was shifted. The battle lasted until 9 o'clock that evening, and repeated impetuous assaults by the enemy, in an effort to take the hill, were repulsed. The Twentieth slept on the field of battle and then marched ten miles to an encampment at Harrison's Landing. The "Seven Days" was done.

Although both Colonel Lee and Lieutenant-Colonel Francis W. Palfrey had been wounded, and although the total Union loss in killed, wounded and missing was nearly sixteen thousand, as against more than twenty thousand for the enemy, Captain Holmes, often in the thick of shell and bullets, escaped injury. July 4 the regiment moved out of the rain and mud at Harrison's Landing to higher ground, with a brook nearby and a pond accessible for bathing, where it threw up fortifications and settled down. Four days later President Lincoln visited the camp, and soon thereafter the Twentieth had its first dress parade in many weeks. Batches of recruits were welded into the depleted ranks from time to time. Colonel Lee was still too weak to resume command, and Major Paul Revere temporarily took charge. By marches and by boat trips the regiment made its way toward Germantown and the bloody fields of Antietam.

General Lee, who had forced the Army of the Potomac from within four miles of Richmond to encampments thirty miles away, proposed to Jefferson Davis on September 3, 1862, that he invade Maryland and possibly Pennsylvania. The Army of Virginia he had "turned inside out and upside down," but he had no intention of trying to take Washington, around which both Union armies were entrenched.[11] He had recovered Virginia's fields as the harvests were about to ripen, and he wished to "carry the war into the enemy's country."

The Twentieth, on September 6, marched out to a point near Rockville, where it drew up in battle line and threw out pickets. The expected attack did not materialize. Let Lieutenant-Colonel Palfrey, who returned from Washington that day to rejoin the regiment, contrast the appearance of the capital with the force he found under arms.

"Nothing could have been more peaceful than the appearance of Washington as I left it on a lovely afternoon. The signs of war were always plenty there of course, but there was absolutely nothing to indicate the neighborhood of an enemy. Everyone seemed to be absorbed in the pursuits of peaceful business and secure pleasure as if the blast of war had not been heard in the land. On foot, on horseback, in carriages, everyone seemed to be out of doors, and enjoying, whether working or playing, the perfect close of a perfect day. I had not ridden many miles when I met a squad of prisoners, and learned that they had been taken that morning in a skirmish on the Maryland side of the Potomac. So Lee, or some of Lee's men, had invaded a loyal State, and there was every prospect that there would soon be wigs on the green. Proceeding a few miles further, I found the regiment, part of a line sleeping on its arms in order of battle, and supporting some batteries, of which the guns were unlimbered, with the gunners lying at the trails of the pieces. The report was that Jackson, with a largely superior force, was close at hand, and apparently proposing to attack in the morning. It was a dramatic changing of scene, from the comfort and careless gaiety of Washington to a starlit bivouac, with every preparation made for meeting an impending attack.[12]

"Washington and its environments presented singular sights in the early days of September, 1862. The

luxury and refinements of peace contrasted sharply with
the privations and squalor of war. There are few pret-
tier suburban drives than those in the neighborhood
of Washington, and no weather is more delightful
than that of late Summer there, when a cooler air comes
with the shortening days. As the shadows lengthen in
the golden afternoon, well-appointed carriages rolled
along those charming drives, bearing fair women in
cool and fresh costumes, and by their side the ragged,
dusty, sunburnt regiments from the Peninsula trudged
along. Rest, cleanliness, ice, food, drink, every indul-
gence of civilized life within reach of hand, but our
hands could not be stretched out to grasp them. Military discipline was the dragon that guarded the golden
apples of the Hesperides. They were so near and yet
so far. The mythic Tantalus must have been present to
the minds of many of those who then marched by the
road which leads from Washington to the Chain
Bridge. The carriages returned to their stables, the fair
ladies returned to the enjoyment of every pleasure that
Washington could confer, but the Army of the Potomac moved steadily northward, to bivouac under the
stars or the clouds, and to march again in its tatters
through the dust and the sunshine, through the rain
and the mud."[13]

Let the Colonel contrast also the conditions under which the
Twentieth Regiment was now functioning with the hardships
which had encompassed the men on the Peninsula. He continues:

"Fortunately we had by this time become soldiers
in something more than the name; we had learned to
make much out of little, we were cheered by the more
wholesome air and the more variegated country, we
were glad to get out of the wilderness of the Peninsula.
It was pleasant, too, to be once more in a country that
was at least nominally friendly. Whatever the real feel-

ings of the Marylanders might be, the Stars and Stripes might often be seen in other places than above the heads of the color guards. Whether the natives sold to us gladly or not, they had much to sell, and that in itself was a most agreeable novelty to us. In the Peninsula, the country afforded us nothing, and the change from the land where our meat was fat pork, or odious beef served quivering from an animal heated by the long day's march and killed as soon as the day's march was ended, to a land where fresh vegetables and poultry were not rare, was very cheering. Money was not scarce. The pay of the army was liberal, and we had had no chance to spend money on the Peninsula. So our march was pleasant. Wood and water were easy to find, instead of requiring weary searches at the end of a weary day. We no longer had to send the pioneers to search for stakes, and then to fit them toilsomely in the hard, bare earth with their picks, before we could unsaddle and let our horses' bridles go. The foragers found forage for the poor beasts in abundance, and the little tins in which we had learned to cook so cleverly had often something in them better than the hard bread, water, salt, pepper, and ration meat."

By easy stages the regiment marched to the Monocacy, crossed the stream the afternoon of September 13, and then paraded through Frederick City, amid the applause of civilians and women. Maryland had refused Lee's invitation a week earlier to join the Confederacy, and the village was glad to be rid of his ragged soldiery. Two days after the Twentieth marched through the village, the Union forces at Harper's Ferry surrendered more than 12,000 men, with large supplies; however, Lee's circular order to his subordinates, issued earlier, had fallen into McClellan's hands, revealing the movements of all parts of the Confederate army.

Antietam

The Twentieth moved toward Boonsborough the day Harper's Ferry was surrendered, and then moved off through Keedysville to Antietam Creek. McClellan had in hand for the battle thirty-five brigades of infantry and a strong division of cavalry, while Lee could muster for action only fifteen brigades, fourteen of which had suffered severely at Turner's Gap. The story of Antietam (or Sharpsburg, as the battle is sometimes called) is history, and we need follow here only the fortunes of the Twentieth regiment. Sedgwick's division, to which the regiment belonged, reached the East Wood, a grove of fine oaks, and formed three lines, with the Twentieth in the center. It was subjected to heavy artillery fire as it made its way thence to the West Woods, where, under a sharp musketry fusillade from the enemy, the three lines crowded together. The men of the Twentieth stood leaning on their muskets, and some of the officers began smoking. Suddenly a cry was raised:

"The enemy is behind us!"

It was true. Not twenty yards away were the Confederates, turning the left flank, where the regiments were breaking. The soldiers of the Twentieth faced about promptly, but were so crowded that but few could fire without hitting their own men. An order was given to retreat, and amid fearful loss of life the Twentieth retired by the right flank, at the ordinary step and with their firearms on their shoulders. In less than an hour the division lost more than two thousand men in a vain sacrifice, and General Sedgwick was wounded; but the Twentieth kept steady and maintained its formation throughout. "Neither General McClellan nor any officer or soldier in the army," says the historian of the Twentieth, "thought that night of a victory having been won. It was two days later, after Lee had retreated across the Potomac, that anyone put forward this claim, and in a qualified sense it has been allowed."[14]

Late on the night of the battle, the household of Dr. Oliver Wendell Holmes in Boston was aroused by the loud summons of a telegraph messenger. The Doctor read: "Capt. Holmes

[99]

wounded shot through the neck thought not mortal at Keedys-ville."

Through the neck! Wind-pipe, food-pipe, carotid, jugular, half a dozen smaller but formidable vessels, a great braid of nerves, the spinal cord—a bullet should have killed at once, the Doctor reflected, if at all. He reread the message: "Thought not mortal"; that was better than "not thought mortal." He couldn't place the man whose name was signed to the dispatch. Where was Keedysville? It was a postoffice in Washington County, Maryland. The messenger wanted a dollar and thirteen cents. "Has nobody got thirteen cents? Don't keep that boy waiting—how do we know what messages he has got to carry?"

Subsequently the Doctor wrote the story of "My Hunt After the Captain" (for he set out at once to search for his wounded son), and found some of the things he did as hard "as for one of our young fellows to leave his sweetheart and go into a Peninsular campaign," which was what the son had done. The narrative, although it did not greatly please the hero of it, was full of shrewd observation and interesting reflection.[15] In a New York City hotel "we were not uncivilly treated. . . . If the despot of the Patent-Annunciator is only mildly contemptuous in his manner, let the victim look upon it as a personal favor. . . . One cannot expect an office clerk to embrace tenderly every stranger who comes in with a carpet-bag."

The Doctor moved on to Philadelphia, where he hoped to get news of the wounded man, but inquired in vain; on the way thence to Baltimore he came upon Dr. William Hunt of Philadelphia, who had treated the son for his first wound and was now bound on another errand of surgery. The story is too discursive to permit of extended quotation here, although it has achieved a certain fame. In a hotel in Frederick, Dr. Holmes heard of a wounded officer in an upper chamber, but it proved to be Lieutenant Henry L. Abbott of the Twentieth, who was ill of typhoid fever and had heard nothing of the Captain. Presently there entered the room Lieutenant Henry R. Wilkins of the same regiment, just from the battle-ground and on his way to Boston with

the body of an officer. He thought the Captain's wound less serious than had been supposed at first, but he had heard a rumor,
which he felt he should repeat, that it had been fatal. He assured
Dr. Holmes that the story was not to be taken into account, but
the good Doctor acknowledged a "dull ache in this or that obscurely sensitive region". He hired a man with a team to take him
on.

> "And now, as we emerged from Frederick [he wrote],
> we struck at once upon the trail from the great battle-
> field. The road was filled with straggling and wound-
> ed soldiers. All who could travel on foot—multitudes
> with slight wounds of the upper limbs, the head or
> face—were told to take up their beds—a light burden
> or none at all—and walk. Just as the battlefield sucks
> everything into its red vortex for the conflict, so does it
> drive everything off in long, diverging rays after the
> fierce centripetal forces have met and neutralized each
> other. For more than a week there had been sharp fight-
> ing all along this road. Through the streets of Fred-
> erick, through Crampton's Gap, over South Mountain,
> sweeping at last the hills and the woods that skirt the
> windings of the Antietam, the long battle had traveled,
> like one of those tornadoes which tear their path
> throughout fields and villages.
>
> "The slain of higher condition, now 'embalmed' and
> iron-cased, were sliding off on the railways to their far
> homes; the dead of the rank and file were being gath-
> ered up and committed hastily to the earth; the gravely
> wounded were cared for hard by the scene of conflict or
> pushed a little way along to the neighboring villages;
> while those who could walk were meeting us, as I have
> said, at every step in the road. It was a pitiable sight,
> truly pitiable, yet so vast, so far beyond the possibility
> of relief, that many single sorrows of small dimensions
> have wrought upon my feelings more than the sight of

this great caravan of maimed pilgrims. The companionship of so many seemed to make a joint-stock of their suffering; it was next to impossible to individualize it, and so bring it home, as one can do with a single broken limb or aching wound. Then they were all of the male sex, and in the freshness or the prime of their strength. Though they tramped so wearily along, yet there was rest and kind nursing in store for them. These wounds they bore would be the medals they would show their children and grandchildren by and by. Who would not rather wear his decorations beneath his uniform than on it?

"Yet among them were figures which arrested our attention and sympathy. Delicate boys, with more spirit than strength, flushed with fever or pale with exhaustion or haggard with suffering, dragged their weary limbs along as if each step would exhaust their slender store of strength. At the roadside sat or lay others, quite spent with their journey."[16]

Southern women the Doctor found quite distinguishable "from our New England pattern". He noted that, "soft, sallow, succulent, delicately finished about the mouth and firmly shaped about the chin, dark-eyed, full-throated, they looked as if they had been grown in a land of olives. There was a little toss in their movement, full of muliebrity." John C. Gray, Jr., thanking his mother for a copy of the magazine containing the narrative, which she had sent to him at Sharpsburg, commented somewhat sharply on it (as he had a right to do, being a friend of the Holmes family), and in particular upon the passage just quoted. "He certainly talks more freely about the appearance and character of those he meets than he has any right to do," the young soldier wrote; "but I was very much interested in it and his description of the people and country is wonderfully correct and graphic, considering what a cursory view of them he must have had."

The somewhat rare word "muliebrity", which is used in medical parlance to indicate female puberty, was no stranger to the vocabulary of Dr. Holmes. In *Elsie Venner* he said: "One of the twain is apt to be a pretty bit of muliebrity, with shapes to her, and eyes flying about in all directions."

We need not follow the Doctor on his search through hospitals, churches and houses, always unsuccessfully. He talked with a wounded South Carolinian, "of good family, son of a judge in one of the higher courts of his State, educated, pleasant, gentle, intelligent. One moment's intercourse with such an enemy, lying helpless and wounded among strangers, takes away all personal bitterness towards those with whom we or our children have been but a few hours before in deadly strife. The basest lie which the murderous contrivers of this Rebellion have told is that which tries to make out a difference of race in the men of the North and South. It would be worth a year of battles to abolish this delusion, though the great sponge of war that wiped it out were moistened with the best blood of the land." His "rebel" was "a man finished in the humanities and Christian culture", and "it made my heart ache to see him."

In Keedysville (why the Doctor did not go there first is not made clear), a medical officer replied to a question about Captain Holmes:

"Oh yes; he is staying in that house. I saw him there, doing very well."

The "chorus of hallelujahs" which arose in the good Doctor's soul was diminished when he learned that the "young centurion", whose double-barred shoulder-straps he had never seen, had left in a milk-cart the morning before for Hagerstown. The Doctor was then within ten miles of the Captain, but "no mysterious attraction warned me that the heart warm with the same blood as mine was throbbing so near my own." No, he fared forth several hundred miles before returning to the same neighborhood. How it happened he tells in these words:

"The Captain had gone to Hagerstown, intending to take the cars at once for Philadelphia, as his three friends actually did, and as I took it for granted he certainly would. But as he walked languidly along, some ladies saw him across the street, and seeing, were moved to pity, and pitying, spoke such soft words that he was tempted to accept their invitation and rest awhile beneath their hospitable roof.

"The mansion was old, as the dwellings of gentlefolk should be; the ladies were some of them young, and all were full of kindness; there were gentle cares, and unasked luxuries, and pleasant talk, and music-sprinklings from the piano, with a sweet voice to keep them company—and all this after the swamps of the Chickahominy, the mud and flies of Harrison's Landing, the dragging marches, the desperate battles, the fretting wound, the jolting ambulance, the log-house and the rickety milk-cart! Thanks, uncounted thanks to the angelic ladies whose charming attentions detained him from Saturday to Thursday, to his great advantage and to my infinite bewilderment! As for his wound, how could it do otherwise than well under such hands? The bullet had gone smoothly through, dodging everything but a few nervous branches, which would come right in time and leave him as well as ever."[17]

These facts did not transpire, however, until the Doctor had made his way circuitously to Hagerstown, boarded a belated train and walked through the cars looking to this side and that. In the forward car, on the fourth seat to the right, he saw the Captain, "my first-born, whom I had sought through many cities."

"How are you, Boy?"

"How are you, Dad?"

"Such are the proprieties of life, as they are observed among us Anglo-Saxons of the nineteenth century, decently disguising those natural impulses that made

Joseph, the prime minister of Egypt, weep aloud so that the Egyptians and the house of Pharaoh heard—nay, which had once overcome his shaggy old uncle Esau so entirely that he fell on his brother's neck and cried like a baby in the presence of all the women. But the hidden cisterns of the soul may be filling fast with sweet tears, while the windows through which it looks are un-dimmed by a drop or a film of moisture."

Thus did Captain Holmes, as impassive as his father at their meeting, return to Boston for a second convalescence, briefer this time than before. Again the return was on bedding in railway trains, with a stopover in New York City, where the Doctor saw Central Park for the first time, "an expanse of wild country, well crumpled so as to form ridges which will give views and hollows that will hold water . . . but it cost me four dollars to get there, so far was it beyond the Pillars of Hercules of the fashionable quarter. What it will be by and by depends on circumstances; but at present it is as much central to New York as Brookline is to Boston."

It was a joy to get back at last to Boston and home with the wounded soldier. "Lay him in his own bed, and let him sleep off his aches and weariness. So comes down another night over this household, unbroken by any messenger of evil tidings—a night of peaceful rest and grateful thoughts; for this our son and brother was dead and is alive again, and was lost and is found."

CHAPTER 7

Chancellorsville

IN THE gathering dusk of a December day the redoubtable Twentieth Massachusetts, battered but undiminished in spirit, moved up from the bank of the Rappahannock to take part in the most spectacular event of its career. Ahead lay the rifle-pits of Mississippi sharpshooters, celebrated for their bravery and their uncanny accuracy. Beyond them was Fredericksburg, the cellars of its houses alive with Confederate troops, the crescent of hills behind belching flame from batteries of artillery. In this, the only instance during the Civil War of a deadly contest for a populous town, the regiment confronted dangers for the most part unseen and incalculable.[1]

Moving by the flank in fours, under intrepid leadership, the regiment entered Water Street to face a withering fire from three companies of the Twenty-first Mississippi massed ahead of it, and from the houses on either side. A civilian forced to act as guide was slain by the first volley, and the men swept ahead into the unfamiliar town, shifting into platoons in order not to present so broad a mark to muskets flashing in the gloom on the flanks. Forward it moved to Caroline Street, where one wing turned to the right, the other to the left, each driving the enemy ahead of it.

The town was taken. The way was clear for General Burnside, who had succeeded McClellan after the costly experiment of Antietam, to carry out his foolhardy and disastrous movement against Lee's armies.

"I cannot presume," said the report of the brigade's commanding officer, "to express all that is due the officers and men of this regiment for the unflinching bravery and splendid discipline shown in the execution of the order. Platoon after platoon was swept away, but the head of the column did not falter. Ninety-seven officers and men were killed or wounded in the space of fifty yards."[2]

The streets of the town, from which its population had fled, were in darkness as other Union forces crossed the river by pontoon bridges and made ready to cook a belated meal. A private of the Eighty-ninth New York sat beside a little fire, on which a pot of coffee was boiling, with a roasted chicken on his plate and a jar of jelly at his side. He refilled his cup, placed it on the dead body of a Confederate soldier conveniently at hand, and ate with unaffected appetite. Warfare deadens sensibilities to civilized amenities and niceties.

The day had been warm, but the night became almost bitter, and the men shivered as they explored their prize. Here George Washington had spent a part of his youth, and his mother was buried in a cemetery not far away. To soldiers still flushed with battle this did not seem an impressive fact, nor did their conquest impress them. Somewhere near the picket line a house was fired, and threw a fitful glare upon the shattered town and upon streets littered with dead and wounded. Ninety-eight cannon balls had struck a single residence in Caroline Street; in all the little city there was not an unbroken window. In that dancing light the men became jocund. To the strain of the encounter there succeeded a reckless gaiety.

Suddenly the streets became vocal with the sound of *Yankee Doodle* and *The Star-Spangled Banner*. Here and there a squad organized itself into an impromptu chorus. A fantastic procession, in the costumes of an elder Virginia, marched along the streets. A mule with drooping ears drew the relic of a Colonial coach, its yellow body swaying, its gilded ornamentation tarnished; a grinning private, his face blacked with burnt cork, was its charioteer. Two others, dressed in costumes of Martha Washington's day, sat on the back seat and threw kisses promiscuously, amid the applause of the crowd. Then, when the harlequin spirit was at its height, a detachment of Confederate skirmishers ventured down from Marye's Hill and sent a shower of bullets through the streets. Instantly the revellers threw off their ancient costumes and reappeared in uniform, armed and ready for fight. The night's masquerade was ended.[3]

Captain Holmes, having recovered from the wound inflicted at Antietam, returned to the command of Company G of the Twentieth Regiment on November 19, 1862. He had missed no fighting, he was glad to know, and he was in good time for the adventure of December 11, which preceded by two days the disaster of the Battle of Fredericksburg. For a time he was in hospital, so difficult was it to stomach and digest the kind of rations he got; and as dysentery was wholly incongruous with his notions of soldiering, he told his anxious parents nothing about it. They heard of it, however, through Philadelphia friends to whom he pencilled a five-line note. This attack was even worse than the illness on the Chickahominy.[4]

Ten days before the Captain returned, McClellan had been notified that he was deposed, and Burnside, protesting that he was unequal to the command of so large an army, which proved to be quite true, had succeeded to the post. He said that he would make his headquarters in the saddle; and, this word having leaked through to the Confederate lines, an irreverent buck private observed that it was queer the new commander of the Army of the Potomac was going to have his headquarters where his hindquarters ought to be.[5]

Colonel Lee, commander of the Twentieth, suffered gravely from the illnesses caused by exposure and cold, but would not claim the privileges of age (he was the second oldest man of that rank in the army), would take no leave of absence and would shirk no duty. He was in charge of a brigade, and vowed he would resign if he could not do his whole duty. In an October foray he spent two days in the saddle and two nights in rain and cold without a tent for shelter, and returned to camp dangerously ill—so ill that on the twenty-fifth his death was actually reported in camp —and he was forced to move into dry quarters in a town near Bolivar Heights, where the regiment was stationed.

The regiment had often been on the move that fall, sometimes in beautiful Indian summer weather, but had heard with envy of a dinner at "Parker's" in Boston which Captain Holmes attended with nine other officers of the Twentieth: Lieutenant-Colonel Palfrey, also wounded at Antietam, who never afterward was able to rejoin the regiment; Colonel Lee, who was on reluctant sick leave; Captain William F. Bartlett, who had been wounded in the Peninsula campaign, and afterward became Colonel of the Forty-ninth Massachusetts; Captain John C. Putnam, wounded at Ball's Bluff; Captain Norwood P. Hallowell, wounded at Antietam; Lieutenant Edward N. Hallowell, on sick leave; Surgeon Nathan Hayward, on leave, and Medical Cadet Norton Folsom.[6]

Lieutenant Henry L. Abbott, who had been on sick leave, returned with Captain Holmes while the regiment was in camp at Falmouth. On the next day the regiment moved to an adjacent hill, where it had a better site, and remained there until the move against Fredericksburg.

Around more than one camp-fire it was whispered that the left wing of the Union forces, under Burnside, had not done its full duty at Antietam.[7] The army was disappointed that McClellan had been removed, for the men adored him, and his appearance was invariably the signal for an ovation. His caution, it was said, was succeeded by a rashness on the part of Burnside "that brought the Union cause very near the brink of destruction." And the historian of the Twentieth adds: "All the misfortunes flowing from this premature and ill-considered movement can be traced directly to General Burnside"; while, later, he says: "If the commanding general had arranged, as prudence and a sound military judgment would dictate, for the pontoons and the army to arrive at the same time, the bloody battle of Fredericksburg would never have been fought, and the Army of the Potomac would not have been called upon to suffer a defeat that was not only disastrous, but productive of moral results that months did not wholly remove."

Burnside's maneuvres did not cause Lee to call to his aid General Jackson, who was a hundred miles away. "The calm and unruffled manner," says the historian, "in which General Lee received the information of a new movement against Richmond is in striking contrast to the excitement and panic into which our military authorities were thrown whenever he turned his horse's head toward the upper Potomac."[8]

The main engagement at Fredericksburg was fought on December 13. To the Twentieth Massachusetts had been promised the distinction of leading the forces across the river, and although the plans were altered, in effect this promise was fulfilled. The regiment was quartered on the northern bank, near the Lacy house, where Burnside had his headquarters. This fine old Colonial mansion, fronting a hundred feet along the bluff, and commanding a view of the fertile valley, had been known for a century in Virginia as Chatham. There George Washington met and courted Martha Custis; there, beneath the great oak on the upper terrace, Robert E. Lee plighted his troth with another Miss Custis, and often during the great battle, so it is related, he turned his glass toward that tree, to see whether it was being injured in the bitter artillery duel.[9]

Fredericksburg, extending for a mile along the Rappahannock across from the Lacy house, had fallen into a sort of inertia, and for fifty years had not heard the sound of trowel or hammer in the erection of a new building. Burnside had spent two weeks in the town, and should have known that the crescent of hills back of it, including the Marye and Willis heights, made the task of holding it, if it were taken, well-nigh impossible. Military commentators make a mystery of his reasons for this attack. He lost more than fourteen thousand men, the Confederates less than five thousand; and his army suffered a defeat from which its morale was slow in recuperating.

It is six months later, and the stage is being reset for another crossing of the Rappahannock to Fredericksburg. Burnside has been retired and Hooker is in command. No gloom of a brief December day but the brilliance of a May morning greeted the Twentieth. If, in its earlier adventure, some doubt had been expressed about its possible behavior, owing to the fact of its earlier experience at Ball's Bluff, where it had crossed the Potomac to a gallant but costly defeat, none was felt now; the brigade commander, in his report of the regiment's charge upon the hills, after it cleared the way into the town, had said: "The Twentieth Massachusetts stood firm and returned the fire of the enemy until I had reformed the line and commenced a second advance. The advance was renewed in fine style by the whole line, but gave way on the left. The Twentieth Massachusetts showed the matchless courage and discipline evinced on the previous day"[10]—in the town, two days before.*

General Sedgwick's corps, No. 6, to which the Twentieth was attached, was under orders, delivered May 2, 1863, to cross the Rappahannock, take Fredericksburg, and move out on the Plank Road toward Chancellorsville, ten miles to the west. It was to attack Lee's army from the rear the next morning. The regiment, which was three miles below Fredericksburg, broke camp soon after midnight, and moved along the river to the spot it had occupied the December preceding. Guarding the opposite bank were the same Mississippi sharpshooters of whom it had been said on the earlier occasion: "In two wars the riflemen of Mississippi had been famous for their bravery and the skill and accuracy with which they used their rifles. Here again they gained new laurels, winning applause from both friend and foe."[11]

The pontoons were in readiness to be slid into the water, and apparently the former experience was to be repeated. What had been done once could be done again; the men were in high spirits. As day broke, familiar objects came into view: The handsome Lacy house amid its old oaks, its ruined gardens dropping down in terraces to the river, its trees mutilated, the mansion empty. Through the mists Marye's Height, commanding the Plank Road over which the troops were ordered to make their way, could be

---

* In sketches of Mr. Justice Holmes prepared for the *Congressional Directory* and for *Who's Who* the statement is made that he was wounded the third time at Marye's Hill, Fredericksburg, inadvertently creating a wide-spread impression that the Battle of Fredericksburg is meant; the Justice was injured in the later May maneuver, which was part of the Battle of Chancellorsville.

seen; they must be taken if the command were to be carried out. The army was in three divisions, and the Twentieth was in Gibbon's, on the right.

Gibbon crossed and moved up the river road, but had not proceeded far when he came to a canal from the outskirts of the town to the river. The bridges over the cut had been removed, and as the Twentieth was subjected to a sharp fire from the artillery on the heights, Gibbon directed that the men withdraw to a rise of ground and lie down. It was there that a piece of shrapnel struck Captain Holmes in the heel, splintering the bone and tearing or snapping ligaments and tendons.

It was now ten o'clock in the morning, and the forces were expected at Chancellorsville within a few minutes. Marye's Hill was taken without the firing of another shot; the men relied solely on their bayonets. Within the space of five minutes a thousand prisoners were captured, about the number of the Union killed and wounded.[12] Thus a single division took the hills which had once baffled the entire Army of the Potomac. One General said that if there had been one hundred more Confederates on the hills it would have been impossible to carry them. It was nearly three o'clock that afternoon before the column got into motion toward its main objective, Chancellorsville. Although most authorities give Lee less than half as many men as Hooker commanded—more than 120,000—and although General Jackson was killed, apparently by the fire of his own men, the Federal forces suffered a decisive defeat with a total of more than seventeen thousand killed, wounded and missing. The total of Confederate killed, wounded and missing was thirteen thousand.

Captain Holmes was taken again to Charles Street in Boston, and Dr. Henry J. Bigelow, probing the wound, found part of the bone removable, another part fixed but denuded. After ten days the young man, his father reported, was "in excellent spirits, not at all nervous, as when he was last wounded, very reasonably tractable, avoids stimulants, smokes *not* enormously, feeds pretty well, and has kept tolerably quiet until today, when Dr. Bigelow let him ride out, and is, on the whole, a quite endurable patient."[13]

The surgeon used a carrot to keep the wound open. Doctor Holmes, an incorrigible punster, pinched the heel gently and asked his "young centurion" (as he had called him when wounded the second time) into what vegetable the carrot had been turned. There was no answer.

"Why," said the good Doctor triumphantly, "into a Pa's nip."

The weather was very cold, the elder Holmes reported sadly, and the spring puns were very backward. "The *art o' jokes* don't flourish." He was to report, however, that Bostonians were "some *punkins*" in that field, albeit they had "the demirep-utation of making worse puns and more of them" than "in any other habitable portion of the globe." He thought the tendency hereditary, like all other vices. "Did not Alexander the Great inherit his tendency to get drunk from his father, the notorious Fill-up of Macedon?"

As for the Captain, the Doctor rejoiced to report that he had at last found a man who had inquired about the invalid *"without referring to Achilles!"*

John C. Ropes wrote to John C. Gray, then at Gordon's headquarters in West Point, Va., that Captain Holmes might lose his leg. This was six days after the injury was inflicted; it was after the young man had reached home. But three weeks later Ropes wrote to his friend that he had been at Holmes's and had stayed until 11 o'clock, when visitors were expected to retire. "He is very entertaining as usual." By then the danger that he might lose the leg was past. Less than two months later Holmes acted as pallbearer at the funeral of the brother, Henry Ropes, killed at Gettysburg, July 2, 1863.

After the Captain had been discharged from the army, Ropes wrote to his friend, now transferred to Folly Island, South Carolina, that he was seeing a good deal of Holmes. "He is much the same, but improved on the whole in every way, more quiet and mature. Was introduced by him to General William Dwight. The General is like Doughty (Howard Dwight) when the latter was balmy, that is, he has not Doughty's shrewdness and wariness, or does not seem to have it. . . . He was severe on McClellan."[14]

So was Ropes severe on McClellan, as Captain Holmes could not fail to note. The future historian of the war was more outspoken in his letter to young Gray—an admirer of the General— than in later writings. Early in January of that year he said that McClellan had "displayed none of the qualities of a great commander," and demanded: "Where are the 50,000 victims of the slowness, the mistakes, the gross faults of the Peninsular Campaign?" He heard, too, that Burnside was dilatory at Antietam, as was being whispered around some camp-fires. "Charles R. Lowell, Col. 2d Cavalry," he wrote, "told me that McClellan ordered Burnside to attack first thing in the morning, where the enemy opposite him was weak, but that he delayed, and that McClellan had to send him five aides to hurry him up."[15]

Subsequently Ropes met General McClellan in Boston. "He is a very strong man for a gentleman, and stands well on his pins, looks as if he could stand a great deal, whether drink, dissipation, work, or exposure, or responsibility. . . . There is not a weak line in his face. . . . But he lacks that eye which most really able men have; he has no penetrating glance; there are no signs of reflection, of acute observation, or of any superiority but what comes from a well-balanced mind."[16]

The letter-writer was as severe with President Lincoln as with General McClellan, asserting that he "displayed great incapacity" in his administration of the Peninsular Campaign, "in fact, he acted like a devilish fool, throughout." The "radicals", whose main wish was to abolish slavery rather than preserve the Union, had too much influence with the President, Ropes thought. "Their policy has united the South and has divided the North," he declared. ". . . They keep in office a Secretary of War [Stanton] who is more or less directly the cause of all our woe because he is thoroughly identified with them in policy." Nor was he gentler with the Secretary of State. When Gray wrote him that "Seward is the only salt in the Cabinet," he retorted that he would have "turned him out at any time the last two years had I been Abe. Miserable old humbug that he is, with his pretensions to wisdom!"[17]

If these were irresponsible vaporings there would be no occasion to set them down here. Neither Ropes nor Gray was a negligible person by any means, and the differences of opinion in their letters expressed divergences which were widespread. "There are no subjects," says Colonel Bruce in his history of the Twentieth, "upon which the people are so little capable of forming a correct judgment as those arising out of a great war. The army in the first years of the conflict showed the feelings and partook of this weakness of the nation."[18]

During convalescences in Boston Captain Holmes heard the merits and demerits of commanders and political leaders debated with ardor, but the debates did not dampen his conviction that he must return to the front and do his share of that "job", as he called it. He did return, and was aide-de-camp from January 29, 1864, until mustered out July 17 of that year, on the staff of General H. G. Wright, division commander of the Army of the Potomac when the Captain joined him, but in May of that year put in command of the 6th corps. The aide was made Provost Marshal of Falmouth for awhile, and young Gray, who went over to dine with Captain Herbert C. Mason and Lieutenant Henry Ropes (this was before Gettysburg) saw him there. An excellent officer, his superiors thought Holmes, and brevetted him a Lieutenant-Colonel, but in active service he had no higher title than Captain.

Wounds, illness and the nature of his work kept Captain Holmes from sharing with the others of the Twentieth some of the battles of Gettysburg, Bristol Station, The Wilderness, Spottsylvania, Cold Harbor, Petersburg and Appomatox Court House. The historian of the regiment, speaking of the moment when "the last gun had been fired between the men of the Second Corps and the men of the Army of Northern Virginia," must have warmed the Captain's heart when he wrote:

"At half past four in the afternoon official notice was given to the Army of the Potomac that its great opponent had surrendered. Preparations were being made to celebrate the event by firing a salute of one hundred guns, when General Grant, drop-

ping the rôle of soldier to assume that of statesman, immediately
prohibited it. He did not wish that the brave men who were again
to become our fellow citizens should carry away from Appomatox
the memory of shouts over the fall of such peerless valor."[19]

Soon after the return of the Twentieth a Saint Gaudens lion
was purchased and placed in its honor on the stairway of the Boston Public Library; within the library, in an alcove, are memorial
tablets; and at Gettysburg there is a monument, with a bronze
tablet placed there by a daughter of Colonel Paul Revere, third
to command the regiment, who was killed there. Twice wounded,
Colonel Lee was finally retired on account of his health, and survived until 1892. Of him Captain Holmes said:

> "Three years ago died the old colonel of my regi-
> ment, the Twentieth Massachusetts. He gave our regi-
> ment its soul. No man could falter who heard his 'For-
> ward, Twentieth!' I went to his funeral. From a side
> door of the church a body of little choir-boys came in
> like a flight of careless doves. At the same time the
> doors opened at the front, and up the main aisle ad-
> vanced his coffin, followed by the few gray heads who
> stood for the men of the Twentieth, the rank and file
> whom he had loved, and whom he led for the last time.
> The church was empty. No one remembered the old
> man whom we were burying, no one save those next to
> him, and us. And I said to myself, the Twentieth has
> shrunk to a skeleton, a ghost, a memory, a forgotten
> name which we other old men alone keep in our hearts.
> And then I thought: It is right. It is as the colonel would
> have had it. This also is part of the soldier's faith: Hav-
> ing known great things, to be content with silence. Just
> then there fell into my hands a little song sung by a
> warlike people on the Danube, which seemed to me fit
> for a soldier's last word, another song of the sword, but

a song of the sword in its scabbard, a song of oblivion and peace."

And Captain Holmes, reminding his hearers that a soldier had been buried on the battle-field, recited to them these verses:

> And when the wind in the tree-tops roared,
> The soldier asked from the deep dark grave:
>   "Did the banner flutter then?"
> "Not so, my hero," the wind replied,
> "The fight is done, but the banner won,
> Thy comrades of old have borne it hence,
> Have borne it in triumph hence."
> Then the soldier spake from the deep dark grave:
>   "I am content."
>
> Then he heareth the lovers laughing pass,
>   And the soldier asks once more:
>   "Are these not the voices of them that love,
>   That love—and remember me?"
> "Not so, my hero," the lovers say,
> "We are those that remember not;
> For the Spring has come and the earth has smiled,
>   And the dead must be forgot."
> Then the soldier spake from the deep dark grave:
>   "I am content."[20]

On at least one occasion Captain Holmes himself wrote a war song, this time a requiem for Major Henry Livermore Abbott, killed May 6, 1864. "He was a man to love and admire," said John C. Ropes; and Captain Holmes, still on duty, wrote a sonnet which later was printed anonymously (October 7, 1864) on the editorial page of the *Boston Evening Transcript:*

H. L. A.
Twentieth Massachusetts Volunteers

He steered unquestioning nor turning back,
Into the darkness and the unknown sea;

He vanished in the starless night, and we
Saw but the shining of his luminous wake.
Thou sawest light, but ah, our sky seemed black,
    And all too hard the inscrutable decree,
    Yet, noble heart, full soon to follow thee,
Lit by the deeds that flamed across thy track.

Nay, art thou hid in darkness shall we say,
    Or rather whisper with untrembling lips;
We see thee not, yet trust thou art not far,
    But passing onward from this life's eclipse
Hast vanished only as the morning star,
Into the glory of a perfect day!

In the capacity of Mr. Justice Holmes, the veteran paid another tribute to a departed comrade in the *Transcript* of September 20, 1910, the subject being Captain Gustave Manitzky of Boston, who achieved that rank only a month before Captain Holmes was mustered out, and served until the end of the war. The letter read:

"To the Editor: I was expecting to stop and see Captain Manitzky on going to town this week, when the telephone told me he was dead. Our friendship had lasted for nearly fifty years. He was my First Sergeant when I commanded Company G of the Twentieth Massachusetts in the Civil War, he having recently come to this country from Polish Prussia and having gone into the army upon principle and because of his sympathy with the cause. We made many a heart-breaking march and were in many a battle together, and his gallantry and efficiency gained him a commission in a regiment in which a sergeant had to be a fighting man to keep his chevrons and an unusual man to gain the shoulder-straps. He became a captain, after the war attained some rank in the regular army. When somewhat later I joined Shattuck and Monroe in the practice of law he was already the managing end of the firm, and became one of the best-known figures in legal Boston. The Twentieth was a regiment that never talked much about itself but that stood in the first half-dozen of all the regiments of the North for number of killed and wounded in its ranks.

O. W. HOLMES."

"Look at yonder portrait and yonder bust," said Captain Holmes twenty years after the war was ended, in a speech on Harvard's part in it, "and tell me if stories such as they commemorate do not add a glory to the bare fact that the strongest legions prevailed." (The portrait to which he referred was that of Colonel Robert Gould Shaw, killed July 18, 1863, at Fort Wagner, South Carolina, in command of the Fifty-fourth Massachusetts, colored; the bust was that of Brigadier-General Charles Russell Lowell, who died October 20, 1864, of wounds received the day before at Cedar Creek, Virginia.) He continued: "So it has been since war began. After history has done its best to fix men's thoughts upon strategy and finance, their eyes have turned and rested on some single romantic figure—some Sidney, some Falkland, some Wolfe, some Montcalm, some Shaw. This is that little touch of the superfluous which is necessary. Necessary as art is necessary, and knowledge which serves no mechanical end. Superfluous only as glory is superfluous, or a bit of red ribbon that a man would die to win."[21]

After the Captain was wounded the third time his father, replying to a comment on "My Hunt After the Captain," wrote to F. S. Cozzens: "This last wound will keep him quiet for a while, but probably not leave any permanent lameness. He lies on a couch and receives lots of pretty company, is very jolly and does not seem to think much of his past exposures. . . . I don't think he values himself so much for his military adventures, though he has really been brave and faithful, as [illegible] powers and tastes which he is having a chance to cultivate just now."

Here is a hint at least of the extent to which the dangers, the toil and the tragedy of war burned themselves into the consciousness and spirit of this sensitive young man. More conclusive evidence of how they fixed his attitude towards life and his philosophy of living may be found in excerpts from speeches he has made from time to time. He who runs may read, for the words were fashioned often into literature and were transcribed as spoken.

"You see a battery of guns go by at a trot, and for a moment you are back at White Oak Swamp, or Antietam, or on the Jerusalem Road. You hear a few shots fired in the distance, and for an instant your heart stops as you say to yourself, The skirmishers are at it, and listen for the long roll of fire from the main line. You meet an old comrade after many years of absence; he recalls the moment when you were nearly surrounded by the enemy and again there comes up to you that swift and cunning thinking on which once hung life or freedom—Shall I stand the best chance if I try the pistol or the sabre on that man who means to stop me? [Captain Holmes once had to make such a choice.] Will he get his carbine free before I reach him, or can I kill him first? These and the thousand other events we have known are called up, I say, by accident, and, apart from accident, they lie forgotten. . . .[22]

"I see another youthful lieutenant as I saw him in the Seven Days, when I looked down the line at Glendale. The officers were at the head of their companies. The advance was beginning. We caught each other's eye and saluted. When next I looked, he was gone.

"I see the brother of the last—the flame of genius and daring in his face—as he rode before us into the wood of Antietam, out of which came only dead and deadly wounded men. So, a little later, he rode to his death at the head of his cavalry in the Valley.

"In the portraits of some of those who fell in the civil wars of England, Vandyke has fixed on canvas the type of those who stand before my memory. Young and gracious figures, somewhat remote and proud, but with a melancholy and sweet kindness.

There is upon their faces the shadow of approaching fate, and the glory of generous acceptance of it. I may say of them, as I once heard it said of two Frenchmen, relics of the *ancien régime,* 'They were very gentle. They cared nothing for their lives.' High breeding, romantic chivalry—we who have seen these men can never believe that the power of money or the enervation of pleasure has put an end to them. We know that life may be lifted into poetry and lit with spiritual charm. . . .

"Each of you, as I do, thinks of a hundred such that he has known. I see one—grandson of a hard rider of the Revolution and bearer of his historic name—who was with us at Fair Oaks, and afterwards for five days and nights in front of the enemy the only sleep that he would take was what he could snatch sitting erect in his uniform and resting his back against a hut. He fell at Gettysburg.

"His brother, a surgeon, who rode, as our surgeons so often did, wherever the troops would go, I saw kneeling in ministration to a wounded man just in rear of our line at Antietam, his horse's bridle round his arm—the next moment his ministrations were ended. . . . I see another quiet figure, of virtuous life and silent ways, not much heard of until our left was turned at Petersburg. He was in command of the regiment as he saw our comrades driven in. He threw back his left wing, and the advancing tide of defeat was shattered against his iron wall. He saved an army corps from disaster, and then a round shot ended all for him."

Of another, who had entered the army at nineteen, Captain Holmes said:

"In action he was sublime. His few surviving companions will never forget the awful spectacle of his advance alone with his company in the streets of Fredericksburg. In less than sixty seconds he would become the focus of a hidden and annihilating fire from a semi-circle of houses. His first platoon had vanished under it in an instant, ten men falling dead by his side. He had quietly turned back to where the other half of his company was waiting, had given the order, 'Second platoon, forward!' and was

again moving on in obedience to superior command, to certain
and useless death, when the order he was obeying was counter-
manded. The end was distant only a few seconds; but if you had
seen him with his indifferent carriage, and sword swinging from
his finger like a cane, you never would have suspected that he
was doing more than conducting a company drill on the camp
parade ground. He was little more than a boy, but the grizzled
corps commanders knew and admired him; and for us, who not
only admired but loved, his death seemed to end a portion of our
life also. . . .

"I have spoken of some of the men who were near to me among
others very near and dear, not because their lives have become
historic, but because their lives are the type of what every soldier
has known and seen in his own company. In the great democracy
of self-devotion private and general stand side by side. Unmar-
shalled save by their own deeds, the armies of the dead sweep before us, 'wearing their wounds like stars'. . . .

"Now, at least, and perhaps as long as man dwells upon the
globe, his destiny is battle, and he has to take the chances of war.
If it is our business to fight, the book for the army is a war-song,
not a hospital-sketch. It is not well for soldiers to think much
about wounds. Sooner or later we shall fall; but meantime it is for
us to fix our eyes upon the point to be stormed, and to get there
if we can. . . .[23]

"Most men who know battle know the cynic force with which
the thoughts of common-sense will assail them in times of stress;
but they know that in their greatest moments faith has trampled
those thoughts under foot. If you have been in line, suppose on
Tremont Street Mall, ordered simply to wait and to do nothing,
and have watched the enemy bring their guns to bear upon you
down a gentle slope like that from Beacon Street, have seen the
puffs of the firing, have felt the burst of the spherical case-shot
as it came toward you, have heard and seen the shrieking fragments go tearing through your company, and have known that
the next or the next shot carries your fate; if you have advanced
in line and have seen ahead of you the spot which you must pass

where the rifle bullets are striking; if you have ridden by night
at a walk toward the blue line of fire at the dead angle of Spottsylvania, where for twenty-four hours the soldiers were fighting
on the two sides of an earthwork, and in the morning the dead
and dying lay piled in a row six deep, and as you rode had heard
the bullets splashing in the mud and earth about you; if you
have been on the picket-line at night in a black and unknown
wood, have heard the spat of the bullets upon the trees, and as
you moved have felt your foot slip upon a dead man's body; if
you have had a blind fierce gallop against the enemy, with your
blood up and a pace that left no time for fear,—if, in short, as
some, I hope many, who hear me, have known, you have known
the vicissitudes of terror and of triumph in war, you know that
there is such a thing as the faith I spoke of. You know your own
weakness and are modest; but you know that man has in him
that unspeakable somewhat which makes him capable of mir-
acle, able to lift himself by the might of his own soul, unaided,
able to face annihilation for a blind belief.[24]

"War, when you are at it, is horrible and dull. It is only when
time has passed that you see that its message was divine. I hope it
may be long before we are called again to sit at that master's feet.
But some teacher of the kind we all need. In this snug, over-safe
corner of the world we need it, that we may realize that our comfortable routine is no eternal necessity of things, but merely a
little space of calm in the midst of the tempestuous untamed
streaming of the world, and in order that we may be ready for
danger. We need it in this time of individualistic negations, with
its literature of French and American humor, revolting at discipline, loving flesh-pots, and denying that anything is worthy of
reverence,—in order that we may remember all that buffoons forget. We need it everywhere and at all times. For high and dangerous action teaches us to believe as right beyond dispute things
for which our doubting minds are slow to find words of proof.
Out of heroism grows faith in the worth of heroism. The proof
comes later, and even may never come. Therefore I rejoice at
every dangerous sport which I see pursued. The students at Hei-

delberg, with their sword-slashed faces, inspire me with sincere respect. I gaze with delight upon our polo-players. If once in a while in our rough riding a neck is broken, I regard it, not as a waste, but as a price well paid for the breeding of a race fit for leadership and command."[25]

BOOK II

Jurist and Thinker

CHAPTER 8

Student, Lawyer, Professor

To A young man who became troubled even at eighteen about the mystery of the universe, and concluded reluctantly that it was ingenuous to hope that either Plato or Spinoza had explained it, philosophy was attractive. Oliver Wendell Holmes had the character and the inquiring mind to profit from the study, and to make his study profitable to the world. A boyhood acquaintance with Emerson, moreover, and a warm friendship for William James, were strong influences.

"To be a philosopher," said Emerson's friend Thoreau, "is not merely to have subtle thoughts, nor even to found a school, but so to love wisdom as to live, according to its dictates, a life of simplicity, independence, magnanimity and trust. It is to solve some of the problems of life not only theoretically, but practically."

Although Thoreau died but a year after the young man was graduated, he had the kind of personality Holmes liked. For one thing, there was none of the evangelist about him. He might be transcendental in economics, but he was tough-minded. Holmes chuckled over Emerson's saying, in telling of a long walk, "Take Thoreau's arm? I would as soon take the arm of an elm tree." When Thoreau went into the woods he asked no one to follow him. He regarded philosophy as a way to what was expressed in later idiom as "the good life." Well, Holmes thought that, consciously or unconsciously, all of us strive to make the kind of world we like;[1] and although he agreed with Spinoza that criticism of the past was futile, he saw no good reason why he should not try to make the future congruous with his wishes. He did not mean to sit still and let time run over him. He did not expect to find in philosophy a universal solvent; neither did he agree with the cynical view of his friend Henry Adams that philosophers sought to meet insoluble problems with unintelligible answers. He once asked Henry's father, Charles Francis Adams, whether he thought the law "worthy of the interest of an intelligent man" —he was quite sure philosophy merited that interest—and was somewhat tepidly reassured; and then presently he saw that through philosophy lay a road to the law, that the law itself was "a window looking out on life and destiny".

"The philosophers teach us," he said, "that an idea is the first step toward an act. Beliefs, so far as they bear upon the attainment of a wish (as most beliefs do), lead in the first place to a social attitude, and later to combined social action, that is, law. Hence, ever since it has existed, the law expressed what men most strongly have believed and desired. . . .

"On the other hand, in the history of philosophy and economics we can say with more confidence that we trace cause and effect. The one shows the inward bond between the successive stages of the thought of man; the other the sequence of outward events that have governed his action and (some believe) really have determined his thought. At all events the latter fits the former as the outside of a cathedral fits the inside,—although there are gargoyles and Mephistopheles without and angels and saints within. . . .

"The most obvious moral of what I have said is that the law will furnish philosophical food to philosophical minds. The surgeon of my regiment in the War of Secession used to divide the world into external and internal men. The distinction is as old as Plato. For I take it that what makes the Banquet immortal is not the divine gossip about Aristophanes and Alcibiades and Socrates, but that it and some of the Dialogues are the first articulate expression that has come down to us of what internal men believe, that ideas are more interesting than things."[2]

And again, still later: "For the last thirty years we have been preoccupied with the embryology of legal ideas; and explanations, which, when I was in college, meant a reference to final causes, later came to mean tracing origin and growth. But fashion is as potent in the intellectual world as elsewhere, and there are signs of an inevitable reaction. The reaction, if there is one, seems to me an advance, for it is toward the ultimate question of worth."[3]

After Captain Holmes was mustered out of military service, and returned to Boston, he was resolved to take up the law, although he knew that to most students it was "a ragbag of details". He himself came to regard reports of specific cases as "only the small change of legal thought",[4] and he was a generation in the vanguard when he led the movement toward seeing the subject as a whole rather than as an uncharted ocean. Never did he think it what a professor of law was to call it later—a bramble bush—although more than once he found the going thorny.

"The best approach that I found to general views on the historical side was the first volume of Spence's *Equitable Jurisdiction,* and, on the practical, Walker's *American Law,*" he wrote. "The only philosophy within reach was Austin's *Jurisprudence.* It was not without anguish that one asked oneself whether the subject was worthy the interest of an intelligent man. One saw people whom one respected and admired leaving the study because they thought it narrowed the mind; for which they had the authority of Burke. It required blind faith—faith that could not yet find the formula of justification for itself. The works of foreign scholarship were then inaccessible. One had to spend long days of groping, with the inward fear that if one only knew where to look, one would find that one's difficulties and questions were fifty years behind the times. Now [this was written in 1911], a man can start with the knowledge that he starts fair— that the best results of Europe, as well as of this country and England, are before him. And those results are so illuminating that diligence alone is enough to give him an understanding of how the law came to be what it is, of its broadest generalizations, and (so far as any one yet can state them) of the reasons to be offered for continuing it in its present form or for desiring a change."[5]

Although the Justice spoke thus disparagingly about the state of legal education during his young manhood, the Harvard Law School, when he entered it in 1864, was headed by Joel Parker, former Chief Justice of New Hampshire, whom Holmes regarded as one of the greatest of American judges, and who displayed as a lecturer the qualities which had made him famous on the bench. The school was in the forefront, with a tradition of illustrious lawyers in its faculty; and twenty years after taking a degree there Holmes, then on the bench of the Supreme Judicial Court of the State, gave it unstinted praise. He recalled that among the associates of Dean Parker were "Parsons, almost if not quite a man of genius and gifted with a power of impressive statement which I do not know that I have ever seen equalled; and Washburn, who taught us all to realize the meaning of the phrase . . . the 'enthusiasm of the lecture room'." Washburn, he said, "did more for me than the learning of Coke and the logic of Fearne could have done without his kindly ardor."[6]

Although Holmes thought that the education which students got from others was moral rather than intellectual,[7] and belittled the mere acquisition of infertile facts, he perceived that lawyers were specialists and came to think of the law itself as "more immediately connected with the highest interests of man than any other [branch of human knowledge] which deals with practical affairs".[8]

Even as a student of the law, Holmes perceived that jealousy and envy, anathema to the Puritan tradition, were in fact when sublimated the bases of human justice. He did not carry this to the point of a maudlin sympathy with those who were envious and jealous of persons possessing greater wealth; for he accepted conventional economic theories, however scornfully he might reject some accepted legal theories, and he thought that the possession of great wealth meant increased production by all rather than increased consumption by the rich, and so resulted in a public good. He looked behind primary impulses, such as hunger, sex and vanity, and attempted to perceive their influence in a rational world. "Vanity," he was to say later, "is the most philosophical of those feelings that we are taught to despise. For vanity recognizes that if a man is in a minority of one we lock him up, and therefore longs for an assurance from others that one's work has not been in vain."[9] Acquisition came from the desire for personal recognition and for power; the consequent possession of great wealth meant to Holmes investment, "and investment means the direction of labor towards the production of the greatest returns."[10] A feeling that personal recognition was denied gave rise to envy and jealousy, and out of this sprang the formulation of laws and mores intended to provide a just order in the world.

Assuredly this attitude toward the unequal distribution of wealth was vulnerable, and became more and more unsatisfactory as Holmes grew older, for he witnessed the repeated breakdown of an economic system founded on "rugged" individualism and the free play of competition. But his humane and tolerant posture toward human emotions and appetites was to stand him in good stead as he advanced in legal learning, and came to impress his processes of thought more and more upon the legal world. Back of his approach to the law was a creative philosophy of life.

From the moment Holmes entered the law school he never once scattered his fire. As a writer, as a speaker, as a lawyer, teacher, jurist, every movement and every outgiving was the product of a considered and concentrated attention. "The rule of joy and the law of duty seem to me all one," he wrote. . . . "With all humility, I think, 'Whatsoever thy hand findeth to do, do it with thy might,' infinitely more important than the vain attempt to love one's neighbor as one's self. If you want to hit a bird on the wing . . . you must not be thinking about yourself, and, equally, you must not be thinking about your neighbor; you must be living in your eye on that bird. Every achievement is a bird on the wing."

Thus he found within himself and in the life around him charts and lights for his guidance over "the ocean of the law".[11] He has told us how bewildered he was at first:

"One found oneself plunged in a thick fog of details—in a black and frozen night, in which were no flowers, no spring, no easy joys. Voices of authority warned that in the crush of that ice any craft might sink. One heard Burke saying that law sharpens the mind by narrowing it. One heard in Thackeray of a lawyer bending all the powers of a great mind to a mean profession. One saw that artists and poets shrank from it as from an alien world. . . . And yet one said to oneself, law is human—it is a part of man, and of one world with all the rest. There must be a drift, if one will go prepared and have patience, which will bring one out to daylight and a worthy end. You all have read or heard the story of Nansen and see the parallel which I use. Most men of the college-bred type in some form or other have to go through that experience of sailing for the ice and letting themselves be frozen in. In the first stage one has companions, cold and black though it be, and if he sticks to it, he finds at last that there is a drift as was foretold. When he has found that, he has learned the first part of his lesson, that one is safe in trusting to courage and to time. But he has not yet learned all. So far his trials have been those of his companions. But if he is a man of high ambitions he must leave even his fellow-adventurers and go forth into a deeper solitude and greater trials. He must start for the pole. In plain words he must face the loneliness of original work. No one can cut out new paths in company. He does that alone.

"When he has done that and has turned misgivings into success he is master of himself and knows the secret of achievement."

The secret of achievement, "a bird on the wing", was learned thus in solitude.[12] It was the lesson, Holmes himself said, not of law but of life.

It was in 1866 that Holmes took his degree as Bachelor of Laws; and in that year his father tagged New England blue-bloods with a label which was to cling to them for more than half a century: "The Brahmin Caste", which he used in his most successful novel, *Elsie Venner*. Ten years later Henry Adams pilloried the Brahmins of Boston in a letter to Charles Milnes Gaskell:

"There is no society worth the name, no wit, no intellectual energy or competition, no clash of minds or of schools, no interests, no masculine self-assertion or ambition. Everything is respectable, and nothing amusing. There are no outlaws. There are not only no convictions, but no strong wants. Dr. Holmes, who does the wit for the city of three hundred thousand, is allowed to talk as he will—wild atheism commonly—and no one objects. I am allowed to sit in my chair at Harvard College [where Adams taught history and Holmes was an instructor in Constitutional law] and rail at everything which the college respects, and no one cares. . . . But when a society has reached this point, it acquires a self-complacency which is wildly exasperating. My fingers itch to puncture it; to do something which will sting it into impropriety."

In the same letter, written at Beverly Farms, Adams spoke of having talked with Holmes about the theory of the Constitution.

After Holmes, no longer young, had left Harvard and ascended the bench of the State's highest tribunal—in 1886, Doctor Holmes was on a triumphal tour of England, and was being honored with higher degrees. He had not been abroad since he had studied medicine, and he was known to Englishmen as a writer, not a physician. Cambridge made him a Doctor of Letters, while the undergraduates roared, to the appropriate melody, "Holmes, Sweet Holmes"; and when Oxford made him a D. C. L. the galleries were even more obstreperous, although the fun was directed at the Vice-Chancellor, who was conferring degrees on John Bright and the Doctor, among others, rather than at the wearers of the red robes. The Doctor listened with a broad grin, heartily amused at the chaffing, and was still more amused when, parchment in hand, he turned toward the well-filled bench where the other honorees were seated: "Give the Autocrat a seat," yelled the galleries; "Room, room!"; "Come, show your manners, gentlemen—is there no place for Wendell Holmes to sit?"

Edinburgh made the Doctor an LL. D., and his British friends overwhelmed him with hospitalities. "He is enjoying himself immensely," wrote James Russell Lowell, who was in London, "and takes as keen an interest in everything as he would have done at twenty. I almost envy him this freshness of genius. Everybody is charmed with him, as it is natural they should be." The Doctor was then nearing fifty-seven, and he was accompanied on the trip by his daughter, Mrs. Turner Sargent. He was so pleased with his trip that he wrote a book about it, *Our Hundred Days in Europe*.[13]

The younger Holmes had been looking forward to a trip to Europe. In the preceding fall he had talked it over with his father, and had inquired whether he would ask John Lothrop Motley (this was before Motley went to England to live), for letters of introduction to John Stuart Mill and to Thomas Hughes; the latter was to be made Queen's Counsel three years later, and still later a judge; he was, moreover, to lecture in this country and to found the "Rugby Colony" in Tennessee; already he had written *Tom Brown's School Days* and *Tom Brown at Oxford*. In asking for the introductions, the good Doctor adopted the deprecatory note one might expect from a New England parent who suspected that he might be overproud of his first-born. "He is a presentable youth," ventured the Doctor, "with fair antecedents, and is more familiar with Mill's writings than most fellows of his years. If it like your Excellency to send me two brief notes for him, it would please us both, but not if it is a trouble to you."[14]

Young Holmes did not need the formal letters of introduction. He had the qualities within himself to win warm friends, and his first morning in London was such as few Americans in their middle twenties ever experience. He had breakfast with Leslie Stephen, and the two of them had lunch with Frederick Pollock.

Frederick Pollock, it so happened, was not to inherit a baronetcy until 1888, and Leslie Stephen had not yet been made a Knight Commander of the Bath, a distinction much above a mere knighthood. Each, however, had made his mark, the one in English law, the other in English letters. These two friendships proved, indeed, the closest and richest the younger Oliver Wendell Holmes formed abroad, although he was to become an intimate of Frederick W. Maitland, who later collaborated with Sir Frederick Pollock on a *History of English Law* (1895); of Sir Henry J. S. Maine, Lord Haldane, and Sidney Webb; and he became acquainted with such men as Lord Bryce, Joseph Chamberlain, Lord Sankey, Lord Alverstone and Lord Bowen. He made other trips to Europe in the summers of 1896 and 1901.

The special bond between Pollock and Holmes was that they took a like large view of the law and its relation to life, and both were interested in the degree to which precedents might illuminate new problems, or history afford a guide to the future. The special bond between Stephen and Holmes was that both (although either might have denied it) were stylists in letters, and that each put "nerve and dagger" into his writings. Sir Leslie introduced the American at the Alpine Club in London, and together they took a long walking tour of England, encountering amusing misadventures. They did much mountain climbing in Switzerland with alpenstocks and ice-axes, exulting in the exposure, hardship and danger.

Pollack and Maitland were to do for English law much what Holmes was to do for American law and the common law in general; for one thing they delved into legal administration after the Norman Conquest, when for centuries the King of England and his subjects spoke French, when the laws were written in French and judicial pronouncements were in French and the Year Books were written in that language; their researches revealed there, as did the studies of Holmes in this country, conditions and documents long forgotten or ignored.

Holmes was admitted to the bar in 1867, but had still to undergo an apprenticeship, and he read in the office of his kinsman, Robert M. Morse, at 7 Pemberton Square. Subsequently he practiced briefly with his brother, Edward Jackson Holmes; afterward he was with Chandler, Shattuck and Thayer at 4 Court Street; then was associated with George Otis Shattuck of that office and William A. Munroe at 35 Court Square, in the firm of Shattuck, Holmes and Munroe; and the head of the firm became not only one of his closest friends but an adviser to whom he often turned. It will not be amiss, as revealing what this association meant to him, to quote in part what he said after his friend died, in 1897:

"I owe Mr. Shattuck more than I ever have owed to any one else in the world, outside my immediate family. From the time when I was a student in his office until he died, he was my intimate friend. He taught me unrepeatable lessons. He did me unnumbered kindnesses. To live while still young in daily contact with his sweeping, all-compelling force, his might of temperament, his swiftness (rarely found with such might), his insight, tact, and subtlety, was to receive an imprint never to be effaced. My education would have been but a thin and poor thing had I missed that great experience. The things he did for me in other practical ways even gratitude cannot commemorate or remember. It seemed to me that he could not find any one near him without interesting himself in his fortunes and his fate.

"You cannot expect from me a critical analysis and estimate. I could not sit coldly down to measure and weigh his qualities, to 'peep and botanize' upon his grave. He was my dear and honored friend. I can do little more than repeat that. . . .

"At the time to which I refer, when I first knew him, and while he still tried many cases, he was a great man with the jury in every way. His addresses carried everything before them like a victorious cavalry charge, sometimes, as it seemed to me, sweeping the judge along with the rest in the rout. Latterly his most successful appearances were in arguments of law. He had learned the all too rarely learned lesson of pointed brevity. . . .

"He was no less eminent in his work out of court. He was one of the wisest and most far-seeing of advisers. I know of splendidly victorious men who have said that but for his help when the battle was turning against them they would have gone down in the fight. . . .

"I have had much delight in his companionship. Whether driving over the sandy roads of the Cape, or sailing in his yacht, or dining at his house, or at some later and less regular entertainment in the garret in which I used to live, he had a kind of benevolent beaming in his face and heart which gave unction to enjoyment."[15]

Thus did Mr. Justice Holmes, then sitting in the Supreme Judicial Court of his State, pay his personal tribute to an associate who had done much to shape and guide his younger years. It was to be expected that he would endeavor, also, to put somewhat into perspective the life of which he was speaking; and so we find him saying:

"People often speak of correcting the judgment of the time by that of posterity. I think it quite as true to say that we must correct the judgment of posterity by that of the time. A small man may be remembered for some little felicity which enabled him to write a successful lyric, or in some way to charm the senses or emotions of a world always readier with its rewards for pleasures than for great thoughts or deeds. But I know of no true measure of men except the total of human energy which they embody—counting everything, with due allowance for quality, from Nansen's power to digest blubber or to resist cold, up to his courage, or to Wordsworth's power to express the unutterable, or to Kant's speculative reach. The final test of this energy is battle in some form—actual war—the crush of Arctic ice—the fight for mastery in the market or the court. Many of those who are remembered have spared themselves this supreme trial, and have fostered a faculty at the expense of their total life. It is one thing to utter a happy phrase from a protected cloister; another to think under fire—to think for action upon which great interests depend. The most powerful men are apt to go into the mêlée and fall or come out generals. The great problems are questions of here and now. Questions of here and now occupy nine hundred and ninety-nine thousandths of the ability of the world; and when the now has passed and has given place to another now, the heads and hands that built the organic structure of society are forgotten from the speech of their fellows, and live only in the tissue of their work.

"Such may be the fate of the man whom today we remember and honor. But remembered or forgotten, few indeed, I believe, of those whom I have seen, counted for as much in the hardest work of the day. I do not regret that it should be known by few. What is any remembrance of men to our high ambition? Sooner or later the race of men will die; but we demand an eternal record. We have it. What we have done is woven forever in the great vibrating web of the world. The eye that can read the import of its motion can decipher the story of all our deeds, of all our thoughts. To that eye I am content to leave the recognition and the memory of this great head and heart."[16]

The speaker's Stoic recognition of contemporary appraisal and applause as ephemeral and fugitive has dignified his whole life. It accounted for the distaste he manifested from the first for publicity, and for his reluctance to accept honorary dinners and similar affairs, although more than once he was drawn into them.

The "garret" in which Holmes used to live, and to which he referred in his eulogy of Shattuck, was in fact a smallish room on the top floor of the house his father had built at 296 Beacon Street. A brother occupied a similar room adjoining; and the two places made a garret such as no young man need despise, for it was airy and well-lighted, and from the window one looked out over the placid waters of the Charles. Yet so disinclined was young Oliver Wendell Holmes to take advantage of the favored position he had by reason of birth, of his father's eminence in the life of the city and the substantial competence he now reaped from his pen, that he worked as though he feared to starve in his garret. More than once apprehension was expressed lest he impair his health permanently by his long hours; or, "Wendell is going to kill himself with overwork," his friends sometimes told one another.

Holmes was an instructor in constitutional law in Harvard College in 1870-71; thereafter he was first a lecturer and then a full professor, until 1882, in the Law School; from 1870 to 1873 he was an editor of the *American Law Journal,* and contributed articles and unsigned editorials which revealed the exceptional caliber of his mind. His work in editing the twelfth edition of Kent's four-volume *Commentaries on American Law* (1873), showed such industry and erudition that the edition became straightway a classic, and for more than half a century has continued a favorite. At the Lowell Institute he delivered, in the winter of 1880-81, a series of lectures on the common law which he elaborated subsequently into a book. He wrote the lectures, but seldom referred to the manuscript. His students were surprised and delighted to find him talking to them as though he had a good story to tell.

Doctor Holmes was not alone in his perception that his tall young son was attractive to young ladies. His quip about his "white Othello" and the circle of admiring Desdemonas can be matched by the statement, much later, of Bishop William Lawrence, that Captain Holmes "was seen on the streets of Boston, a handsome invalid, to the great delectation of the girls of the city. He was a romantic hero, built for it."[17] Boston was still a bit provincial socially, and the young ladies, in their tight waists and long skirts and bustles, could not be insensible of this good-looking young Harvard man, who was so quickly making his mark in the law, although he need not have bestirred himself so vigorously, in view of the grateful securities which were rightfully his. He was a great talker, too, nor did his erudition make him for one moment a bore. He was fond of feminine society, but inclined to rail at social exactions.

Already the life of the younger Oliver Wendell Holmes had been profoundly affected by a feminine influence; his devotion to his mother and hers to him were exemplified each time he was taken home wounded during the Civil War, when she proved herself as courageous as he. "The kindest, gentlest and tenderest of women," John T. Morse, Jr., called her in his *Life and Letters* of the Doctor; and there can be no doubt that she contributed largely not only to her husband's success but to her son's. She was a daughter of an Associate Justice of the Supreme Judicial Court of the State, a post to which the son was to ascend five years before her death in the winter of 1887-88; in time the son became Chief Justice.

This petted but unspoiled young war hero did not rush into marriage. He would have been welcome, undoubtedly, at his father's Beacon Street house if he had taken a bride thither, but he had a pride and independence which made that course impossible; not he, to ride the wave of his father's success. And when, at the age of thirty-one, he married Miss Fanny Dixwell, fate smiled upon him in that the second woman who entered his life was to exercise over it an influence even more beneficent and more prolonged than the first.

When William James met Miss Dixwell he vowed that she was "decidedly A 1, and (so far) the best girl I have known." This was in 1866. "I should like, if possible," said James, "to confine my whole life to her, Ellen Hooper, Sara Sedgwick, Holmes, Harry [his brother, Henry] and the Medical School, for an indefinite period, letting no breath of extraneous air enter. There, I hope that's a confession of faith."[18]

Miss Dixwell was to become the bride of the Holmes he was talking about, Miss Hooper was to become Mrs. E. W. Gurney and Miss Sedgwick, Mrs. William E. Darwin.

Long afterward, James wrote from Nauheim in 1901 to Miss Frances Morse about a panel Mrs. Holmes had executed, and declared that the inscription on it "sums up the attitude towards life of a good philosophic pluralist," which he hoped to be.[19] The inscription was her translation of an epitaph in the Greek Anthology:

> 'A shipwrecked sailor buried on this coast
>   Bids thee take sail.
> Full many a gallant ship, when we were lost,
>   Weathered the gale.

The occasion of the mention by James of the carved panel and its inscription was that Holmes, then Chief Justice in Massachusetts, gave it to the town of Gloucester, but with no indication on it of the identity of the giver. The panel was more than seven feet long and nearly four feet wide, and was a carving representing a piece of hatchway with a spar afloat, the water breaking over it. The inscription was on the hatchway.

"My wife had a Sargent connection," wrote Chief Justice Holmes. "who lived in Gloucester and was a sea captain before she was born, which serves as a somewhat more special reason than the fact that we know the neighborhood and love the shore." The Sargent connection was through the father of Mrs. Holmes; and it happened that a sister of Holmes, Amelia, had married a Sargent.

Miss Dixwell became Mrs. Holmes on June 17, 1872, and the couple went to live in a modest apartment above a drug store next to the Athenaeum. The bride prepared the breakfast, and the two went out almost invariably to dinner at "Parker's". They were too unconventional to care for the formalities of Back Bay society, but both loved good conversation, and both could contribute generously to it. The rapier wit of Mrs. Holmes was as flexible and flashing as her husband's, and already it was being said of him that his private speech was as good as his written work, if not better. They shared a lively humor and an appreciation of novel ideas, and their life together was a continual raillery at each other. Each was high-spirited and each was gifted with an invincible personal charm. Of an evening, while the husband pored over his law books or wrote diligently, Mrs. Holmes often worked what her friends called "creating a new art", in worsted on silk. Neither of them was loath to quit the task on hand for a good lark; even after Holmes achieved the dignity of a place in the United States Supreme Court, they sometimes ran to fires together.

Fond as Mrs. Holmes was of good fun, she could be a severe task-mistress. She created exactly the environment her hard-working husband needed. Her gaiety and her unaffected admiration for him did not prevent her from bringing him sharply to book on occasion. When she died, on April 30, 1929, friends of the Holmeses said that a fifty-six-year honeymoon was ended. He was then eighty-eight years old.

At the time of the marriage Holmes was an editor of the *American Law Review* (his work is to be found in Volumes V, VI and VII), and he soon became a member of the Board of Overseers of Harvard, a post he held for six years; but aside from his practice his main concern was his course of lectures at Harvard. It seemed odd to him that Sir James Stephen, most conspicuous of the advocates of a codification of legal principles, and Professor Langdell, who originated the method of teaching from specific cases, should have started from the same premises—that the number of legal principles was small—to reach divergent conclusions. He thought that if competent men could be found to do the codifying it would be highly useful, but for his own part he adopted the Langdell method.

"Why," he said, "look at it simply in the light of human nature. Does not a man remember a concrete instance more vividly than a general principle? And is not a principle more exactly and intimately grasped as the unexpressed major premise of the half-dozen examples which mark its extent and its limits than it can be in any abstract form of words? Expressed or unexpressed, is it not better known when you have studied its embryology and the lines of its growth than when you see it lying dead before you on the printed page?"[20]

One of the lecturer's duties was to instruct a first-year class in Torts, and he struck out boldly to make Torts a separate branch of law, a distinction now generally recognized. He plunged the students into a collection of cases, and discussed them with better results than he had expected, for he had undertaken the work with some misgivings. After a week or so he was encouraged to find his pupils examining the questions before them "with an accuracy of view which they never could have learned from text-books, and which often exceeded that to be found in text-books." He even asserted that he himself gained a good deal from these daily encounters.

Holmes appreciated the warning not to know too much law, but his friend, law partner and preceptor, George Otis Shattuck, told him that "the business of a lawyer is to know law", and he undertook to ground his classes in that policy. He thought that the profession should be taught in so far as possible "in the grand manner", but in his own case drudgery was the gray angel of success, and he did not intend that pupils who fell under his care should escape their share of it. He hoped they would "go forth in their turn, not to imitate what their masters have done, but to live their own lives more freely for the ferment imparted to them here. The men trained in this School may not always be the most knowing in the ways of getting on. The noblest of them must often feel that they are committed to lives of proud dependence —the dependence of men who command no factitious aids to success, but rely upon unadvertised knowledge and silent devotion; dependence upon finding an appreciation which they cannot seek, but dependence proud in the conviction that the knowledge to which their lives are consecrated is of things which it concerns the world to know. It is the dependence of abstract thought, of science, of beauty, of poetry and art, of every flower of civilization, upon finding a soil generous enough to support it. If it does not, it must die. But the world needs the flower more than the flower needs life."

Lawyers, Holmes insisted, were specialists.

"I once heard a Russian say that in the middle class of Russia there were many specialists; in the upper class there were civilized men. Civilized men who are nothing else are a little apt to think that they cannot breathe the American atmosphere. But if a man is a specialist, it is most desirable that he should also be civilized; that he should have laid in the outline of the other sciences, as well as the light and shade of his own; that he should be reasonable, and see things in their proportion. Nay more, that he should be passionate, as well as reasonable—that he should be able not only to explain, but to feel; that the ardors of intellectual pursuit should be relieved by the charms of art, should be succeeded by the joy of life become an end in itself."[21]

Such were the standards and the ideals of this man who was helping to teach the young idea in law at Harvard to shoot. He was not only talking in the classroom; he was writing, and his early work in that direction gave good earnest of the fields he was to furrow and the forests he was to fell in later years.

CHAPTER 9

Early Writings: "The Common Law"

MANY STUDENTS of law and many who write about it are unable to see the forest for the trees. It was a special gift of Holmes that he could take the large view, even while noting the origins of oak and elm, fir and pine, and that he could differentiate between the deciduous and the evergreen. To the examination of origins he brought a scholarly, critical and sometimes prophetic intelligence; to the determination of what was evanescent and what perennial he brought a lively sense of social values.

It was remarkable that the student was able to concentrate so intensely as he did upon the subject he had chosen. In the early seventies of the Nineteenth Century, when he began his legal writing, the South which he had helped so recently to conquer was still being "reconstructed"; the Fifteenth Amendment to the Constitution, prohibiting color restrictions in voting, was ratified and promulgated in 1870, and could not have failed to interest him deeply. Abroad, the situation was even more exciting to a man recently come through a bitter war; the Franco-Prussian conflict was on, the Third Republic was succeeding an Empire, and the German Empire was being proclaimed.

But, although the metaphor of the battle-field was to reappear continually in the Holmes articles, lectures and speeches, he turned his eyes resolutely away from scenes at home and abroad to fasten them upon the intricately patterned and inadequately documented material which he had undertaken to clarify and illuminate. His earlier legal writings are accessible, although they have not been gathered verbatim into a book and although part of them is unsigned.*

---

*A bibliography of this material, anonymous and signed, will be found in Appendix I. Comment on some of it, not always favorable, accompanies Professor

In those days Holmes was preoccupied with the origins of the law and the theory of legal history; he was concerned also, as a lecturer, with the rules by which one might apply such a theory to professional teaching and study. But he was no bookworm merely; there was clearly foreshadowed his interest in the formulation of law to accord with realistic public policy and social conditions. The articles and editorials which he wrote as one of the editors of the law journal, he rewrote later and incorporated in his first book, *The Common Law,* which, had he achieved no other work, would remain an enduring monument.

Even then new conditions, due to the coming of the Machine Age, confronted a body of law written to conform with the notions of Ricardo and Adam Smith. Technological advances and changing social conceptions had introduced into legal problems unforeseen facts and conflicts. The old pat phrases were futile in the presence of mass production and altered business relationships. Holmes was among the earliest to perceive that the new wine could not be poured into old bottles, and to find fresh containers. Thus even his early work became part of the foundation on which was erected the present realistic tendency in jurisprudence.

That we experience a good many of the same passions and feelings as the barbarian, Holmes clearly perceived.[1] He saw to what extent social demand in terms of the greatest common denominator, and the driving force of group or mass emotion, had counted in the formulation and growth of the law, and that the law must help a community reach the social end desired by the majority, or by the governing element, of whomsoever it might be composed; subsequently he put that perception neatly into

Karl N. Llewellyn's article, "What Price Contract?—An Essay in Perspective," in the *Columbia Law Journal* of March, 1931 (Vol. XL, No. 5); in footnotes Professor Llewellyn says of passages he cites: "the paternity of which has been acknowledged in personal communication." Professor Felix Frankfurter of the Harvard Law School has also done painstaking work in that field, as recorded in the *Harvard Law Review* of the same month (Vol. XLIV, No. 5), from which the appendix was taken. Professor Frankfurter noted that "the *American Law Review* printed six essays and at least sixty reviews and comments which, although unsigned, bear the unmistakable *imprimatur* of its editor's thought and style."

words.[2] His concern with psychology has prompted one of his admirers to say that "Holmes was conscious of the rôle of the unconscious a generation before Freud began to re-orient modern psychology;"[3] but this does not mean that Holmes was an isolated pioneer. His friend William James was deriding the current attempt to reinterpret religion in terms of sex, and others by the dozen were exploring the subconscious. Freud merely expanded and overemphasized what the others had found. It was characteristic of Holmes that he should be out in front, with the shock troops.

Since the earlier writings foreshadowed the later, and in some instances were recast, let us compare two brief passages in order to observe how this master workman in words refashioned his own phrases. In the passage to follow he stepped over into the domain of his father, who was then lecturing on anatomy at Harvard, and lifted therefrom for an illuminating simile a rudimentary bone found in cats and dogs which, when the clavicles unite, becomes the merrythought (wish-bone) of birds. As printed in "Common Carriers and the Common Law", a signed article in the law journal, he said:

> "The official theory is that each new decision follows syllogistically from existing precedents. But as precedents survive like the clavicle in the cat, long after the use they once served is at an end, and the reason for them has been forgotten, the result of following them must often be failure and confusion from the merely logical point of view. It is easy for the scholar to show that reasons have been misapprehended and precedents misapplied."[4]

In "Early Forms of Liability", the first chapter of *The Common Law*, Holmes altered this but slightly on page 35:

> "The official theory is that each new decision follows syllogistically from existing precedents. But just as the

clavicle in the cat only tells of the existence of some earlier creature to which a collar-bone was useful, precedents survive in the law long after the use they once served is at an end and the reason for them has been forgotten. The result of following them must often be failure and confusion from the merely logical point of view."[5]

The next paragraph is noteworthy for three reasons. It differentiates discerningly and subtly between the form and substance of the law, it is a touchstone of the writer's attitude toward legal history and legal philosophy, and it is taken verbatim (excepting for a negligible alteration) from the earlier paper. Holmes, who had even then a deceptive air of ease in writing, heightened that impression by the prodigality with which he threw aside whole pages of his earlier work. One may fancy him examining a page over which he had labored faithfully and consigning it scornfully to limbo; this paragraph he saved:

"On the other hand, in substance the growth of the law is legislative. And this in a deeper sense than that what the courts declare to have always been the law is in fact new. It is legislative in its grounds. The very considerations which judges most rarely mention, and always with an apology, are the secret root from which the law draws all the juices of life. I mean, of course, considerations of what is expedient for the community concerned. Every important principle which is developed by litigation is in fact and at bottom the result of more or less definitely understood views of public policy; most generally, to be sure, under our practice and traditions, the unconscious result of instinctive preferences and inarticulate convictions, but none the less traceable to views of public policy in the last analysis. And as the law is administered by able and experienced men, who know too much to sacrifice good sense to a syllogism, it will be found that, when ancient rules maintain themselves in the way that has been and will be shown in this book, new reasons more fitted to the time have been found for them, and that they gradually receive a new content, and at last a new form, from the grounds to which they had been transplanted."[6]

When Holmes spoke of the way that had been shown in the book, he referred presumably to a passage on pages 1-2: "The substance of the law at any given time pretty nearly corresponds, so far as it goes, with what is then understood to be convenient; but its form and machinery, and the degree to which it is able to work out desired results, depend very much upon its past." To make clear that he had no respect for the mere uninspired digger after antiquarian conditions and views, it is pertinent to quote three brief sentences written more than a quarter of a century later: "The man of science in the law is not merely a bookworm. To a microscopic eye for detail he must unite an insight which tells him what details are significant. Not every maker of exact investigation counts, but only he who directs his investigation to a crucial point."[7] And again, in that same paper: "History is the means by which we measure the power which the past has had to govern the present in spite of ourselves, so to speak, by imposing traditions which no longer meet their original end. History sets us free and enables us to make up our minds dispassionately whether the survival which we are enforcing answers any new purpose when it has ceased to answer the old."[8]

History set Holmes free. "It is revolting," he said, "to have no better reason for a rule of law than that it so was laid down in the time of Henry IV. It is still more revolting if the grounds upon which it was laid down have vanished long since, and the rule simply persists through blind imitation of the past."

Holmes is so identified in many minds with his work as a legal historian that it may not be amiss to quote more at length from the vivid pages in which that passage occurs. If we want to know why a rule of law has taken its present shape, or why it is in existence, he said, "we go to tradition", and:

> "We follow it into the Year Books, and perhaps beyond them to the customs of the Salian Franks, and somewhere in the past, in the German forests, in the needs of Norman kings, in the assumptions of a dominant class, in the absence of generalized ideas, we find out the practical motive for what now best is justified by the mere fact of its acceptance and that men are accustomed to it. The rational study of the law is still to a large extent the study of history. History must be a part of the study, because without it we cannot know the precise scope of rules which it is our business to know. It is a part of the rational study, because it is the first step toward an enlightened skepticism, that is, towards a deliberate reconsideration of the worth of those rules. When you get the dragon out of his cave onto the plain and in the daylight, you can count his teeth and claws, and see just what is his strength. But to get him out is only the first step. The next is either to kill him, or to tame him and make him a useful animal. For the rational study of the law the black-letter man may be the man of the present, but the man of the future is the man of statistics and the master of economics."[9]

One conspicuous service which Holmes, the student of history, rendered to law, was that he helped it live down its past.

In the first chapter a passage was quoted from the early writings of Holmes as revealing that, although he accepted the Austinian definition of law as the fiat of a sovereign, it was with qualifications. How account, under such a definition, for international law, regulating more than one sovereign, none acknowledging fealty to a superior? Austin slid from under that query by denying that such regulations were law. How determine what the sovereign actually is, when an invisible complex of forces is at work? (John C. Gray, whom Holmes knew and admired, thought the real rulers of society were undiscoverable.) Or, for that matter, how was one to determine in this republic the exact nature of the sovereign or the State, and to determine its relation to the law?

The anecdote about the French peasant who wandered about the streets of Paris inquiring where he might see *l'Etat* could never have been told of any American, provincial or urban. Louis XIV might say, "I am the State," but no American President would have the temerity. One of the consequences of what Elihu Root called "organized self-control", and a consequence seldom the subject of comment in this country, is that the government, the State, local or national, is seldom present as an entity in the mind of the citizen. The voter does not feel a distinct relation to the State and he is too cynical about politics to feel responsibility for it. As for the President, he is usually the choice of interested cliques, or the consequence of an Act of God, as has happened on five occasions. In such a setting the "blandishments of the Emperor's wife" could have no force, but other and sometimes more potent extra-legal influences come into play.

Yet, after summarizing Montesquieu's conception of the State, Holmes asked, "What have two hundred years added?" This was in his witty introduction, written in 1900, to a reprint of the *Esprit des Lois*. "It is true," he comments, "that Montesquieu limits his remarks to trifles. They [the French] readily will admit that other people are wiser, if you will grant them that they are better dressed. . . . After things of this sort, two pages further on we read that the most perfect government is that which attains its ends with the least cost, so that the one which leads men in the way most according to their inclination is best. . . . What proximate test of excellence can be found except correspondence to the actual equilibrium of forces in the community—that is, conformity to the wishes of the dominant power?"[10]

Harold J. Laski, a warm friend of Mr. Justice Holmes and the best-equipped commentator on his status as a statesman, thinks he would echo Spinoza's dictum that "freedom and strength of mind are virtues in private men, but the virtue of government is safety"; and that he would echo from the same thinker that "a government is best under which men lead a peaceable life, by which I mean that life of man which consisteth not only in the circulation of the blood and other properties common to all animals, but whose chief part is reason and the true life and excellence of the mind."[11] To provide safety and peaceableness the State must enforce the law, but it can do so only by demonstrating its power to command obedience; and the justification of the code must be found, as Holmes put it, "in some help which the law brings towards reaching a social end which the governing power of the community has made up its mind that it wants."[12]

It was not a moral justification. Although freely avowing: "The law is the witness and external deposit of our moral life. Its history is the history of the moral development of the race";[13] and although believing that the practice of the law as a profession, "in spite of popular jests", tended to make good citizens, he yet emphasized the difference between the law and morals and thought the distinction of vital importance. To assume that moral rights are legal rights would result, he perceived, in confusion; and he illustrated this point, as so often he did, in homely terms.

> "If you want to know the law and nothing else, you must look at it as a bad man, who cares only for the material consequences which such knowledge enables him to predict, not as a good one, who finds his reasons for conduct, whether inside the law or outside of it, in the vaguer sanctions of conscience. The theoretical importance of the distinction is no less, if you would reason on your subject aright. The law is full of phraseology drawn from morals, and by the mere force of language continually invites us to pass from one domain to the other without perceiving it, as we are sure to do unless we have the boundary constantly before

our minds. The law talks about rights, and duties, and malice, and intent, and negligence, and so forth, and nothing is easier, or, I may say, more common in legal reasoning, than to take these words in their moral sense, at some stage of the argument, and so to drop into fallacy. For instance, when we speak of the rights of man in a moral sense, we mean to mark the limits of interference with individual freedom which we think are prescribed by conscience, by our ideal, however reached. Yet it is certain that many laws have been enforced in the past, and it is likely that some are enforced now, which are condemned by the most enlightened opinion of the time, or which at all events pass the limit of interference as many consciences would draw it."[14]

The bad man whom Holmes conjured up wouldn't care two straws about ethical considerations or moral axioms; he would want to know only what the courts were going to do. If he did certain things he would be subjected to certain disagreeable consequences, perhaps the compulsory payment of a fine. "But from his point of view, what is the difference between being fined and being taxed a certain sum for doing a certain thing?"[15] When the law imposes a financial liability the courts debate whether it constitutes a fine or a tax.

Men and corporations, whether good or bad, like to know how they will stand in reference to the law if they undertake certain courses of conduct, and what the courts are likely to do to them. Often they consult lawyers, and the lawyer as counsellor sometimes becomes an unofficial law-giver, or law-maker. Case books, treatises and statutes, in this country and abroad, covering six or seven centuries and multiplying at a great rate, are the attorney's main reliance. To what extent is the course of the law predictable?

The law, Holmes felt, was not a mystery, despite this multitude of straws in the wind, but a recognized profession with established limits, and with certain principles at its core not too numerous to be manageable. He discussed the possibility of predicting the incidence of the public power and authority, through the courts, on the basis of accumulated data, with a whimsical aside upon the fact that the dramatic element (the "human interest") was eliminated from these documents.

"In these sibylline leaves are gathered the scattered prophecies of the past upon the cases in which the axe will fall. These are what properly have been called the oracles of the law. Far the most important and pretty nearly the whole meaning of every new effort of legal thought is to make these prophecies more precise, and to generalize them into a thoroughly connected system. The process is one, from a lawyer's statement of the case, eliminating as it does all the dramatic elements with which his client's story has clothed it, and retaining only the facts of legal import, up to the final analyses and abstract universals of theoretic jurisprudence. The reason why a lawyer does not mention that his client wore a white hat when he made a contract, while Mrs. Quickly would be sure to dwell upon it along with the parcel gilt goblet and the sea-coal fire, is that he foresees that the public force will act in the same way whatever his client had upon his head. It is to make the prophecies easier to be remembered and to be understood that the teachings of the decisions of the past are put into general propositions and gathered into text-books, or that statutes are passed in a general form. The primary rights and duties with which jurisprudence busies itself again are nothing but prophecies. One of the many evil effects of the confusion between legal and moral ideas . . . is that theory is apt to get the cart before the horse, and to consider the right or the duty as something existing apart from and independent of the consequences of its breach, to which certain sanctions are added afterward. But, as I shall try to show, a legal duty so called is nothing but a prediction that if a man does or omits certain things he will be made to suffer in this or that way by judgment of the court; and so of a legal right."[16]

Max Weber has observed that ethics founded on expediency are less reliable than those founded on tradition; the ethics of those who endeavor to regulate their deportment and policy on predictions of the law appear to be founded on both.

It has seemed advisable here, in order to body forth more clearly the Holmes philosophy of the law, to quote from time to time from later writings as well as from his earlier work, in which his position was but foreshadowed. Although he often wrote in flashing epigrams, and sometimes, under the hydraulic pressure of his thought, compressed centuries into a paragraph or even a sentence, none could be more meticulous than he in dealing with his material. While he was editing the law journal he was editing also Kent's *Commentaries,* and he said in the preface to the twelfth edition, as illustrative of the care he exercised:

"I have devoted more than three years to the attempt to bring this work down through the quarter of a century which has elapsed since the author's death. While it has been in progress I have tried to keep the various subjects before my mind, so far as to see the bearing upon them of any new decision in this country or in England. Almost all my more important notes have been partially or wholly rewritten—many more than once—in the light of cases which have appeared since their first preparation; and every case cited has been carefully examined in the original report."

So scrupulous was the editor, that when the new edition was printed from the last he compared it with the sixth edition, which contained the author's last corrections, and so revised the citations. He had watched decisions not only in this country but in England; and in preparing this book for the public, as well as in his own legal writing, he had taken account of Continental legal processes as well. In this connection an outburst by Professor Karl N. Llewellyn of the Columbia law faculty, in dealing with methods quite dissimilar from the methods of Holmes, is enlightening as showing how common the other is.

> "It is high time," [said the Professor] "that American legal thinking should arrive at a conscious and sociologically defensible working position in regard to European legal thought. We have flea-jumped back and forth between the extremes of deliberate ignorance and uninformed contempt or dismissal, and the opposite extreme of undigested indiscriminate gulping. There is little profit in either. It is almost universally true that our case-training and earthy *ad hoc* legal sense offer important addition to a continental theory. It is very commonly true that even a wholly sound continental theory calls for remodeling in the light of our own data before it is adequate for description of our law or of the processes of our law. It is also very commonly true that even an unsound continental theory holds stimulus for the understanding of our law."[17]

The good professor then finds fault with Holmes, "our foremost and least tradition-ridden jurist", for accepting a Roman concept of *obligatio* in relation to tort, but admits a moment later that Holmes had "a better insight" in an article written in 1872 for the *American Law Review*. "The home-grown color of his mind", and his "heterodox insight", Professor Llewellyn thought, appeared in "its true creative power" in a highly technical discussion of the "Elements of Contract", on page 302 of *The Common Law*.

At another point in the same paper Professor Llewellyn examined a statement made by Holmes in this book: "To explain how mankind first learned to promise, we must go to metaphysics, and find out how it ever came to frame a future tense."[18] Both ancient Hebrew and modern German, Professor Llewellyn notes, manage promises with a present tense. "Insight does not always need exact verbal symbols, although symbols both further and limit insight. One might risk the suggestion: as law to life, so language to thought." It might be interpolated that in a legal opinion Holmes had put the last thought, or something akin to it, rather more neatly than his critic: "A word is not a crystal, transparent and unchanged; it is the skin of a living thought and may vary greatly in color and content according to the circumstances and the time in which it is used."[19]

If Holmes perceived in the sublimation of envy and jealousy the bases of human justice, he saw also, as many others had seen, the element of revenge in early law and the forms in which it had persisted. "It is commonly known," he wrote, "that the early forms of legal procedure were grounded in vengeance. Modern writers have thought that the Roman law started from the blood feud, and all the authorities agree that the German law began in that way. The feud led to the composition, at first optional, then compulsory, by which the feud was bought off. The gradual encroachment of the composition may be traced in the Anglo-Saxon laws and the feud was pretty well broken up, though not extinguished, by the time of William the Conqueror. The killings and houseburnings of an earlier day became the appeal of mayhem and arson.... Vengeance imports a feeling of blame, and an opinion, however distorted by passion, that a wrong has been done. It can hardly go very far beyond the case of a harm intentionally inflicted; even a dog distinguishes between being stumbled over and being kicked."[20]

At that time trespass had been much more discussed in legal literature than the original principles of liability for harm inflicted by some person or thing, and it was natural that Holmes should devote special attention to them. They had their root, he was persuaded, in revenge, and were gradually changed in form. In this phase he found an illuminating example of how "the law has grown, without a break, from barbarism to civilization". Let us glance at his discussion of ancient and independent systems of law.

> "There is a well-known passage in Exodus which we shall have to remember later: 'If an ox gore a man or a woman, that they die: then the ox shall be surely stoned, and his flesh shall not be eaten; but the owner of the ox shall be quit.' When we turn from the Jews to the Greeks, we find the principle of the passage just quoted erected into a system. Plutarch, in his Solon, tells us that a dog that had bitten a man was to be delivered up bound to a log four cubits long. Plato made elaborate provisions in his Laws for many such cases. If a slave killed a man, he was to be given up to the relatives of the deceased. If he wounded a man, he was to be given up to the relatives of the deceased. . . . Nor was this an ideal creation of merely imagined law, for it was said in one of the speeches of Aeschines, that 'we banish beyond our borders stocks and stones and steel, voiceless and mindless things, if they chance to kill a man; and if a man commit suicide, bury the hand that struck the blow afar from its body.' This is mentioned quite as an every-day matter, evidently without thinking it at all extraordinary, only to point an antithesis to the honors heaped upon Demosthenes. As late as the second century after Christ the traveller Pausanias observed with some surprise that they still sat in judgment on inanimate things in the Prytaneum. Plutarch attributes the institution to Draco."

Not only was the ox in Exodus to be stoned; a tree from which a man fell was to be chopped to pieces; the deodand was accursed. In those days the liability was not with the owner but with his property, whether living or inanimate. In early Roman law the scholar found embodiments of "the hatred for anything giving us pain, which wreaks itself on the manifest cause, and which leads even civilized man to kick a door when it pinches his fingers."[21] But, one may ask, what bearing could these old customs have upon present-day law? "So far as concerns the influence of the Roman law upon our own," Holmes wrote, "especially the Roman law of master and servant, the evidence of it is to be found in every book that has been written for the last five hundred years. It has been stated already that we still repeat the reasoning of the Roman lawyers, empty as it is, to the present day." He traced analogies also to German and even to Asian law. But on its formal side, although going back to discernible roots, Holmes could find no logical cohesion of part with part in the body of law. "The truth is," he wrote, "that the law is always approaching and never reaching, consistency. It is forever adopting new principles from life at one end, and it always retains old ones from history at the other, which have not yet been absorbed or sloughed off. It will become entirely consistent only when it ceases to grow."[22] Codification would be "but a phase in a continuous growth". He saw in the very inconsistency due to growth a merit. "If truth were not often suggested by error, if old implements could not be adjusted to new uses, human progress would be slow."

Published in 1881, when Holmes was just forty, but representing a decade of preparation, *The Common Law* was hailed by the London *Spectator* as "the most original work of legal speculation which has appeared in English since the publication of Sir Henry Maine's *Ancient Law*". Other critics here and abroad were equally emphatic in their praise. Sir Frederick Pollock reminds us that the book was published "when English-speaking law schools were in their infancy and serious law reviews, in English at any rate, not yet born, when current text-books were with few exceptions merely empirical, and most practicing lawyers believed that law could be learnt only by rule of thumb (as some still do) and that professed teachers of law were no better than impostors (as indeed some were not)."[23] He wrote for the London *Saturday Review* an unsigned criticism of the book in which he forecast that it would become a most valuable—"we should almost say an indispensable"—companion of legal students. It is one of the few text-books which the courts have recognized. It was translated almost at once into German, French and Italian. Chairs of legal history began to be founded in the schools. The patient drudgery and the high intelligence which had gone into the book bore fruit speedily.

An unsigned review which Holmes wrote for the *American Law Review* in 1873 dealt with an article on "Class Legislation" in the London *Fortnightly Review,* growing out of the prosecution for conspiracy of the leaders of the London gas-stokers' strike in the previous year. Drastic sentences were imposed, and the speech of Mr. Justice Brett in imposing them so stirred British opinion as to cause a reconsideration of the English law on combinations. The law brought to bear on the gas-stokers was class legislation, and was strongly denounced on that ground. The Holmes comment is noteworthy as revealing the independent and incisive quality of his thought in that day.

"But it is no sufficient condemnation of legislation," Holmes wrote, "that it favors one class at the expense of another; for much or all legislation does that; and none the less when the *bona fide* object is the greatest good of the greatest number. Why should the greatest number be preferred? Why not the greatest good of the most intelligent and most highly developed? The greatest good of a minority of our generation may be the greatest good of the greatest number in the long run. But if the welfare of all future ages is to be considered, legislation may as well be abandoned for the present. If the welfare of the living majority is paramount, it can only be on the ground that the majority have the power in their hands. The fact is that legislation in this country, as well as elsewhere, is empirical. It is necessarily made a means by which a body, having the power, put burdens which are disagreeable to them on the shoulders of somebody else. Communism would no more get rid of the difficulty than any other system, unless it limited or put a stop to the propagation of the species. And it may be doubted whether that solution would not be as disagreeable as any other."[24]

Already the student was pondering whether the welfare of a living majority or of problematic future generations should be paramount. He was given to the long view as well as to the large view. "The law has got to be stated over again," he said; "and I venture to say that in fifty years we shall have it in a form of which no man could have dreamed fifty years ago."[25] Forty-five years of that half century had elapsed when Mr. Justice Holmes was ninety years old; and, as he anticipated, a thousand heads had been analyzing and generalizing the rules of the law and the grounds for them; yet it could hardly be said that no man could have foreseen what the result would be, for he himself had foreseen and foretold its essences. His noble conception of a realistic and rationalized science of law was as yet unrealized. He had blazed the path. He had been a leader in pressing forward on it.

CHAPTER 10

Harvard or the Bench?

NOT UNTIL 1882, after the publication of *The Common Law*, did Holmes become a full professor of the Harvard Law School. The elevation brought him face to face with a major decision, which was to affect profoundly his later life; a decision more important, we may well believe, than his determination to study law rather than devote himself to the academic pursuit of philosophy. Associate Justice Otis P. Lord of the Supreme Judicial Court of Massachusetts had made it known that he must resign soon, on account of failing health; and Governor Long had Holmes in mind as his successor. Should he leave Harvard for the bench?

Such were the ponderable factors on both sides that no man could consider the issue lightly. Holmes loved "every limb of old Harvard College", and never ceased to speak glowingly of its Law School.[1] The first Royall Professor of that School had been a Chief Justice of the State Supreme Court; Joseph Story had taught there from 1811 to 1845, while an Associate Justice of the United States Supreme Court. Its faculty lists were studded with illustrious names; among its Bachelors were Sumner and Phillips and James Russell Lowell, with scores of others hardly less famous.

Holmes knew how often collaboration between teachers and pupils in this school had contributed to the enrichment of legal literature. He knew that as teacher he would occupy a proud position and he knew that he would have a body of students of whom any teacher might be proud. He was not too far from his Latin to recall that Cicero had found an art not only in knowing a thing but a certain art in teaching it, and had inquired what greater or better gift any man could give a republic than to instruct its youth. To help young men become fit governors of their generation seemed to Holmes a noble work; and there was more-over a strong personal tug to remain where he was. It was not merely that his father, after a distinguished service as lecturer on anatomy, had just been made professor emeritus; the faculty included also warm friends of the younger man. Charles S. Peirce was lecturing on logic there; in his room and in William James's, Holmes and a few others had been wont to gather for long dis-cussions, largely metaphysical.[2] The atmosphere and the person-nel and the prospect of frequent encounter with active searching minds drew Holmes strongly. He appreciated, too, the opportu-nities, the possibilities, which lay open to the teacher. He had formulated, and he was to express to a later student body, the scope and the limitations of such instruction.

"A law school does not undertake to teach success," he said. "That combination of tact and will which gives a man immediate prominence among his fellows comes from nature, not from in-struction; and if it can be helped at all by advice, such advice is not offered here. . . .

"Education, other than self-education, lies mainly in the shap-ing of men's interests and aims. If you convince a man that an-other way of looking at things is more profound, another form of pleasure more subtle than that to which he has been accustomed —if you make him really see it—the very nature of man is such that he will desire the profounder thought and the subtiler joy. So I say the business of a law school is not sufficiently described when you merely say that it is to teach law, or to make lawyers. It is to teach law in the grand manner, and to make great lawyers.

"Our country needs such teaching very much. I think we should all agree that the passion for equality has passed far be-yond the political or even the social sphere. We are not only unwilling to admit that any class of society is better than that in which we move, but our customary attitude towards everyone in authority of any kind is that he is only the lucky recipient of honor or salary above the average, which any average man might as well receive as he. When the effervescence of democratic nega-tion extends its workings beyond the abolition of external distinctions of rank to spiritual things—when the passion for equality is not content with founding social intercourse upon universal human sympathy and a community of interests in which all may share, but attacks the lines of Nature which establish orders and degrees among the souls of men—they are not only wrong, but ignobly wrong. Modesty and reverence are no less virtues of freemen than the democratic feeling which will submit neither to arrogance nor to servility.

"To inculcate those virtues, to correct the ignoble excess of a noble feeling to which I have referred, I know of no teachers so powerful and persuasive as the little army of specialists. They carry no banners, they beat no drums; but where they are, men learn that bustle and push are not the equals of quiet genius and serene mastery. They compel others who need their help, or who are enlightened by their teaching, to obedience and respect. They set the examples themselves; for they furnish in the intellectual world a perfect type of the union of democracy with discipline. They bow to no one who seeks to impose his authority by foreign aid; they hold that science like courage is never beyond the necessity of proof, but must always be ready to prove itself against all challengers. . . .

"Lawyers, too, were among the first specialists to be needed and to appear in America. And I believe it would be hard to exaggerate the goodness of their influence in favor of sane and orderly thinking. But lawyers feel the spirit of the times like other people. They, like others, are forever trying to discover cheap and agreeable substitutes for real things. I fear that the bar has done its full share to exalt that most hateful of American words and ideals, 'smartness', as against dignity of moral feeling and profundity of knowledge. It is from within the bar, not from outside, that I have heard the new gospel that learning is out of date, and that the man for the times is no longer the thinker and the scholar, but the smart man, unencumbered with other artillery than the latest edition of the Digest and the latest revision of the Statutes.

"The aim of a law school should be, the aim of the Harvard

Law School has been, not to make men smart, but to make them wise in their calling—to start them on a road which will lead them to the abode of their masters. A law school should be at once the workshop and the nursery of specialists in the sense which I have explained. It should obtain for teachers men in each generation who are producing the best work of that generation. Teaching should not stop, but rather should foster, production. The 'enthusiasm of the lecture room', the contagious interest of companionship, should make the students partners in their teachers' work. The ferment of genius in its creative moment is quickly imparted. If a man is great, he makes others believe in greatness; he makes them incapable of mean ideals and easy self-satisfaction. His pupils will accept no substitute for realities; but at the same time they learn that the only coin with which realities can be bought is life."[3]

Holmes, to paraphrase his own expression, was one of the men in his generation who was producing the best work in that generation, and was to produce the best of the generation yet ahead of his. He had other characteristics and qualities which fitted him to be a great teacher.

Yet the bench exercised an attraction certainly not less potent, even when Holmes first began to debate his choice. As an editor, as a lecturer at Harvard and at the Lowell Institute, and as an author, he had arrived at quite definite notions about the function of the jurist as an interpreter, law-maker, statesman, philosopher. In the early flush of his work as editor he had alluded to Lord Mansfield's advice to a business man, suddenly elevated to the bench, that he should state conclusions but not reasons, because his judgments would be right, probably, whereas his reasoning would surely be wrong. With this as a premise, Holmes continued:

> "It is only after a series of determinations on the subject matter, that it becomes necessary to 'reconcile the cases', as it is called, that is, by a true induction to

state the principle which has until then been obscurely felt. And this statement is often modified more than once by new decisions before the abstracted general rule takes its final shape. A well-settled legal doctrine embodies the work of many minds, and has been tested in form as well as substance by trained critics whose practical interest it is to resist it at every step."[4]

Holmes was discussing "Codes, and the Arrangement of the Law". It was in this paper that he first insisted on codification, not on the basis of rights, the prevailing method, but on the basis of duties, which "precede rights logically and chronologically". His gift of phrasing cropped out there, but his deep-cutting insight, not to be distracted by current and long-established custom, was more significant.

"The very words of the court" were employed whenever possible in those legal books on which a code might possibly be modelled. Holmes perceived how far-reaching was the work of the jurist, and to what extent that work affected the teacher and the student. "The perfect lawyer," he said, "is he who commands all the ties between a given case and all others. But few lawyers are perfect, and all have to learn their business."[5]

And in *The Common Law* he had written:

"Since the ancient forms have disappeared, a broader treatment of the subject ought to be possible. Ignorance is the best of law reformers. People are glad to discuss a question on general principles, when they have forgotten the special knowledge necessary for technical reasoning. But the present unwillingness to generalize is founded on more than merely negative grounds. The philosophical habit of the day, the frequency of legislation, and the ease with which the law may be changed to meet the opinions and wishes of the public, all make it natural and unavoidable that judges as well as others should openly discuss the legislative principles upon which their decisions must always rest in the end, and should base their judgments upon broad considerations of policy to which the traditions of the bench would hardly have tolerated a reference fifty years ago."[6]

Holmes perceived, too, the jurist's obligation to interpret history and legal precedents in the light of current conditions, and the fashion in which the courts had sometimes failed to do this. Much later, in dedicating the new hall of the Boston University School of Law, he illustrated the point so aptly that it will be well to set down the passage here:

"Let me take an illustration, which can be stated in a few words, to show how the social end which is aimed at by a rule of law is obscured and only partially attained in consequence of the fact that the rule owes its form to a gradual historical development, instead of being reshaped as a whole, with conscious articulate reference to the end in view. We think it desirable to prevent one man's property being misappropriated by another, and so we make larceny a crime. The evil is the same whether the misappropriation is made by a man into whose hands the owner has put the property, or by one who wrongfully takes it away. But primitive law in its weakness did not get much beyond an effort to prevent violence, and very naturally made a wrongful taking, a trespass, part of its definition of the crime. In modern times the judges enlarged the definition a little by holding that, if the wrong-doer gets possession by a trick or device, the crime is committed. This really was giving up the requirement of a trespass, and it would have been more logical, as well as truer to the present object of the law, to abandon the requirement altogether. That, however, would have seemed too bold, and was left to statute. Statutes were passed making embezzlement a crime. But the force of tradition caused the crime of embezzlement to be regarded as so

far distinct from larceny that to this day, in some juris-
dictions at least, a slip corner is kept open for thieves
to contend, if indicted for larceny, that they should
have been indicted for embezzlement, and if indicted
for embezzlement, that they should have been indicted
for larceny, and to escape on that ground.

"Far more fundamental questions still await a better
answer than that we do as our fathers have done. What
have we better than a blind guess to show that the criminal law in its present form does more good than harm?
I do not stop to refer to the effect which it has had in
degrading prisoners and in plunging them further
into crime, or to the question whether fine and imprisonment do not fall more heavily on a criminal's wife
and children than on himself. I have in mind more
far-reaching questions. Does punishment deter? Do we
deal with criminals on proper principles? . . .

"The impediments to rational generalization, which
I illustrated from the law of larceny, are shown in the
other branches of the law, as well as in that of crime."[7]

Holmes debated earnestly whether he could live a fuller and
more useful life in a chair at Harvard or on the bench of the
Supreme Court, and in his doubt turned to that valued friend,
his senior law partner—for he was still practicing law—George O.
Shattuck. He must give up his practice, obviously, if he went
upon the bench. His law partner perceived how weighty were
the arguments on both sides, yet his advice was unqualified: he
urged that the wider field was in the court. And he counselled
his young friend, pending that appointment, to accept the professorship in the Law School, but to have an understanding in
writing that he would be free to resign if the post of Associate
Justice were tendered to him. This Holmes did.

By now Charles W. Eliot had been for a little more than twelve
years President of Harvard, and from the moment of his acces-
sion he had dominated the university to an extent theretofore

for two centuries unknown. His innovations and his firmness were described, not without humor, by the elder Oliver Wendell Holmes:

> "Mr. Eliot makes the Corporation meet *twice* a month instead of once. He comes to the meeting of every Faculty, ours [the medical] among the rest, and keeps us up to eleven and twelve o'clock at night discussing new arrangements. He shows an extraordinary knowledge of all that relates to every department of the University, and presides with an *aplomb*, a quiet, imperturbable, serious good-humor, that it is impossible not to admire. We are, some of us, disposed to think that he is a little too much in a hurry with some of his innovations, and take care to let the Corporation know it. . . . I cannot help being amused at some of the scenes we have in our Medical Faculty—this cool, grave young man proposing in the calmest way to turn everything topsy-turvy, taking the reins in his hands and driving as if he were the first man that ever sat on the box. I say amused, because I do not really care much about most of the changes he proposes, and I look on a little as I would at a rather serious comedy.
>
> " 'How is it? I should like to ask,' said one of our number the other evening, 'that this Faculty has gone on for eighty years, managing its own affairs and doing it well—for the Medical School is the most flourishing department connected with the college—how is it that we have been going on so well in the same orderly path for eighty years, and now *within three or four months* it is proposed to change all our modes of carrying on the school—it seems very extraordinary, and I should like to know how it happens.'
>
> " 'I can answer Dr. ——'s question very easily,' said the bland, grave young man: 'there is a new president'."[8]

No longer a new president, but still distinctly in charge, Doctor Eliot wanted to retain in the law faculty the brilliant son of the medical lecturer who had chuckled at his calm assurance in those earlier faculty meetings. The younger man had made a place for himself, on his own merit. His book had been received with a critical accord which amounted to an ovation. His lectures at Harvard and at the Lowell Institute had made friends and admirers of the students who heard them. By birth and achievement he was altogether desirable from the viewpoint of the university. Doctor Eliot, however, did not press the point in person, but through members of the law faculty, in particular James Barr Ames, then a professor but later to become Dean. Well, Fisher Ames, an ancestor of Professor Ames, had declined the Presidency of Harvard in 1804; to decline continuance of a professorship could hardly be stigmatized as downright treason. The weight of Shattuck's word counted heavily in the scales of temporary indecision; and when, on December 8 of that year, Governor Long announced the appointment of Holmes, it was with the knowledge that the post would be accepted.

In the opinion of certain Harvard faculty members, this step was little less than an affront. Possibly that attitude was reflected in the fact that, although Yale University made Holmes a Doctor of Laws in 1886, Harvard did not so honor him until 1895.

For twenty years Holmes was to sit in the Supreme Judicial Court, for the last three years of that period as Chief Justice; when the time came for him to move onward to Washington and the Supreme Court of the United States, he gave utterance to an emotion and a faith which may have been not unlike what he felt when he left Harvard. The members of the Middlesex Bar gave a dinner in his honor, and he closed his speech to them with the words:

"I have felt very sad at the thought of all that I leave, and sad with the wonder whether the work of twenty years on which I have spent the passion of my heart will be adjudged to have been nobly done. I have felt sad, too, with a different sadness in thinking of the future. It is an adventure into the unknown. No man can go far who never sets down his foot until he knows that the sidewalk is under it.

"But, gentlemen, it is a great adventure, and that thought brings with it a mighty joy. To have the chance to do one's share in shaping the laws of the whole country, spreads over one the hush that one used to feel when one was awaiting the beginning of a battle. . . .

"We will not falter. We will not fail. We will reach the earthworks if we live, and if we fail we will leave our spirit in those who follow, and they will not turn back. All is ready. Bugler, blow the charge."[9]

When Holmes left the academic shades to ascend his State's supreme bench it was because he heard the bugler's signal. He left knowing full well that he had incurred pedagogic displeasure, but he left believing, and rightly, that the adventure in front of him was worth whatever price he must pay for it. Whether he could have served his profession and his fellow man the better in the educational field must remain problematical; it is certain that his work as a jurist contributed largely to the education of younger generations of lawyers. It is possible to say of him, what he said afterward of Frederick William Maitland, who occupied in the British world of law and letters a place similar to his own in North America:

"His profound knowledge of the sources of English law equipped him, as perhaps no other was equipped, to illustrate and explain the present. His knowledge was only a tool to his good sense. His good sense and insight were illuminated and made vivid by his power of statement and gift of narrative, so that any reasonably prepared reader of his writings, even those dealing with what one would have expected to be dry details, is sure to become interested, absorbed and charmed."[19]

The intellectual discipline and realistic philosophy which had come to Holmes as a result of his studies, writing and teaching, were to be manifest in his work on the bench in Massachusetts. His decisions there, but little noticed by his contemporaries, were to presage his decisions in the higher court for which he was destined. The balance of his justice, the width of his erudition, the discernment of the "crucial point" involved in dusty chronicles, both in dissent and in accord with the majority of the court, were to prefigure the whole body, excepting strictly constitutional decisions, of his contribution to jurisprudence.

CHAPTER 11

Judge Holmes and Social Questions

MASSACHUSETTS JUDGES should be "as free, impartial and independent as the lot of humanity will admit", according to the State Constitution.[1] Judge Oliver Wendell Holmes, as a member of the Supreme Judicial Court, exemplified this admonition. He once recalled that James Otis, in a legal argument, had helped lay the foundations of the instrument under which he functioned.

"As we walk down Court street," he said, "in the midst of a jostling crowd, intent like us upon today and its affairs, our eyes are like to fall upon the small, dark building that stands at the head of State Street, and, like an ominous reef, divides the stream of business in its course to the gray cliffs that tower beyond. And, whoever we may be, we may chance to pause and forget our hurry for a moment, as we remember that the first waves that foretold the coming storm of the Revolution broke around that reef. But, if we are lawyers, our memories and our reverence grow more profound. In the old State House, we remember, James Otis argued the case of the writs of assistance, and in that argument laid one of the foundations for American constitutional law. Just as that little building is not diminished, but rather is enhanced and glorified, by the vast structures which somehow it turns into a background, so the beginnings of our national life, whether in battle or in law, lose none of their greatness by contrast with all the mighty things of later date, beside which, by every law of number and measure, they ought to seem so small. To us who took part in the Civil War, the greatest battle of the Revolution seems little more than a reconnaissance in force, and Lexington and Concord were mere skirmishes that would not find mention in the newspapers. Yet veterans who have known battle on a modern scale are not less aware of the spiritual significance of those little fights, I venture to say, than the enlightened children of commerce who tell us that soon war is to be no more."[2]

James Otis was a contributor to the Massachusetts Constitution, but John Adams wrote it, and then sailed for Europe in 1799, before it was debated in convention. He had been guided not by Otis alone, but by the charter of the Province, by the writings of Europeans, and by the thought of several New Englanders. Samuel Adams, Theophilus Parsons and Thomas Allen were among those whose knowledge of legal principles and practice contributed to this document, of which Judge Holmes, in his new capacity, became an interpreter.

Although appointed to the Supreme Judicial Court on December 15, 1882, Judge Holmes did not take his seat until the following January 3, at a term of the court then being held in Boston. Subsequently he was to amplify somewhat the Constitutional description of a judge by telling his own conception of the qualities which should be manifest in the office. After the death on June 4, 1891, of Judge William Allen, who had been an Associate Justice of the Court since September 5, 1881, Judge Holmes said in open court:

"The bar found him very silent upon the bench. He was not so in the consultation room. There he expressed himself freely and at times, notwithstanding his quiet manner, with the warmth of a hearty and somewhat impulsive temperament, so that there was no question that we knew not only his opinions, but the man behind them.

"He seemed to me a typical New Englander, both in character and in ways of thinking; a characteristic product of one of those inland towns which have been our glory—centers large enough to have a society and a culture of their own, and, formerly at least, remote enough to have local traditions, and local rather than cosmopolitan standards and responsibilities. As with others whom I have known that were brought up in similar surroundings, his Yankee caution and sound judgment were leavened with a touch of enthusiasm capable of becoming radical at moments, and his cultivation had destroyed rather than fostered his respect for the old merely as such. He was very kind. He was always perfectly considerate and reasonable, as well as warm of feeling. In ill health as in good he took his share of work without a word or hint of what it cost him until he died. He had the subtlety of a Calvinist theologian, and as sound a training in the common law as was to be found in Massachusetts; but he was saved from becoming over-technical by his good sense, his humanitarian turn, and the occasional slight touch of radicalism which I have noted. I never felt quite sure that nothing had been overlooked in a statement of facts until his eye had scrutinized it. In discussion, if you did not agree with him, you always reached an exact issue,.and escape in generalities was impossible. I know few qualities which seem to me more desirable in a judge of a court of last resort than this accuracy of thought, and the habit of keeping one's eye on the things for which words stand. Many men, especially as they grow older, resent attempts to push analysis beyond consecrated phrases, or to formulate anew. Such attempts disturb the intellectual rest for which we long. Our ideal is repose, perhaps because our destiny is effort, just as the eyes see green after gazing at the sun. Judge Allen had none of this weakness, but went on without rest to the end.

"Great places make great men. The electric current of large affairs turns even common mold to diamond, and traditions of ancient honor impart something of their dignity to those who inherit them. No man of any loftiness of soul could be long a Justice of this Court without rising to his full height. . . .

"Our prevailing ideals are somewhat coarse. Com-

paratively few imaginations are educated to aspire beyond money and the immediate forms of power. I have
no doubt that vulgar conceptions of life at the top are
one of the causes of discontent at the bottom of society.
Unless we are to accept decadence as the necessary end
of civilization, we should be grateful to all men like
William Allen, whose ambition, if it can be called so,
looks only to remote and mediated command; who do
not ask to say to anyone, Go, and he goeth, so long as in
truthful imagination they wield, according to their degree, that most subtle and intoxicating authority
which controls the future from within by shaping the
thoughts and speech of a later time.

"Such men are to be honored, not by regiments moving with high heads to martial music, but by a few
others, lonely as themselves, walking apart in medita-
tive silence, and dreaming in their turn the dream of
spiritual reign."[3]

William Crowninshield Endicott, who had been for nine years
an Associate Justice of the court, and had left it but a few months
before Judge Holmes was appointed, died in Boston, May 6, 1900.
He had been a leader of the Essex bar when Holmes began practice, and had once called Holmes into a case which he was to try
in Boston. It was a complicated action involving deals of builders
and contractors, and Holmes said afterward that he feared he had
never quite understood it. But the contact with an eminent and
ardent pleader had its value for him, and the distinguished consideration which his elder accorded him taught him, so he said,
"that a lawyer will try his case like a gentleman without giving up
any portion of his energy and force." Afterward Holmes saw
Judge Endicott upon the bench.

"He was sitting in the old equity court room in
Court Square [Judge Holmes said after the death], and
I remember thinking at the time, as I still think, that
he represented in the superlative degree my notion of

the proper bearing and conduct of a judge. Distinguished in person, with the look of race in his countenance which in more ways than one suggested a resemblance to that first Endicott to whom Massachusetts owes so much, he sat without a thought of self, without even the unconscious pride or aloofness which seemed, nay, was his right, serenely absorbed in the problems of the matter in hand, impersonal yet human, the living image of justice, weighing as if the elements in the balance were dead matter, but discerning and collecting those elements by the help of a noble and tender heart. . . .

"He was not less successful in the performance of his other duties as a judge. He was thought to have great power over juries—a matter of more importance in this court then than now, as in his day more jury cases were tried here. Among other causes, the jurisdiction in actions of tort still was retained, and murders continued to be tried before two judges of this bench until long after I came to it.

"Even under our unfortunate legislation, in his mode of presenting the different hypotheses and stating the law according to which the jury may find, a judge inevitably adopts such an order and such emphasis as to bring to their attention what he deems the important elements of the case, and by doing so inevitably in some degree helps to lead them to what he thinks the proper result. I never heard Judge Endicott complained of as going too far, but I think it was recognized that the jury was likely to come out in the way that he thought right.

"As a writer of decisions of the full court, I cannot estimate him as accurately as I could wish, because my other duties have not allowed me time to study his work with a view to critical appreciation. When one reads cases in the way of business, one is intent upon other things than the personality of the man who happens to express the judgment of the court. I think of him as not avoiding the difficulties of a case, as not seeking refuge in generalities, as clear in exposition and as agreeable to read. Beyond that I should not undertake to speak. I have been led to surmise that he found the labor of writing too great, and that this was the reason for his resignation. That is a matter of temperament. The work here has killed some men who took it too hard. But I should not have supposed that Judge Endicott found it other than easy, from his style. . . . Of the many interesting, powerful and impressive figures that are now only memories, his stands out unique in dignity and charm."[4]

At the turn of the Twentieth Century, with three busy decades still ahead of him, Judge Holmes was moved to say, at the outset of his speech to the full court about Mr. Endicott: "It is November and the last leaves are falling that once screened my generation from the sky." His associates on the bench began to fall like leaves, or to resign from the heavy work, soon after he took his seat. Waldo Colburn, who had been an Associate Justice since 1882, died at his home in Dedham on September 26, 1885, and was succeeded by William Sewall Gardner, who took his seat October 20 of that year, while the court was sitting at Plymouth. William Sewall Gardner resigned in September, 1887; Charles Devens, who had been an Associate Justice for eighteen years, died January 7, 1891, and was succeeded three weeks later by John Lathrop, who had been on the bench of the Superior Court. A week later Marcus Morton, who had been an Associate Justice from 1869, and Chief Justice until August 27, 1890, died on February 10, 1891; James M. Barker succeeded as an Associate Justice. William Allen, an Associate Justice for ten years, died on June 4, 1891; and it was his death which occasioned the speech by Judge Holmes from which quotation has been made. Charles

Allen resigned from the court in 1898 and was succeeded by John W. Hammond.

How Judge Holmes "was saved from becoming over-technical", and how he kept his eye "on the things for which words stand", we shall see as we examine some of his decisions. His attitude toward social questions, however, toward the Machine Age, labor unions and the unequal distribution of wealth, and his reluctance to dissent from the majority of the court, are better illustrated by other cases. He had issued a preliminary injunction, for example, forbidding threats and acts of violence during a strike, but permitting picketing. The majority of the court held that picketing was utilized for intimidation, and was illegal. In his report for the consideration of the full court, Judge Holmes, after a hearing, set forth certain facts either admitted or proved, that the plaintiff's workmen had struck, and had conspired to prevent him from getting other workers, so as to prevent him from carrying on his business and compel his adoption of a certain schedule of prices. The means adopted consisted of the picket, or patrol, which relied upon persuasion and social presence, and which he held to be lawful; threats of unlawful harm, and the actions of pickets in so far as they interfered with the employer or his workmen, or any conspiracy to interfere by threats, he held to be illegal.

Chief Justice Walbridge Abner Field dissented, with Judge Holmes, from the position of the majority. He noted that the practice of issuing injunctions in such cases was of recent origin, and added: "I am not convinced that to persuade one man not to enter into the employment of another, by telling the truth to him about such person and his business, is actionable at common law, whatever the motive may be." And again:

> "In the present case, if the establishment of a patrol is using intimidation or force within the meaning of our statutes, it is illegal and criminal; if it does not amount to intimidation or force, but is carried to such a degree

as to interfere with the use by the plaintiff of his property, it may be illegal and actionable, but something
more is necessary to issue an injunction. . . ."[5]

What Judge Holmes had to say in his separate dissent has attracted more attention than any other of his Massachusetts opinions, and by some lawyers is held to be classic. It laid the foundation, moreover, for certain subsequent pronouncements, and
merits quotation more fully than some which are to be noted
later:

> "In a case like the present, it seems to me that what-
> ever the true result may be, it will be of advantage to
> sound thinking to have the less popular view of the law
> stated, and therefore, although when I have been un-
> able to bring my brethren to share my convictions, my
> almost invariable practice is to defer to them in silence,
> I depart from that practice in this case, notwithstand-
> ing my unwillingness to do so in support of an already
> rendered judgment of my own. . . .
>
> "It appears to me that the judgment of the majority
> turns in part on the assumption that the patrol neces-
> sarily carries with it a threat of bodily harm. That as-
> sumption I think unwarranted. . . . I may add, that I
> think the more intelligent workmen believe as fully as
> I do that they can no more be permitted to usurp the
> State's prerogative of force than can their opponents in
> their controversies. . . .
>
> "The true grounds of decision are considerations of
> policy and of social advantage, and it is vain to suppose
> that solutions can be attained merely by logic and the
> general propositions of law which nobody disputes.
> Propositions as to public policy rarely are unanimously
> accepted, and still more rarely, if ever, are capable of
> unanswerable proof. They require a special training
> to enable any one even to form an intelligent opinion

AN EARLIER PORTRAIT OF MR. JUSTICE HOLMES
BY CHARLES HOPKINSON

This portrait, completed in 1930, hangs in the library of the Harvard Law School. It is reproduced through the courtesy of Mr. Hopkinson.

CHIEF JUSTICE HUGHES AND MR. JUSTICE HOLMES

Photographed on Mr. Holmes's ninetieth birthday, March 8, 1931

about them. In the early stages of the law, at least, they generally are acted on rather as inarticulate instincts than as definite ideas for which a rational defense is ready.

"To illustrate what I have said in the last paragraph, it has been the law for centuries that a man may set up a business in a country town too small to support more than one, although he expects and intends thereby to ruin some one already there, and succeeds in his intent. In such a case he is not held to act 'unlawfully and without justifiable cause.' . . . The reason of course is that the doctrine generally has been accepted that free competition is worth more to society than it costs, and that on this ground the infliction of damage is privileged.

"I have chosen this illustration partly with reference to what I have to say next. It shows without the need of further authority that the policy of allowing free competition justifies the intentional inflicting of temporal damage, including the damage of interference with a man's business, by some means, when the damage is done not for its own sake, but as an instrumentality in reaching the end of victory in the battle of trade. . . .

"I have seen the suggestion that the conflict between employers and employed is not competition. But I venture to assume that none of my brethren would rely on that suggestion. If the policy on which our law is founded is too narrowly expressed in the term free competition, we may substitute free struggle for life. Certainly the policy is not limited to struggles between persons of the same class competing for the same end. It applies to all conflicts of temporal interests. . . .

"But it is not necessary to cite cases; it is plain from the slightest consideration of practical affairs, or the most superficial reading of industrial history, that free competition means combination, and that the organization of the world, now going on so fast, means an ever increasing might and scope of combination. It seems to me futile to set our faces against this tendency. Whether beneficial, as I think it is, or detrimental, it is inevitable, unless the fundamental axioms of society, and even the fundamental conditions of life, are to be changed.

"One of the eternal conflicts out of which life is made up is that between the effort of every man to get the most he can for his services, and that of society, disguised under the name of capital, to get his services for the least possible return. Combination on the one side is potent and powerful. Combination on the other side is the necessary and desirable counterpart, if the battle is to be carried on in a fair and equal way. . . .

"If it be true that workingmen may combine with a view, among other things, to getting as much as they can for their labor, just as capital may combine with a view to getting the greatest possible return, it must be true that when combined they have the same liberty that combined capital has to support their interests by argument, persuasion, and the bestowal or refusal of those advantages which they otherwise lawfully control. I can remember when many people thought that, apart from violence or breach of contract, strikes were wicked, or organized refusals to work. I suppose that intelligent economists and legislators have given up that notion today. I feel pretty confident that they equally will abandon the idea that an organized refusal by workmen of social intercourse with a man who shall enter their antagonist's employ is wrong, if it is dissociated from any threat of violence, and is made for the sole object of prevailing if possible in a contest with their employer about the rate of wages. The fact that the immediate object of the act by which the benefit to themselves is to be gained is to injure their antagonist, does not necessarily make it unlawful, any more than when a great house lowers the price of certain goods for the purpose, and with the effect, of driving a smaller antagonist from the business."[6]

Here Judge Holmes upheld what lawyers call a "primary boycott", the refusal of an individual or a group to deal with a person or corporation during a controversy, and although his position was, as he said, unpopular then, such a boycott is now generally considered legal. A little later he upheld what is called a "secondary boycott", involving a refusal to deal with persons having dealings with the object of a "primary boycott", and this is now held generally to be malicious and unlawful. Again he was in dissent.

This case involved, anti-unionists might say, an example of labor's inhumanity to labor. Rival organizations were in a contest for supremacy. One of them threatened an employer with boycott unless he discharged men of the other. The majority of the court granted an injunction forbidding this and forbidding threats against the employer's business, holding that this was no dispute between capital and labor, and that the right to contract freely for one's labor is entitled to legal protection. Thus Judge Hammond said in the majority decision:

> "It is well to see what is the meaning of this threat to strike when taken in connection with the intimation that the employer 'may expect trouble'. It means more than that the strikers will cease to work. This is only the preliminary skirmish. It means that those who have ceased to work will, by strong, persistent, and organized persuasion and social pressure of every description do all they.can to prevent the employer from procuring workmen to take their places. It means much more. It means that, if peaceful measures fail, the employer may reasonably expect that unlawful physical injury may be done to his property; that attempts in all the ways practiced by organized labor will be made to injure him in his business, even to his ruin, if possible. . . ."[7]

After citing an English decision in regard to the right to personal liberty, "liberty of the mind and will", Judge Hammond continued:

> "It was not the intention of the defendants to give fairly to the employer the option to employ them or the plaintiffs, but to compel the latter against their will to join the association, and to that end to molest and interfere with them in their efforts to procure work by acts and threats well calculated by their coercive and intimidating nature to overcome the will."[8]

In dissenting, Judge Holmes exhibited both his reluctance to assume that rôle and his hesitation in judicial "law-making".

> "When a question has been decided by the court, I think it proper as a rule that a dissenting judge, however strong his convictions may be, should thereafter accept the law from the majority and leave the remedy to the Legislature if that body sees fit to interfere. . . . But much to my satisfaction, if I may say so, the court has seen fit to adopt the mode of approaching the question which I believe to be the correct one, and to open an issue which otherwise I might have thought closed. The difference between my brethren and me now seems to be a difference of degree, and the line of reasoning followed makes it proper for me to explain where the difference lies. . . .

> "I agree, for instance, that if a boycott or a strike is intended to override the jurisdiction of the courts by the action of a private association it may be illegal. On the other hand, I infer that a majority of my brethren would admit that a boycott or a strike intended to raise wages directly might be lawful, if it did not embrace in its scheme or intent violence, breach of contract, or other conduct unlawful on grounds independent of the mere fact that the action of the defendants was combined. . . .

"That purpose was not directly concerned with wages. It was one degree more remote. The immediate object and motive was to strengthen the defendants' society as a preliminary and means to enable it to make a better fight on questions of wages or other matters of clashing interests. I differ from my brethren in thinking that the threats were as lawful for this preliminary purpose as for the final one to which strengthening the union was a means. I think that unity or organization is necessary to make control of labor effectual, and that societies of laborers lawfully may employ in their preparation the means which they might use in the final contest.

"Although this is not the place for economic discussion, and although the law may not always reach ultimate economic conceptions, I think it well to add that I cherish no illusions as to the meaning and effect of strikes. While I think the strike a lawful instrument in the universal struggle of life, I think it pure phantasy to suppose that there is a body of capital of which labor as a whole secures a larger share by that means. The annual product, subject to an infinitesimal deduction for the luxuries of the few, is directed to consumption by the multitude, and is consumed by the multitude always. Organization and strikes may get a larger share for the members of an organization, but, if they do, they get it at the expense of the less organized and less powerful portion of the laboring mass. They do not create something out of nothing. It is only by divesting our minds of questions of ownership and other machinery of distribution, and by looking solely at the question of consumption—asking ourselves what is the natural product, who consumes it, and what changes would or could we make—that we keep in the world of realities. But, subject to the qualifications which I have expressed, I think it lawful for a body of workmen to

try by combination to get more than they are now getting, although they do it at the expense of their fellows,
and to that end to strengthen their union by the boycott and the strike."[9]

In this opinion Judge Holmes advanced from the earlier dissent by holding that the strengthening of a labor union justified
an act which might be actionable otherwise, and that in these circumstances a "secondary boycott" was lawful. He did not open
the door to illegal acts, but only to conduct undertaken for justifiable motives. It is worth noting that, years afterward, he and
Mr. Justice Brandeis dissented in another labor case, in which the
United States Supreme Court granted an injunction forbidding
labor organizers to function in a mine where the contract stipulated that the workers should not join a union. The organizers
had been dissuading men from working unless the employers
would consent to unionization. Justices Holmes and Brandeis
did not regard this as malicious interference, which was the view
of the majority, but held that the purpose justified the methods
utilized.

Judge Holmes applied his conception of the law as rigorously
to Massachusetts unions as to corporations and to individuals. In
another dissent, where damages were sought on the ground that
the defendants had conspired to induce a woman to break a labor
contract, a demurrer was sustained in the lower court and by a
majority of the Supreme Judicial Court on the ground that the
complaint did not "set out the words or substance of the words
of the false and malicious statements". Judge Holmes believed
that the case should have been heard strictly on its merits. "An action will lie for depriving a man of custom," he said, "that is, of
possible contracts, as well when the result is effected by persuasion as when it is accomplished by fraud or force, if the harm is
inflicted simply from malevolence and without some justifiable
cause, such as competition in trade."[10] And in another similar
case, later, he held an inducement to violate a labor contract unlawful because it did not reveal the justification on which he had
insisted in earlier instances.[11]

Judge Holmes commented on the precarious position of the employe in industry in another case, although he did not hold the employer liable for damages. A workman, at the suggestion of another employe, undertook to repair a machine—this was outside his regular duties—and was injured. "If the servant is acting within the scope of his regular employment," said Judge Holmes, "or in obedience to special orders, the fear of losing his place may take away his choice so far that he cannot be said freely to take the risk upon himself." He was in sympathy with the collection of employers' liability, but not in these special circumstances.

It so happened that the first dissent Judge Holmes wrote was to set forth his view in regard to the constitutionality of a statute prohibiting employers from imposing fines on laborers for inferior work. It may be worth while to digress a moment here on behalf of an anecdote the Judge was fond of repeating in later years. He said he had heard the story of a man who had a valet to whom he paid high wages, subject to deduction for faults. "One of his deductions was, 'For lack of imagination, five dollars.'" Judge Holmes thought this lack was not confined to valets. In the case now to be discussed, however, something more tangible was involved.

A State law prohibited the imposition of fines for imperfect work. The majority of the Supreme Judicial Court held that this interfered with liberty of contract, and was therefore unconstitutional. Judge Holmes agreed that the legislature might regulate the method of payment, according to an earlier decision, and insisted that its judgment should be binding in this case. Judge Knowlton, who wrote the majority opinion, said:

> "It might well be held that, if the legislature should determine it to be for the best interests of the people that a certain class of employes should not be permitted to subject themselves to an arbitrary imposition of a fine or penalty by their employer, it might pass a law to that effect. But when an attempt is made to compel payment under a contract of the price for good work

when only inferior work is done, a different question is presented."[12]

The statute, passed in 1891, provided in its first section that "No employer shall impose a fine or withhold the wages or any part of the wages of an employe engaged at weaving for imperfection that may arise during the process of weaving." A woolen manufacturer was found guilty in a lower court and contested the decision on the ground that the law traversed the Constitution.

Judge Knowlton referred to Article I, Section 10, of the Constitution of the United States, providing that no State should pass any "law impairing the obligation of contracts. The right to acquire, possess and protect property includes the right to make reasonable contracts, which shall be under the protection of the law." He continued:

> "The manufacture of cloth is an important industry, essential to the welfare of the community. There is no reason why men should not be permitted to engage in it. Indeed, the statute before us recognizes it as a legitimate business, into which anybody may freely enter. The right to employ weavers, and to make proper contracts with them, is therefore protected by our Constitution; and a statute which forbids the making of such contracts, or attempts to nullify them, or impair the obligation of them, violates fundamental principles of right which are expressly recognized by our Constitution."

Judge Holmes, alone in his dissent, called it a "misfortune to disagree with my brethren", but continued:

> "So far as it has been pointed out to me, I do not see that it [the statute in question] interferes with the right of acquiring, possessing and protecting property any more than the laws against usury. . . . In truth I do not think that the clause of the Bill of Rights has any application. It might be urged, perhaps, that the power

to make reasonable laws impliedly prohibits the making of unreasonable ones, and that this law is unreasonable. If I assume that this construction of the Constitution is correct, and that, speaking as a political economist, I should agree in condemning the law, still I should not be willing or think myself authorized to overturn legislation on that ground, unless I thought that an honest difference of opinion was impossible, or pretty nearly so. . . .

"This, however, is not all. I do not confine myself to technical considerations. I suppose that this act was passed because the operatives, or some of them, thought that they were cheated out of a part of their wages under a false pretense that the work done by them was imperfect, and persuaded that the Legislature had the right to deprive the employers of an honest tool which they were using for a dishonest purpose, and I cannot pronounce the legislation void, as based on a false presumption, since I know nothing of the matter one way or another. The statute, however construed, leaves the employers their remedy for imperfect work by action. I doubt if we are at liberty to consider the objection that this remedy is practically worthless; but if we are, then the same objection is equally true, although for different reasons, if the workmen were left to their remedy for wages wrongfully withheld."[13]

This lone dissent on a constitutional question, the first written by Judge Holmes, came nearly ten years after he was appointed to the Supreme Judicial Court. (The dissents already noted were of later date.) In five years there were but two expressed dissents, one written by Judge Field, afterward Chief Justice, when Judge Holmes wrote the majority opinion;[14] in the other, when Judge Knowlton wrote the dissenting opinion, Judge Holmes was with the majority but did not write the opinion. There had been several cases, however, in which the phrase occurred: "A majority of the court are of the opinion that . . .", as though there were a minority opinion, which remained unexpressed.[15] There was a tacit understanding on the bench that there would be no written disagreement except in extreme cases, but this restriction became less effective as the personnel of the court changed. It is possible, too, that Judge Holmes, despite his disinclination to voice minority opinion in unimportant instances, may have exercised some influence in that direction. A Boston lawyer once said of him, "Holmes is like rum to the other judges."[16]

Judge Holmes was with the majority four times as often as he was in dissent, and wrote the majority opinions in one-third of the cases where there were opposing views expressed. When in the minority, although he wrote two-thirds of the opinions, he was much less likely to raise a controversy, or to express a difference, than Judge Field. On constitutional questions he thought it more important to learn what benefits the framers of the instrument sought to confer, or what evils they sought to avert, when they wrote an affirmative clause, than what they would have tried to avoid if they had cast it in negative form. He did not speculate about possibilities, and he did not like generalities. This dislike was expressed in a majority opinion he wrote, when Judge Knowlton wrote a dissent and Judge Allen concurred:

> "We think that the case at bar is not beyond our competence to decide. The greatest danger in attempting to do so is that of being misled by ready-made generalizations, and of thinking only in phrases to which as lawyers the judges have been accustomed, instead of looking straight at things and regarding the facts in all their concreteness as a jury would do. Too broadly generalized conceptions are a constant source of fallacy."[17]

In another majority opinion, in which Judge Devens wrote the dissent, with the concurrence of Judges C. Allen and Knowlton, Judge Holmes threw a striking sidelight upon interpretation of constitutional provisions. A statute had been enacted providing for the killing of animals diseased with glanders, without compensation to the owner; an action was brought by an owner whose animal was killed although it did not in fact have the disease, and the majority held compensation should be paid.

"Still it may be asked," said Judge Holmes, "if self-protection required the act [the killing of the animal] why should not the owner bear the loss? It may be answered, that self-protection does not require all that is believed to be necessary to that end, nor even all that is reasonably believed to be necessary for that end. It only requires what is actually necessary. It would seem doubtful, at least, whether actual necessity ought not to be the limit when the question arises under the Constitution between the public and an individual."[18]

In an action for fraud, founded on a charge of false representations, Judge Holmes, dissenting from the majority view, said:

> "If I were making the law, I should not hold a man answerable for representations made in the common affairs of life without bad faith in some sense, if no consideration was given for them. . . . But the proposition, even if accepted, seems to me to apply in this case. . . . The representation was made in casual talk, but in a business matter, for the very purpose of inducing others to lay out their money on the faith of it. . . . I can see no difference in principle between an invitation by words and an invitation by other acts, such as opening the gates of a railroad crossing. . . .
>
> "I am of opinion as I have stated that in a case like the present a man takes the risk of the interpretation of his words as it may afterward be settled by the court."[19]

The court was asked for an opinion, in 1896, about the constitutionality of a statute giving preference to veterans—obviously Civil War veterans—in State civil service employment. A section of the statute authorized veterans to apply for such positions, and provided that if they passed the examination they should be preferred in appointment over any other males. On this the court divided. Chief Justice Field, and Judges Holmes, Knowlton and Morton held the law was constitutional; Judges Allen, Lathrop and Barker viewed it as unconstitutional. In the majority opinion it was said:

> "The General Court may have been of the opinion that a person who served in the army or navy of the United States in the time of the War of the Rebellion, and had been honorably discharged therefrom, or who was a citizen of Massachusetts and had distinguished himself by valiant and heroic conduct in the army and navy of the United States, and had received a medal of honor from the President of the United States, is a person who has shown such qualities of character that it is for the interests of the Commonwealth to appoint him to certain offices or employments in preference to other male persons if he is found otherwise qualified to perform the duties. The General Court may have so thought, on the ground either that such a person would be likely to possess courage, constancy, habits of obedience, and fidelity, which are valuable qualifications for any public office or employment, or that the recognition of the services of veterans in the way provided for by the statute would promote that love of country and devotion to the welfare of the State which it concerns the Commonwealth to foster. If such was the opinion of the General Court, we cannot say that it was beyond the constitutional power to enact this section. Of the wisdom of the legislation we are not made the judges."[20]

In the dissent, Judges Allen, Lathrop and Barker made the point that the fact of being a veteran, as defined in the statute, did not "bear such a relation to the duties of the present offices or employment in the civil service of the Commonwealth that it can be made a decisive test in the selection of persons for such offices or employment," and added:

"A veteran may or may not have special fitness for such positions. Certainly to have served honorably in the army or navy is not the only way in which one can acquire such fitness. However useful the training may be which many of the veterans received in the army or navy, it cannot be laid down as a universal proposition that every veteran who can pass the examination to which all applicants are subjected is better qualified for such office or employment than any other person now is or can become. The appointing power cannot be required to pass by cases of conspicuous fitness, and to accept service of a lower character, simply because a veteran applies for the position. In requiring this to be done, the statute sets apart a class of persons who, in consequence of what they did in the war, and irrespective of present qualifications, are to be preferred, so that nobody else, however well fitted or however meritorious by reason of valuable or distinguished services in other occupations calling for fidelity and fortitude, can be considered as eligible for appointment, or can be eligible in the future, in competition with them. No matter what may have been the training, services and discipline, or what may be the natural ability or acquired skill of others, the power of selecting them for public office or employment is cut off. This involves a compulsory disregard of actual fitness and qualifications, to the detriment of the public service.

"Nor can the fact that a veteran has passed the prescribed examination be made a decisive test in favor of his appointment. This may merely show that he has the minimum qualifications required, but cannot be made to entitle him to compulsory preference over those who are better qualified."[21]

In another instance the Massachusetts House of Representatives asked the advice of the court as to whether it would be constitutional to enact a statute empowering cities and towns to buy and sell fuel, or to establish and maintain municipal fuel yards. The majority reported unfavorably. Judge Barker wrote a dissenting opinion, holding that such a law would be constitutional, and Judge Holmes submitted a supplementary minority view.

Nowadays such legislation might be called socialistic, but this happened in 1892, and the term then used was "populistic". In the early nineties the words "Populist" and "Populite" were used in derision of a political gospel which was sweeping the agricultural regions of the South, West and Midwest; it was in 1892, indeed, that the word Populists was formally adopted as a party designation. The movement had its beginnings in the decade after the Civil War, during the railroad boom, heightened immigration, land speculation and land-grabbing. The Patrons of Husbandry and the Grange were early organizations, and were followed by a widespread crop of kindred groups. In the upper Mississippi Valley and further south, in Illinois and at nearly all points west, discontent cast about for governmental panaceas. The State elections of 1890 revealed the numerical strength of the movement and its ardor. Its candidates for Governor, or candidates whom it supported, were elected in South Carolina, Georgia, Tennessee and Texas; the Legislatures of eight Southern States were within its grasp and it had forty Representatives in Congress. In 1892, despite the fact that the demand was to shift within four years to the "free and unlimited" coinage of silver at sixteen to one, the earlier platforms were still intact, and the Populists nominated General James B. Weaver for the Presidency. In the East there was a distinct uneasiness at the strength of the demand for paternalism and "trust-busting".

The proposal, therefore, of Massachusetts Representatives that municipalities be empowered to deal in fuel for the general advantage was stigmatized in some quarters as due to the infection of these political notions. Chief Justice Field, with Judges Allen, Knowlton, Morton and Lathrop, held that the proposal was illegal, and concluded their opinion with these words:

"If there be any advantage to the inhabitants in buy-
ing and selling coal and wood for fuel at the risk of the
community on a large scale, and on what has been
called the cooperative plan, we are of the opinion that
the Constitution does not contemplate this as one of
the ends for which the government was established, or
as a public service for which cities and towns may be
authorized to tax their inhabitants."[22]

The main dissent from this view was written by Judge Barker;
Judge Holmes wrote a supplementary opinion, in which he said
that when money was taken to enable a public body to offer for
sale an article of general necessity, "the purpose is no less public
when that article is coal or wood than when it is water, or gas, or
electricity, or education, to say nothing of cases like the support
of paupers or the taking of land for railroads or public markets."
Whether the legislation was needed, or whether it was expedient,
he did not think the Court was called on to consider. He could
see no reason for overruling the legislation.[23]

Let no one suppose that these words betrayed a fondness for
Populist or socialist theories. They manifested only a large tolerance of social experiments and a conviction, often reaffirmed
thereafter, that no judge should permit his personal prejudices to
interfere with his judgment, even though the theory being tested
was personally obnoxious, so long as there was no actual ban
against it. "I believe that the wholesale regeneration which so
many now seem to expect," he wrote afterward, "if it can be
helped by conscious, coordinated human effort, cannot be
affected appreciably by tinkering with the institution of property, but only by taking in hand life, and trying to build a new
race. That would be my starting point for an ideal for the law.
The notion that with socialized property we should have women
free and a piano for everybody seems to me an empty humbug."[24]

And the judge may have had in the back of his mind, a score
of years later, the very bill to empower municipalities to sell fuel,
when he said:

"When twenty years ago a vague terror went over the earth and the word socialism began to be heard, I thought and still think that fear was translated into doctrines that had no proper place in the Constitution or the common law. Judges are apt to be naïf, simple-minded men, and they need something of Mephistopheles. We too need education in the obvious—to learn to transcend our own convictions and to leave room for much that we hold dear to be done away with short of revolution by the orderly change of law.

"I have no belief in panaceas and almost none in sudden ruin. I believe with Montesquieu that if the chance of a battle—I may add, the passage of a law—has ruined a State, there was a general cause at work that made the State ready to perish by a single battle or law. Hence I am not interested one way or another in the nostrums now so strenuously urged."[25]

Montesquieu, whom Holmes called one of "the high priests of thought", admitted to his philosophy no such thing as an accident in the usual sense. "The main current carries with it all the special accidents."[26] Holmes has subscribed to this belief, and united with it a belief in the wholesomeness and rightness of the main current of American government and life. If that main current were muddy or misguided or malignant, we must meet and accept the outcome we merited. As Judge and Justice, Holmes has had faith in our future.

THE SUPREME COURT OF THE UNITED STATES, OCTOBER, 1930

Left to right, front row, seated: Justices McReynolds, Holmes, Chief Justice Hughes, Justices Van Devanter and Brandeis. Rear row, standing: Justices Stone, Sutherland, Butler and Roberts.

MR. JUSTICE HOLMES IN HIS STUDY

This photograph was taken on March 6, 1926

CHAPTER 12

Interpretations

RECOGNIZING THAT we live by symbols, Judge Holmes searched the symbols which are words with exceptional discrimination and wariness. More than one commentator has noted that Judge Holmes, himself expert in the use of words and a past master of phrase-making, strives always to find intentions and meanings in documents and advises others to "think things". Judge Benjamin N. Cardozo has praised him on that score with the discernment and appreciation of a man who exercises, on his own account, a skill comparable with the skill of Holmes himself.

"No one," says Judge Cardozo, "has been able to combat more effectively than he the repression of a formula, the tyranny of tags and tickets. Is it a question of the competence of a legislature to respond by novel legislation to the call of an emergent need? Fettered by the word, we are too often satisfied to say that competence exists if it can be brought within a cliché, 'the police power' of the State; and at home in the protective phrase we settled back at peace. Is it a question of the quality of the need, the pressure of the emergency, that will bring the power into play? We say the need must have relation to an activity 'affected with a public interest'; and again at home in the protective phrase, we are happy in the thought that while we keep within that shelter there can come no damage to the State. The familiar form beguiles into an assurance of security. Danger as well as deception may indeed be lurking ill-concealed, danger as well as deception in a false appearance of exactitude. The threat is too remote to jolt us out of the deeply-cloven ruts. In the end we may find we have been sinking a little deeper than we willed. For a cliché is not a barrier to power intent upon its aims, although sluggishness of thought may lead us for a season to act as if it were. A label is not a dyke or dam' that will repel the onset of the flood—the rush of an emergent need—though it may breed a sense of safety till the flood has swept beyond. All this the great master has been quick to see. He had seen it when, paternally indulgent, he has been willing for the hour to let the cramping phrases pass, to let them pass with a word of warning that the need may yet arrive to throw them over or expand them, to pull out of the rut at whatever cost of pain and effort. The repetition of a catchword can hold analysis in fetters for fifty years or more."[1]

Neat distinctions between words and nice discussions of phrases cropped out of the decisions Judge Holmes wrote while in the Supreme Judicial Court of Massachusetts. He once illuminated the historical and pragmatic significance of the words "porch" and "portico" in litigation in equity arising from a deed which stipulated that porticos were permitted but that "no projections in the nature of a bay window, circular front or octagonal front" was to be permitted on a building. A stone porch was added to the structure; Judge Holmes held that it was not prohibited under the deed, saying:

"If this porch was not permitted under the head of porticos and other usual projections it was not permitted at all.

"Etymologically the words 'porch' and 'porticos' are one. Formerly, porch was used as synonymous with portico in its classic sense. 'And he made a porch of pillars; the length thereof was fifty cubits.' (I Kings, vii 6.) The tendency in modern times has been to diminish 'porch' to the shelter in front of a building, and we are very willing to assume that, with the constant growth of distinctions and nice discriminations in the meanings of words, 'porticos' retains more of the original suggestion of length and of a roof supported by pillars, among architects and scholarly persons, and that porch is more specially appropriated to a smaller structure, generally with closed sides. But the distinction is not carefully preserved in common speech. With us portico, as well as porch, has shrunk, and usually means a shelter in front of a door. (See Dyche & Pardon's Dictionary, 1754; also Imperial Dictionary, 1882, 'Portico.') When porticos are cut down to the little structures which we all know, we think that a special reference to the mode of support has vanished almost as completely as to the length. The parties to this deed did not mean by portico 'a walk covered with a roof'. They meant the shelter to the door of a building, familiar to Massachusetts and Boston. We are of the opinion that they used it as a generic word, including a shelter with closed sides, as well as one with pillars. We agree that in determining the scope of the word we must look at the object of the restrictions and exceptions to it. But, as we have said, the permission extends to more serious structures, with closed sides, and therefore there is no reason for excluding porches."[2]

Not only a catchword, as suggested by Judge Cardozo, but general maxims can "hold analysis in fetters". A case in torts arose in connection with the interpretation of an Employers' Liability Act, and Judge Holmes observed that "general maxims are oftener an excuse for the want of accurate analysis than a help in determining the extent of a duty or the construction of a statute. But certainly with such a statute as this, we agree that common law rights are not to be taken away by doubtful implications and affirmative words."[3] In two unrelated will cases he insisted on a literal acceptance of wording. "The only safe course," he said in one instance, "is to confine ourselves to the words used in the particular limitation, when those words have a plain meaning";[4] and in the other: "The description of the fund is so definite as to exclude this construction, which could be reached only by a somewhat violent transposition of language which is plain as it stands."[5]

That emotional conditions affect our understanding of words Judge Holmes saw plainly, and called attention to it when, in deciding an action based on representations said to have been fraudulent, he wrote: "The rule of law is hardly to be regretted, when it is considered how easily and insensibly words of hope or expectation are converted by an interested memory into statements of quality and value when the expectation has been disappointed."[6] Not emotions alone, obviously, but circumstances might have an influence. "The meaning of the words," said Judge Holmes in another case, "might vary according to circumstances, and the interpretation of them is a question for the instructed imagination, taking the facts just as they are."[7]

One watch company sought to prevent another from marking its output conspicuously with a word commonly associated with the former's timepieces. For this purpose it sought an injunction, and Judge Holmes was prompted to deliver a little homily on the sense of verbal proprietorship:

> "It is true that a man cannot appropriate a geographical name but neither can he a color, or any part of the English language or even a proper name to the exclusion of others whose names are like his. Yet a color in connection with a sufficiently complex combination of other things may be recognized as saying so circumstantially that the defendant's goods are the plaintiff's as to pass the injunction line. . . .
>
> "So although the plaintiff has no copyright on the dictionary or any part of it, he can exclude a defendant from a part of the free field of the English language, even from the mere use of generic words unqualified and unexplained, when they would mislead the plaintiff's customers to another shop. . . .
>
> "Whatever might have been the doubts some years ago, we think that now it is pretty well settled that the plaintiff merely on the strength of having been first in the field may put later comers to the trouble of taking such reasonable precautions as are commercially practicable to prevent their lawful names and advertise-

ments from deceitfully diverting the plaintiff's custom."[8]

Criticism of the phrasing used by the judge in a lower court brought a rebuke from Judge Holmes. This was a case for personal injuries, and the defendant asked the court to charge that "if the jury find that the plaintiff was more or less drunk, and that this state was a contributing cause to the injury, the plaintiff cannot recover." The instruction threw the conditional phrase into the negative form: "If without drunkenness he would not have been injured, then he cannot recover," and exception was taken to this.

"If there is any difference in the shade of meaning," said Judge Holmes, "it is not such as would strike the lay mind, and evidently at the time did not strike anyone's mind, as no attention was called to it. The judge having given all that was asked by way of addition to or correction of his charge, the defendant's general exception does not warrant going back to what had been said before, and picking out phrases for minute criticism."[9]

In a case involving the interpretation of a law, Judge Holmes said:

> "Legislation is often tentative, beginning with the most obvious case, and not going beyond it, or the full length of the principle upon which its act must be justified. In laws about settlement and analogous questions, which are matters of arbitrary statute, it would be very unsafe to extend the words beyond their fair meaning."[10]

And in a somewhat similar case, when a question arose about a statute forbidding any company to "lay or erect wires . . . for the purpose of carrying on its business without the consent of the Mayor", and so on, Judge Holmes granted an injunction against a concern which sought to evade the law.

> "Without wasting time upon useless generalities about the construction of statutes, it is enough to say

that the statute before us had that consideration in view, and must be construed accordingly. We agree that we cannot supply a *casus omissus*. But the fair scope and meaning of the words used, and the number of cases included, will vary more or less according to the purpose of the act. . . .

"It is suggested that in some of these cases the company did not sell electric light because it did not own the device at the customer's end by which the electricity furnished took the form of light—that the company sold only electricity. We think it quite clear that the Legislature took no such nice distinctions, and that a wire is prohibited equally when used to furnish electricity for the purpose of conversion into light at the end of the wire."[11]

The "natural meanings" of words should be attributed to them. Judge Holmes refused to accept an interpretation which altered a deed "by giving a special and unusual meaning to a covenant in daily use, the interpretation of which is as well settled as that of any words in the language."[12] There was another instance of this in his decision not to grant an injunction against the town of Taunton to prevent its spending money for public musical concerts. The statute authorized appropriations for armories, the celebrations of holidays, "and for other purposes". The City Council appropriated money for concerts, and although the sum involved was small a resident attempted to prevent its expenditure. "The word 'other'," said Judge Holmes, "implies that the celebration of holidays is a public purpose within the meaning of the act, and indicates that purposes which are public only in that sense are included within its scope, although they look rather more obviously to increasing the picturesqueness and interest of life than to the satisfaction of rudimentary wants, which alone we generally recognize as necessary."[13]

Judge Holmes attributed to human imitativeness fads of phrases and doctrines, and saw its humorous aspects as well as its gravity. A short time before he became Chief Justice in Massachusetts he addressed the New York State Bar Association, and began by saying that "the law of fashion is the law of life." Digressing presently to passing waves of fancy for certain words and phrases, he said:

> "Lately have we not all been bored to death with *volenti non fit injuria,* and with Lord Bowen's remark that it is *volenti* and not *scienti?* . . . Do we not hear every day of taking the risk—an expression which we never heard used as it now is until within a very few years? Do we not hear constantly of invitation and trap —which came into vogue within the memory of many, if not most of those who are here? Heaven forbid that I should find fault with an expression because it is new, or with the last mentioned expressions on any ground! Judges commonly are elderly men, and are more likely to hate at sight any analysis to which they are not accustomed, and which disturbs repose of mind, than to fall in love with novelties. Every living sentence which shows a mind at work for itself is to be welcomed. It is not the first use but the tiresome repetition of inadequate catchwords which I am observing— phrases which originally were contributions, but which, by their very felicity, delay further analysis for fifty years."[14]

It was this speech which served as a text for Judge Cardozo. But there were times when Judge Holmes spoke so seriously as fully to justify the solemnity with which Judge Cardozo treated the topic. "By the theory of our language," Judge Holmes once said, "while other words may mean different things, a proper name means one person or thing and no other. If language perfectly performed its function, as Bentham wanted to make it, it would point out the person or thing in every case. But under our random system it sometimes happens that your name is *idem sonans* with mine, and it may be the same even in spelling. But it never means you or me indifferently. In theory of speech your name means you and my name means me, and the two names are different. They are different words. *Licet idem sit nomen, tamen diversum est propter diversitatem personae.*[15] In such a case we let in evidence of intention not to help out what theory recognizes as an uncertainty in speech, and to read what the writer meant into what he has tried but failed to say, but, recognizing that he has spoken with theoretic certainty, we inquire what he meant in order to find out what he has said. It is on this ground that there is no contract when the proper name used by one party means one ship, and that used by the other means another. The mere difference of intent as such is immaterial.

"In the use of common names and words a plea of different meaning from that adopted by the court would be bad, but here the parties have said different things and never have expressed a contract. If the donor, instead of saying 'Blackacre' had said 'my gold watch' and had owned more than one, inasmuch as the words, though singular, purport to describe any such watch belonging to the speaker, I suppose that no evidence of intention would be admitted. But I dare say that evidence of circumstances sufficient to show that the normal speaker of English would have meant a particular watch would be let in.

"I have stated what I suppose to be our general theory of construction. . . . For each party to a contract has notice that the other will understand his words according to the usage of the normal speaker of English under the circumstances, and therefore cannot complain if his words are taken in that sense.*

" . . . I do not suppose that you could prove, for purposes of construction as distinguished from avoidance, an oral declaration or even an agreement that words in a dispositive instrument making sense as they stand should have a different meaning from the common one; for instance, that the parties to a contract

---

*Judge Holmes thought, in Nash v. Minnesota Title Insurance and Trust Co., 163 Mass., 574, that this principle should be carried further than the majority of the Supreme Judicial Court was willing to go.

orally agreed that when they wrote five hundred feet it should mean one hundred inches, or at Bunker Hill Monument should signify Old South Church.[16] On the other hand, when you have the security of a local or class custom or habit of speech, it may be presumed that the writer conforms to the usage of his place or class when that is what a normal person in his situation would do."[17]

The word "malicious", Judge Holmes said on another occasion, had nothing to do with motives, or even with the attitude toward the future, but signified only "that the tendency of his conduct under the known circumstances was very plainly to cause the plaintiff temporal harm." He had in mind then, and at one point of the speech from which a longer quotation has been given, a libel suit against a Boston newspaper of which the use of the wrong man's name was the basis, although no charge was brought of deliberate malice in the usual sense. The news story said that "H. P. Hanson, a real estate and insurance broker of South Boston, emerged from the seething mass of humanity that filled the dock and indulged in a wordy bout with Policeman B," and so on; the story was about a Municipal Court proceeding. H. P. Hanson was in fact a real estate and insurance broker in South Boston; but the man actually involved was A. P. H. Hanson, who was in the same business in the same community. The newspaper reporter used the wrong initials by mistake. The lower court, without a jury, found that the libel was not published about H. P. Hanson, who was not present; and the majority of the Supreme Judicial Court, Judge Knowlton writing the opinion, sustained this view. Judges Holmes, Morton and Barker dissented, and Judge Holmes wrote their opinion.

> "I am unable to agree with the decision of the majority of the court, and as the question is of some importance in its bearing on legal principles, and as I am not alone in my views, I think it proper to state the considerations which have occurred to me. . . .

"On general principles of tort, the private intent of the defendant would not exonerate it. It knew that it was publishing statements purporting to be serious, which would be hurtful to a man if applied to him. It knew it was using as the subject of those statements words which purported to designate a particular man, and would be understood by its readers to designate one. . . . Without special reason, it would have no right to assume that there was no one within the sphere of its influence to whom the description answered. The case would be very like firing a gun into the street, and, when a man falls, setting up that no one was known to be there.

"So, when the description which points out the plaintiff is supposed by the defendant to point out another man whom in fact it does not describe, the defendant is equally liable as when the description is supposed to point out nobody. On the general principles of tort, the publication is so manifestly detrimental that the defendant publishes it at the peril of being able to justify it in the sense in which the public will understand it.

"I feel some difficulty in putting my finger on the precise point of difference between the minority and the majority of the court. I understand, however, that a somewhat unwilling assent is yielded to the general views which I have endeavored to justify, and I should gather that the exact issue was to be found in the statement that the article was one describing the conduct of a prisoner brought before the Municipal Court of Boston, coupled with the later statement that the language, taken in connection with the publicly known circumstances under which it was written, showed at once that the article referred to A. P. H. Hanson, and that the name of H. P. Hanson was used by mistake. I have shown why it seems to me that these statements are misleading. I only will add on this point, that I do not know what the publicly known circumstances are.

"I think it is a mistake of fact to suppose that the public generally know who was before the Municipal Criminal Court on a given day. I think it is a mistake of law to say that, because a small part of the public have that knowledge, the plaintiff cannot recover for the harm done him in the eyes of the greater part of the public, probably including all his acquaintances who are ignorant about the matter, and I also think it is no sufficient answer to say that they might consult the criminal records, and find out that probably there was some error. . . .

"Even if the plaintiff and A. P. H. Hanson had borne the same name, and the article identified its subject only by a proper name, very possibly that would not be enough to raise the question. For, as everyone knows, a proper name always purports to designate one person and no other, and although, through the imperfection of our system of naming, the same combination of letters and sounds may be applied to two or more, the name of each, in theory of law, is distinct, although there is no way of finding out which person was named by inquiring which was meant."[18]

In that case there came uppermost the prolonged thought which Judge Holmes had given to words and their interpretation, their function as a tool of the law and the rigorous caution which must be exercised in dealing with them.

Judge Holmes had clear-cut notions about the function and responsibility of the daily press. In another libel action, based on newspaper stories about a custom house broker, where a newspaper defended itself on the ground that there was good reason to believe its allegations to be true, he wrote:

"When private inquiries are made about a private person, a servant, for example, it is often impossible to answer them properly without stating facts, and those who settled the law thought it more important to preserve a reasonable freedom in giving necessary information than to insure people against occasional unintended injustice, confined as it generally is to one or two persons. But what the interest of the private citizen in public requires is freedom of discussion rather than that of statement. Moreover, the statements about such matters which come before the courts are generally public statements, where the harm done by a falsehood is much greater than in the other case. If one private citizen wrote to another that a high official had taken a bribe, no one would think good faith a sufficient answer to an action."[19]

But, admitting the value of publicity to the proper administration of justice, Judge Holmes would not excuse premature publication of charges. In the case of an attorney who sued a Boston newspaper for printing a petition for his removal prior to official action, the main question was whether the daily was privileged to publish the accusations.

"No binding authority has been called to our attention which precisely determines this case," Judge Holmes wrote, "and we must be governed in our conclusions mainly by a consideration of the reasons upon which admitted principles have been established. . . . The chief advantage to the country which we can discern . . . is the security which publicity gives for the proper administration of justice. . . .

"It is desirable that the trial of causes should take place under the public eye, not because the controversies of one citizen with another are of public concern, but because it is of the highest moment that those who administer justice should always act under a sense of public responsibility, and that every citizen should be able to satisfy himself with his own eyes as to the mode in which a public duty is performed. . . ."

Judge Holmes drew a distinction between a trial in an open court, which a newspaper is privileged to report, and the filing in the clerk's office of a petition to disbar a lawyer, which he did not regard as "privileged".

"For the purpose of the present case," he said, "it is enough to mark the plain distinction between what takes place in open court, and that which is done out of court by one person alone, or more exactly, as we have already said, the contents of a paper filed by him in the clerk's office."[20] The publication of accusations, presenting only one side of the story, Judge Holmes thought likely to lead to "trial by press" rather than trial by jury.

In still another libel action, theater owners objected because a newspaper had said a performance was indecent, and introduced evidence that the costumes worn by women dancers were the kind usually worn on such occasions. This testimony was properly excluded, Judge Holmes held.

"Every man in the world," he said, "knows that the costumes worn upon the stage by dancing women vary so widely, not only in measure but in suggestion, that in this case a reference to what is usual would be wholly uninstructive. A witness who could testify upon that point could testify to what the actual costumes were. The rest was for the jury."[21]

When questions arose regarding the weight of evidence or the admissibility of testimony, and fell under the hand of Judge Holmes, the literature of law was sometimes enriched and it is possible that the others on that bench were enlightened. In an unimportant mental-capacity case he found occasion, for example, to declare in majestic terms the supreme nature of the acts of the court. "A judgment *in rem,*" he said, "is an act of the sovereign power; and, as such, its effect cannot be disputed, at least within the jurisdiction. If a competent court declares a vessel forfeited, or orders it sold free of all claims, or divorces a couple, or establishes a will . . . a paramount title is passed, the couple is divorced, the will is established, as against all the world, whether parties or not, because the sovereign has said it shall be so."[22] This pronouncement was somewhat in accord with the Austinian definition of law as the fiat of a sovereign, although Judge Holmes accepted the definition only with qualifications.

In a quite different case, a prosecution for the sale of liquor, Judge Holmes noted that the presumptions and inferences of jurors must be derived from proved facts and from their own experience of life. "It is true in most cases," he said, "that, when a fact in issue is to be inferred from facts proved, the court cannot instruct the jury as to probabilities or presumptions of fact, but can only determine that, if the jury draw the inference upon the presumptions which they have learned from their experience of life, they will be warranted so far as the court knows, and will not be making a mere guess without adequate data.

"It does not appear that we have all the evidence before us. But it does appear that the room from which the cellar was entered was a bar-room, with a contrivance which might be used to prevent surprise, that the beer was concealed and in considerable quantity, and that there were drippings of spirituous liquor in half a barrel of empty bottles called smugglers. We cannot pronounce the inference that the beer was kept for sale so little warranted by the teachings of experience as to be but a mere guess."[23]

The reason for cross-examination, and its value, emerged from another decision in which Judge Holmes discussed monetary valuations.

"No doubt the actual amount of damage expressed in dollars is theoretically certain, and is a fact. But it is a fact which neither can be observed directly by the senses . . . nor can be deduced from the facts directly observed by simple mathematical computation, without assuming other facts not the subject of direct observation. What a particular man will think the amount of damage may differ widely from the actual amount, and, as experience shows, is likely to differ from the opinion of others, because it will not depend upon what he sees, but upon a number of other facts which he arrives at by inexact and undisclosed methods. An opinion upon such a question, however honestly formed and by however competent a man, is too remote from the indisputable data of the senses to be admitted without being subject to cross-examination."[24]

Although scornful of opinions maintained merely because others had cherished them in the past, Judge Holmes could say a good word on occasion for precedent. Thus there was a case in which intoxicating liquor was delivered to a minor, although the sale had been made to his mother, for her use. Under an amendment to the statute an effort was made to show that the sale was to a minor. "The attempt to measure the degree of certainty necessary to a verdict," said Judge Holmes, "like the attempt to fix the quantity of evidence, although familiar to the civilians, is not consonant to the general practice of our law, and may well be confined to the limits set by precedent." He continued:

> "If, before the amendment of the other section, the plain purpose and scope . . . was to prevent sales to minors for their own use, that is still its purpose. The words still mean what they meant when they were first enacted; and, if any inference is to be drawn from the subsequent action of the Legislature, it is that they were contented with the construction given to this section by the court."[25]

Another liquor case drew from Judge Holmes what was, for him, a somewhat lengthy discussion of the evidence and the inferences to be drawn from it.

> "There was evidence that many men had been seen going into a side door in the ell of the defendant's house and that some of them were under the influence of liquor when they came out. From this side door there was a path to a side door in the ell of another

house. In this ell was a room locked with a brass padlock, and in the room on February 19, 1893, was a
three-gallon jug nearly full of whiskey. A key fitting
the padlock was in the defendant's house. Exceptions
were taken to the admission of evidence that on the
same day the defendant's daughter, a girl sixteen or
seventeen years old, who lived with her, after looking
up and down the street in front of the house, was seen
to go from the defendant's side door to the other several times, in a loose dress, and to return holding her
dress as if she had something under it; that an officer
seized this object from the outside of the dress and
found it a hard substance in size and shape like a quart
bottle; that the defendant was present and ordered the
officer to let the girl go; that he said, 'Let me see what
that is,' and that the defendant answered, 'No, I won't.'

"The defendant's answer may have been dictated by
other reasons, but the jury were at liberty to find that
it was due to unwillingness on her own account to let
the officer know what the object in the bottle was. The
evidence was admissible in connection with other facts.
The mode in which the officer got his knowledge of
what the girl had in her hand did not make the fact
inadmissible."[26]

This was written in 1893; nearly forty years later the Supreme
Court of the United States, Mr. Justice Holmes emphatically dissenting, was to justify even wire-tapping in the procuring of
similar evidence.[27]

In ruling upon cases involving marital and sexual relations,
Judge Holmes was as unsentimental as could be expected of a
man happily married and unaffectedly an admirer of pretty and
witty women. "It is said," he commented on one occasion, "that
marriage operates as an oblivion of all that is passed. But there is
no reason for making of this rule a veil of fiction which prevents

the facts from throwing their natural light on subsequent events." In a criminal charge of adultery, Judge Holmes gave a decision reminiscent of the famous "paternoster case", in which it was held that if a man spent a night in a hotel with a woman it was not to be presumed that they wished only to say their prayers. In the lower court the judge first instructed the jury that "if they occupied together the room known as the parlor, that is evidence enough to warrant you in finding adultery. That is as strong evidence as is usually found in adultery cases." Exception was taken to this, and the judge said: "I withdraw those instructions and instruct the jury as follows: If a married man is found with a woman not his wife, in a room with a bed in it, and stays through the night with her there, that is sufficient to warrant a finding of adultery against him." To this also exception was taken. Said Judge Holmes, on the appeal:

> "The first instruction did not express any opinion as to whether the facts testified to were proved, but went to the inferences to be drawn from those facts by way of presumption in case they were proved. Such inferences, however, are for the jury as a general rule, as well as the truth of the testimony. But if the language first used went too far the judge at once expressly withdrew and corrected it upon his attention being drawn to it, and limited his statement to the proposition that the supposed facts, if proved, would be sufficient to warrant a finding of guilty. Even the latter form of expression might be used in such a way as to prejudice the jury; but on its face, it only means that there is evidence to be considered by the jury. . . . The correction left the defendant without ground of complaint."[28]

In one of the earliest opinions written by Judge Holmes, he reflected a view then prevalent in Massachusetts, as borrowed from the common law, of the unity of man and wife. A woman was living apart from her husband without means of support, and a man who delivered milk to her sought to collect from her husband. Judge Holmes said this was a case where "the law authorizes a wife to pledge her husband's credit, even against his will; it creates a compulsory agency and her request is his request."[29] Handed down on March 3, 1883, this decision was in thorough accord with the law at the time, but changed social conditions have modified the concept of marital unity, and in some States have actually dissolved it.

A husband based an action on a charge that others had enticed his wife to live apart from him, and Judge Holmes in his decision gave expression to humane wisdom as well as to the law. "For a married woman to leave her husband without cause," he observed, "is not a great crime. It is legal if with his consent, and if against his will it is only illegal in the sense that, if she keeps away from him for three years, he may get a divorce. A married woman must be supposed to be capable of receiving advice to separate from her husband without losing her reason or responsibility. . . . Good intentions are no excuse for spreading slanders. But in order to make a man who has no special influence or authority answerable for mere advice of this kind because it is followed, we think it ought to appear that the advice was not honestly given, that it did not represent his real opinions, or that it was given from malevolent motives. . . . Evidence of the plaintiff's statement that he was going to make as dirty a case of it as he could for certain of the defendants, was admissible as tending to show bias and discredit his testimony."[30]

The validity of a marriage was in question. The marriage and a subsequent divorce had taken place in California. "It would be inconvenient," Judge Holmes said, "for parties to be divorced as between themselves, and yet married towards the world. The same convenience makes it desirable that the effect should be the same wherever the question arises, whether within the jurisdiction or without it, and therefore, in the case of a decree which would be void outside the jurisdiction, that it should not be held conclusive within. The decree if binding in California would be binding everywhere. . . . But especially in this country, where changes of residence from State to State are frequent, every court must strive so far as possible to bring the local view of a citizen's status into accord with that which would prevail generally elsewhere."[31]

In a case where a man and woman had been married in New Hampshire, then had returned separately and lived separately in Massachusetts, their divorce case was taken to the Supreme Judicial Court because the statute provided that they must have lived together as man and wife if they were to be subject to that jurisdiction. Said Judge Holmes:

> "Their having lived in the State separately was not
> enough. We cannot escape from the literal meaning of
> the statute, which is not satisfied with residence mere-
> ly, but requires the parties to have 'lived together as
> husband and wife'. If the result was an unintended
> anomaly the remedy is with the Legislature."[32]

Construing the statute literally, even though it caused an absurd situation, Judge Holmes adhered to his policy to leave legislation, whenever possible, in the hands of the Legislature.

Construing a contract strictly, Judge Holmes gave a decision the effect of which was to deny to Bates College a gift of $100,000.[33] Similarly, he insisted on respecting the ruling of a master in chancery, in a mortgage case, and held that a boiler and engine attached to realty only by a shafting were personal property, not a part of the real estate, although he observed that it would have averted some perplexity if "the rule of the common law had been adhered to more strictly, that whatever is attached to the freehold by the owner becomes a part of the realty." He thought it more important "to respect decisions upon a question of property than to preserve a simple test."[34]

Nuggets of wisdom will be found by those who read these opinions. "The law does not trouble itself very much with philosophic difficulties," said Judge Holmes. "The practical uncertainty aris- ing from the ignorance of men is enough to be uncertainty in its eyes. . . .If theoretic uncertainty of the event gave character to the act, the length of time would make no difference."[35] And again: "Whatever practical uncertainty courts may have felt upon a subject [the promotion of a lottery] with which they are less well acquainted than some others of the community, in theory of law there is no uncertainty, and the sooner the question is relieved from doubt the better."[36]

The manufacturer of a decoction prepared according to a secret formula died, and there were two claimants of the right to exploit the medicine. The medicine was called "Dr. Spencer's Queen of Pain", and Judge Holmes held that the man who devised it had no exclusive right to the use of the formula. The old rule had been that things must be passed to a claimant by deed if not delivered by hand. "But the formalities required by the early common law have been broken in upon a good deal, although more in England than in this State", and from this he passed to the question of sole proprietorship of the formula.

> "The exclusive right to particular combinations of words or figures, after they have been published, for purposes not less useful than advertising—for poetry, for the communication of truths discovered for the first time by the writer, for art or mechanical design—now at least is a creature of statute, and is narrowly limited in time. When the common law developed the doctrine of trade-marks and trade names, it was creating a property in advertisements more absolute than it would have allowed the author of *Paradise Lost*; but the meaning was to prevent one man from palming off his goods as another's, from getting another's business by unfair means, and, perhaps, from defrauding the public."[37]

A man was indicted for mixing rat-poison with tea, with the intention of killing another man, who, however, did not drink the brew. "We assume," said Judge Holmes, "that an act may be done which is expected and intended to accomplish a crime, which is not near enough to the result to constitute an attempt to commit it, as in the classic instance of shooting at a post supposed to be a man. As the aim of the law is not to punish sins, but is to prevent certain external results, the act must come pretty near to accomplishing that result before the law will notice it."[38]

In an action for damages against the New York, New Haven and Hartford Railroad Company, on account of the death of a boy four years old, the road introduced evidence that the mother of the child was poor and alone in the house, and therefore negligent of him. Judge Holmes overruled this defense. He held that "the circumstances and limited powers of a large part of the community" must be considered. "The poor can not always keep their children in the house or always see that they are attended when out of doors."[39]

Against a street car company a passenger brought the complaint that she had suffered injury and fright when a drunken person was removed from the car, although she undertook to show that the conductor knew she was a particularly sensitive person. Judge Holmes held that the cars must be operated with reference to ordinary sensibilities. "The liability of their proprietors can not be increased simply by a passenger's notifying the conductor that he has unstable nerves."[40]

One of the many epigrams for which Judge Holmes was to become famous was embedded in his opinion on an unimportant action against a street railway company for personal injuries. A passenger on a horse car said that if the driver had gone a little faster the rear platform would have cleared the collision, or that the driver might have avoided it by stopping at a certain intersection.

"A horse car," said Judge Holmes, "cannot be handled like a rapier."[41]

Yale University conferred upon Judge Holmes, on June 30, 1886, the degree of Doctor of Laws.

"I know of no mark of honor," he said in accepting the degree, "which this country has to offer that I should value so highly as

[217]

this which you have conferred upon me. I accept it proudly as an accolade, like the little blow upon the shoulder from the sword of a master of war which in ancient days adjudged that a soldier had won his spurs and pledged his life to decline no combat in the future.

"The power of honor to bind men's lives is not less now than it was in the Middle Ages. Now as then it is the breath of our nostrils; it is that for which we live, for which, if need be, we are willing to die. It is that which makes the man whose gift is the power to gain riches sacrifice health and even life in the pursuit. It is that which makes the scholar feel that he cannot afford to be rich....

"... I am enough of a Puritan, I think, to conceive the exalted joy of those who look upon themselves only as instruments in the hands of a higher power to work out its designs. But I think that most men do and must reach the same result under the illusion of self-seeking. If the love of honor is a form of that illusion, it is no ignoble one. If it does not lift a man on wings to the sky, at least it carries him above the earth and teaches him those high and secret pathways across the branches of the forest the travellers on which are only less than winged.

"Not the least service of this great University and its sister from which I come is, that by their separate teaching and by their mutual rivalry they have fostered that lofty feeling among their graduates. You have done all that a university can to fan the spark in me. I will try to maintain the honor you have bestowed."[42]

Judge Holmes was then forty-five years old. Many other distinctions were to be showered upon him in the long span of life to come, but few which were to call from him a deeper evidence of appreciation.

CHAPTER 13

Chief Justice of Massachusetts

WALBRIDGE ABNER FIELD, Chief Justice of the Massachusetts Supreme Judicial Court, died in Boston on July 15, 1899. He had been an associate on that bench from February 21, 1881, to September 4, 1890, when he was elevated to Chief. Judge Holmes was chosen on August 2 to succeed him, and took his seat in that capacity on September 12, at the term of court held in Pittsfield. It was there, in Berkshire County, that he took the oath; and he may have reflected on how ancient was the ritual, one of the earliest forms of contract known to our law. He had suggested that it might run back as far as covenant and debt, usually supposed to be the earliest forms of contract. "The judge swears that he will execute justice according to the law," he had said, "the juryman that he will find his verdict according to law and the evidence, the newly adopted citizen that he will bear true faith and allegiance to the government of his choice."[1]

He was to "execute justice according to the law", but with the understanding, as he candidly admitted, that the law sometimes was inept. None was more brusque, even cavalier, in brushing aside legal technicalities. On occasion he could turn a shaft of wit on a fine point of pleading, as when he said that "a specialty deriving its validity from an estoppel in pais is perhaps like Nebuchadnezzar's image with a head of gold supported by feet of clay."[2] This was in an opinion in a probate bond action involving a contract, unimportant enough; the first opinion Chief Justice Holmes wrote, indeed, dealt with an unimportant contract case, and need not detain us here.[3]

How many of those cases, to take advantage of a later phrase of the jurist, were "ragbags of detail". Almost one-fifth of his opinions in Massachusetts dealt with torts: three times as many as dealt with criminal law, or evidence or property or procedure or contracts or equity. It was natural that torts should fall to him, since he had done more than any other one man to demonstrate that this constituted a separate branch of the law. Until the sec, ond half of the Nineteenth Century there had not been any attempt, even, to systematize the principles of the common law on torts; and as late as 1871 an American reviewer of Addison's pioneer text in England vowed that "We are inclined to think that torts is not a proper subject for a law book."[4] To the layman that affirmation may not seem far-fetched even now.

Hundreds of the cases which fell under the Judge's hand, indeed, involved dry-as-dust detail. Six months after he was elevated to head the bench he examined the book in which he kept a docket of the decisions he had written, and noted that there were about a thousand cases. "A thousand cases," he exclaimed, "many of them upon trifling or transitory matters, to represent nearly half a lifetime! A thousand cases, when one would have liked to study to the bottom and to say his say on every question which the law has ever presented, and then to go on and invent new problems which should be the test of doctrine, and then to generalize it all and write it in continuous, logical, philosophic exposition, setting forth the whole corpus with its roots in history and its justifications of expedience real or supposed!

"Alas, gentlemen, that is life. I often imagine Shakespeare or Napoleon summing himself up and thinking: 'Yes, I have written five thousand lines of solid gold and a good deal of padding—I, who would have covered the Milky Way with words which outshone the stars!' 'Yes, I beat the Austrians in Italy and elsewhere I made a few brilliant campaigns, and I ended in middle life in a *cul-de-sac*—I, who dreamed of a world monarchy and Asiatic power.' We are lucky enough if we can give a sample of our best, and if in our hearts we can feel that it has been nobly done."[5]

Well, it was true of executing justice, as Holmes said it was true of life, that it was like an artichoke: only the tips of the leaves were edible. Hadn't an eminent English barrister advised a youthful aspirant to legal honors that he would succeed if he could eat sawdust without butter? The new Chief Justice took his torts and stodgy contract cases uncomplainingly along with the other sawdust; nay, he took them with avidity. Once in every so often he found a nugget of butter. None could deny his right to feel that his work was "nobly done"; and it was not long before an opportunity arose for him to indicate his view of the dignity and importance of the post he occupied.

In response to resolutions of the bar, Chief Justice Holmes on November 25, 1899, delivered from the bench a speech about his predecessor. The very first case Holmes had as a young lawyer was tried in the Superior Court before Judge Lord, whom Holmes succeeded in the Supreme Judicial Court; and it was argued in the higher court with Mr. Field on the other side. Afterward the two men were associated for nearly seventeen years in that court, and Chief Justice Holmes admitted that it was difficult to speak from the bench about an event so close to him as the death of Chief Justice Field. "Long association," he said, "makes friendship, as it makes property and belief, a part of our being. When it is wrenched from us, roots are torn and broken that bleed like veins."

In the consultation room Judge Field had a tendency to explore every side issue of principle or fact, rather than pass it by, and in order to satisfy his conscience, did much work which never appeared in the record. His successor felt that the element of time was imperative. "One has to try to strike the jugular and let the rest go." As to Chief Justice Field's qualifications as a jurist, he continued:

> "I have said that, although of skeptical temperament, he had convictions. The fact led to a curious result in his way of regarding the authority of decided cases. I am not sure how he would have expressed it, or indeed whether the notion was articulate in his mind, but he seemed to me to conceive of the law as ideally, at least, embodying absolute right. If a case appeared to him to run against some general principle which he thought was or ought to be a part of the law, the fact

that it was decided seemed to make but little impression on his mind. He did not hesitate to throw doubt upon it or to disregard it. I do not think that he would have been content to regard the law as an empirical product of history, the particular forms of which are venerable mainly because they are—because in fact these and not something else which would seem to be as good or better if only the world were accustomed to it, are what our part of the world has come out on. Perhaps it was the same point of view that made him more ready than some judges to hold rather a tight rein upon the actual practices of the community. If a contract struck him as aiming at a gambling result, he would not enforce it, however much his refusal might encounter the daily practice of a whole board of brokers. He had his views of policy, and he did not doubt that the law agreed with him.

"It was part of the same general habit of mind that he should be free to the point of innovation in applying convenient analogies to new cases. He sometimes seemed to me to go not only beyond but against tradition in his wish to render more perfect justice. He was less interested in the embryology of the law as an object of abstract speculation, or in the logical outcome of precedent, than he was in making sure that every interest should be represented before the court, and in extending useful remedies—a good fault, if it be a fault at all. He had an accomplished knowledge of the present state of the law, and a good deal of curious and useful information about our local history, for which I have envied him often. I doubt if any lawyer whom I have known, except his honored predecessor, from whom we still learn upon another bench, was his equal in this regard. . . .

"Gentlemen, for all of us this is a solemn moment. For me, it is almost oppressively solemn. It would be serious enough were I only to remember the line of great, gifted, and good men whose place I have been called on to fill. But it is sadly, yes, awfully solemn, when I remember that with our beloved chief vanishes the last of those who were upon the bench when I took my seat, and so realize the swift, monotonous iteration of death.

"We sometimes wonder at the interest of mankind in platitudes. It is because truths realized are truths rediscovered, and each of us with advancing years realizes in his own experience what he always has admitted, but never before had felt. The careless boy admits that life is short, but he feels that a term in college, a summer vacation, a day, is long. We gray-haired men hear in our ears the roar of the cataract, and know that we are very near. The cry of personal anguish is almost drowned by the resounding echo of universal faith. It has become easier for us to imagine even the time when the cataract will be still, the race of men will be no more, and the great silence shall be supreme. What then may be the value of our judgments of significance and worth I know not. But I do firmly believe that if those judgments are not, as they may be, themselves the *flammantia moenia mundi,* the bounds and governance of all being, it is only because they are swallowed up and dissolved in something unimaginable and greater out of which they emerged. Our last word about the unfathomable universe must be in terms of thought. If we believe that anything is, we must believe in that, because we can go no further. We may accept its canons even while we admit that we do not know that we know the truth of truth. Accepting them, we accept our destiny to work, to fight, to die for ideal aims. At the grave of a hero who has done these things we end not with sorrow at the inevitable loss, but with the contagion of his courage; and with a kind of desperate joy we go back to the fight."[6]

The sole survivor of those who had made up that bench in 1882, when appointed, Holmes was to remain Chief Justice but three years; yet there was still ahead of him a long career in a court even higher.

In an opinion handed down not long before leaving the Massachusetts bench, Chief Justice Holmes revealed his disinclination to undertake even "interstitial" legislation; he preferred to leave law-making to the Legislature whenever he could, although he had seen from the first that the courts divided with the Legislature the guardianship both of private and of public law. His clear conception of private law as an organic and flexible body, which must be maintained in vigor and freshness, and of Constitutional law as containing certain affirmations of perennial worth which should not be tampered with, and certain other provisions which, if made definite and certain to begin with, should not be warped by doctrinaire opinions, had already emerged from the widespreading body of decisions he had written. The opinion to which reference has been made dealt with an instance where a *prima facie* case had been established, and a demand had been set up for further proof. Chief Justice Holmes showed that the common law contained no precedent for such an order, nor had the chancery courts in England.

Specifically, this was an action for personal damages against the New York, New Haven and Hartford Railroad, in which the road asked for an order compelling the injured man to submit to a physical examination by a physician of its choosing. The plaintiff asserted that this doctor was hostile to him, but offered to undergo examination by any other physician the company might name. The main consideration of the Supreme Judicial Court was the propriety of issuing an order for further medical examination, whether by the railroad's chosen doctor or any other.

Chief Justice Holmes noted that "when the plaintiff coupled

with his objection an offer to accept any other doctor whom the defendant might choose to send, bearing in mind the large possibilities that were open by telegraph and rail, he had a plain right to have his personality respected to the small extent that he asked"; and passed from that to the larger issue of ignoring accepted rules and requiring further evidence when the case had been established:

> "We do not forget the continuous process of developing the law that goes on through the courts, in the form of deduction, or deny that in a clear case it might be possible even to break away from a line of decisions in favor of some rule generally admitted to be based upon a deeper insight into the present wants of society. But the improvements made by the courts are made, almost invariably, by very slow degrees and by very short steps. Their general duty is not to change but to work out the principles already sanctioned by the practice of the past. No one supposes that a judge is at liberty to decide with sole reference even to his strongest convictions of policy and right. His duty in general is to develop the principles which he finds, with such consistency as he may be able to maintain. . . .
>
> "In the present case we perceive no such pressing need of our anticipating the Legislature as to justify our departure from what we can not doubt is the settled tradition of the common law to a point beyond that which we believe to have been reached by equity, and beyond any to which our statutes dealing with kindred subjects ever have seen fit to go. It will be seen that we put our decision not upon the impolicy of admitting such a power, but on the ground that it would be too great a step of judicial legislation to be justified by the necessities of the case."[7]

In an earlier instance, not involving litigation but by request of the Legislature, Judge Holmes expressed even more fully his

Justice Oliver Wendell Holmes

views as to judicial legislation and, it so happened, the function of the voter himself as taking part in legislation.[8] Massachusetts is unique in providing that its Supreme Court must give such advice. This was in response to an order from the House of Representatives in regard to a statute granting the right to women to vote in town and city elections, and involved three points: Whether such a law would be constitutional if it were framed (1) to take effect in town or city upon its acceptance by the majority of the voters in the State; (2) to take effect in a community upon its acceptance by a majority of the voters there; (3) to take effect throughout the State if ratified by a majority of the voters plus women specially authorized to register and vote on this question alone.

Chief Justice Field, with Judges Allen, Morton and Lathrop, held that such a law would be unconstitutional. Judges Holmes and Barker held that it would be constitutional on any of the three counts. Judge Knowlton agreed with the majority that the first and third provisions would be unconstitutional, but disagreed with them as to the second. "The substance of the transaction," Judge Knowlton wrote, "is that the legislative department declines to take the responsibility of passing the law; but the law has force, if at all, in consequence of the votes of the people; they ultimately are the legislators. It seems to us that by the Constitution the Senate and the House of Representatives have been made the legislative department of the government, and that there has not been reserved to the people any direct part in legislation."[9]

Judge Holmes, speaking for himself and Judge Barker, observed that the House had addressed its questions to the court as individuals, and that individual replies were required. He had no doubt of the Legislature's power to grant to women the right to vote. On the three points raised he wrote:

> "I admit that the Constitution establishes a representative government, not a pure democracy. It establishes a General Court which is to be the law-making

sult the grant might become a law against the will of a majority of the male voters. I answer this question, also, Yes."[10]

From the first Judge Holmes was reluctant to legislate unless it was unavoidable, and manifested a disposition to brush aside technicalities, as well as to avoid hard and fast rules, although he respected rules when they were justified by current conditions or when there seemed no good reason for disregarding them. In an unimportant action on a promissory note he observed that the rule as stated by the courts in all similar cases applied with equal force in that. "If we were to depart from that rule . . . we should be legislating, instead of following precedents, and legislating in very doubtful accord with the contracts of the parties."[11] He wished to respect the policies of the Legislature when possible. "If we are right in our understanding of the policy established by the Legislature," he said on another occasion, "it is our duty to carry it out so far as we can do so without coming into conflict with paramount principles."[12] In one case he even carried this so far as to respect the action of a Legislature in another State.[13]

This was a personal injury action in which Massachusetts made no provision for the recovery of damages, but the other State did; and the injury had been suffered in the other State. "The mere existence of a slight variance of view in the forum resorted to," said Judge Holmes, "not amounting to a fundamental difference of policy, should not prevent an enforcement of the obligation admitted to have arisen by the law which governed the conduct of the parties. It is unnecessary to consider whether we should be prepared to adopt to its full extent what is thought by the learned editor of Story, *Conflict of Laws* (eighth edition), Section 625, note *a*, to be the true doctrine—that 'whether the domestic law provides for redress in like cases should in principle be immaterial, so long as the right is a reasonable one and not opposed to the interests of the State'."

In a liquor case, where the seller knew that the purchaser intended to resell in another State in violation of its laws, Judge

Holmes said: "Of course it would be possible for an independent State to enforce all contracts made and to be performed within its territory, without regard to how much they might contravene the policy of its neighbors' laws. But in fact no State pursues such a course of barbarous isolation."[14]

"Local precedent," said Judge Holmes in a comparatively inconsequential equity case, "is more important than abstract theory in determining this question, at least so far as the State Constitution is concerned; and if it is true, as it may be, that the difference between uses which are public within the requirements of the Constitution and those which are not is one of degree, that is no novelty."

On the ground of general reasoning, Judge Holmes refused to disturb a rule of property which had long been established;[15] all legal lines, he observed in another instance, "are more or less arbitrary as to the precise place of their incidence, although the distinctions of which they are the inevitable outcome are plain and undeniable."[16] A lawyer argued for his client, who disputed the right of a railroad company to remove her infant when its fare was not paid, that the child stood on the same footing as a parasol. The law was specific as to the removal and arrest of persons who refused to pay fare, but in this case no arrest was made. "There is no doubt of the company's right to put off the infant," said Judge Holmes, "whether the contract for her carriage, if any, was made with her or her mother. She was a passenger, and as such was not entitled to be carried unless paid for." He pushed aside the comparison with a parasol.[17] In another instance, when a woman, less than five months in pregnancy, fell upon a defective highway and was prematurely delivered, the infant survived but a few minutes. The question arose as to whether this morsel of unborn humanity was a "person" for whose life an administrator could be appointed, to sue the town for its death. "This court," said Judge Holmes, "requires that a child shall have reached some degree of quasi-independent life." Here he was dealing with a technical question as to when a "child" becomes a "person".[18]

Many technicalities and close distinctions arose for his consideration. In a tax case, itself not important, he ruled: "There may be
nice distinctions between the facts of the cases cited and those before us, but the principle is laid down in general terms";[19] and he
destroyed a close technical defense in another action, brought by
a person who stepped into a drain running across the sidewalk of
a city street, stumbled and fell over an embankment where there
was no protective railing. The statute required that notice be
given to the city—in this case, Worcester—and the city maintained
that the notice was defective because it gave the lack of a railing
as the cause of the injury, with no mention of the defective drain.

"It does not appear," said Judge Holmes, "that the plaintiff
would have been hurt if he had not fallen into the sewer; and,
even if we were to assume that the drain across the sidewalk was
a defect, as well as a necessary condition of the injury, we think it
would be interpreting the statute with too great strictness and excessive refinement to say that it was not satisfied by stating the
proximate cause of the injury complained of."[20]

Even though harmful rather than beneficial, the truth could
not be blinked in a Holmes opinion. Scattering sentences from
one of his earliest Massachusetts decisions throw light on the mental attitude in which he approached his task. "The court," he
said, "can hardly be asked to close its eyes upon the truth in order
to lay down a rule which can only be justified on the ground that
it is beneficial. . . . But we are not only required to start with a
fiction. As the next step, we must lay down a fixed and arbitrary
rule for what is really in a constant state of fluctuation. . . . We
think, then, that it would be inexpedient and unjust to lay down
a sweeping general principle as is contended for."[21] On another
occasion, again avoiding a hard and fast rule, he said: "The extent of duty under such circumstances is a matter of expediency
and degree, which different minds might fix at different points."[22]

A seaman brought an action to recover a balance of wages he
said was due, and the defense was set up that he had signed a formal release. The seaman said he did not know what he was signing. "It is contrary to first principles," Judge Holmes protested

in his decision, "to allow a person whose overt acts have expressed assent to deny their effect on the ground of an undisclosed state of his mind for which no one else was responsible. The common law makes no exception to these principles in favor of seamen, nor do we see any evidence that the statute meant to make one."[23]

In the examination of these opinions and decisions, without regard to chronological order, it sometimes happens that sentences relating to cases quite different in their legal nature reveal a kindred phase or state of mind on the part of Judge—or Chief Justice Holmes. Thus in a case in torts we find him saying coldly: "The standard of good faith required in sales is somewhat low, not only out of the allowance for the weakness of human nature, but because it is not desirable to interfere too much for the purpose of helping men in their voluntary transactions more than they help themselves";[24] and much later, in an action involving quite disparate legal principles: "We agree that if the sale was in terms of the vote, and those terms were legal, it would be none the worse that the transaction came very near to illegality and was framed so as to avoid it. One meaning of drawing a line between the lawful and the unlawful is that you have a right to get as near the line as you can if you do not cross it."[25] In a dispute over payment for a system of heating in a mill, the "enlightened skepticism", of which Mr. Justice Holmes was to speak later, reappeared. "In view of modern modes of business," he wrote, "it is not surprising that in some cases eager sellers or selling agents should be found taking that degree of risk with unwilling purchasers, especially where taste is involved. . . . We are of the opinion that the satisfactoriness of the system and the risk taken by the plaintiff were to be determined by the mind of a reasonable man, and by the external measures set forth in the contract, not by the private taste or liking of the defendant."[26]

That the law itself may be misused and its provisions abused appeared in an opinion Judge Holmes wrote in a mortgage case, in which one man promised another orally to bid on the property for him, and under foreclosure received a deed for the property, for which he gave a mortgage, a promissory note and cash, part of which he had received from the owner. Judge Holmes held that no trust could be charged with respect to the land in favor of the owner, on the basis of an oral agreement. Justices Allen and Knowlton dissented.

"The statute of frauds," said Judge Holmes, "may be made an instrument of fraud. But that always is true, whenever the law prescribes a form for an obligation. The very meaning of such a requirement is that a man relies at his peril on what purports to be such an obligation without that form. If the present case suggests the possibility that wrong may be accomplished through the forms of law, it equally suggests the danger which the statute was intended to meet."[27]

In an insolvency case involving a charge of fraud, Judge Holmes noted that crime was a matter not for private vengeance but of public interest. A debtor was found guilty of two charges, but acquitted of a third charge, that he had contracted the debt with no intention of paying it. The creditor appealed from the acquittal.

"The sentence, to be sure," said Judge Holmes, "might have been heavier upon a conviction of all the charges, but a creditor has no private interest in the sentence, although it is incident to a proceeding in his private interest; and it is contrary to the analogies of the law to allow an appeal for the sole purpose of enhancing the punishment."[28]

A standard of legally responsible moral deportment was established by Judge Holmes in one of the early cases which came before him, involving a singular instance of medical practice. A physician prescribed that the clothes of a woman patient be kept saturated with kerosene. The patient died, and a charge of malpractice under the criminal law was lodged against the physician.

"Recklessness in a moral sense," said Judge Holmes, "means a certain state of consciousness with reference to the consequence of one's acts. No matter whether defined as indifference to what those consequences may be, or as failure to consider their nature or probability as fully as the party might and ought to have done, it is understood to depend on the actual condition of the individual's mind with regard to consequences, as distinguished from mere knowledge of present or past facts or circumstances from which some one or everybody else might be led to anticipate or apprehend them if the supposed act were done. We have to determine whether recklessness in this sense was necessary to make the defendant guilty of felonious homicide, or whether his acts are to be judged by the external standard of what would be morally reckless, under circumstances known to him, in a man of reasonable prudence. . . .

"Unless he can bring himself within some broadly defined exception to general rules, the law deliberately leaves his idiosyncracies out of account, and peremptorily assumes that he has as much capacity to judge and foresee consequences as a man of ordinary prudence would have in the same situation. . . .

"We cannot recognize a privilege to do acts manifestly endangering human life, on the ground of good intentions alone. . . .

"But if the dangers are characteristic of the class according to common experience, then he who uses an article of the class upon another cannot escape on the ground that he had less than the common experience."[29]

With what care Judge Holmes considered both sides of a case before arriving at his decision was revealed in an unimportant action in torts, in which a corporation was formed to promote a dental preparation intended to allay pain; it was charged that the decoction was useless for that purpose, and that the stock of the corporation was fraudulently represented. Judge Holmes thought the objection to certain testimony "a purely practical one, a concession to the shortness of life", and saw no objection to admitting it. "If a dozen patients should testify," he said, "that when the defendant used his Naboli, he filled their teeth without hurting them, and that he hurt them a good deal when he did not use it, supposing the testimony to be believed, and not to be explained by fancy and a general disposition on the part of the witnesses to think well of new nostrums, it would go far towards proving that Naboli had some tendency to deaden pain. Filling teeth, however skillfully done, is generally unpleasant. If it is found to be wholly painless when a certain compound is used, as the witnesses testified, probably the compound is at least in part the cause."

But the jury might have discovered that the so-called invention was in fact "an empirical mixture of known sedatives", and that it had gained no new quality of value, but that the compounding might even have neutralized to some extent the qualities of the ingredients. "If they [the jury] believed thus, they might have found that to mix the ingredients was an expedient obvious to any person knowing their respective effects, and was not patentable. If the patent was worthless, the stock was worthless."[30]

On one occasion Judge Holmes spoke of the right to till the land almost as though it were a "natural" right, but by and large he revealed a disposition to cast this whole category into outer darkness, and with it, by indirection, Rousseau's attempt to found human freedom on nature rather than on culture. In his clear and unsentimental view there appeared to be only such rights as could be enforced, and the rights of the individual were subordinate to community rights.

It so happened that many of the cases in which the contours of these views took shape fell to Judge Holmes early in his work on the Massachusetts bench. They shaped his attitude as Chief Justice there, and his position in later years when a member of the Supreme Court of the United States. No running commentary upon them is appropriate; they are better expressed in his own words than in the words of another. They are of such importance to his whole judicial posture that excerpts from his decisions, even when dealing with actions in themselves of minor consequence, shall be set down here somewhat elaborately.

The owner of a slope, running down to a mill-pond, fertilized it and cultivated it in the usual ways, and considerable quantities of solid matter were carried by surface drainage into the water. The owner of the mill-pond sought to restrain the farmer by injunction. Judge Holmes found for the right to cultivate the land, saying in part:

> "The respective rights and liabilities of adjoining land-owners cannot be determined in advance by a mathematical line or a given formula, certainly not by a simple test of whether the obvious and necessary consequence of a given act by one is damage to the other. The fact that the drainage is foreseen, or even intended, is not decisive apart from the statute. Some damage a man must put up with, however plainly his neighbor foresees it before bringing it to pass. . . . Liability depends upon the nature of the act, and the kind and degree of harm done, considered in the light of expediency and usage. For certain kinds there is no liability, no matter what the extent of the harm. A man may lose half the value of his house by the obstruction of his view, and yet be without a remedy. In other cases his rights depend upon the degree of the damage, or rather of its cause. He must endure a certain amount of noise, smells, shaking, percolation, surface drainage, and so forth. . . .
>
> "The present case presents one of those questions of degree. . . . We are of the opinion that a man has a right to cultivate his land in the usual and reasonable way, as well upon a hill as in the plain, and that drainage to the lower proprietor of the kind complained of is something that he must protect himself against as best he may. The plaintiff says that a wall would stop the trouble. If so, it can build one upon its own land."[31]

The loss of value from obstructing part of the view from a house was involved in another case, in which complaint was made of a "spite fence". The litigation was taken to the Supreme Judicial Court under the "due process" clause. "It is plain," said Judge Holmes, "that the right to use one's property for the sole purpose of injuring others is not one of the immediate rights of ownership; it is not a right for the sake of which property is recognized by the law, but is only a more or less necessary incident of rights which are established for very different ends. It has been thought by respectable authorities that even at common law the extent of a man's rights in cases like the present might depend upon the motive with which he acted." And he continued:

"We do not so understand the common law, and we concede further, that to a large extent the power to use one's property malevolently, in any way which would be lawful for other ends, is an incident of property which cannot be taken away even by legislation. . . .

"But it does not follow that the rule is the same for a boundary fence unnecessarily built more than six feet high. It may be said that the difference is only one of degree: most differences are when nicely analyzed. At any rate, the difference of degree is one of the distinctions by which the right of the Legislature to exercise the police power is determined. Some small limitations of previous rights incident to property are imposed for the sake of preventing a manifest evil; larger ones could not be, except by the exercise of the right of eminent domain. . . .

"A man cannot be punished for malevolently maintaining a fence for the purpose of annoying his neighbors merely because he feels pleasure at the thought he is giving annoyance, if that pleasure alone would not induce him to maintain it, or if he would maintain it for other reasons even if that pleasure should be denied him. If the height above six feet is really necessary for any reason, there is no liability, whatever the motives of the owner in erecting it. If he thinks it necessary, and acts upon his opinion, he is not liable because he acts malevolently.

"We are of the opinion that the statute thus construed is within the limits of the police power, and is constitutional, so far as it regulates the subsequent erection of the fence. To that extent it is simply a noxious use of the owner's premises, and although the use is not directly injurious to the public at large, there is a public interest to restrain this kind of aggressive annoyance of one neighbor by another, and to mark a definite limit beyond which it is not lawful to go."[32]

As for "moral rights", the law knows nothing of them as such, Judge Holmes held in a majority opinion, from which Judges Field and Allen dissented. Judge Holmes supported his position by certain citations not found in law books, which gives an added interest to what he said. "It must be remembered," he wrote, "whenever a new statute comes up for consideration, that although it may be found by construction to give what it gives as if in pursuance of a legal duty, there is no such legal duty in fact, and no antecedent rights on the part of the persons who receive its benefits. It is only tautologous to say that the law knows nothing of moral rights unless they are also legal rights, and from before the day of Hobbes the argument has been public property that there is no such thing as a right created by law, as against the sovereign who makes the law by which the right is to be created. Hobbes, *De Cive,* c. 6, paragraph 14 (Op. Lat. ii 227); *Leviathan,* c. 26 (English Works iii 250-252); Sir John Eliot, *De Jure Maiestatis,* c. 3; Bodin, *De Republica,* I, c. 8; Bentham, *Fragment on Government,* c. 5 (Works I, 292-293); Austin, *Jurisprudence,* Lecture 6, pp. 286, 287 (third ed.)."[33]

In the decision regarding drainage into a mill-pond, Judge Holmes spoke of noise, smells and so on as incidental annoyances. Even earlier he had decided that a piggery was a nuisance. A man was charged with keeping some five hundred swine near some dwellings, and it was duly set down that there were "large quantities of noisome, noxious and unwholesome smokes, smells and stenches." Said Judge Holmes: "A piggery in which swine are kept in such numbers that their natural odors fill the air thereabouts, and make the occupation of the neighboring houses and passages over the adjacent highways disagreeable or worse, is a nuisance." In commenting on a complaint that the judge in the lower court had not sufficiently and correctly instructed the jury, Judge Holmes thought it enough to say of the instructions: "It would have been well if they had impressed more fully on the jury that the question was one of degree."[34]

It became necessary to draw a line between the conflicting rights of two tenants in the same building, one of them a manufacturing company, the other a merchant. The merchant complained that sands and acids leaked through from the floor above upon his goods, and Judge Holmes said at once there was no right to invade the lower premises in that fashion; then he added:

> "As any line of adjustment between conflicting rights must be drawn on practical grounds, there is no doubt that it may vary under different circumstances. For instance, in England, in view of the national importance of their great manufactures, juries are instructed that, in counties where great works are carried on, parties must not stand on extreme rights. . . . No doubt, when once it is decided that a certain liability or risk shall be attached to a voluntary relation, the party entering into that relation takes that risk. But what risks shall be attached to any relation is a pure question of policy in the first instance."[35]

The early morning ringing of a bell on a mill was held to be a nuisance, and was enjoined, but subsequently a bill was passed authorizing the ringing of bells of a certain size. The mill owner then sought to have the injunction modified. Judge Allen wrote an opinion, in which Judge Holmes concurred, that the Legislature could invade to a certain extent the "natural rights of individuals" in exercising its police power "with a view to the general good".[36] It became increasingly clear as time went on that Judge Holmes held individual privileges and rights as subsidiary to "the general good", or to the exercise of group authority. Thus, when a man whose horse was frightened by the firing of a cannon on the Boston Common brought suit against the city, Judge Holmes held that the community was not liable. The Common was held not for emolument or revenue, he found, but for the public benefit, and the ordinance authorizing the firing of the cannon was a police regulation of the use of a public place. "Perhaps," he added, 'it will save future litigation if we go one step further, and intimate that as the subject matter was within the city's authority to regulate by by-law, and as the by-law, so far as appears, is reasonable, those who act under it are justified in doing what we all know extra-judicially to have been done upon the Common time out of mind."[37]

Another Boston ordinance forbade public speaking on the city grounds except by a permit from the Mayor. In some quarters it was suspected that this was intended to prevent unorthodox sermons. Judge Holmes held that the ordinance was not an interference with free speech but a proper regulation of public grounds.

> "That such an ordinance is constitutional . . . does not appear to us to be open to doubt. To say that it is unconstitutional means that, even if the Legislature has purported to authorize it, the attempt was vain. . . . It assumes that the ordinance is directed against free speech generally . . . whereas in fact it is directed toward the modes in which Boston Common may be used. . . .
>
> "For the Legislature absolutely or conditionally to forbid public speaking in a highway or public park is no more an infringement of the rights of a member of the public than for the owner of a private house to forbid it in his house. When no proprietary right interferes the Legislature may end the right of the public to enter upon the public place by putting an end to the dedication to public uses. So it may take the lesser step of limiting the public use to certain purposes. . . ."[38]

Judge Holmes did not believe that the ordinance was directed especially against free preaching of the Gospel, "as certain Western ordinances, seemingly general, have been held to be directed against the Chinese." He held it to have been passed for its ostensible purpose, the proper regulation of a public place.

Whenever "the general benefit and improvement" of the community conflicted with the interest of the individual, "wholly one of sentiment and temper", Judge Holmes upheld the police power in protection of the former. When the owner of a lot in a cemetery owned by the town of Lawrence complained that the city had built a wall and terrace in front of his lot and had closed the avenue, Judge Holmes refused to require the restoration of the place to its condition at the time of the purchase, saying:

> "It has been said that rights of burial in public burial grounds are peculiar, and are not very dissimilar to rights in pews; that they are so far public that private interests in them are subject to the control of the public authorities having charge of police regulations. . . .
>
> ". . . and when the master finds that the pecuniary loss to him is nothing, and that the injury or damage, if any, is wholly one to be counted among the trifles which the law does not regard, and when it further appears that the plaintiff has lain by and taken no action other than to protest, while the city has expended in the work in question a large sum of money manifestly to the general improvement and benefit of the cemetery, and the cost of removing or opening the wall and terrace across the avenue would largely exceed the amount or value of the plaintiff's individual interest in the premises, we are clearly of the opinion that the plaintiff has no claim to equitable relief."[39]

In the city of Newton a man who owned swine and other animals was asked to remove this source of pollution of the water supply, and refused. Judge Holmes held that the city had the right to take the land and rid itself of this nuisance. "There are no sacramental words," he observed, "which must be used in a statutory power to take and hold lands"; and, a little later: "It would be an unjust refinement to say that the right is only to do such things from time to time as a court or jury may think necessary then."[40]

Again, when part of a street was discontinued in another town, and a property owner sought damages for the loss of access and because the diversion of traffic adversely affected the value of his site, Judge Holmes said:

> "It is intelligible for them to say that only the loss of access, the comparatively palpable injury, should be paid for, and not the advantage which the land owner had had the luck to enjoy of being where the crowd was; somewhat in the same way that the common law refuses to recognize the damage, often very great even measured in money, caused by cutting off a view."[41]

A prodigious circuit of reading, a deep study of the origins and principles of law, and an alert sense of justice, lay back of the consistent pattern of decisions Holmes cut while Judge and Chief Justice in Massachusetts. Taken together, his opinions embrace a philosophy of law. They express, too, a philosophy of life; for behind the detail of the cases which fell to his hand he saw the stuff and circumstance of life's drama. His seat on the bench enabled him to look through a window on the human struggle. In the "sawdust" of the law he found not only nuggets of butter but the very juices of mankind.

BOOK III

Statesman and Philosopher

CHAPTER 14

Holmes and Roosevelt

I T WAS by a hairbreadth that Oliver Wendell Holmes became an Associate Justice of the Supreme Court of the United States. How narrow was the margin has seldom been discussed; yet it illumines the processes of our politics, the folkways of our society, and the temperaments of two great men. The other actor in the drama was Theodore Roosevelt, and the circumstances cast an ominous light on the coercions of the Presidential office.

In June of 1902 Associate Justice Horace Gray, who had been appointed in 1881 and overwhelmingly confirmed the following day, decided reluctantly that his failing health required his resignation. Roosevelt was told of this, and began casting about for a successor, but the resignation did not reach him until a month later, and was made dependent upon his pleasure.

Mr. Justice Gray was a Massachusetts man, and had served as a Judge of the Supreme Judicial Court of that State for ten years, then as Chief Justice there for seven years. In the Supreme Court at Washington he had written the majority decision—with but a single dissent—in the celebrated and far-reaching legal tender case of 1884. It is worth recalling that Justice Stephen J. Field, in his dissenting opinion, lamented:

> "What was in 1862 called 'the medicine of the Constitution' has now become its daily bread. So it always happens that whenever a wrong principle of conduct, political or personal, is adopted on the plea of necessity, it will afterwards be followed on the plea of convenience. . . . From the decision of the court I see only evil to follow."[1]

Not until Grover Cleveland's day was that evil remedied; I have interjected the quotation from this dissent because of its indirect bearing on other dissents which were to follow, though not from the pen of Mr. Justice Field. It was the first dissent of Mr. Justice Holmes (quite different in temper from the Field dissent) which estranged Roosevelt from him.

Merely by the psychological law of association, with Mr. Justice Gray about to retire, it was congruous that Roosevelt should turn to another Chief Justice of the Massachusetts Supreme Court. That man proved to be Holmes. The President had been educated at Harvard, he was a close friend of Henry Cabot Lodge and on terms of intimacy with many of the Back Bay aristocracy. Of Holmes he wrote to Lodge:

> "He possesses the high character and the high reputation both of which should if possible attach to any man who is to go upon the highest court of the entire civilized world. His father's name entitles the son to honor; and if the father had been an utterly unknown man the son would nevertheless now have won the highest honor. The position of Chief Justice of Massachusetts is in itself a guarantee of the highest professional standing. Moreover, Judge Holmes has behind him the kind of career and possesses the kind of personality which make a good American proud of him as a representative of our country. He has been a most gallant soldier, a most able and upright public servant, and in public and private life alike a citizen whom we like to think of as typical of the American character at its best. The labor decisions which have been criticized by some of the big railroad men and other members of large corporations constitute to my mind a strong point in Judge Holmes' favor.
>
> "The ablest lawyers and greatest judges are men whose past has naturally brought them into close relationship with the wealthiest and most powerful clients, and I am glad when I can find a judge who has been

able to preserve his aloofness of mind so as to keep his broad humanity of feeling and his sympathy for the class from which he has not drawn his clients. I think it eminently desirable that our Supreme Court should show in unmistakable fashion their entire sympathy with all proper effect to secure the most favorable possible consideration for the men who most need that consideration.

"Finally, Judge Holmes' whole mental attitude ... is such that I should naturally expect him to be in favor of those principles in which I so earnestly believe."[2]

What could have happened to dampen this high ardor? What had altered the enthusiasm which made Roosevelt proud of Holmes "as a representative of our country", which made the decisions on capital and labor a strong point in his favor, which dimmed the expectation that the Judge would be "in favor of those principles in which I so earnestly believe"?

Roosevelt had just become acquainted with a speech which Holmes had made eighteen months earlier. How he became acquainted with it after that lapse of time he does not tell us. On February 4, 1901, the centennial of the day on which John Marshall took his seat as Chief Justice of the Supreme Court, a motion was made that the Massachusetts Court adjourn in recognition of the day. The motion was not unexpected, and Holmes had written a speech for the occasion, before passing on it favorably. That we may know with some precision what he thought of the most famous Chief Justice who has occupied that seat, let us see in part what he said.

"If I were to think of John Marshall simply by number and measure in the abstract," he read, "I might hesitate in my superlatives, just as I should hesitate over the battle of the Brandywine if I thought of it apart from its place in the line of historic cause. But such thinking is empty in the same proportion that it is abstract. It is most idle to take a man apart from the circumstances which, in fact, were his. . . . A great man represents a great ganglion in the nerves of society, or, to vary the figure, a strategic point in the campaign of history, and part of his greatness consists in his being *there*. . . . When we celebrate John Marshall we celebrate at the same time and indivisibly the inevitable fact that the oneness of the nation and the supremacy of the national Constitution were declared to govern the dealings of man with man by the judgments and decrees of the most august of courts.

" . . . What I have said does not mean that I shall join in this celebration or in granting the motion before the court in any half-hearted way. Not only do I recur to what I said in the beginning, and remembering that you cannot separate a man from his place, remember also that there fell to Marshall perhaps the greatest place that ever was filled by a judge; but when I consider his might, his justice, and his wisdom, I do fully believe that if American law were to be represented by a single figure, sceptic and worshipper alike would agree without dispute that the figure could be one alone, and that one, John Marshall."[3]

There was more, quite as eloquent. I cannot resist quoting a fragment near the end, that Marshall's "unhelped thought may one day mount a throne, and without armies, or even with them, may shoot across the world the electric despotism of an unresisted power. It is all a symbol, if you like, but so is the flag. The flag is but a bit of bunting to one who insists on prose. Yet, thanks to Marshall and to the men of his generation—and for this above all we celebrate him and them—its red is our lifeblood, its stars our world, its blue our heaven. It owns our land. At will it throws away our lives."

To Theodore Roosevelt the speech from which these excerpts were taken was "unworthy of the subject", and showed "a total incapacity to grasp what Marshall did". He continued, in his letter to Lodge:

> "In the ordinary and low sense which we attach to the words, 'partisan' and 'politician', a judge of the Supreme Court should be neither."

To this Senator Lodge, who edited the correspondence, thought fit to append a footnote: "No man is fit to be in the Supreme Court if he is not a Constitutional lawyer, in the sense that Marshall was; a Constitutional statesman believing in great party principles, and willing to continue the Constitution so that the nation can develop on the broadest lines." Having got past this interpolation, let us proceed with Roosevelt's letter:

"But in the higher sense, in the proper sense, he is not in my judgment fitted for the position unless he is a party man, a constructive statesman, constantly keeping in mind his adherence to the principles and policies under which this nation has been built up and in accordance with which it must go on; and keeping in mind also his relations with his fellow statesmen who in other branches of the government are striving in cooperation with him to advance the ends of government. Marshall rendered such invaluable service because he was a statesman of the national type, like Adams who appointed him, like Washington whose mantle fell upon him.

"Taney was a curse to our national life because he belonged to the wrong party and faithfully carried out the criminal and foolish views of the party which stood for such a construction of the Constitution as would have rendered it impossible even to preserve the national life. The Supreme Court of the sixties was good exactly in so far as its members fitly represented the spirit of Lincoln.

"This is true at the present day. The majority of the present Court who have, although without satisfactory unanimity, upheld the principles of President McKinley and the Republican party in Congress, have rendered a great service to mankind and to this nation. The minority—a minority so large as to lack but one vote of being a majority—have stood for such reactionary folly as would have hampered well-nigh hopelessly this people in doing efficient and honorable work for the national welfare, and for the welfare of the islands themselves, in Porto Rico and the Philippines. No doubt they have possessed excellent motives and without doubt they are men of excellent personal character; but this no more excuses them than the same conditions excused the various upright and honorable men who took part in the wicked folly of secession in 1860 and 1861.

"Now I should like to know that Judge Holmes was in entire sympathy with our views. . . . I should hold myself as guilty of an irreparable wrong to the nation if I should put in his [Judge Gray's] place any man who was not absolutely sane and sound on the great national policies for which we stand in public life."[4]

To speak of Holmes as upholding the principles of President McKinley, the creature of Marcus A. Hanna, has almost a touch of comedy; to assume that he would support Roosevelt's "great national policies" of imperialism in Porto Rico and the Philippines, and to rate him an ungenerous foe who would stigmatize secession as "wicked folly"—yea, that knight who could say in a Harvard speech that neither North nor South needed colleges in which to learn "the greatest qualities of the race"; and at another time could say that "those who stood against us held just as sacred convictions that were the opposite of ours"—these unbuttoned utterances give glimpses of the gulf between Roosevelt's estimate and the true Holmes. In regard to the more martial of the speeches Holmes made about the Civil War, Roosevelt, an incorrigible fire-eater, wrote Lodge (this was in 1895, when Roosevelt was Police Commissioner in New York City): "By Jove, that speech of Holmes was fine; I wish he could make Edward Atkinson learn it by heart and force him to repeat it forwards and backwards every time he makes a peace oration." Atkinson was a Brookline economist of pacifist leanings.

Whatever reassurances, if any, Roosevelt may have received from Lodge, he held up the appointment of Holmes for a month after he had received the resignation of the dying Justice Gray. It was not until August 11, 1902, that he wrote Lodge: "I have had a very nice letter from Hoar [Senator George Frisbie Hoar of Massachusetts] and shall announce Judge Holmes' appointment today." He did announce it and Lodge congratulated him on the "chorus of praise" in the press. Mr. Justice Gray died in the middle of September of that year, and the appointment was sent to the Senate for confirmation the following December 2. It was confirmed straightway. Mr. Justice Holmes took his seat on December 6.

Having taken the plunge, President Roosevelt appeared determined to make the most of it. The new Justice and Mrs. Holmes were in great demand as diners-out in Washington, nowhere in greater demand than for dinners and lunches at the White House. It cannot be said that the Justice admired Roosevelt as unreservedly as the President admired him, and Mrs. Holmes sometimes made "Teddy" the object of her alert and not invariably kindly wit. Yet things went along swimmingly until 1903, when Mr. Justice Holmes wrote the dissent for a minority of four in the Northern Securities case. This was a cause quite close to Roosevelt's heart. On hearing that Holmes had written the dissent he exclaimed that he could carve out of a banana a Justice with more backbone than that.

But before we go into this, the first dissent by Mr. Justice Holmes—and one in which Chief Justice Fuller, with Mr. Justice White and Mr. Justice Peckham, concurred—let us clear up certain possible misconceptions regarding Roosevelt's hesitancy in appointing to the bench a judge who did not espouse his views—and the views of McKinley.

Few have understood more clearly than Roosevelt that an occupant of the supreme bench of this country must be not only a jurist but a statesman as well. Nearly a century ago de Tocqueville wrote: "The Supreme Court is placed at the head of all known tribunals, both by the nature of its rights and the class of justiciable parties which it controls. The peace, the prosperity and the very existence of the Union are placed in the hands of the Judges."[5] And Theodore Roosevelt, at a dinner to Mr. Justice Harlan in 1902, echoed:

> "In not one serious study of American political life will it be possible to omit the immense part played by the Supreme Court in the creation, not merely the modification, of the great policies, through and by means of which the country has moved on to her present position. . . . The Judges of the Supreme Court of the land must be not only great jurists, they must be great constructive statesmen, and the truth of what I say is illustrated by every study of American statesmanship."

Statesmanship! Yes, to be sure; but this was the Theodore Roosevelt who, evidently bearing in mind the numerous five-to-four decisions of the Court, replied, when he was asked whether it would be possible to enforce in this country a tax as deep-cutting as Lloyd George's 1909 budget for England:
"It would depend on whether a Judge of the Supreme Court came down heads or tails."

One associates "heads or tails" with a childish game of chance. The aleatory metaphor revealed the Rooseveltian state of mind regarding the Court some six years after four of its members, with Holmes at their head—or at least as their spokesman—in the Northern Securities case, had held views contrary to his own.[6] He had chosen only one member of that Court, and the choice had been made with due regard, as he thought, to acquiescence in his opinions and in his general political theory.

Presidents have been influenced usually by geographical and political considerations in filling vacancies in the Supreme Court. Roosevelt was not alone nor unique in feeling that the bench should represent the opinion of the prevailing political party.

He was elected by that party, and the Senate which must confirm or reject his choice was and is a partisan body. As a fact, Presidents have nearly always found it expedient or necessary to choose men from their own party. John Adams, a Federalist, appointed as Chief Justice John Marshall, a good Hamiltonian Federalist. After thirty-four years of service, Marshall died during the administration of Andrew Jackson, who was opposed politically to nearly everything Adams had advocated. Would Jackson appoint a Jacksonian Democrat? It may be as well to glance back and see what was thought of this emergency.

Lawyers, editors and the country at large awaited with anxiety the selection of Marshall's successor. The Democrats hoped for a man who would stem practices tending, as they put it, to "prostrate" the States. The Whigs, predecessors in political thought of the present Republicans, feared that Jackson would be governed solely by politics, and thought that the Chief Justiceship would fall within his avowed unashamed policy that to the victor belong the spoils. Whig organs trembled at the prospect of "a new era in affairs which may result most calamitously for the country", and vowed that "the majesty and utility of that great tribunal" might be destroyed. John Quincy Adams, recalling that the appointment of Marshall was the last act of his father's administration, "and one of the most important services rendered by him to his country," asserted that the Chief Justice had "cemented the Union which the crafty and quixotic democracy of Jefferson had a perpetual tendency to dissolve. Jefferson hated and dreaded him." As to Jackson: "He has not yet made one good appointment. His Chief Justice will be no better than the rest."

Those who foresaw a partisan appointment were justified in their Jackson; those whose premonitions envisaged the dissolution and ruin of the Union were destined to be disappointed. The man Jackson chose was Roger B. Taney, a Marylander and former Federalist politician, who had deserted to the Jackson banner and had been rewarded with the office of United States Attorney General, then Secretary of the Treasury. He had been nominated an Associate Justice of the Supreme Court in 1835, but had been rejected by the Senate; a year later a Senate of different composition confirmed him as Chief Justice. He was an eminent lawyer, but the Whig opposition delayed his confirmation by ten weeks. During the delay the Court sat with no Chief Justice (Associate Joseph Story acting in that capacity), and with the chair of another Associate Justice vacant. Few cases of importance were presented.

If Marshall has been called "the Supreme Conservative", then Taney might be called "the Supreme Jeffersonian". Many historians attribute wholly to Taney the decision in the Dred Scott case, which has even been said falsely to have been "fabricated" by the slavery party. When Taney wrote this decision, Lincoln said he thought it erroneous. "We know that the Court that made it has often overruled its decision," he said, "and we shall do what we can to have it overrule this."[7] When Taney died in 1864 the President replaced him with Salmon P. Chase, who had been his Secretary of the Treasury and was a Presidential aspirant; but he wanted to be sure before making the appointment how Chase felt about the Civil War.

Chief Justice Taft was appointed by a President of his own party, and Chief Justice Hughes likewise. It is true that Taft, when President, elevated to the Chief Justiceship a Louisianian who had been a Democratic United States Senator and was a former rebel soldier; but—and here, I surmise, we come to the nub of the matter—Taft and Edward Douglass White were not markedly disparate in their economic and social attitudes.

We arrive then, though without documentary evidence to support the position, at this terminus: That for Taft to have appointed Oliver Wendell Holmes or Louis D. Brandeis would have been out of keeping with his ways of thought; just as it would have been out of drawing for Roosevelt, who appointed Holmes, or Woodrow Wilson, who appointed Brandeis, to choose for the bench a jurist regarded as a rock-bound conservative. Even in the White House one must keep house with oneself. That Roosevelt took an extreme posture in a private letter to Senator Lodge, subsequently made common property in the publication of their correspondence, is no reflection either on the Presidency or on the Court. It is merely a reminder of the political pressures brought to bear in Washington, and of the frequency of five-to-four decisions during the last third of a century.

Political pressures and Roosevelt's political prestige were factors in his anger at Holmes after the Northern Securities dissent. Not only was this case close to the President's heart; it was an integral part of his reputation as a "trust-buster". That we may understand his emotional reactions it is necessary to recapitulate the circumstances briefly.

By the tragic accuracy of an assassin's bullet, Roosevelt became President September 14, 1901; in six months, on February 20, 1902, he caused his Attorney General, Philander C. Knox, whom he had inherited from the slain McKinley, to sue for the dissolution of the Northern Securities Company, a holding corporation chartered in New Jersey by the elder J. Pierpont Morgan and James J. Hill to consolidate the Northern Pacific, the Great Northern, and the Chicago, Burlington and Quincy railroads.

Although the filing of the suit burst like a thunderclap, and caused something very like a panic on the New York Stock Exchange, it had been under discussion for weeks in Washington. Roosevelt inquired, for one thing, whether the name of Morgan couldn't be omitted from the list of defendants; Knox said he could do it if the President so directed, but that he would not sign such a bill of complaint, because he did not propose to have half the lawyers in the United States laughing at him.

Here was the man who had set out deliberately to bring to book the "malefactors of great wealth", being balked in a kindly intention to spare a multimillionaire by a Cabinet member who, Big Business thought, would be "a steadying influence" in the administration. Knox was an incorrigible conservative, he had been Andrew Carnegie's counsel for years, he had learned law chiefly in writing briefs for corporate enterprises. He had been the friend and servant of captains of industry; yet when he was told over the telephone by a member of the House of Morgan about the stock market flurry he had the effrontery to reply: "The stock ticker does not tick in the Department of Justice."

Morgan suggested to Roosevelt that he send Knox to see one of the Morgan lawyers. "They can fix it up," he said. "That can't be done," Roosevelt replied.[8] He had once dubbed Knox, who measured five feet five, a "sawed-off cherub"; and evidently he meant to garner for himself the glory of this warfare he was about to wage against "predatory interests". He knew the temper of the electorate toward the "public-be-damned" attitude of dynastic industrial barons.

The suit was brought under that clause of the Sherman Act forbidding a "combination in the form of a trust or otherwise . . . in restraint of commerce among the several States or with foreign nations." A majority of five of the Supreme Court, in a decision written by Justice John M. Harlan, held that the Sherman Act recognized the rule of free competition, and that the Northern Securities scheme would deprive the public of advantages which would accrue under competition. A summary of the decision and the full text of the dissent, in which Chief Justice Fuller, Mr. Justice White and Mr. Justice Peckham concurred, is available in *The Dissenting Opinions of Mr. Justice Holmes*, and merits prolonged attention.[9] Of the majority, Mr. Justice Brewer alone held that the Sherman Act included only *unreasonable* restraints of trade; this will explain certain references by Mr. Justice Holmes to a "minority" as holding certain views, although these four subscribed to the majority decision. At the risk of presenting an inadequate account of a legal document which is justly held to be both great law and great literature, I wish to quote certain passages from it. Mr. Justice Holmes said at the outset that "although I think it useless and undesirable, as a rule, to express dissent, I feel bound to do so in this case and to give my reasons for it." And he added, in the course of his close and cogent reasoning:

> "Great cases like hard cases make bad law. For great
> cases are called great not by reason of their real im-

portance in shaping the law of the future but because of some accident of immediate overwhelming interest which appeals to the feelings and distorts the judgment. These immediate interests exercise a kind of hydraulic pressure which makes what previously was clear seem doubtful, and before which even well-settled principles of law will bend.

"What we have to do in this case is to find the meaning of some not very difficult words. We must try, I have tried, to do it with the same freedom of natural and spontaneous interpretation that one would be sure of if the same question arose upon an indictment for a similar act which excited no public attention and was of importance only to a prisoner before the court. Furthermore, while at times judges need for their work the training of economists and statesmen, and must act in view of their foresight of consequences, yet when their task is to interpret and apply the words of a statute, their function is merely academic to begin with —to read English intelligently—and a consideration of consequences comes into play, if at all, only when the meaning of the words is open to reasonable doubt. . .

"I stick to the exact words used. The words hit two classes of cases, and only two—Contracts in restraint of trade and combinations or conspiracies in restraint of trade, and we have to consider what these respectively are. . . .

". . . It would seem to me impossible to say that the words, 'every contract in restraint of trade is a crime punishable with imprisonment' would send the members of a partnership between, or a consolidation of, two trading corporations to prison—still more impossible to say that it forbade one man or corporation to purchase as much stock as he liked in both. . . .

"According to popular speech, every concern monopolizes whatever business it does, and if that business is trade between two States it monopolizes a part of the trade between States. Of course the statute does not forbid that. It does not mean that all business must cease. A single railroad down a narrow valley or through a mountain gorge monopolizes all the railroad transportation through that valley or gorge. Indeed, every railroad monopolizes, in a popular sense, the trade of some area. . . .

"There is a natural feeling that somehow or other the statute meant to strike at combinations great enough to cause just anxiety on the part of those who love their country more than money, while it viewed such little ones as I have supposed with just indifference. This notion, it may be said, somehow breathes from the pores of the Act, although it seems to be contradicted in every way by the words in detail. And it has occurred to me that it might be that when a combination reached a certain size it might have attributed to it more of the character of a monopoly merely by virtue of its size than would be attributed to a smaller one.

"The law, I repeat, says nothing about competition and only prevents its suppression by contracts or combinations in restraint of trade, and such contracts or combinations derive their character as restraining trade from other features than the suppression of competition alone. . . .

". . . I am happy to know that only a minority of my brethren adopt an interpretation of the law which in my opinion would make eternal the *bellum omnium contra omnes* and disintegrate society so far as it could into individual atoms. . . . [Such a law] would be an attempt to reconstruct society."

The crux of the division in the Supreme Court in this case was as to whether the Sherman Act was intended to provide, or did provide, for the maintenance of free competition. Although the

statute made no use of the word "competition", the majority held
that it was meant to maintain competition. As time went on the
evils of competing transportation lines which were inadequate to
meet national demands became more and more evident, even to
farmers and manufacturers and political spellbinders; and so we
had, in the Railway Act of 1920, Congressional legislation which
may seem to a layman a vindication of Mr. Justice Holmes and
his brethren in their dissent.

When the act was passed the aggregate capital of railroads in
this country—some of it represented by "watered" stock, to be
sure—was estimated at twenty billions of dollars. The World War
had taught among many lessons this: That consolidation and centralized planned direction might be a blessing rather than an un-
mixed evil; and it was perceived that the pressing transportation
problem of the United States must be met either by government
ownership or by consolidation into fewer groups. To weld a
thousand disjointed systems into a few strong groups was the intention of the Act of 1920. Although it made a verbal flourish
about the preservation of competition, its main provisions were
that existing channels of commerce should be preserved and that
due attention should be paid to the financial structure of the
mergers. The Interstate Commerce Commission, upon which
was imposed the task of planning the regrouping, proposed after
more than a year of cogitation that nineteen strong systems
should replace the thousand in existence; and any one of the
nineteen, under centralized management, clearly must be a more
momentous and more portentous consolidation than Hill, Morgan and their associates contemplated in the Northern Securities
Company.

Over the dissent of Mr. Justice Holmes and his three brethren
the Northern Securities merger was dissolved as evil and illegal;
the authorization by Congress of much bigger railroad mergers
was hailed as highly progressive. "It really seemed hard," said
Hill, on learning of the Northern Securities decision, "when we
look back on what we have done, that we should be compelled to
fight for our lives against political adventurers who have never

done anything but pose and draw a salary." This whining, coming from any captain of industry, has a familiar sound. Capitalists often feel, or pretend to feel, that they are misunderstood and mistreated; but at any rate the arguments of the capitalist battery of lawyers in defense of the Northern Securities merger appear to have been justified by later events.

Owen Wister, in his absorbing volume, *Roosevelt: The Story of a Friendship,* places the Northern Securities suit "at the top of all Roosevelt's great and courageous strokes in the domain of domestic statesmanship". He thinks the warfare thus inaugurated was "a stroke of genius", and that it "marked the turn of a rising tide". Doubtless it was an admirable and useful thing, at a time when Big Business was at the peak of its power, cynicism and arrogance, that it should be put in its place. Yet Mr. Wister picks up from the passages I have quoted a striking phrase, and himself speaks of "the 'hydraulic pressure' turned on by Roosevelt";[10] and he tells of a conversation he had in later years with Mr. Justice Holmes, whom he regarded as "altogether the most important figure among the Roosevelt Familiars." That Roosevelt was angered by the dissent he freely owns, but he is impressed that Holmes, "true to form, sat tight."

> " 'Can you understand,' I asked him twenty-seven years later, 'how I'm able absolutely to agree with you in the Northern Securities, and at the same time be very glad that Roosevelt won that suit?'
> " 'Perfectly,' he said.
> " 'And,' I continued, 'once that object lesson had been put across, to divorce the Union and Southern Pacific [alluding to a later Supreme Court decision] was a needless step.'
> "He thought so too, naturally; he had declined to break up the merger of the other two railroads."

The Union and Southern Pacific were Harriman lines which were dissolved in 1906, "much to my disgust," Mr. Wister says.

Holmes and Roosevelt

It is worth noting that the first reluctant dissent by Mr. Justice Holmes at Washington would be classified in the loose terminology of the sociologist as "conservative" rather than "liberal"; that is to say, he took the side of capital when it was under attack by its avowed enemy and a public figure who was later to lead the Progressive Party to defeat.

Holmes himself was quite untroubled, it is safe to say, as to whether the outcome of his deliberations when a case was before him for adjudication was going to be regarded as liberal or conservative. I doubt whether the words were to be found in his legal lexicon. Nor do I suppose that he greatly cared whether he, as a famous figure in his world, was classified either by those within that world or by outsiders as belonging to one camp or to the other. His attitude of aloofness from personal feeling or individual predilections in functioning as a judge was pronounced and was unmistakable. The Court was and is there for the interpretation of the Constitution and not for the expression of emotion, of social theories or of political practices. Its statesmanship is not a matter of "heads or tails"; and if Roosevelt said that Holmes had no backbone, at the time of the Northern Securities dissent, there are others who will say that, in resisting "hydraulic pressure" and in contravening the opinion of the man who so short a while before had elevated him to the bench, he displayed a spirit and a courage of high order.

CHAPTER 15

In the Supreme Court

JUST BEFORE Theodore Roosevelt told Senator Lodge he would appoint Oliver Wendell Holmes to the Supreme Court vacancy, and while he was debating about sending the name to the Senate for confirmation, the then Chief Justice of Massachusetts delivered two noteworthy speeches. Neither was to echo so loudly in his career as the discussion of John Marshall, and one of them passed almost unnoticed at the time, although it expressed with great felicity his abiding love for his New England, and ended on a note of that metaphysical faith which was his guiding star. It was made at the unveiling of memorial tablets at Ipswich, Massachusetts, on July 31, 1902.

"We are told by scholars," said Chief Justice Holmes, "that the Greeks and Romans built up their cities and their civilization on the worship of their ancestors and care for the shadowy needs of the dead. That ancient religion has vanished, but the reverence for venerable traditions remains. I feel it to my finger tips, but with the just change from personal and family story to the larger, vaguer, but not less inspiring belief that we tread a sacred soil. I have been too busy trying to account for myself to stop to account for my ancestors. I have the poems of Anne Bradstreet [from whom he was descended on his mother's side], that pale passion flower of our first Spring, but I do not read them often, and I cannot say much more of Governor Dudley than that what I once wrongly thought his portrait, in modest form, hangs in my house. But I love every brick and shingle of the old Massachusetts where once they worked and prayed, and I think it a noble and pious thing to do whatever we may by written word and moulded bronze and sculptured stone to keep our memories, our reverence and our love alive and to hand them on to new generations all too ready to forget."

"A noble and *pious* thing", the speaker said. It was characteristic of his richly-stored mind that, having begun with an illusion to Greek and Roman civilization, he should fall thus into the classical meaning of a word, which prompted Vergil to call the Trojan son of Anchises and Aphrodite, because of his filial devotion, "the pious Aeneas". He continued: "It may be that we are to be replaced by other races that come here with other traditions and to whom at first the great past of Massachusetts seems, as they sometimes proclaim it, but the doings in a corner of a little band of provincial heretics. But I am bold to hope that the mighty leaven that swelled the hearts of the founders of this Commonwealth still works and will work even under altered forms—that their successors will keep the State what the founders made it, a hearthstone of sacred fire.

"We all, the most unbelieving of us, walk by faith. We do our work and live our lives not merely to vent and realize our inner force, but with a blind and trembling hope that somehow the world will be a little better for our striving. Our faith must not be limited to our personal task; to the present, or even to the future. It must include the past and bring all, past, present and future, into the unity of a single continuous life. . . .

"Modest as they are, the monuments now unveiled seem to me trumpets which two hundred years from now may blow the great battle-calls of life, as two hundred years ago those whom they commemorate heard them in their hearts. And to many a gallant spirit, two hundred years from now as two hundred years ago, the white sands of Ipswich, terrible as engulfing graves, lovely as the opal flash of fairy walls, will gleam in the horizon, the image of man's mysterious goal."[1]

How true-blue to Boston its ancient stock remains has often been a matter of comment. "To value aright the affection which the old Bostonian had for Boston," said William Dean Howells, "one must conceive of something like the patriotism of men in the times when a man's city was a man's country, something Athenian, something Florentine." In Holmes the sense of loyalty was wide enough to embrace New England as well as his city-state, nor was Washington to alter it by one tittle.

In the other address Chief Justice Holmes discussed the "wasteful" aspect of artistic effort and the importance to mankind of uneconomic aspiration and production. This was at the dedication of the Northwestern University Law School Building in Chicago, on October 20, 1902. It is well worth setting down here in part, as indicating how many-sided and sensitive was the man then on his way to our highest tribunal, and as revealing again that touch of the metaphysical.

> "Nature has but one judgment on wrong conduct—if you can call that a judgment which seemingly has no reference to conduct as such—the judgment of death. That is the judgment or the consequence which follows uneconomical expenditure if carried far enough. If you waste too much food you starve; too much fuel, you freeze; too much nerve tissue, you collapse. And so it might seem that the law of life is the law of the herd; that man should produce food and raiment in order that he might produce yet other food and other raiment to the end of time. Yet who does not rebel at that conclusion? Accepting the premises, I nevertheless almost am prepared to say that every joy that gives to life its inspiration consists in an excursion toward death, although wisely stopping short of its goal. Art, philosophy, charity, the search for the north pole, the delirium of every great moment in man's experience—all alike mean uneconomic expenditure—mean waste—mean a step toward death. The justification of art is not that it offers prizes to those who succeed in the economic struggle, to those who in an economic sense have produced the most, and that thus by indirection it increases the supply of wine and oil. The justification is in art itself, whatever its economic ef-

fect. It gratifies an appetite which in some noble spirits is stronger than the appetite for food. The principle might be pressed even further and be found to furnish art with one of its laws. For it might be said, as I often have said, and as I have been gratified to find elaborated by that true poet, Coventry Patmore, that one of the grounds of aesthetic pleasure is waste. I need not refer to Charles Lamb's well-known comments on the fallacy that enough is as good as a feast. Who does not know how his delight has been increased to find some treasure of carving upon a mediaeval cathedral in a back alley—to see that the artist has been generous as well as great, and has not confined his best to the places where it could be seen to most advantage? Who does not recognize the superior charm of a square-hewed beam over a joist set on edge which would be enough for the work? . . . If I wished to make you smile, I might even ask whether life did not gain an enrichment from neglected opportunities which would be missed in the snug filling out of every chance. But I am not here to press a paradox. I only mean to insist on the importance of the uneconomic to man as he actually feels today. You may philosophize about the honors of leisure as a survival; you may, if you like, describe in the same way, as I have heard them described, the ideals which burn in the center of our hearts. None the less they are there. They are categorical imperatives. They hold their own against hunger and thirst; they scorn to be classed as mere indirect supports of our bodily needs, which rather they defy; and our friends the economists would do well to take account of them, as some great writers like M. Tarde would take account of them, if they are to deal with man as he is. . . .

"Mr. Ruskin's first rule for learning to draw, you will remember, was, Be born with genius. It is the first rule for everything else. If a man is adequate in native force, he probably will be happy in the deepest sense, whatever his fate. But we must not undervalue effort, even if it is the lesser half. . . . Our tastes are finalities, and it has been recognized since the days of Rome that there is not much use disputing about them. If some professor should proclaim that what he wanted was a strictly economic world, I should see no more use in debating with him than I do in arguing with those who despise the ideals which we owe to war. But most men . . . want to press philosophy to the uttermost edge of the articulate, and to try forever after some spiritual ray outside the spectrum that will bring a message to them from behind phenomena. They love the gallant adventures which yield no visible return. I think it is the glory of that university which I know best, that under whatever reserves of manner they may hide it, its graduates have the romantic passion in their hearts."[2]

These excerpts are peepholes upon the temper and the temperament of the man about whose appointment Roosevelt was debating. When finally the name was sent to the Senate it was promptly confirmed, and Oliver Wendell Holmes took his seat as an Associate Justice on December 6. He arrived in Washington the day before, was measured for his silk robe, and took the two oaths which are a part of the induction, one in the robing room and the other on the bench. Both were administered by Chief Justice Melville Weston Fuller, who was eight years older than the new member, and had sat on that bench since July 20, 1888. During four years—an unusual stretch of time in this case—there had been no change in the personnel of the Court. In fact, during the first ten years of Chief Justice Fuller's incumbency there had been a change almost annually.[3] President Harrison had appointed four men to the bench. By a sort of tacit custom, nine-tenths of those chosen to serve in the Court were in their fifties; Mr. Justice Holmes was sixty-one. All were white-haired save Edward Doug-

lass White, whom Cleveland had appointed in 1894 and whom
the Senate, after rejecting two other names the President had submitted, confirmed immediately. White was a Civil War veteran,
a former Louisiana jurist and United States Senator, and was
the second man to be advanced from Associate Justice to Chief
Justice; the first was William Cushing of Massachusetts, in 1796,
and he, owing partly to advancing years, declined after the Senate
had confirmed the choice. Benjamin R. Curtis of Boston, Associate Justice from 1851 to 1857 (he took his seat two weeks before
the Senate acted on the appointment), resigned soon after the
Dred Scott decision, from which he had dissented, because he felt,
regretfully, that "he could no longer expect to see the Court act
on Constitutional questions with freedom from political considerations".[4] George Ticknor Curtis, his brother, had argued the
case ably before the Court. The name of Curtis is distinguished
in the history of the Court; so are the Massachusetts names of
Joseph Story and Horace Gray.

When resigning in 1906, Henry Billings Brown wrote of the
Court to his associates (and the letter illuminates the earlier Curtis complaint):

> "The antagonisms, sometimes almost fierce, which
> were developed during the earliest decades of its his-
> tory and at one time threatened to impair its usefulness,
> are happily forgotten; and the now universal acqui-
> escence in its decisions, though sometimes reached by
> a bare majority of its members, is a magnificent tribute
> to that respect for the law inherent in the Anglo-Saxon
> race, and contains within itself the strongest assurance
> of the stability of our institution."[5]

Mr. Justice Billings was not of Massachusetts, but a Maine
man. As for Mr. Justice Gray, whom Holmes succeeded, an enthusiastic anonymous contributor to the *American Law Review*
described him, a short time before his death, as "the greatest
judge, we submit, that the processes of judicial evolution have yet
reared in our country, not excepting Marshall."[6] Certainly the

new member of the Court had no reason to be ashamed of his predecessors from Massachusetts.

Oddly mingling informality with august ritual was the atmosphere into which the new member was introduced. The Saturday conferences of the Chief Justice and his eight associates were held in a shabby room adjoining the Senate barber shop; the manner there was of easy or emphatic give and take, the manners, despite the urbanity of the judges, sometimes jocular or teasing. But once seated behind their long bench, black-robed and conscious of the weight of what they were doing, the members assumed that grave and reverend air which impressed deeply those who were admitted at intervals from the corridor outside, as spectators left and made room for others in the small, semi-circular room. Beneath this lighted dome for more than half a century prior to 1859 the United States Senate, until its growth from the admission of new States required the addition of a wing to the Capitol, had functioned.

These gray walls and marble pillars had resounded to the oratory of Webster and Calhoun and Clay and Crittenden. Here Aaron Burr had presided and the Hayes-Tilden contest had been heard. Above the judicial bench, ranged along the straight wall, was the old Senate gallery, and topping the archway beneath its central point an eagle stretched his gilded wings and glared down at the Justices. At noon, between cords drawn across the Capitol corridor, the Justices, headed by their Chief, marched from the robing room into the court, passed between crimson curtains and beneath the marble busts of dead Chief Justices, behind a screen and so to their seats, the spectators meanwhile respectfully standing. "Oyez! Oyez! Oyez!" intoned the crier in his frock coat. "All persons having business before the honorable judges of the Supreme Court of the United States are admonished to draw near and give their attention, for the court is now sitting. God save the United States and this honorable court."

The audience seated itself and the ponderous wheels of the law, in its most imposing sanctuary, began to turn.

Mr. Justice Holmes did not entertain, when he took his seat, what has been called "the basic myth" that the law expresses a certainty or that its operation can be inevitably sure.[7] On the Massachusetts bench he had made evident his freedom from that thought. Nor did he suppose that the nation was an organic unit, embracing whole-heartedly and in its entirety the will of the majority. State Legislatures, he perceived, functioned in separate compartments and undertook to meet community demands or problems in some cases peculiar to their own sections. But he well knew that he had arrived at a terminal which represented the highest juridical ambition of any lawyer in his country. Let us call the roll of those associated with him.

Chief Justice Fuller, of Illinois, born February 11, 1833, had been without previous judicial experience when appointed by President Cleveland and confirmed by the Senate on July 20, 1888. He was to preside for twenty-two years, until his death, July 4, 1910.[8]

Mr. Justice White, who succeeded Fuller as Chief Justice, was born November 3, 1845, and his appointment as Associate was confirmed February 19, 1894.[9] Joseph McKenna of California, born on August 10, 1843, had been appointed by President McKinley and confirmed on January 21, 1898; he was to resign on January 5, 1925.[10] Mr. Justice Brown of Michigan was born March 21, 1836, had been appointed by President Harrison and confirmed on December 29, 1890; he resigned May 28, 1906, and was to live until September 4, 1913 (when Mr. Justice Holmes entered the Court this Associate had already lost an eye through overwork).[11] David Josiah Brewer of Kansas was born January 20, 1837, was appointed by Harrison and confirmed December 18, 1889. He was a nephew through his mother of former Associate Justice Stephen Johnson Field, who died in 1889; and he had been a classmate at Yale of Mr. Justice Brown.[12] John Marshall Harlan, born June 1, 1833, had been appointed by President Hayes and confirmed November 29, 1877; he lived until October 14, 1911, a year and a half longer than Mr. Justice Brewer.[13] A giant in stature, Mr. Justice Harlan once astonished his colleagues, in delivering a dissent in an anti-trust case, by turning upon them, his long arms outstretched, and declaring that he had lived to see the Court twice reverse itself upon a single issue. George Shiras, Jr., of Pennsylvania, born January 26, 1832, had been appointed by Harrison and confirmed July 26, 1892; he was to resign a little more than a year after Mr. Justice Holmes took his seat, but lived until August 21, 1924.[14] Wheeler Hazard Peckham of New York, born January 1, 1833, had been appointed by Cleveland and rejected February 16, 1894; he was to live until September 27, 1905. Of these, Mr. Justice McKenna had served three terms in the lower house of Congress, had been a judge of the United States Circuit Court, and had served for a time as Attorney General.

This recital of dates of births, resignations and deaths suffices to make clear that nearly all of the Court were the juniors of Mr. Justice Holmes and that he survived all of them on that bench, as well as outlived all of them. Here, as in Massachusetts, the "monotonous iteration" of the brevity of life was borne in upon him.

When Mr. Justice Shiras resigned, Roosevelt appointed in his place William R. Day of Ohio, a wisp of a man. His son, a former football player and a six-footer, once argued a case before his father and the others of the Court. Mr. Justice Holmes surveyed the upstanding dimensions of this offshoot of his associate and passed a pencilled note along the bench: "He is a block of the old chip."

When Mr. Justice Brown resigned, Roosevelt appointed William H. Moody of Massachusetts, who had been a Representative in Congress, Secretary of the Navy and Attorney General; and when Mr. Justice Peckham died, Taft appointed Horace H. Lurton of Tennessee, a Confederate veteran of the Civil War.[15] As the stately procession passed behind the screen in the courtroom, Mr. Justice Holmes invariably turned to his associate and former enemy in arms, and gave a military salute.

The fact that a Republican President advanced Mr. Justice White, a Democrat, to succeed Chief Justice Fuller attracted much attention at the time. Yet, as Charles Warren notes in his work, *The Supreme Court in United States History,* partisan influences were slight: "The mental attitude of the Judge had far more to do with the conclusions of his opinion than had his political attitude. Certainly no decision could have been forecast by a consideration of party lines in the Court." And he quotes, as illustrating how slight was the importance of party designations during the incumbency of Chief Justice Fuller, this passage:

> "In view of the number of vacancies which will be filled by President Taft and the Senate, and the many statements which have been made concerning the political importance of these appointments, in more than eighteen years since the decision in Field v. Clark, in 1892, there has been but one case which involved a question of constitutional law and in which all the Republican members of the Court took one position and all the Democratic members took a contrary position; that case (Snyder v. Bettman, 190 U. S. 249, in 1903) was whether a Federal inheritance tax, which was collected while the property was in the hands of an executor, could constitutionally be applied to a bequest to a municipality for public purposes; the Court upheld the tax, against the dissents of the Chief Justice and Justices White and Peckham; this decision will not be of much practical importance, until the people of the United States have become far more eager to make bequests to municipalities than they are today."[16]

During those eighteen years, Mr. Warren reminds us, there was only one other case in which the Republicans and the Democrats in the Court faced one another on opposing sides.[17] It was from the Court of Claims, and did not involve constitutional interpretation. In the cases which engendered political excitement, such as the Insular Cases and the Northern Securities Case, Republican and Democratic judges were to be found on both sides.

What the general attitude of Mr. Justice Holmes would be in his new work had been foreshadowed in his Massachusetts opinions. Even his vigorous position in regard to the Fourteenth Amendment, and in particular its "due process" clause, regarding which some of his more noteworthy opinions were to be delivered, could have been foreseen. The cases before the Supreme Court involving interpretation of the United States Constitution fall into three general classes: what may be called "State rights" cases, involving the conflict between the authority of the Federal Government and the rights reserved to the States; the "natural" or other rights of individuals as against the authority of the States of which they are citizens or in which they happen to become involved in litigation; the powers of the Federal Government in areas where the States have no authority unless by Congressional enactment. The first and second of these classes have arisen for the most part under the Commerce Clause of the Constitution and the Fourteenth Amendment.

Mr. Justice Holmes had manifested, while in Massachusetts, his reluctance either to void statutory legislation or to read into the law the personal predilections or prejudices of the jurist. From these two attitudes arose, in the main, his dissents in the Supreme Court. Many persons, including many members of the United States Senate, felt that he was opposing a tendency on the part of a "conservative" majority in the Court to color Constitutional interpretation with private social and economic opinions. In *The Dissenting Opinions of Mr. Justice Holmes* are two score citations of the Fourteenth Amendment, but the most emphatic pronouncement in regard to it came on May 26, 1930, after the publication of that volume. Although the opinion is incorporated in *Representative Opinions of Mr. Justice Holmes,* published in 1931, it should be quoted here also because of its frank criticism of the majority's attitude and because to several commentators it recalled the famous dissent of Mr.

Justice Curtis in the Dred Scott Case. Mr. Justice Holmes was considering a case in which the majority held that a State had no right to enforce its transfer or inheritance taxes on bonds and bank credits in that State, where they were not taxable when they were owned by a resident who had lived in another State. The enforcement of the inheritance and transfer tax was held to violate "due process". Said Mr. Justice Holmes, in the course of an opinion in which Justices Brandeis and Stone dissented with him:

> "I have not yet adequately expressed the more than anxiety that I feel at the ever-increasing scope given to the Fourteenth Amendment in cutting down what I believe to be the constitutional rights of the States. As the decisions now stand, I can hardly see any limit but the sky to the invalidating of those rights if they happen to strike a majority of this Court as for any reason undesirable. I cannot believe that the Amendment was intended to give us *carte blanche* to embody our economic or moral beliefs in its prohibitions. Yet I can think of no narrower reason that seems to me to justify the present and the earlier decisions to which I have referred. Of course the words 'due process of law', if taken in their literal meaning, have no application to this case; and while it is too late to deny that they have been given a much more extended and artificial signification, still we ought to remember the great caution shown by the Constitution in limiting the power of the States, and should be slow to construe the clause in the Fourteenth Amendment as committing to the Court, with no guide but the Court's own discretion, the validity of whatever laws the States may pass. . . . It seems to me to be exceeding our powers to declare such a tax a denial of due process of law.
>
> "And what are the grounds? Simply, so far as I can see, that it is disagreeable to a bondholder to be taxed

in two places. Very probably it might be good policy to restrict taxation to a single place, and perhaps the technical conception of domicile may be the best determinant. But it seems to me that if that result is to be reached it should be reached through understanding among the States, by uniform legislation or otherwise, not by evoking a constitutional prohibition from the void of 'due process of law', when logic, tradition and authority have united to declare the right of the State to lay the now prohibited tax."[18]

It cannot be assumed, from this forthright utterance, that Mr. Justice Holmes was a rampant "State rights" man. He thought that the Constitution was an experiment, as all life is an experiment; and he thought that legislators, whether State or Federal, should have a relatively free hand in social and economic experiments to meet special conditions, even when the laws they enacted were personally obnoxious to him; but in this case he wished, clearly, to protect a State from an infringement of its declared rights, and he expressed the wish in terms which might have gratified any good Jeffersonian.

The "due process" clause was the only fragment of the Fourteenth Amendment still effective when Mr. Justice Holmes began attacking it. The Thirteenth, Fourteenth and Fifteenth amendments, adopted as part of the reconstruction program after the Civil War, had been nullified, and all the enabling legislation had been repealed finally by 1894. When the Fourteenth Amendment was first offered it was rejected even by three States which had not seceded from the Union, and its acceptance by the South was forced by the threat of martial law—which was soon in operation anyhow—unless the former Confederate States would ratify it. They knuckled under, but the real purpose of the amendment, and its most elaborate section, providing for the enfranchisement of the Negro, was ignored in the North and South. It provided for the limitation of Congressional representation in any State unless Negroes were admitted to the polls,

and not all Northern States were willing to enforce such a reduction.

The limitation of State rights, to which Mr. Justice Holmes
objected, was the real purpose of the "due process" clause, which
had no connection with the apparent object of the Amendment,
and was slipped into it by a corporation lawyer then in the
House, John A. Bingham of Ohio.

> "No State shall make or enforce any law which shall
> abridge the privileges or immunities of citizens of the
> United States [it reads]; nor shall any State deprive
> any person of life, liberty, or property without due
> process of law, nor deny to any person within its juris-
> diction the equal protection of the laws."

Representative Bingham explained afterward on the floor of
the House that the first ten Amendments to the Constitution
(the "Bill of Rights") limited the authority of the Congress but
not of the States, and that his purpose was to remedy this condition. Roscoe Conkling, who had served on the joint committee
which accepted the singular clause, vowed they had "wrought
in grave sincerity".[19] Long after the Amendment had become a
laughing stock the clause, which needed no "force bill" but de-
pended upon the temper of a Supreme Court majority, was effective for the protection of criminals on trial, the justification
of lawyers defending men they knew to be guilty, and the defense of high corporation dividends. Again the "strong medicine of the Constitution" had become "its daily bread". What
had been adopted "on a plea of necessity", as Mr. Justice Field
had put it in dissenting from another majority attitude, was
again being followed "on a plea of convenience".

So long as the Supreme Court majority held in reverence the
sanctity of corporation convenience and dividends, the clause
was a Golconda for Big Business and the lawyers who served it.
Mr. Justice Holmes made his first assault upon it in 1904, and
on that occasion—the situation has in it a touch of humor—subscribed to a dissent written by Mr. Justice Harlan, "the last of

the tobacco-spittin' judges." Justices White and Day also subscribed to the dissent, and Holmes wrote a separate minority opinion upon the practice of invoking "the equal protection of the laws" on behalf of "an economic theory which a large part of the country does not entertain." This was the Lochner Case, in which Mr. Justice Holmes uttered his famous epigram: "The Fourteenth Amendment does not enact Mr. Herbert Spencer's *Social Statics.*"

In 1910, when Associate Justice White became Chief Justice, James M. Beck, perhaps as illiberal as any lawyer who has ever served as Solicitor General of the United States, was writing on "Nullification by Indirection", and said of the expansion of centralized powers:

> "The insistence upon the reserved rights of the States has become little more than a political platitude. There is little, if any, real popular sentiment of sufficient strength to protect the States against the encroachment of the Federal Government. . . . Men have been trained by imperative economic influences to look to the Central Government as the real political government, and to the States as little more than subordinate provinces, useful for the purposes of local police regulation and nothing more."[20]

During the incumbency of Chief Justice Fuller, centralized power had been sustained by the Supreme Court in the case of a Federal law which, violating a treaty, prohibited the entry of Chinese laborers;[21] in one of these cases Mr. Justice Brewer, dissenting, had asserted that the majority was striking "a blow against constitutional liberty", and that the decision contained "the germs of an assertion of unlimited and arbitrary power, in general incompatible with the immutable principles of justice, inconsistent with the nature of our government."[22] But the Court pursued its policy, and broadened the national power still further by holding that it was possible to regulate the alien inheritance of lands in the States.[23] It upheld the power of the President to instruct United States marshals to protect the lives of Federal judges,[24] and declared that a marshal who had shot a man in defense of Judge Field was acting "in pursuance of a law of the United States", a statement regarded as "the broadest interpretation yet given to implied powers of the National Government under the Constitution."[25] The power of Congress over the Territories was upheld in a sweeping decision,[26] and the power to regulate interstate commerce was further emphasized.[27] There were many other instances of the tendency, both economic and governmental, as noted by Charles Warren, and one consequence was the outbreak of "bitter attacks upon the court".[28]

During the first term of Chief Justice White this tendency appeared to be checked. Teeth were put into the Sherman Act by the decisions dissolving the oil and tobacco trusts. In the second of these cases a lawyer, hopeful of demonstrating the minuteness of foreign competition, asserted before the Court that "nobody but dudes and fools smoke foreign cigarettes." Mr. Justice Holmes interrupted gently from the bench. "Are you sure?" he inquired. "I have smoked them, and I am sure I am not a dude."

The Sherman Act, forbidding combinations in restraint of foreign and interstate trade, was passed in 1890, but did not damp the daring or the ardor of promoters. Their operations, Charles A. Beard has noted, would have amazed their predecessors of the seventies and the eighties.

> "In 1899, the Standard Oil Company took the place of the old trust; about the same time the Copper Trust and the Smelters' Trust were formed under the beneficent laws of New Jersey. The next year the National Refining Company came into existence with a capital greater than the total national debt in Washington's day; and at the opening of the new century that towering genius of finance, J. P. Morgan, completed the edifice of the United States Steel Corporation with more than a billion dollars in outstanding paper. As the

chief element in these operations was the ability to float huge issues of stocks and bonds, primacy in such matters passed to large banking houses and heavy investors. So an immense collection of great and small interests was knit into a compact fabric under the management of two or three potent financial groups in New York. . . . .

"Even the investors who relied with child-like faith on the legerdemain of financial wizards had grounds for complaints. Either through inadvertence or calculation, some of the gigantic corporate structures revealed distressing flaws in their masonry. For instance, the New York, New Haven and Hartford Railway combination, effected under Morgan's tutelage, was so loaded with stocks and bonds that it collapsed with an awful crash, spreading ruin far and wide among widows, orphans and other security holders in New England and giving an awful shock to those who had bought common shares at a high figure in the old days of prudence."[29]

Taft, who instituted forty-five indictments under the Sherman Act to but twenty-five by Roosevelt, was in the White House when the oil and tobacco monopolies were disbanded into friendly units. The decisions caused national excitement "and revived the hopes, somewhat shaken by previous decisions, that the National power was adequate to deal with the trusts".[30] In that same year the Court held that a peonage statute was contrary to the Thirteenth Amendment, validating that document for the first time in its history,[31] and in the next year refused to interfere with a State's adoption of the initiative and referendum, holding that this was a political and not a judicial issue.[32] The Court now had what is commonly called a more "liberal" tinge.

The personnel of the Court, moreover, was undergoing rapid changes. President Taft appointed five members, a majority.

In the Supreme Court

Within seven years after Chief Justice White took his seat Justices Peckham, Brewer, Harlan, Lurton, Lamar and Hughes had died or resigned. President Wilson appointed three members, including Louis Dembitz Brandeis; and it was not until then that the voice of the minority began to be heard through the land, not until later that the majority of the Court could be called "liberal".

CHAPTER 16
Holmes and Brandeis

A PREGNANT PHRASE sank after 1916 into the common consciousness of the United States. Even newspaper readers became familiar, in reports of Supreme Court procedure, with what newspaper men might call the "snapper"; Holmes and Brandeis dissenting. John Hessin Clarke, who was to resign in 1922 to devote his life to work for the League of Nations, was sometimes associated with them. He was an Ohio man and former Federal judge there, and like Brandeis he was a Wilson appointee. Others sometimes supported them. Chief Justice Taft joined the minority in 1922 in protesting against voiding a minimum wage act for the District of Columbia, although he did not agree "with some general observations in the forcible opinion of Mr. Justice Holmes".[1]

From widely separated points, Holmes and Brandeis traveled converging roads which led them almost always to the same conclusions. Differing in method and attitude, they were spiritually akin. Possibly Judge Holmes of Massachusetts had Brandeis in mind in 1897 when he said that "for the rational study of the law ... the man of the future is the master of statistics and the master of economics."[2] He, who, for all his persistent delving in the "ragbag of details", could not quite bring himself to a diligent study of graphs and charts, could not have framed a phrase more accurately describing one side of his future associate on the highest bench of the land. After they came together there, Mr. Justice Brandeis once told his friend that a study of statistics would be good for him.

"Well, you pick out the right books and send them up to me," said Mr. Justice Holmes, and presently took his leave for his summer place at Beverly Farms. There, in due time, was delivered a box of books. A servant opened it, and revealed a formidable array, ranging from monographs to tomes, on the eight-hour day, the textile industry, the employment of women, employers' liability, and so on. Mr. Justice Holmes gazed at the box in unaffected dismay.

"Just nail it up," he told the man, "and send it back to him." And then, with a sigh of relief, he immersed himself in Plato.

On another occasion, much later, when a decision was pending in a case involving the constitutionality of the California "criminal syndicalism" statute, Mr. Justice Brandeis called at the Washington home of his associate for a protracted discussion of the issues involved. After he had left, Mr. Justice Holmes observed to his secretary: "I'm afraid Brandeis has the crusading spirit. He talks like one of those upward-and-onward fellows."

Louis Dembitz Brandeis was so distinctly upward-and-onward that when he was nominated to the Supreme Court a tremendous hullabaloo was set up by Captains of industry, the satellites of Big Business and the staid elements of the legal profession. Elihu Root, President A. Lawrence Lowell of Harvard (Brandeis is a Harvard man), Joseph Choate and William Howard Taft joined the chorus, vowing that the nominee was "unfit" and "lacking in judicial temperament", and the American Bar Association felt it a "painful duty" to oppose him. Said the *New York World,* in those days alive and fighting:

> "His public services have won him the hearty detestation of certain powerful corporations and financial interests. They hate him not merely because he is a radical, but because he is enormously able and efficient. To them it is indecent that a lawyer with such extraordinary ability should wantonly and deliberately use his talent to promote the social welfare of the American people when he might command princely fees in the service of privilege."

At the time of the appointment, January 28, 1916, to succeed Justice Joseph R. Lamar, Brandeis was fifty-nine years old and had seen no previous service on the bench. Born and reared in Louisville, he had a Cavalier background, while the background of his ancestors was European. His parents, migrating to the Land of the Free from Bohemia after the attempted revolutions of 1848, established themselves comfortably, and named their son for a maternal uncle who was to vote for Abraham Lincoln at the Chicago Presidential Convention of 1860, when the boy was four years old. Adolph Brandeis, the father, a substantial merchant, was strongly Unionist. (Kentucky remained neutral, and gave about as many soldiers to the North as to the South.) The son was educated at the University of Louisville, was sent to Dresden, and then, the family fortune having disappeared in a panic, worked his way to his LL.B. at Harvard in 1877. He was admitted to the bar in Louisville the next year, but soon moved to Boston and practiced there until he went to Washington. In 1891 he married Miss Alice Goldmark of New York. Already he had acted as counsel for employers as well as for workingmen, and on occasion as arbitrator between them, and he had made up his mind what his course was to be. Miss Goldmark became Mrs. Brandeis knowing that this man was a fighter, and that he had elected to fight for the minority.

Whether in the courtroom or out of it, Brandeis never learned the technique of bluff. He brought into action a Big Bertha charged with devastating facts and figures. His mental machinery was cool, comprehensive and efficient, and he was as incapable of bulldozing an opponent or a witness as of appealing to the emotions of a jury. He mastered words as he mastered statistics, and developed English which was clean cut and muscular. As counsel in the Ballinger-Pinchot investigation, before the Interstate Commerce Commission and afterward on its behalf for the Government in Washington and for the people in Oregon, California and Boston, for workingmen in insurance cases, and in opposing the New Haven's effort to monopolize New England transportation, he became a national figure. Railroad magnates and Captains of Industry thought him a sinister figure.

Long and bitter was the fight in the United States Senate

against the appointment of Brandeis to the Supreme Court. President Wilson took a hand.

> "I nominated Mr. Brandeis for the Supreme Court [he said in a public statement] because it was and is my deliberate judgment that, of all the men now at the bar, whom it has been my privilege to observe, test and know, he is exceptionally qualified. I cannot speak too highly of his impartial, impersonal, orderly and constructive mind, his rare analytical powers, his deep human sympathy, his profound acquaintance with the historical roots of our institutions and insight into their spirit, or of the many evidences he has given of being imbued, to the very heart, with our American ideals of justice and equality of opportunity . . . or of his genius in getting persons to unite in common harmonious action and look with frank and kindly eyes into each other's minds, who had before been heated antagonists. This friend of justice and of men will ornament the High Court of which we are all so justly proud."

How right Wilson was, how wofully wrong were Root, Lowell, Choate and the twenty-two Senators who voted on June 1, 1916, against the confirmation, was manifest in the outcome. Debating another nomination to the Supreme Court, Senator Shipstead once illuminated retroactively—perhaps without intention—the fears and motives which had guided his colleagues in the Brandeis nomination, before he took his seat. "Hegel at one time said that humanity cannot learn from history anything except that it cannot learn from history," he said. "It has been customary at all times in human history that those who are concerned with the good or ill of humanity have gone back to the scrap piles, to the dump heaps of the past, very often, and taken an old, discarded tin can in the form of an idea, given it a coat of paint and a nice label and sold it to humanity as a container for a hitherto unknown but benign cure for political and economic ills.

"Russia has such a tin can and it is labeled 'Communism'. Italy has such a tin can and it is labeled 'Fascism'. We have such a tin can and we call it 'equity'. All of these are repudiations of parliamentary government or government by law."

Senator Shipstead said that the tin can of equity was covered by the mantle of the judiciary and that the mantle covered also a sword. Yet something was learned from history as Mr. Justice Brandeis and his brethren made it, whether or not they wore swords. Testimony as to what had been learned was given on November 13, 1931, when the Justice was seventy-five years old. President Hoover sent him a message commenting on "a heart and mind which have made the nation your debtor", and scores of others offered their felicitations. Said the staid *New York Times*:

> "The storm against him at the time of his appointment seems almost incredible now. From the first he vindicated the wisdom of President Wilson, disappointed and surprised his opponents. Year by year his stature as a judge has increased. He has come to be regarded with general respect and affection such as surrounds his elder brother, Mr. Justice Holmes, his intimate friend, often his companion in dissent, though as strong and independent characters they not infrequently dissent from each other. . . .
>
> "But his logic, his learning, the lucid order of his reasoning, the exactness of his language, his extraordinary penetration of facts, his intellectual energy, have long marked him as one destined to be memorable in the front row of great judges."

And the *New York Herald Tribune,* almost as conservative as its contemporary, echoed:

> "In light of the respect with which the country now regards Mr. Justice Brandeis, who has just celebrated his seventy-fifth birthday, it is interesting to recall the

misconceptions caused by his appointment to the Supreme Court fifteen years ago. In his recently published *Reminiscences* Mr. William G. McAdoo writes that "the uproar over President Wilson's appointment of Louis D. Brandeis . . . filled the air during the early months of 1916, and for a while the pro-and-con clamor over the qualities of Brandeis as a man, a citizen, a lawyer and a judge made the news of the World War sound like a whisper. . . .

"Justice Brandeis has now long been considered one of the outstanding figures on the Supreme bench and not the less so because he has been so often bracketed with Mr. Justice Holmes in dissenting from majority opinions. The country has come to look to him, as to Justice Holmes, for a welcome vigor and courage in the interpretation of the Constitution. . . .

"We know that we are echoing a nation-wide sentiment in expressing the hope that Mr. Justice Brandeis will long be spared to honor his court and his country."

What oil had Mr. Justice Brandeis poured on the troubled waters? What had he done to quell the storm of conservative opposition?

Despite the urbane serenity of Mr. Justice Brandeis, there is nothing oily about him. What he poured on the troubled waters was the quieting influence of a great mind and a tranquil spirit. At seventy-five he was still a fighter, "with a wallop in either fist", as one newspaper commentator noted. He understood and he exemplified in a high sense the juristic function of statesmanship. He differed from Mr. Justice Holmes in experience and in specialized knowledge, and they did not entertain identical conceptions of public policy; until their early manhood they had occupied disparate atmospheres and environment, and a part of the dissimilarity was that New England began the earlier to watch the concentration of business interests into larger units.

Mr. Justice Brandeis appeared even in his later years to entertain some of his youthful ideals about small business and independent enterprise. Thus, in the introduction to *The Social and
Economic Views of Mr. Justice Brandeis,* we find Charles A.
Beard, that fertile and effective critic of American institutions,
saying:

> "American society, as Mr. Brandeis then conceived
> it, should not be dominated by huge monopolies and
> trusts, but should be the home of 'the new freedom',
> in which small, individual enterprises can flourish un-
> der the defensive arm of the government. The rela-
> tions of the great utilities and the public should be ad-
> justed on principles of prudent investment, efficient
> capitalization, scientific management, and fair earn-
> ings equitably shared with the public under sliding-
> scale rules. Trade unions are necessary to the uphold-
> ing of decent living standards among the mass of work-
> ers, and in the weighing of judicial opinion they
> should be given the benefit of the doubt unless the
> mandate of the law is too clear to be mistaken or the
> end sought is undesirable as ascertained by an inquiry
> into the facts. . . .
>
> "And what of his place in American constitutional
> development? That, as of every other statesman, will
> depend not upon the purity of his spirit, the logic of
> his mind, nor his arrangement of materials, but upon
> the degree to which he has divined the future—the up-
> shot of the things in which he has been immersed. Is
> the America of tomorrow to be the society of 'the new
> freedom' so effectively portrayed by Mr. Brandeis and
> the President who appointed him? Or will the march
> of integration in finance and industry override the
> small enterprises which they sought to preserve against
> extinction? Here we all see through a glass darkly.
> Those who have thought most about it may be in-

clined to say with Henry Adams that, given our ignorance, silence is best. And yet, even though the year 2000 may be far from the picture which Mr. Brandeis has idealized in his mind, we may be sure that the realistic, fact-burdened method which he has employed in all his thinking about legal and economic affairs will have an increasing influence on coming generations of students, lawyers and judges. Humanity and ideas, as well as things, are facts, and a jurisprudence which takes them into account cannot perish from the earth."[3]

Mr. Justice Holmes once said to a visitor: "Bigness is the curse of this country", but he had in mind at the moment the complexity and size which made it impossible for appointed and elected officials to exert to the full their personal powers. Even members of Congress, he observed, were thus handicapped. On the Supreme Court bench, it may be said in passing, he and Mr. Justice Brandeis, although one employed a "judicial process" dissimilar from the "legal method" of the other, exerted their powers to the full, often in unison.

A certain difference in attitude between the two Justices may be illustrated by a familiar anecdote about James McNeill Whistler. Thomas Humphry Ward, then art critic for the London *Times,* after inspecting some etchings, said: "That, my dear Whistler, is bad, very bad; but this is good, *quite* good." Whereupon the artist protested: "Now if you don't like that, say so; and if you do like this, say so; but don't tell *me* they're good or bad. Here—have a brandy and soda. You'll know whether that's good or bad."

Mr. Justice Holmes held himself aloof from questions of goodness or badness, certainly from any personal emotional reaction. He considered that as a jurist he was not concerned with such issues. He considered cases on their legal merits without going into those prolonged and searching inquiries regarding the need of a remedy and the adequacy of proposed legislation which Mr.

Justice Brandeis pursued with ardor. To the latter, the law is an agency of good, an avenue to justice, an instrument of public service.

The unlikeness of judicial approach between Justices Holmes and Brandeis cannot be illustrated better than by a case in which they took opposite positions. The owners of land in Pennsylvania had made contracts with a mining company permitting operations under their homes, and the Legislature subsequently enacted a law forbidding mining beneath dwellings; the owners, when the company gave notice that it intended under its contract to proceed with excavations under the houses, sued to enforce the statute and were upheld in the lower court, whereupon the company appealed to the Supreme Court. Mr. Justice Holmes wrote the opinion reversing the case, and Mr. Justice Brandeis dissented. Admitting that the Pennsylvania statute destroyed previously existing rights of property and contract, Mr. Justice Holmes, who had been generous in dealing with the police power of the States, and had extended its area, denied that in this case it could be stretched so far:

> "Government hardly could go on if to some extent values incident to property could not be diminished without paying for every such change in the general law. As long recognized, some values are enjoyed under an implied limitation and must yield to the police power. But obviously the implied limitation must have its limits, or the contract and due process clauses are gone. . . .

> "The protection of private property in the Fifth Amendment presupposes that it is wanted for public use, but provides that it shall not be taken for such use without compensation. A similar assumption is made in the decisions upon the Fourteenth Amendment. . . . When this seemingly absolute protection is found to be qualified by the police power, the na-

tural tendency of human nature is to extend the qualification more and more until at last private property
disappears. But it cannot be accomplished in this way
under the Constitution of the United States. . . .

"We are in danger of forgetting that a strong public
desire to improve the public condition is not enough
to warrant achieving the desire by a shorter cut than
the constitutional way of paying for the change."[4]

The coal was still in the ground, Mr. Justice Brandeis argued
in his dissent, so that nothing was being taken away from the
mining company; all that was sought to be prevented was a
"noxious use".

"Every restriction [he wrote] upon the use of property imposed in the exercise of the police power de-
prives the owner of some right theretofore enjoyed,
and is, in that sense, an abridgement by the State of
rights in property without making compensation. But
restriction imposed to protect the public health, safety, or morals from dangers threatened is not a taking.
The restriction here in question is merely the prohibition of a noxious use."

As for the diminution in value, Mr. Justice Brandeis noted
that "values are relative", and added: "I suppose no one would
contend that by selling his interest above one hundred feet from
the surface he could prevent the State from limiting, by the police power, the height of structures in a city. And why should a
sale of underground rights bar the State's power?" He thought,
too, that the Supreme Court should defer to the State court's
greater familiarity with local conditions. Contracts between private individuals, he maintained, could not prevent the exercise
of the police power. He saw no reason for considering "recipro-
city of advantage", save that the mine operators had "the advantage of living and doing business in a civilized community".

Mr. Justice Brandeis was concerned with the private rights

and the safety of homes in a civilized community; Mr. Justice Holmes was concerned with the application of constitutional principles. He might have echoed John Marshall: "It is a Constitution we are expounding."

The effect of a decision upon the community and the persons involved, and upon the future, engross Mr. Justice Brandeis. Within the contours of the law he perceives organic benisons or evils, and by exhaustless inquiry he satisfies himself as to their nature. His realism is largely in terms of accountancy. The realism of Mr. Justice Holmes is philosophic and abstract. One is concerned with social justice in the concrete, the other is animated by a large tolerance. Both, however, revealed in the opinions held in common that they thought of the law as something devised for mankind's advantage, not its enslavement; both were unwilling to attach undue importance to precedents merely as such, and both realized that the Supreme Court must not only "umpire the Federal system" but function to some extent in the control of social and governmental affairs. Thus they were often in accord, especially where the Fourteenth Amendment and the Commerce Clause were concerned.

A fairly good cross-section of the methods and mentalities of the two Justices can be obtained by an examination of another case in which they agreed substantially but wrote separate opinions. It was a five-to-four labor decision, in which Justices Pitney and Clarke also dissented. In 1916 the employes of a restaurant in Bisbee, Arizona, struck; and by picketing, handbills and banners they informed the public that the employer was "unfair". The owner vainly sought an injunction and appealed to the Supreme Court, invoking the "due process" clause of the Fourteenth Amendment.[5]

Chief Justice Taft wrote the majority opinion, setting forth that the business was a property right, that it was reduced from $55,000 to $12,000 a year, and that the abusive epithets and libellous attacks, although there was no violence, were illegal.

Mr. Justice Brandeis noted that the employer had a legal right to carry on his business for profit, and to buy merchandise or labor at such prices as he chose.

"This right to carry on business—be it called liberty or property—has value, and he who interferes with the right without cause renders himself liable. But for cause the right may be interfered with and even be destroyed. Such cause exists when, in the pursuit of an equal right to further their several interests, his competitors make inroads upon his trade, or when suppliers of merchandise or of labor make inroads upon his profits. What methods and means are permissible in this struggle of contending forces is determined in part by decisions of the courts, in part by acts of the Legislature. The rules governing the contest necessarily change from time to time. For conditions change, and furthermore, the rules evolved being merely experiments in government, must be discarded when they prove to be failures.

"Practically every change in the law governing the relation of employer and employe must abridge, in some respect, the liberty or property of one of the parties, if liberty and property be measured by the standard of the law theretofore prevailing. If such changes are made by acts of the Legislature, we call the modification an exercise of the police power. And, although the change may involve interference with existing liberty or property of individuals, the statute will not be declared a violation of the due process clause, unless the Court finds that the interference is arbitrary or unreasonable or that, considered as a means, the measure has no real or substantial relation of cause to a permissible end. Nor will such changes in the law governing contests between employer and employe be held to be violative of the equal protection clause merely because the liberty or property of individuals in other relations to each other (for instance, as competitors in trade or as vendor and purchaser) would not, under similar circumstances, be subject to like abridgment. Few laws are of universal application. It is of the nature of our law that it has dealt, not with man in general, but with him in relationships. . . .

"Whether a law enacted in the exercise of the police power is justly subject to the charge of being unreasonable or arbitrary can ordinarily be determined only by a consideration of the contemporary conditions, social, industrial, and political, of the community to be affected thereby. Resort to such facts is necessary, among other things, in order to appreciate the evils sought to be remedied and the possible effects of the remedies proposed."[6]

Mr. Justice Brandeis reviewed at some length the application of the common law to the struggle between employers and employes, peaceful picketing and boycotting, and the situation in England from early days. He dissented from the majority view on the ground that the employer had not been deprived of property without "due process" nor had he been denied equal protection of the laws. These brief excerpts give no adequate notion of the close reasoning and wide knowledge which went into the document.

Mr. Justice Holmes, agreeing with "the more elaborate expositions of my brothers Pitney and Brandeis", wrote certain observations which exhibited his expertness as a verbal fencer, from which only one or two brief excerpts need be repeated here:

"The dangers of a delusive exactness in the application of the Fourteenth Amendment have been adverted to before now. . . . Delusive exactness is a source of fallacy throughout the law. By calling a business 'property' you make it seem like land, and lead up to the conclusion that a statute cannot substantially cut down the advantages of ownership existing before the statute was passed. An established business no doubt may have pecuniary value and commonly is protected by law against various unjustified injuries. But you cannot give it definiteness of contour by calling it a thing. It is a course of conduct and like other conduct is subject to substantial modification according to time and circumstances both in itself and in regard to what shall justify doing it a harm. . . .

"I must add one general consideration. There is nothing I more deprecate than the use of the Fourteenth Amendment beyond the absolute compulsion of its words to prevent the making of social experiments that an important part of the community desires, in the insulated chambers afforded by the several States, even though the experiments may seem futile or even noxious to me and to those whose judgment I most respect."[7]

In another five-to-four decision Justices Holmes and Brandeis were found together in the minority, although the majority rested mainly on an earlier opinion Mr. Justice Holmes himself had written. Under the Revenue Act of 1916, Congress made stock dividends subject to the income tax, and a woman holding stock in the Standard Oil Company of California, when in 1916 it declared a stock dividend totalling some $25,000,000, paid her tax but sued to recover. Mr. Justice Pitney, writing the opinion for the majority of five, held that stock dividends were an increase in capital investment and not income, and cited as authority an opinion which had been written by Mr. Justice Holmes and which dealt with an earlier Revenue Act, passed in 1913.[8] Mr. Justice Brandeis, with Mr. Justice Clarke concurring, wrote a lengthy analysis and interpretation which revealed afresh (this was in 1920) his extraordinary mastery of corporate methods and fiscal machinery. "But it is contended," he wrote, "that, because the simple method was adopted of having the new stock issued direct to the stockholders as paid-up stock, the new stock is not to be deemed income, whether she retained it or converted it into cash by sale. If such a different result can flow merely from the difference in the method pursued, it must be because Congress is without power to tax as income of the stockholder either the stock received under the latter method or the proceeds of its sale; . . . Is there anything in the phraseology of the Sixteenth Amendment or in the nature of corporate dividends which should lead to a departure from these rules of construction and compel this Court to hold that Congress is powerless to prevent a result so extraordinary as is here contended for by the stockholder?" It seemed clear to him that Congress had the power to make dividends representing profits taxable as income, whether the medium of payment was cash or stock. "It surely is not clear," he added, "that the enact-ment exceeds the power granted by the Sixteenth Amendment. And as this Court has so often said, the high prerogative of declaring an Act of Congress invalid should never be exercised except in a clear case."[9]

Mr. Justice Holmes thought it needful to add a word regarding the earlier decision he had written. "I think that Towne *v.* Eisner was right in its reasoning and result," he said, "and that on sound principles the stock dividend was not income. But it was clearly intimated in that case that the construction of the statute then before the Court might be different from that of the Constitution. . . . I think that the word 'incomes' in the Sixteenth Amendment should be read in 'a sense most obvious to the common understanding at the time of its adoption.' . . . For it was for public adoption that it was proposed. . . .

"The known purpose of this Amendment was to get rid of nice questions as to what might be direct taxes, and I cannot doubt that most people not lawyers would suppose when they voted for it that they put a question like the present to rest. I am of opinion that the Amendment justifies the tax."[10]

In nearly three score dissents Justices Brandeis and Holmes

have fully agreed, one signing the other's opinion. Neither is a chronic objector. Each agrees with the majority far oftener than he agrees with the other in a minority position. It so happened that they fully agreed in a case which came up soon after Mr. Justice Brandeis ascended the bench, a child-labor act to prohibit the interstate shipment of goods made by children less than fourteen years of age. Mr. Justice Day, for the majority, said that the act did not regulate transportation "but aims to standardize the ages at which children may be employed in mining and manufacturing within the States." He thought that Congress had overstepped its authority, and that if it were not held invalid the powers of local government might finally be crushed and "our system of government be practically destroyed."

Justices Brandeis, McKenna and Clarke joined Mr. Justice Holmes, who wrote:

> "It would not be argued today that the power to regulate does not include the power to prohibit. Regulation means the prohibition of something, and when interstate commerce is the matter to be regulated, I cannot doubt that the regulation may prohibit any part of such commerce that Congress sees fit to forbid. . . .
>
> "The notion that prohibition is any less prohibition when applied to things now thought evil I do not understand. But if there is any matter upon which civilized countries have agreed—far more unanimously than they have with regard to intoxicants and some other matters over which this country is now emotionally aroused—it is the evil of premature and excessive child labor. I should have thought that if we were to introduce our own moral conceptions where in my opinion they do not belong, this was preëminently a case for upholding the exercise of all its powers by the United States.

> "... It is not for this Court to pronounce when pro-
> hibition is necessary to regulation if it ever may be ne-
> cessary—to say that it is permissible as against strong
> drink but not as against the product of ruined
> lives."[11]

It is easy to see how Mr. Justice Brandeis, with his passion for
social justice, could sign that flaming opinion with a good conscience. Both these men, whatever their fine intellectual equilibrium, have on occasion "burned to and fro in fury beautiful".
Twice the majority of the Supreme Court had overridden the
will of Congress in regard to child labor; and so the Sixty-eighth
Congress, in 1924, had recourse to a device adopted early in the
history of this country to circumvent that tribunal: it proposed
as a joint resolution the adoption of the Twentieth Amendment
to the Constitution, giving it the power to "limit, regulate, and
prohibit the labor of persons under eighteen years of age".

There were times, too, when Mr. Justice Brandeis, particularly if free speech were at issue, could write in a fashion to
which Mr. Justice Holmes could subscribe with a good conscience. The record here is eloquent and copious. Even though
passages torn from their context lose much of their value, let us
consider excerpts from such opinions, written by Mr. Justice
Brandeis, in which Mr. Justice Holmes could concur without
qualification of so much as a phrase.

Officials and editors of the Philadelphia *Tageblatt* were sentenced, under the Espionage Act of 1917, for the publication of
reports held to promote the success of this nation's enemies.[12]
Mr. Justice McKenna, voicing the view of the majority, observed that free speech was not an absolute right and that this
case afforded the "curious spectacle" of men invoking the Constitution "to justify the activities of anarchy". Mr. Justice Clarke
dissented, not because he thought the right of free expression
was in danger but because he thought the men had not been
fairly tried. Mr. Justice Brandeis quoted from an earlier unani-
mous decision of the Court, written by Mr. Justice Holmes, that

the question at issue in such instances was whether words had been so used "as to create a clear and present danger" of the sort Congress had a right to prevent.[13]

> "This [said Mr. Justice Brandeis] is a rule of reason. Correctly applied, it will preserve the right of free speech both from suppression by tyrannous, well-meaning majorities, and from abuse by irresponsible, fanatical minorities. Like many other rules for human conduct, it can be applied correctly only by the exercise of good judgment; and to the exercise of good judgment calmness is, in times of deep feeling and on subjects which excite passion, as essential as fearlessness and honesty. . . .
>
> "The jury which found men guilty of publishing news items or editorials like those here in question must have supposed it to be within their province to condemn men, not merely for disloyal acts, but for a disloyal heart; provided only that the heart was evidenced by some utterance. To prosecute men for such publications reminds of the days when men were hanged for constructive treason. . . . To hold that such publications can be suppressed as false reports, subjects to new perils the constitutional liberty of the press, already seriously curtailed in practice under powers assumed to have been conferred upon the postal authorities. Nor will this grave danger end with the passing of the war. The constitutional right of free speech has been declared to be the same in peace and war. . . . Convictions such as these, besides abridging freedom of speech, threaten freedom of thought and belief."[14]

Justices Holmes and Brandeis were staunch defenders of the freedom of the press, although minority defenders. What they were saying in those days was destined in time to become the majority opinion of the Court. If President Wilson had carried out his original intention of taking Brandeis into his Cabinet, preferably as Attorney General, the administration might have been spared, through council-table discussion, the embarrassment inflicted upon it by the flag-waving and intolerant Postmaster General, Albert Sidney Burleson. Mr. Burleson closed the mails arbitrarily against Victor Berger's Socialist *Milwaukee Leader,* and Mr. Justice Clarke, who delivered the Court's decision, held that the Postmaster General had that power, because of the paper's "willful attempt to cause disloyalty and refusal of duty in the military and naval forces and to obstruct the recruiting and enlistment service".[15] Justices Holmes and Brandeis wrote separate opinions.

"The United States may give up the Post Office when it sees fit," said Mr. Justice Holmes, "but while it carries on, the use of the mails is almost as much a part of free speech as the right to use our tongues, and it would take very strong language to convince me that Congress ever intended to give such a practically despotic power to any one man. There is no pretense that it has done so. . . . When I consider the ease with which the power claimed by the Postmaster could be used to interfere with very sacred rights, I am of the opinion that the refusal to allow the relator the rate to which it was entitled whenever its newspaper was carried, on the ground that the paper ought not to have been carried at all, was unjustified by the statute and was a serious attack upon the liberties that not even the war induced Congress to infringe."[16]

The power claimed by Burleson was not a war power, Mr. Justice Brandeis insisted. "There is no question of its necessity to protect the country from insidious domestic foes." To that end Congress had conferred enormous power on the Postmaster General. "But it did not confer—and the Postmaster General concedes that it did not confer—the vague and absolute authority practically to deny circulation to any publication which in his opinion is likely to violate in the future any postal law. The grant of that power is construed into a postal statute passed forty years ago which has never before been suspected of containing such implications. . . . If, under the Constitution, administrative officers may, as a mere incident of the peace-time administration of their departments, be vested with the power to issue such orders as this, there is little of substance in our Bill of Rights, and in every extension of governmental functions lurks a new danger to civil liberty."[17]

Freedom of assembly and individual freedom of thought, opinion and speech were close to the hearts of both these great jurists. In the famous case of Charlotte Anita Whitney, convicted under the California "criminal syndicalism" statute because she helped organize a branch of the Communist Labor Party in Oakland,[18] Mr. Justice Brandeis, with Mr. Justice Holmes concurring, sided with the majority but wrote a separate opinion which had a Holmesian quality of thought and expression:

> "Those who won our independence believed that the final end of the State was to make men free to develop their faculties, and that in its government the deliberative forces should prevail over the arbitrary. They valued liberty both as an end and as a means. They believed liberty to be the secret of happiness and courage to be the secret of liberty. They believed that freedom to think as you will and to speak as you think are means indispensable to the discovery and spread of political truth; that without free speech and assembly discussion would be futile; that with them, discussion affords ordinarily adequate protection against the dissemination of noxious doctrines; that the greatest menace to freedom is an inert people; that public discussion is a political duty; and that this should be a fundamental principle of the American government. They recognized the risks to which all human institutions are subject. But they knew that

order cannot be secured merely through fear of punishment for its infraction; that it is hazardous to discourage thought, hope, and imagination; that fear breeds repression; that repression breeds hate; that hate menaces stable government; that the path of safety lies in the opportunity to discuss freely supposed grievances and proposed remedies; and that the fitting remedy for evil counsels is good ones. Believing in the power of reason as applied through public discussion, they eschewed silence coerced by law—the argument of force in its worst form. Recognizing the occasional tyrannies of governing majorities, they amended the Constitution so that free speech and assembly should be guaranteed.

"Fear of serious injury cannot alone justify suppression of free speech and assembly. Men feared witches and burned women. It is the function of speech to free men from the bondage of irrational fears."[19]

Never were the plans, purposes and ideals of the Founding Fathers more thoroughly aired in Supreme Court opinions than in a relatively insignificant case which happened to involve a delicate Constitutional question unclarified in some 136 years. A postmaster who had been removed by the President without Senate action sued to recover his salary, and the question was whether the executive authority could be conditioned by Congress.[20] The opinions of Chief Justice Taft, who wrote the majority decision, and of Justices McReynolds, Brandeis and Holmes, who wrote separate dissents, give excellent documented pictures of the early debates on the power of the President and of legislation about the removal of his subordinates. The framers of the Constitution, deeply influenced by Montesquieu, who thought that the British government of his day owed its strength mainly to the separation of powers, executive, legislative and judicial, provided for "checks and balances". Yet there grew up in Washington scores of commissions, bureaus and other units which exercised one or more of these powers.

Mr. Justice Holmes, emphasizing his agreement with the conclusions reached by his brothers after "exhaustive research", thought that the arguments drawn from the executive power appeared but "spiders' webs inadequate to control the dominant facts". The dominant fact was: "We have to deal with an office that owes its existence to Congress and that Congress may abolish tomorrow. . . . Congress alone confers on the President the power to appoint to it and at any time may transfer the power to other hands."[21] Mr. Justice Brandeis, in a somewhat lengthier opinion, discussed the separation of the powers of government as not making each branch completely autonomous. "It left each in some measure dependent upon the others, as it left to each power to exercise, in some respects, functions in their nature executive, legislative and judicial." The document is packed with wise observations on our government. "Checks and balances were established in order that this should be 'a government of laws and not of men'." The purpose was "not to avoid friction, but, by means of the inevitable friction incident to the distribution of governmental powers among three departments, to save the people from autocracy." In the Constitutional Convention at Philadelphia every proposal to confer "uncontrollable power upon the President was rejected"; and he concluded: "In America, as in England, the conviction prevailed then that the people must look to representative assemblies for the protection of their liberties. And protection of the individual, even if he be an official, from the arbitrary or capricious exercise of power was then believed to be an essential of free government."[22]

In dissent every Justice may speak more freely than when he is expressing the point of view of five or more men who have arrived, as a rule, at a compromise, or at least a general position tenable by all. It may well be said that the majority opinions of Justices Holmes and Brandeis are more representative and more important than their dissents; but it still is true that when in the minority they have given us striking passages of judicial courage and wisdom.

As the years went on, thanks to changes in the personnel of the Court, Justices Holmes and Brandeis were to find themselves strangely among the majority. There was a new "conservative" minority. It would be pleasant to suppose that those two, uniting in a "pincers" intellectual strategy upon an obstinate entrenched bloc, finally prevailed by the unassisted might of their thought and the overpowering right of their position. The truth is that mysterious forces are always at work on the side of great historical minorities. "The stars in their courses fought against Sisera"; the commander-in-chief of Jabin's army of Canaanites, routed by Barak, was treacherously slain by Jael when he sought refuge in her tent. The fate of Abraham and the cities of the plain, of Elijah, the general Biblical dogma of Numbers and the Remnant, confirm that story; and in secular history Galileo, despite the Inquisition, Jeanne d'Arc despite the Bishop of Beauvais and the fagots, Patrick Henry despite the cries of "Treason!" in the House of Burgesses, have triumphed in the end.

"How much more the world is governed today," says Mr. Justice Holmes, "by Kant than by Bonaparte."[23]

CHAPTER 17

Washington and Beverly Farms

AFTER MOVING to Washington, Mr. Justice Holmes settled into a routine of life which must have seemed to outsiders laborious and monotonous. For twenty-four years he did not miss a session of the Supreme Court. His birthday anniversaries were no more sacred to him than other days, and unless the eighth of March fell on a Sunday, or on a Saturday, when the Court conferred about cases before it, he was to be found on the bench, as diligently attentive as at any other time. As in Massachusetts, he kept his separate docket, in longhand, with copious notes. At seventy he could have retired with pay. When he was questioned about rumors that he would resign on account of his age, he was accustomed to reply that he would not resign until the work ceased to be fun. When Mr. Justice Brandeis ascended the bench he was next in age, and he was fifteen years the junior; Mr. Justice Homes, however, disposed of more cases than most of his associates, and he attacked each of them with high spirit and an unquenchable zest.

Until the Justice was eighty-six years old he walked to and from the Capitol, more than two miles each way. Thereafter he sometimes used a hired automobile, and sometimes accepted a lift from one of his associates. Even when he was well past sixty, he and Mrs. Holmes, so sprightly were they, used to run together to fires. In the Washington home, at 1720 I Street, there were pieces of antique furniture, of which Mrs. Holmes was fond, and some valuable rugs. Beneath the old-fashioned chandelier with its large glass globes, in the library, hung a toy skeleton, which Mrs. Holmes sometimes agitated while twitting the Justice about his age. She was as high-spirited as he, and as fun-loving.

[303]

Mr. Justice Holmes was in the habit of rising early, breaking his fast with fruit, cereal, toast and coffee, and working in his library until 11:30 o'clock, when it was time to set out for the Court. The members allowed themselves but half an hour for lunch, and when the afternoon session was at an end scattered for their residences, which served also as their offices. Mr. Justice Holmes was by way of working until close to seven, and even until after eleven o'clock on busy evenings. On October 4, 1928, when he was eighty-seven years, six months and twenty-nine days old, he became the oldest Justice ever to serve there; before that it had been Chief Justice Roger Brooke Taney, successor to John Marshall.

The willingness of Mr. Justice Holmes to take all the cases assigned to him amounted to little less than greediness. His prodigious capacity for work and his fondness for it astounded his younger and less energetic associates, whom he sometimes addressed as "Infant". He was fond of reading, as well as of work, and he was fond of conversation, according always to younger men a deferential and inquiring attention which they found most flattering. His duties, however, left him less time than he might have wished for companionship and books other than legal. As he grew older he grew especially to like Pepys's *Diary*, but he was still old-fashioned enough to cling, when he could, to "naughty" French novels. (The adjective was applied to them by Mrs. Holmes.) The heyday of the French novel was in the nineties, of course, but even four decades later the Justice's appetite for them was unabated. A visitor reported to him that one of these books had been represented to him as "the most sophisticated novel ever put between covers, and not in the least nasty." The Justice pricked up his ears at once. "Have you read it?" In due season it was passed along to him.

One need no longer be considered somewhat "fast", as was a character in *Little Women*, merely because one reads the deft and witty descriptions of life as depicted by French authors. American authors are no more reticent than they, although perhaps not quite so oblique. To Mr. Justice Holmes a mere alteration in general reading habits could not act as a deterrent; he continued when he could find time to indulge in this frivolous and light-hearted diversion. That is but one way of saying that he continues, even past ninety, to evince a lively interest in the foibles of men as well as in their weightier struggles.

Residence in Washington during the summer is well-nigh insupportable to those not inured to the climate, and the Supreme Court Justices leave for homes in more habitable areas, if they have them, from June to October, during what is ostensibly a vacation. Actually it is a period well filled with work, for the members of the Court must pass on whether cases shall be admitted to the coming docket. Sacks full of writs of certiorari go out from Washington to them, for nearly every lawyer, when his client can afford it, would like to get a case into the Supreme Court. If all the writs offered sufficient cause and were granted the tribunal could never wade through its work, even with an amplified personnel. But each case must be examined painstakingly, and much of the "vacation" of each Justice is spent in poring and pondering over the questions thus presented.

From the first Mr. Justice Holmes went to his place at Beverly Farms, Massachusetts. Thus he escaped the official and social conventions of the capital as well as its heat. The elder Oliver Wendell Holmes had bought this place when it was known as "Screeching Beach" and when the nearby islands were called "Big and Little Misery". As it became fashionable the names were changed to "Singing Beach" and "Mystery Isles", to the great amusement of the Justice. The residents thereabout regarded him as a native (which was as high a compliment as they could have paid him), and the old watchman at the railroad station, of the family of the poet, Lucy Larcom (born there in 1826), was one of his cronies. His housekeeper, Anne, had been there since his father's day.

In this brown frame house, Victorian and simple, approached by a gravel drive beside formal flower-beds of roses and cannas and petunias and marigolds—the work of Mrs. Holmes—the Justice called to his aid his secretary, each year a new sprig from the Harvard Law School, in passing on the multitude of cases that fell to his attention. The appointment to serve as secretary to the Justice was from the first a feather in the cap of any man, and the year proved to be rich in memories. At once a relation was established by the Justice, not of master and man but of bantering friendship. One of the secretaries was reading *Tristram Shandy* when he was summoned to discuss a point, and suggested a case which he remembered from his Harvard training. That, he supposed, was all, and he returned to his book. After five minutes he heard from the adjoining room: "Do you think you might spare me a moment from your cultivated leisure to look out that citation?"

In an obscure prohibition case (this happened in Washington, not at Beverly Farms) Mr. Justice Holmes wrote: "The decisions under the revenue acts have little weight as against legislation under the afflatus of the Eighteenth Amendment."[1] The secretary thought the word "afflatus" might cause comment, and reminded the Justice that a good many people thought he rather delighted in using terms not commonly understood. "Yes," said Mr. Justice Holmes, "I felt myself that it was rather a cabriole word." He let it stand.

The same secretary once objected that the last paragraph of an opinion was not quite clear. "What the hell do you mean?—not clear! Give it to me. Well, if you don't understand it, there may be some other damn fool who won't. So I would better change it."

The former secretaries, who adore the Justice, delight in such stories. One of them objected to the phrasing of a certain opinion, maintaining that the shading given to one word meant that "there isn't more than one man in a thousand who will understand it."

"I write for that man," the Justice retorted.

Even at an age when others find their hands shaking, Mr. Justice Holmes continued to write his opinions and all his correspondence in longhand; and as he objected to having a typewriter in the house, his secretaries used longhand, too. Fortunately, it may be, the Justice was gifted with a valuable brevity. He could dispose even of complex and highly technical questions in laconic terms. Of an especially prolix and verbose associate he used to say that he was "poly-epic". Of another, that the premise of his opinion and the conclusion stood forth like precipices, with a roaring torrent of precedents between, but that he never quite understood how his associate got across.

Beverly Farms, which is on the north shore, is remote from Cape Cod and Chatham, where Mr. Justice Brandeis lives in summer, but the two managed to continue during their "vacation" the contact which they maintained in Washington. Before the death of Mrs. Holmes, she and the Justice used to ride about the countryside in a favorite brougham, and later in an automobile. Even after her death the Justice was fond of long morning walks, especially to West Beach, a swimming place near his home, less frequented than most of the others. Either there or elsewhere, and especially in the village, he often heard unsolicited opinions from his fellow townsmen about the state of the nation and of the world.

It was at Beverly Farms, in 1916, that Harold J. Laski was presented to the Justice, who took an immediate and lasting liking for the young English lecturer and writer. The two did not see each other again for ten years, but corresponded regularly; and in 1919 Mr. Laski edited the *Collected Legal Papers,* published the following year. In an introductory note to the book Mr. Justice Holmes thanked his friend "for gathering these little fragments of my fleece that I have left upon the hedges of life". He was glad, he said, to see these essays and speeches put together into a book. "A later generation has carried on the work that I began nearly half a century ago, and it is a great pleasure to an old warrior who cannot expect to bear arms much longer, that the brilliant young soldiers still give him a place in their councils of war." This was from a man, mind you, then not yet eighty, and younger mentally than most men in their prime.

It was at Beverly Farms, on August 20, 1927, that Mr. Justice
Holmes received Arthur Dehon Hill, counsel in the Sacco-Vanzetti case, to hear his application for a stay of execution.
Throughout Europe as well as in the United States feeling ran
high over this celebrated trial. Bartolomeo Vanzetti was convicted and sentenced to fifteen years in the penitentiary for an
abortive hold-up at Bridgewater, Mass., in which no one was
hurt and no money was stolen. He and Nicolo Sacco were convicted of a subsequent hold-up at South Braintree, Massachusetts, in which two men were killed and a payroll of nearly
$16,000 was taken. After they had been executed, two men made
sworn confessions to the Bridgewater crime, exonerating Vanzetti, and the facts of the confessions were supported in large
measure by independent investigation. Among those convinced
of the innocence of Sacco and Vanzetti it is now believed that the
South Braintree murders were the work of a gang having its
headquarters in Providence, Rhode Island. Prior to the execution there was a widespread feeling that the men, who were anar-
chists, were being made the victims of political prejudice. In ex-
plaining why there was no basis for interference by United States
Courts, Mr. Justice Holmes said:

> "This is a case of a crime charged under State laws
> and tried by a State Court. I have absolutely no author-
> ity as a Judge of the United States to meddle with it. If
> the proceedings were void in a legal sense, as when the
> forms of a trial are gone through in a Court surrounded
> and invaded by an infuriated mob ready to lynch pris-
> oner, counsel and jury if there is not a prompt convic-
> tion, in such a case no doubt I might issue a habeas cor-
> pus—not because I was a Judge of the United States,
> but simply as anyone having authority to issue the writ
> might do so, on the ground that a void proceeding was
> no warrant for the detention of the accused. No one
> who knows anything of the law would hold that the
> trial of Sacco and Vanzetti was a void proceeding. They

might argue that it was voidable and ought to be set aside by those having power to do it, but until set aside, the proceeding must stand. That is the difference between void and voidable—and I have no power to set the proceeding aside—that, subject to the exception that I shall mention, rests wholly with the State. I have received many letters from people who seem to suppose that I have a general discretion to see that justice is done. They are written with the confidence that sometimes goes with ignorance of the law. Of course, as I have said, I have no such power. The relation of the United States and the Courts of the United States to the States and the Courts of the States, is a very delicate matter that has occupied the thoughts of statesmen and judges for a hundred years and cannot be disposed of by a summary statement that justice requires me to cut red tape and to intervene. For stronger cases than this have arisen with regard to the blacks, when the Supreme Court has denied its power.

"A State decision may be set aside by the Supreme Court of the United States—not by a single Justice of that Court—if the record of the case shows that the Constitution has been infringed in specific ways. An application for a writ of certiorari has been filed on the ground that the record shows such an infringement; and the writ of habeas corpus having been denied, I am asked to grant a stay of execution until that application can be considered by the full Court. I assume that under the Statute my power extends to this case although I am not free from doubt. But it is a power rarely exercised and I should not be doing my duty if I exercised it unless I thought that there was a reasonable chance that the Court would entertain the application and ultimately reverse the judgment. This I cannot bring myself to believe. The essential fact of record that is relied upon is that the question of Judge

Thayer's prejudice, raised and it is said discovered only after the trial and verdict, was left to Judge Thayer and not to another Judge. But as I put it to counsel if the Constitution of Massachusetts had provided that a trial before a single Judge should be final, without appeal, it would have been consistent with the Constitution of the United States. In such a case there would be no (5516) remedy for prejudice on the part of the Judge except Executive Clemency. Massachusetts has done more than that. I see nothing in the Constitution warranting a complaint that it has not done more still.

"It is asked how it would be if the Judge were subsequently shown to have been corruptly interested or insane. I will not attempt to decide at what point a judgment might be held to be absolutely void on these grounds. It is perfectly plain that although strong language is used in the present application the judgment was not void even if I interpret the affidavits as proving all that the petitioners think they prove—which is somewhat more than I have drawn from them. I do not consider that I am at liberty to deal with this case differently from the way in which I should treat one that excited no public interest and that was less powerfully presented. I cannot say that I have a doubt and therefore I must deny the stay. But although I must act on my convictions I do so without prejudice to an application to another of the Justices which I should be very glad to see made, as I am far from saying that I think counsel was not warranted in presenting the question raised in the application by this and the previous writ. (5517)."[2]

Mr. Justice Brandeis on the next day refused to take any action in the case, because "of personal relations with some of the people interested". Mrs. Brandeis and a daughter had shown their interest in the case. Mr. Justice Stone was on an island off the coast of Maine, and on the next day also declined to take action. "I concur," he said, "in the view expressed by Justice Holmes as to the merits of the application and action of counsel in presenting it." Chief Justice Taft was in Canada, and refused, as three others of the Court were available, to cross the border and consider an application.

Both at Beverly Farms and in Washington the dinner table of Mr. Justice Holmes (in Washington he and Mrs. Holmes often ate at the old Shoreham Hotel) was a gathering place of distinguished men and women. A certain Britisher was a guest in 1916 and Senator Henry Cabot Lodge, who was there, told the Englishman that his heart was with Great Britain in the war.

"But," said the Britisher, "I thought you were fond of twisting the lion's tail."

"Since 1914," Mrs. Holmes interrupted, "he has worn it as a girdle."

Just before the outbreak of the World War Mr. Justice Holmes returned from a trip to England with the first Viscount Haldane, author and Liberal statesman, at the time Lord High Chancellor, who was coming to this country to deliver an address before the American Bar Association. The two were much together aboard ship, and Lord Haldane afterward called Mr. Justice Holmes "the founder of American jurisprudence", linking his name with the name of Blackstone.

Permission has been given to quote here a letter written when Arthur Garfield Hayes sent to the Justice, in the Spring of 1928, a copy of his book, *Let Freedom Ring*. The lawyer-author received in return a "word of caution".

> "My dear Sir: The duties of my occupation make it impossible for me to do more than glance through your book, but the kind inscription and the spirit that moves you lead me to venture a line or two. I cannot but suspect that you are a little over-wrought upon your theme. I can remember the time before the Civil

War when I was deeply moved by the abolition cause —so deeply that a Negro minstrel show shocked me and the morality of Pickwick seemed to me painfully blunt. I have no right to an opinion as to public conditions for I am a recluse and don't even read the papers. Moreover, at times I have felt as you do. Nevertheless, I rather more than hope that there is more intelligent and high minded thinking on public matters than ever before. One has to remember that when one's interest is keenly excited evidence gathers from all sides around the magnetic point, and that one must mistrust the suggested conclusion. Just after the Civil War there appeared on the fences and everywhere S T 1560 X. I believe it was an advertisement, perhaps of bitters, which then had a locus standi. I said and proved to myself that if one should accept that as a revelation of the secret of the universe one would be astonished by the corroboration that a fortnight would furnish. I think that a type of the way our minds act. I venture this word of caution from the experience of an old man.

Very sincerely yours,
O. W. HOLMES."

Despite an irrepressible gaiety, Mr. Justice Holmes had long been accustomed, when this letter was written, to speak of himself as "an old man", however unwilling his friends and admirers might be to admit that the years had so much as touched him. Sir Frederick Pollock, writing under the title, *"Ad Multos Annos"*, said that the Justice "does resemble Savigny not only in being a great master of the law but in being a master of style"; and, "relying on the privilege of ancient men to be discursive" (he is the lively junior of the Justice by six years), he amplified the point:

"Everyone who is acquainted with our law books [he said] must perceive the difference between those

learned persons who care only to get their meaning expressed somehow and those who take pains to clothe
it in well-turned English. A striking example may be
seen in John and William Scott, two brothers who
were great builders of the law in their distinct
branches. Lord Eldon had no style at all, and if any
man ever read a judgment of his for pleasure, his taste
must have been odd. Lord Stowell's judgments are
models of classical exposition. . . . The difference between the artist and the plain conscientious workman
lurks in a legendary dialogue between the two;
'Brother John,' said Stowell, 'this port is good.'
'Brother William,' said Eldon, 'all port is good, but
some port is better than other.' Evidently Lord Stowell's taste in port, as in English, was the finer. In a later
generation there is a similar contrast between Jessel,
M. R., the greatest equity judge of his time except
Lord Cairns, and Lord Bowen, who was second to
none in the Common Law; the one a downright, clear-
headed, exact and common-sense lawyer, with his
knowledge always ready and never elaborated (in fact
his judgments were seldom written); the other a finished scholar, whose judgments are not only landmarks
of the law, but excellent literature. Mr. Justice
Holmes is of the fellowship of Stowell and Bowen;
and this is not a matter of mere delight or ornament,
for one result is that even readers who are not learned
in the law can learn much of its broader reasons and
policy by following the main currents of his thought.
. . . But he can glorify the law, too, with the imagination of a poet."[3]

Among the "hoarded treasures" of Judge Benjamin N. Cardozo is a letter from the Justice, and he has quoted from it these
excerpts: "I have always thought that not place or power or popu-
larity makes the success that one desires, but the trembling hope

that one has come near to an ideal. The only ground that warrants a man for thinking that he is not in a fool's paradise if he ventures such a hope is the voice of a few masters. . . . I feel it so much that I don't want to talk about it."

"This," said Judge Cardozo, "from the great overlord of the law and its philosophy.

"One does not know where to match the thought in its perfection and engaging modesty unless in the 'trembling hope' of another worshipper of truth and beauty. The wistful words of Keats re-echo through the spaces of a century. 'I think I shall be among the English poets after my death.'

"There was no 'fool's paradise' for Keats, nor will there be for Holmes."[4]

CHAPTER 18

His Ninetieth Milestone

WHEN MR. JUSTICE HOLMES was ninety years old he received tributes such as seldom come to any man during his lifetime. The law reviews of three universities, Harvard, Yale and Columbia, dedicated issues to him; over a nation-wide radio hook-up the Chief Justice of the United States, the president of the American Bar Association, and the dean of the Yale Law School united in praise; the Old World conferred upon him one of its highest distinctions by making him an honorary bencher of the Honorable Society of Lincoln's Inn of London, linking his name thus with the names of William Pitt, Oliver Cromwell, Benjamin Disraeli and William Gladstone; the International Mark Twain Society presented its silver medal to him, and a special book, a symposium of praiseful estimates, was published and presented to him as a birthday gift. His home (for the anniversary fell on a Sunday, March 8, 1931) was flooded with telegrams and letters of congratulation.

Cyril Clemens of Webster Groves, a suburb of St. Louis, asked the Justice whether he would accept the Mark Twain medal in recognition of his work, and he replied that he would be proud to have it "though I hardly know what I have done to deserve it." The day it arrived he wrote that he thought it "quite charming" and that he would keep it "so long as I can keep anything on earth." He put it with a copy of *Innocents Abroad,* which Samuel Clemens had sent to the elder Oliver Wendell Holmes many years before.

The editors of the *Yale Law Journal* dedicated their issue to the Justice as "preëminent in the legal world," and presented articles by Harold J. Laski and Hessel E. Yntema; in the *Columbia Law Review* were articles by Sir Frederick Pollock and Morris R. Cohen; and in *The Harvard Graduates' Magazine* the leading article, by Arthur Dehon Hill, was a biographical sketch and glowing estimate of "the most distinguished Harvard Graduate now in public life." The contributors to the *Harvard Law Review* were Lord Sankey and Sir William Jowitt, the Lord High Chancellor and Attorney General of Great Britain, and Sir Frederick Pollock, then Judge of the Cinque Ports; Chief Judge Benjamin N. Cardozo of the New York Court of Appeals; Chief Justice Charles Evans Hughes, Roscoe Pound, dean of the Law School, Theodore F. T. Plucknett, assistant professor of Legal History, and Felix Frankfurter, Byrne Professor of Administrative Law there.[1] With the help of Henry M. Hart, Jr., Dr. Frankfurter prepared as an appendix a "synoptic table" of all the decisions handed down by Holmes while Judge and Chief Justice of the Massachusetts Supreme Judicial Court. The editors of the publication spoke of Mr. Justice Holmes as "one who finds in the law a constant adventure, ministering to an eternal youthfulness of spirit. Perhaps it is this quality, above all else, which has won for him the peculiar admiration and affection of students of the law. The young soldiers do not merely give him a place in their councils of war; they look to him as their leader in thought and action."

Dr. Frankfurter edited also the symposium, *Mr. Justice Holmes,* reprinting most of the contributions to the Harvard periodical and others extending over a decade.[2] What Chief Justice Hughes wrote for the journal, as Dr. Frankfurter made clear later, was not included because it was not received in time. Reviewing the book for the *Journal* of the American Bar Association, George W. Wickersham alluded to a sentence in the Hughes contribution,—to the journal, not the book: "Nor am I one of those, in exploring that rich garden of utility and beauty, with its rare cultivation, who would be content merely with culling the roses that bloom among the thorns of dissent."

When this was written the Chief Justice was already ranked with the new "liberal" majority in the Supreme Court, but it was perhaps natural that he should speak of "the thorns of dissent", and should be unwilling to cull only roses from among them. Mr. Wickersham said of the symposium that "most of the writers of the essays in this volume were affected with no such scruples," and quoted Buffon's aphorism: *"Le style c'est l'homme."* These writers, he thought, dwelt as much on the style of Mr. Justice Holmes as on his other accomplishments or attributes. "His greatest title to an enduring place in the history of American jurisprudence," said Mr. Wickersham, "is to be found, not in the list of his dissents, but in the great volume of sound well-considered judgments in which he expressed the decisions of the court."

The contributors to the symposium, Mr. Wickersham thought, represented a school of thought to which, in general, the majority of the Supreme Court had been opposed. "This volume," he added, "can hardly be accepted as an appraisal. It is a dithyrambic of applause on the part of enthusiastic admirers of a common school of thought. Its value is as a *memoire pour servir*."[3]

Other critics might think that the essays were neither so vehement nor so wildly lyrical as a dithyramb is generally supposed to be; and to maintain that, since the volume was meant to be a tribute, there was no reason to expect in its pages that note of vigorous dissent from other concurrent views for which Justices Holmes and Brandeis—disproportionately, perhaps—had become widely known. Mr. Wickersham, in fact, conceded that the work of Chief Judge Cardozo, one of the contributors, closely resembled that of Mr. Justice Holmes in the beauty and clarity of its English. The list of names in the title of contents was of wide range and distinction.

The editors of the law reviews arranged for the radio broadcast the evening of the Justice's birthday, and he spoke, for the first time through that medium, over a microphone installed in his study. "In this symposium," he said, "my part is only to sit in silence. To express one's feelings as the end draws near is too intimate a task.

"But I may mention one thought that comes to me as a listener-in. The riders in a race do not stop short when they reach the goal. There is a little finishing canter before coming to a standstill. There is time to hear the kind voice of friends and to say to one's self: 'The work is done.'

"But just as one says that, the answer comes: 'The race is over, but the work never is done while the power to work remains.'

"The canter that brings you to a standstill need not be only coming to rest. It cannot be, while you still live. For to live is to function. That is all there is in living.

"And so I end with a line from a Latin poet who uttered the message more than fifteen hundred years ago:

" 'Death plucks my ear and says "Live, I am coming." ' "

The Justice repudiated the metaphor of "a little finishing canter" not only verbally to his impromptu audience of millions, but by proving that in his case the power to work remained unabated. During the next three months he did more than his share of the intense mental labor involved in clearing the Supreme Court calendar, so that when he left for Beverly Farms the congestion which a few years before had slowed its machinery was relieved. The Court, instead of adjourning for the summer with more than one thousand cases on its docket, had but an insignificant carry-over, quickly disposed of when the members reconvened, with every prospect that they could keep abreast of the business presented.

To this result Congress had contributed somewhat by enacting, in 1925, legislation amending the judicial code and more clearly defining the jurisdiction of the Circuit Courts of Appeals and of the Supreme Court; and in 1928, two years before his death, Chief Justice Taft had taken the lead in a revision of the rules of the Court, which still further facilitated its work. Before that, the Court had been considering nearly fifteen hundred cases each year, and for more than a decade had not been quite able to catch up. Ordinarily it was two years after the filing of a case before it could be argued and decided. After the reforms were effected, two or three months often sufficed, in spite of formal allowances of time for the filing of briefs and of printed statements and the printing of the record, sometimes running to thousands of pages. Upon the record, containing incidentally the judgments of lower courts, the Justices relied for the laws involved and the facts. Each member of the higher tribunal received and examined such a record in each case; and the nonagenarian on the bench was as industrious as his associates. Unless one takes into account a wider experience and knowledge and a faster-working mind, he was, on the face of the record, more industrious than the others.

That line from a Latin poet, "death plucks my ear", set thousands to thumbing books of quotations, translations, anthologies and indexes. Fifteen hundred years ago! Decimus Magnus Ausonius, who had died in France about 394, might qualify; and so might Aurelius Clemens Prudentius, who died about 400, and who was the chief Christian poet of the early Church. Neither of these filled the bill. But, exclaimed the sharp-witted, the Justice said "more than fifteen hundred years". Well, in one of those pastoral verselets in which shepherds speak, Tityus declares that Apollo "plucked my ear" and warned him that shepherds should feed fat sheep "and sing a thin-spun song". Milton, for that matter, had used the metaphor in his elegiac *Lycidas* when he wrote: "Phoebus replied and touched my trembling ears." But none of these would do. The searchers of dictionaries of quotations found what they wanted in *The Syrian Dancing Girl,* certainly not the sort of verse to have been written by the pious Prudentius. The poem is attributed to Vergil, despite its note of disenchantment, and its last line reads: *"Mors aurem vellens, 'Vivite,' ait, 'venio'."*

The girl was dancing to castanets in a tavern on a hot day. Helen Waddell, in *Medieval Latin Lyrics,* translates the poem sensitively and gives to her version that pagan modern note so unlike Vergil and so congruous with the taste of a Justice who was still reading his Latin, not in translations but in the original:

confined to such a category. . . . We place upon his brow the laurel crown of the highest distinction. But this will not suffice us for him. We honor him, but, what is more, we love him. We give him tonight the homage of our hearts."

This was the Chief Justice whose confirmation to that eminence had been fought in the Senate on the ground that, as counsel for many rich and powerful corporations, his attitude had been so influenced that he would add to the weight of reactionary opinion in the Supreme Court. Some of the grave and reverend seignors of that august body of debate were wrong again, although not so far wrong as when, misled in part by organized propaganda, a minority in the chamber had voted against Louis Dembitz Brandeis. They might indeed have looked into the record of Charles Evans Hughes and determined for themselves where he would fall, in the familiar cataloguing of Supreme Court members as "liberal" or "conservative". No hard and fast line can be drawn; but the life, opinions and times of Mr. Hughes should have made the Senators aware that he must be classified generally on the liberal side. It was true that he had argued skillfully and learnedly for the rights of property; it was true that his great powers had been commanded on occasion by "predatory" corporations; it was distinctly not true that on the bench he would be "the tool of the interests".

As Governor of New York the man proposed as Chief Justice had displayed convictions and qualities denounced at that time as "radical". His voice was raised afterward in protest—vain protest, it proved—against the exclusion from the New York Legislature of elected Socialists. He had first become a national figure, when past his fortieth year, by acting as counsel for successive committees of the State Legislature which were investigating the gas companies and the insurance companies. And although as Secretary of State for four years under Presidents Harding and Coolidge, and when he was a candidate for the Presidency in 1916, he may have exhibited somewhat the point of view of "the great aggregations of capital in this country", and exemplified to some extent "the influence of powerful combinations in the political and financial world", both of which charges were made against him as blanket indictments in the Senate debate, nevertheless the temper and mentality of the man were flexible and tolerant.

During six years as Associate Justice, Mr. Hughes had voted only about thirty times with the minority, but many of his majority opinions were distinctly liberal. He had joined in decisions or opinions upholding statutes limiting the hours of labor for women and children, penalizing "yellow dog" contracts against unions, fixing a minimum wage for women, and holding employers responsible for industrial injuries. When his name was offered for the Chief Justiceship he was fourteen years older, and it seemed to be taken for granted by the bloc in opposition that he had suffered in the meantime a sort of mental sclerosis. He disappointed these somewhat over-vigilant guardians of civil liberties by signing, soon after he took his post, measures wherein he agreed with Justices Holmes and Brandeis, and himself wrote some of the opinions. In the defense of the freedom of the daily press he was as upstanding and outspoken as were they. He wrote the majority opinion in the "Minnesota gag case".

Thus Mr. Justice Holmes, at ninety, after serving twenty years on the Massachusetts bench and twenty-eight in the highest tribunal of the land, not infrequently in favor of causes opposed by the majority of this Court or that, found himself one of a juristic *Trois Mousquetaires;* not without cause had he been compared to the Athos of that immortal trio. But oftener than not there were more than three of them. Oftener than not they were a majority of five. There was a new set of "dissenters" in the Supreme Court of the United States. They were the "conservative" dissenters.

Let us look back to June 10, 1916, when Mr. Justice Hughes resigned from the Court to accept nomination as the Republican candidate for the Presidency. President Wilson appointed in his place John Hessin Clarke, who, as we saw in an earlier chapter, resigned in 1922. William Howard Taft, appointed Chief Justice in 1921, died March 8, 1930. George Sutherland, appointed in 1922 by President Harding, had been born in England and educated in Utah, which he had represented in the Senate. Pierce Butler of Minnesota, also appointed in 1922 (although he did not take his seat until January 2, 1923) was another new member. Edward Terry Sanford of Tennessee was appointed in 1923 by Harding, but died March 8, 1930. (Both he and Chief Justice Taft, it will be noted, died on the same birthday anniversary of Mr. Justice Holmes.) Harlan Fiske Stone of New Hampshire, Attorney General under Coolidge, was appointed by that President in 1925.[4] Owen Josephus Roberts of Pennsylvania, who had made a reputation throughout the United States by his prosecution of the "oil cases" during the Coolidge administration, was appointed to the Court by President Hoover in May, 1930.

Chief Justice Hughes and Mr. Justice Roberts, both Hoover appointees, turned the judicial tide in favor of Justices Holmes and Brandeis, with the frequent concurrence of Mr. Justice Stone. In the popular notion the new dissenters were Justices Sutherland, Butler, Van Devanter and McReynolds; as a fact, Justices Sutherland and Van Devanter sided with the majority in the California "red flag case" and there were other instances where one or more of the Court stepped from one side of the line to the other. Thus, although changes in the personnel of the Court did bring a change in the general trend of decisions, and although the Court does act to some extent as a law-making body in addition to being a tribunal of interpretation, still it could not be said, reversing an old aphorism, that in this institution ours had become a government of men and not of laws. For it has never been true that a majority of the Court, or even a section of it, attempted persistently to enforce its own economic or governmental ideas in the interpretation of the law.

"We are very quiet there," Mr. Justice Holmes once said, "but it is the quiet of a storm center, as we all know."[5] Winds of doctrine and persuasion made the storm, or, to shift the metaphor, the conflict of ideas. Elsewhere, in a book review written for an

English publication and all too little noted, Mr. Justice Holmes
has discussed with philosophic acumen the struggle between
ideas, and the relation to it of the law.

"Attention has been called before now," he noted, "to the
struggle for life carried on among ideas; to the result that some
perish and others put on the livery of the conqueror; and to the
fact that law only ends with a theory, but begins with a concrete
case. But so far as I know these considerations have not been
much attended to heretofore. . . . Ecclesiastical penalties for
perjury in the breach of promissory oath continue to a late
period [here he cited Chaucer's *Frere's Tale* in regard to "pun-
isshinge of . . . difamacioun . . . and of testaments, of contractes,
and of lakke of sacraments" etc.] and although the opinion has
been controverted, I think that there are signs that ecclesiastical
chancellors hesitated before they denied a remedy for breach of
faith."

Turning again to the struggle between ideas, the Justice
wrote:

> "If the development of ideas and their struggle for
> life are the interests of the day, the interest of the fu-
> ture, the final and most important question in the law
> is that of their worth. I mean their worth in a more far-
> reaching sense than that of expressing the *de facto*
> will of the community for the time. On this as yet no
> one has much to say. To answer it we should have in
> the first place to establish the ideals upon which our
> judgments of worth depend; and the statement of such
> ideals by different classes would differ, at least in
> form. But suppose that we had agreed that the end of
> the law was, for instance, the survival of a certain type
> of man, still we should have made very little way to-
> ward the founding of a scientific code. Statistics would
> leave the effect of the criminal law open to doubt. Who
> can prove that the doctrine of master and servant, or
> the theory of consideration, helps to attain the ideal

assumed? The attitude of the State toward marriage and divorce is governed more by church and tradition than by facts. Wherever we turn we find that what are called good laws are apt to be called so because men see that they promote a result that they fancy desirable, and do not see the bill that has to be paid in reactions that are relatively obscure. One fancies that one could invent a different code under which men would have been as well off as they are now, if they had happened to adopt it. But that *if* is a very great one. The tree has grown as we know it. The practical question is what is to be the next organic step. No doubt the history of the law encourages skepticism when one sees how a rule or a doctrine has grown up, or when one notices the *naïveté* with which social prejudices are taken for eternal principles. But it also leads to an unconvinced conservatism.

"For it points out that almost the only thing that can be assumed as certainly to be wished is that men should know the rules by which the game will be played. Doubt as to the value of some of those rules is no sufficient reason why they should not be followed by the courts. Legislation gives notice at least if it makes a change. And after all, those of us who believe with Mr. Lester Ward, the sociologist, in the superiority of the artificial to the natural, may see in what has been done some ground for believing that mankind yet may take its own destiny consciously and intelligently in hand."[6]

Mr. Justice Holmes, practicing an "enlightened skepticism", may have had in mind the mistaking of social prejudices for eternal principles when he spoke of judges as being often naïf; to what extent his mode of thought influenced his associates must remain problematic, despite the assurance of some of his admirers that several of his earlier dissents became the position in time of the majority. At any rate, the shifting of the Court's center of gravity from the right toward the left encouraged some liberals—not all of them professional liberals—to perceive therein a symptom that mankind "may yet take its own destiny consciously and intelligently in hand."

A paleontologist may be able to reconstruct from a single fossil the skeleton of a prehistoric mammoth, but no one can chart the outlines of a jurist's attitude from one of his opinions or decisions. It is impossible to characterize Justices Van Devanter, McReynolds, Sutherland and Butler by individual outgivings. Yet it is true that, since the news associations and the daily press follow the procedure of the Supreme Court rather closely, each Justice is likely to be associated in the public mind with particular cases. Without unfairness to them, certain of these cases may be indicated here. In that way we may get the more speedily a picture of the Court as it was when Mr. Justice Holmes turned his ninetieth milestone.

Justice Van Devanter, the senior of the four "conservatives" in service on the bench, wrote the decisions of the Court upholding the validity of the Eighteenth Amendment in 1920;[7] he set the tone of friendliness, that is to say, toward the "experiment noble in purpose". He has opposed State "welfare acts", and dissented, under the "due process" clause, when the Court upheld a zoning ordinance.[8] He wrote the decision holding that the Constitution protected a Federal judge from the income tax;[9] and he wrote the decision voiding West Virginia's attempt to satisfy the needs of her citizens for natural gas before the gas could be shipped to another State.

The majority decided the last-named case under the commerce clause of the Constitution, and since Mr. Justice Holmes wrote a dissenting opinion, it merits further attention here as illustrating a diverging point of view. It should be said that a big business was being transacted by piping gas to Pittsburgh, Cleveland, Cincinnati and Toledo. The States containing those cities protested that the West Virginia statute was an attempt to regulate interstate commerce, which Congress alone was empowered to control. Mr. Justice McReynolds (it is well worth noting since he is classified as one of the "conservatives"), also dissented, but wrote a separate opinion, based on the contention that even though West Virginians first got what natural gas they needed, there still might be enough to supply the imperative needs of nearby States. Mr. Justice Brandeis thought the case should be dismissed without passing on its constitutionality. Mr. Justice Holmes said in part:

> "The statute seeks to reach natural gas before it has begun to move in commerce of any kind. . . . I think that the products of a State until they are actually started to a point outside it may be regulated by the State notwithstanding the commerce clause. . . . A state law was sustained that made it criminal to sell or offer for shipment citrus fruits that were immature or otherwise unfit for consumption. That, upon the grounds of local policy, intercepted before it got into the stream what would have been an object of interstate commerce.
>
> "The local interest in this case is greater and more obvious than in that of green oranges. Again, the power of the State to preserve a food supply for its people by game laws notwithstanding an indirect interference with interstate commerce is established. . . .
>
> "I see nothing in the commerce clause to prevent a State from giving a preference to its inhabitants in the enjoyment of its natural advantages. If the gas were used only by private persons for their own purposes I know of no power in Congress to require them to devote it to public use or to transport it across State lines."[10]

It is difficult to understand how an obdurate majority withstood in the conference room such reasoning as this, supported as it was by numerous earlier majority decisions of that Court not noted in the excerpts. The opinion illustrates, too, the adroit use by Mr. Justice Holmes of the double negative in argument. He knew of "no power in Congress" to prevent the private use of natural gas. By saying that statutes were "not unconstitutional" he often put his associates hard to it.

Mr. Justice McReynolds, as in this case, was found not infrequently on the side of the "liberals", as Justices Holmes and Brandeis came to be called. Although he thought that an automobile should not be searched for liquor without a warrant, dissenting from the majority view, he sided with the majority in upholding the tapping of telephone wires to get evidence. In the latter case Mr. Justice Butler, usually ranked as conservative, thought there ought to be a new trial in the lower courts; Mr. Justice Holmes wrote the main dissent, in which Justices Brandeis and Stone concurred.[11]

Mr. Justice McReynolds, although a Democrat appointed by Woodrow Wilson, has manifested a belief in the further centralization of Federal power and a fondness for technicalities. He held that a seaman could not recover for an injury under a New York statute, because only Congress could regulate the conditions of maritime work;[12] and then, when Congress provided that State compensation laws should apply in such instances, he wrote the opinion of the Court voiding the Act, on the ground that Congress should not transfer a Federal power.[13]

Mr. Justice McReynolds wrote the majority opinion annulling the Wisconsin statute to collect inheritance taxes on gifts made within a certain period of death, on the ground that they were made "in contemplation of death".[14] He wrote the opinion voiding the attempts of Minnesota and Missouri to tax bonds and bank accounts of nonresidents, overruling a prior opinion of Mr. Justice Holmes; and he wrote the decision in the famous O'Fallon railroad valuation case, enabling the lines to set their own high valuation as against estimates—generous but more moderate—by the Interstate Commerce Commission. From this Justices Brandeis, Holmes and Stone dissented.[15]

Soon after President Harding sent Mr. Justice Sutherland to

the Court, the Justice wrote the majority opinion upsetting the attempt to establish a minimum wage for women workers in the District of Columbia,[16] to which reference has been made. He wrote the Court's majority view voiding State attempts to regulate the prices charged by theater-ticket brokers,[17] by dairy proprietors and by employment agencies.[18] In tax and labor cases his conservative—if not reactionary—point of view has been clearly indicated. In these cases, almost without exception, he had the support of Mr. Justice Butler; but the latter was a lone dissenter in the case where the Court upheld the right of the State—Virginia, in this case—to sterilize imbeciles. Mr. Justice Butler, who is of Roman Catholic origin, wrote no opinion; the majority opinion was written by Mr. Justice Holmes. In this case an attempt was made to prevent the operation of salpingectomy on the daughter of a feeble-minded woman, who herself had become the mother of an illegitimate feeble-minded child; all were inmates of a Virginia institution. It was admitted that the woman could be sexually sterilized without detriment to her health, and to her own advantage as well as the general advantage of society. "Three generations of imbeciles are enough," said Mr. Justice Holmes, and continued:

> "But, it is said, however it might be if this reasoning were applied generally, it fails when it is confined to the small number who are in the institutions named and is not applied to the multitudes outside. It is the usual last resort of constitutional arguments to point out shortcomings of this sort. But the answer is that the law does all that is needed when it does all that it can, indicates a policy, applies to all within the lines, and seeks to bring within the lines all similarly situated so far and so fast as its means allow. Of course so far as the operations enable those who otherwise must be kept confined to be returned to the world, and thus open the asylum to others, the equality aimed at will be more nearly reached.[19]

Like Mr. Justice Sutherland, Mr. Justice Butler expressed in his opinions a predilection for Federal centralization, and even held that an oil company which sold gasoline to the Coast Guard need not pay a State tax because in selling it became a federal agency. He upheld the power of California and New York, however, to pass "criminal syndicalism" statutes, in the Whitney and Gitlow[20] cases; that is, where the conflict was between State rights and freedom of political opinion, he favored the State. He voted to deny citizenship to Rosika Schwimmer, Dr. Douglas Clyde Macintosh of Yale and Miss Marie Averill Bland, because they had scruples against bearing arms.

Charles Evans Hughes was not a member of the Court when the Schwimmer case was decided in 1928. A woman pacifist fifty years old, denying that she had any sense of nationalism, wanted to become a citizen but refused to bear arms. Of course she couldn't bear arms in any event, but Mr. Justice Butler thought she lacked the necessary "attachment to the principles of the Constitution", and held it a fundamental duty to be willing to defend the Government. Mr. Justice Holmes, in his dissenting opinion—in which Mr. Justice Brandeis concurred—said in part:

> "Surely it does not show lack of attachment to the principles of the Constitution that she thinks it can be improved. I suppose that most intelligent people think that it might be. . . . She is an optimist and states in strong, and, I do not doubt, sincere words her belief that war will disappear and that the impending destiny of mankind is to unite in peaceful leagues.
> "I do not share that optimism, nor do I think that a philosophic view of the world would regard war as absurd. . . . The notion that the applicant's optimistic anticipations would make her a worse citizen is sufficiently answered by her examination, which seems to me a better argument for her admission than any I can offer. Some of her answers might excite popular prejudice, but if there is any principle of the Constitu-

tion that more imperatively calls for attachment than any other it is the principle of free thought—not free thought for those who agree with us but freedom for the thought that we hate. . . .

"I would suggest that the Quakers have done their share to make the country what it is, that many citizens agree with the applicant's belief and that I had not supposed hitherto that we regretted our inability to expel them because they believe more than some of us do in the teachings of the Sermon on the Mount."[21]

Chief Justice Hughes was on the bench when the other citizenship cases were decided, and wrote the dissenting opinion, in which Justices Holmes, Brandeis and Stone concurred. Dr. Macintosh and Miss Bland refused to say that they would bear arms unless their consciences approved the war being fought. Dr. Macintosh, a Canadian, Dwight professor of theology at Yale, had served in the World War as chaplain both with the British and the American forces, thinking this war was justified. He was not a conscientious objector to all war, as was Miss Schwimmer, and he was fifty-four years old, beyond conscription. If he were a Quaker, he would not be required to serve. Miss Bland, a Canadian and a trained nurse, could hardly be compelled to give military service, and was willing to serve as a nurse in any contingency. Yet the majority of the Court held that these two could not make bargains in asking for citizenship, nor should any alien be admitted who had the slightest scruple against warfare for whatever cause. Mr. Justice Sutherland wrote this decision, and was supported by Justices McReynolds, Roberts, Van Devanter, and Butler. In the pulpit and the press the Court's position was widely criticized.

Chief Justice Hughes, for the minority of four, recognized that an individual might be obligated by "duty to a moral power higher than the State", and insisted that

"there is abundant room for enforcing the requisite authority of the law . . . and for maintaining the con-

ception of the supremacy of law as essential to orderly
government, without demanding that either citizens
or applicants for citizenship shall assume by oath an
obligation to regard allegiance to God as subordinate
to allegiance to civil power."

The passage is cited as reminiscent of the allusion of Mr. Justice Holmes in the Schwimmer case to the Sermon on the Mount.

The "new majority" was strengthened to seven, with only Justices McReynolds and Butler dissenting, in the case of Yetta Stromberg, convicted in California of displaying a red flag "as a sign, symbol or emblem of opposition to organized government or as an invitation or stimulus to anarchist action or as an aid to propaganda that is of a seditious character". Here again Chief Justice Hughes wrote the opinion, declaring that "the maintenance of the opportunity for free political discussion to the end that government may be responsive to the will of the people and that changes may be obtained by lawful means, an opportunity essential to the security of the Republic, is a fundamental principle of our constitutional system."

It was a principle, Mr. Justice Holmes had said in the Schwimmer case, "that more imperatively calls for attachment than any other."

If these opinions and decisions of Chief Justice Hughes were surprising to those who had mistakenly thought that he would be "the tool of the interests", how much more surprising to thousands were those warm words in his address over the radio when Mr. Justice Holmes was ninety years old: "We honor him, but, what is more, we love him." For those who had seen Charles Evans Hughes in action in the courtroom, in Washington and as a political campaigner, regarded him as singularly aloof, even forbidding in demeanor. He had a well-earned reputation for coldness, and he exhibited at times a disdain which approached intellectual snobbery. The truth was that at a dinner table or in other private social gatherings he could unbend; rarely if ever did he unbend in public. The surprising thing was that he told some millions of listeners that he loved Mr. Justice Holmes.

The millions of listeners had a right to know, since it was so, for this birthday was an occasion of national congratulation and rejoicing. To these millions the Justice has assumed an importance outweighing his position in the Supreme Court. He is not only a great jurist, he is a great social scientist, a great philosopher, a great man. He has looked with tolerance even upon opinions and social experiments which were obnoxious to him, he has disdained to magnify his own economic and governmental preconceptions, he has had a proud faith in his countrymen, in his country, and in the power of reason. The Chief Justice himself declined to attempt an estimate of the value of Mr. Justice Holmes to American jurisprudence, and none can estimate his value to American life.

CHAPTER 19

Holmes and Marshall

IN THE reading room of the Harvard Law School the portraits
of Justice Oliver Wendell Holmes and Chief Justice John
Marshall hang *vis-à-vis*. Leaping the arc of a century, the spot-
light of considered opinion has rested upon these two figures as
the greatest in a distinguished line. "We have thought it well
to have it made," Judge Learned Hand said of the picture when
it was unveiled, "and to hang it—to the gratification of its subject—opposite the effigy of the great Chief Justice, before which
it need not flinch."[1] A little later William Allen Jowitt, Attorney
General of Great Britain, said that by English jurists the judgments of Holmes, "both as Justice of the United States Supreme
Court and as Chief Justice of Massachusetts, have been held to
be as authoritative as those of Marshall and Story."[2] And still
later Harold J. Laski:

> "In the last decade, it has become generally recog-
> nized that not since Mr. Chief Justice Marshall has
> the United States possessed a jurist of the insight and
> distinction of Mr. Justice Holmes. Wherever the writ
> of the Common Law runs, there his opinions have
> won for him a standing which places him among the
> classic figures of Anglo-American legal history. It is
> not merely that what he has chosen to say has about it
> an unforgettable literary power. It is not merely,
> either, that he has had a learning and an historical
> penetration unsurpassed and, I venture to think, un-
> equalled upon the American bench. It is not even be-
> cause of his remarkable ability to penetrate through
> the mass of facts to the essential principles they im-
> ply. . . .

"The peculiar importance of Mr. Justice Holmes lies in the marriage of these qualities to a temperament capable of a detachment almost unique in judicial history. It is not that he does not possess a considered and emphatic philosophy. Aristocratic, conservative, sceptical, these marks of a deliberate outlook can be seen in almost everything he has written. But he has never allowed his own special attitude to balance unduly his approach to the law. He has worked within the framework of a judicial system which limits the power of the judge to make himself the master of the Legislature; and, unlike not a few of his colleagues, he has been scrupulous to respect the implications of the system."[3]

John Marshall acknowledged no such limitation upon his authority "to make himself the master of the Legislature." A Virginian, dubbed "the supreme conservative", he was appointed by John Adams, who feared the masses as much as he feared autocracy; Holmes, a Bostonian "liberal", was appointed by a President who liked to be called "the trust-buster". Marshall exalted above the powers of States the principles of Alexander Hamilton, who would have preferred to see this country an elective monarchy; by some Holmes came to be called, a little inaccurately, a "State rights man". Marshall's opinions fell within the platform of his party, the Federalist, and he was openly said to control and to subsidize its organ, the *Washington Federalist;*[4] no one could guess, from the opinions and decisions of Holmes, whether he were a Republican or a Democrat, and, scorning personally the uses of the daily press, he stood uncompromisingly for its freedom from political or other interference or limitation.

Let certain similarities, nevertheless, be conceded. Aside from a comparable mental caliber and power, neither man has accepted the Constitution as a strait-jacket. To move farther afield, it is fair to assume that if Holmes had been alive he would have fought in the Revolution as generously and valiantly as he fought to preserve the Union; Marshall, born in a log cabin on the frontier, was with Washington at Valley Forge[5] and exulted in the French Revolution. "In no part of the globe," he wrote, "was this revolution hailed with more joy than in America." (The free-thinking Thomas Paine declared that "American principles opened the Bastille"; and LaFayette sent the key to the ruined prison to Washington.)[6] And Marshall warned his party against the Alien and Sedition Acts, which subsequently were the chief factor in destroying the Federalists, on the ground that they were calculated to arouse rather than allay discontent";[7] but one doubts whether he would have been hospitable to "freedom for the thought that we hate". Despite sharing a marginal zone of temperament and thought, the men were almost as different as their times.

When Marshall, who was to serve thirty-four years, took his seat in 1801, thirty cases in a single session made a crowded calendar. There were no Federal Circuit Courts west of the Mountains, and there were but six members of the Supreme Court, four constituting a majority.[8] In a lobby back of the bench, plainly to be seen by counsel and spectators, the Chief and his associates donned their black robes, tied at the neck, "in the same manner as a farmer puts on his frock," one observer objected, "or a sportsman his hunting shirt." (In an earlier day the Justices had worn parti-colored robes, red and black, which were considered most impressive.[9]) A fledgling Indiana member of Congress, dropping idly into the Court in 1827, witnessed the public robing. "I had never seen anything like it before," he said; "it reminded me of the man who, having repeated several times that he would die at the stake for the religion of his father, was asked, 'What was your father's religion?' 'I do not exactly know, but it was something very solemn.' So with me; I did not exactly know what the gowns were for, but I thought the Court looked very solemn."[10]

Marshall might never have worn the robes but for two chances. John Rutledge was rejected by the Senate when renom-

inated by Washington—after serving a term—because of a speech
he had made against the Jay Treaty. "As his death did not occur
until the year 1800," says Charles Warren, "the Chief Justiceship, if held by him, would have become vacant at a time when
it is extremely unlikely that President Adams would have appointed John Marshall as his successor. Thus upon the event of
one chance speech regarding a British treaty hinged the future
course of American constitutional law."[11]

The other chance lay in the refusal of Patrick Henry to become Chief Justice before that post was offered to Marshall. If
he had accepted and had been young enough to serve as long as
Marshall (a large *if*, for he died even before Marshall ascended
the bench), we should have today a quite different Constitution,
a different social fabric, and a different set of legalistic disciplines.

Most of us remember Patrick Henry as author of that flaming
phrase, "Give me liberty or give me death." We think of him,
that is to say, much as Thomas Jefferson thought when he wrote
to a friend, "he appears to me to speak as Homer wrote." But
Henry was a great refuser as well as a great orator; he declined to
become Secretary of State under Washington, would not go as
envoy to France, and withheld his name from the Electoral College, in those days that select gathering of Best Minds which,
ignoring the people, chose the President. He was called the
"original" champion of State rights, which is the oldest political
issue in our history; and in the formative days of the Union he
was aligned with Jefferson against Hamilton, Madison and Marshall. He refused to attend the Constitutional Convention at
Philadelphia because, he said, he "smelt a rat".[12] He protested
against "a consolidated government", changing the existent confederacy into "a great national supreme Government".[13] He
came near preventing Virginia's adoption of the Constitution.
"Our rights and privileges are endangered," he cried, "and the
sovereignty of the States will be relinquished. . . . Who authorized them [the Founding Fathers] to speak of *we the people* instead of *we the States?*"

Marshall called the Constitution "an expression of the clear and deliberate will of the whole people", which it was not. John Adams vowed it was "extorted from a reluctant people by a grinding necessity", and it came within an ace of failing of adoption.[14] It is impossible to say what the document might have provided had New Hampshire been represented from the first—her delegates did not put in an appearance for six weeks—and had Rhode Island been represented at all. Provision was made, with the approval of Marshall, for the continuance of slavery during at least twenty years, although his fellow Virginians (what a galaxy was this!) looked upon it with horror: Washington, Jefferson, James Madison, Henry and Richard Henry Lee, John Randolph and Patrick Henry.[15] They led the movement by which Virginia became the first State to denounce the institution. (There were then more than twenty thousand slaves north of what was to become the Mason and Dixon Line; the traffic was profitable to New England skippers.) And the Founding Fathers opposed incorporating in the Constitution a guaranty of freedom of conscience, speech and the press; this was accomplished when Jefferson, on his return from France, led the fight for the first ten amendments, the "Bill of Rights".[16]

Jefferson and Henry were much more of the militant and liberty-loving kidney of Holmes than was Marshall. Let it be said at once that Henry had no such legal learning as the others. He was mentally indolent, the "laziest man in reading" his friend Jefferson had ever known. Yet his biographers assure us that he read Livy through once a year; and the histories, rhetoric and philosophic dialogues of Titus Livius are no soufflé for any literary diet. Henry was admitted to the bar, so informal were they in those days, after having read law only six weeks—on his promise to read some more. Yet Edmund Burke may have had him in mind with scores of others when, warning Britain of the qualities which made the Colonies dangerous, he enumerated among them the love of the legal profession. Certainly Henry, who sounded the keynote of revolution by demanding that Virginia—where he served five terms as Governor—be put in "a state of defense", and who did as much as any other man to precipitate the Revolution, could well be considered dangerous.

Moreover, Henry would never have construed the Tenth Amendment of the Constitution, which reserved to the States or the people the powers not delegated to the United States, as Marshall construed it. Nor, being a "strict constructionist", would he have read into that document a doctrine of "implied powers".[17]

Marshall dominated the Supreme Court during his incumbency by reason of his personal prestige, his learning, his brilliant and profound mind. Three men had preceded him as Chief Justice: John Jay of New York, John Rutledge of South Carolina, and Oliver Ellsworth of Connecticut. They had handed down but six decisions interpreting the Constitution, and only one regarded as highly important. This held that a citizen could sue a sovereign State, and it was promptly offset by the Eleventh Amendment.

Even if the amendment had not been adopted, it is doubtful whether the decision would have stood. "Some doubt has been expressed," says Mr. Justice Holmes, "as to the source of the immunity of a sovereign power from suit without its own permission, but the answer has been public property since before the days of Hobbes. . . . A sovereign is exempt from suit, not because of any formal conception or obsolete theory, but on the logical and practical ground that there can be no legal right as against the authority that makes the law on which the right depends."[18]

Quoting the latter part of this passage, Quincy Wright notes that this consideration "had led Hobbes, John Austin and others to conclude, starting from the premise that the State is the only source of law, that the State cannot be subject to law and consequently international law and treaties impose only moral obligations. Certainly an attempt to apply the two common law principles referred to leads to an apparent contradiction. By the first the State must submit to suit, by the second it cannot be sued."[19]

But in another case Mr. Justice Holmes, putting the matter after his wont into its historical perspective, said:

> "It is true also that in legal theory sovereignty is absolute, and that as against foreign nations, the United States may assert, as Spain asserted, absolute power. But it does not follow that as against the inhabitants of the Philippines the United States asserts that Spain had such power. When theory is left on one side sovereignty is a question of strength and may vary in degree. How far a new sovereign shall insist upon the theoretical relation of the subjects to the head in the past and how far it shall recognize actual facts are matters for it to decide."[20]

Marshall wrote thirty-six of the sixty-two judgments bearing on Constitutional questions during his incumbency, and one of the earliest of these, as well as one of the most momentous, held that the Court could void an Act of Congress.[21]

"If this opinion be sound," exclaimed Jefferson, "then indeed is our Constitution a complete *felo de se*. . . . The Constitution, on this hypothesis, is a mere thing of wax in the hands of the judiciary, which they may twist and shape in any form they please. . . . My construction of the Constitution is very different from that you quote. It is that each department is truly independent of the others, and has an equal right to decide for itself what is the meaning of the Constitution in the cases submitted to its action; and especially, where it is to act ultimately and without appeal."[22]

No power was conferred by the Constitution on the Supreme Court to nullify an Act of Congress, and Marshall cited no precedents. It was enough for him that "a law which is repugnant to the Constitution is void and the courts as well as other departments are bound by that instrument." Undismayed by the thunders of Jefferson and like-minded public men, he proceeded to nullify acts of the Legislatures of Georgia, Maryland, New Hampshire, Virginia, Missouri and Kentucky.[23]

In the Maryland case he upheld the second Bank of the United States, little dreaming that a century later, under the Federal Reserve Act, this country would vindicate him to some extent by setting up in effect fifteen central banks. In the New Hampshire case he voided a State act infringing upon the charter of Dartmouth College, granted by King George: "a spectacular event more important in American educational history than the founding of any single institution of higher learning. By securing the boards of trustees of endowed institutions against political interference, the Dartmouth decision in effect decreed that a large terrain of the higher learning should be forever occupied and controlled by private corporations composed of citizens empowered to select their own successors, collect and disburse money, choose presidents and professors, and more or less directly determine the letter and spirit of the curriculum."[24]

In a Missouri case Marshall voided a statute creating paper "certificates", and again in a Kentucky case; but when the latter came up for a rehearing three years later (because only two others had acted with Marshall, of five who happened to be sitting), the Chief Justice had gone to his reward, and the fiat-money faction for a time had its way. In that case Mr. Justice Story vigorously dissented.[25]

Whatever the merits or demerits of these particular cases, Mr. Justice Holmes has expressed clearly his reluctance to void legislative enactments. "Although research has shown and practice has established," he says, "the futility of the charge that it was a usurpation when this Court undertook to declare an Act of Congress unconstitutional, I suppose we will all agree that to do so is the gravest and most delicate duty that this Court is called on to perform. Upon this as among other considerations, the rule is settled that as between two possible interpretations of a statute, our plain duty is to adopt that which will save the Act. Even to avoid a serious doubt the rule is the same."[26] And again:

"While the courts must exercise a judgment of their own, it by no means is true that every law is void which may seem to the judges who pass upon it excessive, unsuited to its ostensible end, or based upon conceptions of morality with which they disagree. Considerable latitude must be allowed for differences of view as well as for possible peculiar conditions which this Court can know but imperfectly, if at all. Otherwise a constitution, instead of embodying only relatively fundamental rules of right, as generally understood by all English-speaking communities, would become the partisan of a particular set of ethical or economic opinions, which by no means are held *semper ubique et ad omnibus.*

"No court would declare a usury law unconstitutional, even if every member of it believed that Jeremy Bentham had said the last word on that subject, and had shown for all time that such laws did more harm than good.

"The Sunday laws, no doubt, would be sustained by a bench of judges, even if every one of them thought it superstitious to make any day holy."[27]

Mr. Justice Holmes, too, preferred to uphold local courts. "On the other hand," he once said, "while this Court cannot refuse to exercise its own judgment, it naturally will lean toward the interpretation of a local statute adopted by a local court." Indeed, he had shown time and again in Massachusetts his reluctance to nullify statutes or to invade the province of legislatures when it could be avoided.

In the British debts case public opinion was divided along partisan lines, the Federalists espousing the cause of the creditor class.[28] This was before Marshall ascended the bench, and illustrates—for he was of counsel—that as attorney and as judge the same man may hold differing views. For in that case Marshall contended that treaty provisions had no power over State legislation, and referred disdainfully to "those who wish to impair the sovereignty of Virginia."[29] It was decided, after two weeks of argument—for in those days speeches were permitted to run on indefinitely—that the British creditors were entitled to recover; and a fundamental point of law was settled, in that a treaty, if compatible with the Constitution, must supersede State legislation.[30] Marshall's phrase about impairing sovereignty was often quoted against him when, in the interest of manufacturing and commercial classes, he began to nullify State legislation similar in nature to provisions declared void before the Revolution, and for similar reasons, by British judges and the Crown.

The Constitution deals in general terms with the supremacy of treaty provisions. Mr. Justice Holmes wrote the judgment of the Court in a case involving a treaty when the State of Missouri sought to prevent a Federal game warden from enforcing an Act of Congress, passed to carry out a covenant with Great Britain protecting migratory birds which traverse both the United States and Canada. The State contended that what Congress could not do unaided it could not do under a treaty, and that migratory birds were owned by the States in which they happened to be. It was argued that Congress, whatever the treaty, had no power to invade this sovereign ownership.

"Wild birds are not in the possession of anyone," said Mr. Justice Holmes; "and possession is the beginning of ownership. The whole foundation of the State's rights is the presence within their jurisdiction of birds that yesterday had not arrived, tomorrow may be in another State, and in a week a thousand miles away. If we are to be accurate we cannot put the case of the State upon higher ground than that the treaty deals with creatures that for the moment are within the State borders, that it must be carried out by officers of the United States within the same territory, and that but for the treaty the State would be free to regulate this subject itself."[31] He did not refer to the British debts case, but quoted Chief Justice Marshall in another, where he thought differently about impairing sovereignty; and he continued:

"Here a national interest of very nearly the first magnitude is involved. It can be protected only by national action in concert with that of another power. The subject-matter is only transitorily within the State and has no permanent habitat therein. But for the treaty and the statute there soon might be no birds for any powers to deal with. We see nothing in the Constitution that compels the Government to sit by while a food supply is cut off and the protectors of our forests and our crops are destroyed. It is not sufficient to rely upon the States. The reliance is vain, and were it otherwise, the question is whether the United States is forbidden to act. We are of opinion that the treaty and the statute must be upheld."

Mr. Justice Holmes manifested so repeatedly a tolerance toward social and economic experiment on the part of the States that he seemed to some, who failed to take into account his similar attitude toward Congressional legislation, a "State rights man"; but he made it clear that he did not suppose States exercised a sovereignty or enjoyed an authority beyond the bounds of treaty obligations or even beyond the limits of plain common sense.

Between the accessions of Marshall and Holmes the Supreme Court declared unconstitutional thirty-three Acts of Congress, two hundred and twenty-three State laws, and twenty-three municipal ordinances. In the same period it upheld one hundred and eighty-six Congressional acts, six hundred and forty-six statutes, and seventy-three ordinances. Reading between the lines of the Constitution, Marshall set the pace. He was magisterial and imperative. He made much of the "necessary and proper" clause, and it has been said that under his "expansive imagination" it became "a Pandora's box of wonders".[32] In voiding a Virginia law, Marshall said:

"It is to be observed that it is not indispensable to the existence of every power claimed for the Federal Government that it can be found specified in the words of the Constitution, or clearly and directly traceable to some one of the specified powers. Its existence may be deduced fairly from more than one of the substantive powers expressly defined, or from all of them combined. It is allowable to group together any number of them and to infer from them all that the power claimed has been conferred."[33]

This was a sort of *Gestalt* jurisprudence.

Certainly Mr. Justice Holmes has never gone so far. Yet he early perceived that the common law often proceeded from a point of departure not clearly specified, and his perception of what has been called an "inarticulate major premise" applied also to his interpretation of the Constitution. As early as 1870, in an unsigned editorial in the *American Law Review,* he said:

"It is the merit of the common law that it decides the case first and determines the principle afterwards. Looking at the forms of logic it might be inferred that when you have a minor premise and a conclusion, there must be a major, which you are also prepared then and there to assert. But in fact lawyers, like other men, frequently see well enough how they ought to decide on a given state of facts without being very clear as to the *ratio decidendi.* . . . It is only after a series of determinations on the same subject-matter, that it becomes necessary to 'reconcile the cases', as it is called, that is, by a true induction to state the principle which has until then been obscurely felt. And this statement is often modified more than once by new decisions before the abstracted general rule takes its final shape. A well-settled legal doctrine embodies the work of many minds, and has been tested in form as well as substance by trained critics whose practical interest it is to resist it at every step."[34]

Holmes has used the principles of the Constitution, not as a yardstick, but as an avenue of analysis, not as a terminus, but as

a gateway. "You cannot carry a Constitution out with mathematical nicety to logical extremes," he has said.[35] The Fourteenth Amendment (and he would have said the same thing of
any other part), "is not a pedagogical requirement of the impracticable."[36] Because, as he noted in another case, that involving
punishment of Samuel Gompers for contempt of court, "the
provisions of the Constitution are not mathematical formulas
having their essence in their form; they are organic living institutions transplanted from English soil. Their significance is vital
not formal; it is to be gathered not simply by taking the words
and a dictionary, but by considering their origin and the line of
their growth."[37]

Marshall stood at the origin of the line of growth of Constitutional law in this country. He made precedents, and he set an
example of disregarding them on occasion. Mr. Justice Brandeis
has noted that "a doctrine declared by Mr. Justice Story with the
concurrence of Chief Justice Marshall, and approved by Chancellor Kent, was abandoned when found to be erroneous, although it had been acted on for twenty-six years."[38] Thus there
is a long tradition that the findings of the Court are not unshak-
able and immovable outgivings. Abraham Lincoln was outspoken in saying, of Chief Justice Taney's judgment in the Dred
Scott case, "I believe the decision was improperly made, and I
go for reversing it";[39] and again: "We know the Court that made
it has often overruled its decisions, and we shall do what we can
to have it overrule this."[40] It may be said in passing that Taney's
memory is now being cleared of imputations arising from that
decision, and that Chief Justice Hughes has been among his defenders.[41] Taney, as good a Jacksonian Democrat as Marshall
was a good Federalist, became Chief Justice after Marshall's
death.

Some of the earlier dissents of Mr. Justice Holmes appear to
have been vindicated by the later position of his associates.
Whether this was due solely to his influence, or, as we have seen,
to the changing personnel of the Court, it is impossible to say.

His hospitality to social experiments on the part of the States has been justified in the Court's decisions upholding statutes to require transportation companies to carry school children at half fare, compelling prosperous banks to help guarantee the deposits of smaller banks, limiting rents in housing emergencies, providing employers' liability acts, and grade crossing legislation. His stand for freedom of speech and of the press has been upheld in the famous "Minnesota gag law" case. He has gained impressive ground against the erection of the Fourteenth Amendment into a fortress for vested interests. His dissent in the celebrated Leo Frank case in Georgia, on the ground that the court was intimidated by a mob, became the attitude of the Court in 1923, in Moore v. Dempsey, eight years later. Yet it has been said with some truth that his influence has hardly been commensurate with the range of his thought and the depth of his philosophy. His power is certain to be manifest, and he would wish it so, among future generations of lawyers and judges.

If we get no glimpse of the partisan affiliations of this man from his written opinions and decisions, neither do we learn what he thinks of the merits and weaknesses of democratic processes; but to a visitor who once asked him whether he was as sanguine as his friend Lord Bryce about the political experiment this country had undertaken, he indicated his faith in it and in its ultimate triumph.

"Are you in despair?" he demanded. "I'm not."

"Despair is a strong word," the visitor objected; "perhaps downcast would be better."

"I'm not downcast, either," the Justice said. "I look abroad, and see other kinds of governments functioning no better than ours, if as well. And everywhere I see an increasing tendency to refer questions of popular import to the popular will."

Even in decisions and dissents, one could read something of this fine faith of the Justice in the collective common sense and rightness of "reasonable men".

Born, as the saying goes, with a silver spoon in his mouth,

Oliver Wendell Holmes could have gone through life, had he chosen, "sliding with open eyes through liquid bliss." He was not of a temperament which made sliding compatible with bliss, liquid or otherwise; in his young manhood he perceived that the world in which he found himself was a world of conflict and peril, and he declined to let time run over him. The highest form of pleasure he found was in the exertion of his personal powers to the hilt, and he worked so hard, then and later, that his friends feared for his health, even for his life. Each new task, from a battle to a lawsuit, he attacked with a zest approaching rapture. And he formulated as he went along a philosophy of life as well as a philosophy of the law.

Having the true humility of the scientific mind, Holmes did not pretend to incorporate eternal truths in such a philosophy, and he damned the Absolute as emphatically as William James. "We hold these truths to be self-evident," said the signers of the Declaration of Independence. Holmes held no truths to be self-evident, doubted whether there were "certain unalienable rights" and denied the "equal station to which the Laws of Nature and of Nature's God" entitled men. He challenged sentiments and beliefs which had been accepted for centuries by the majority, and asked to see the credentials of standards as well as of institutions. In his essays on *Natural Law* and *Ideals and Doubts*[42] he expressed more fully than elsewhere his general attitude toward the universe around him, but phrases bearing on it are to be found scattered through his writings.

Philosophy, Holmes thought, should release us from prepossessions about eternal values, "natural" rights, duties and moralities, or any all-embracing code for the guidance of mankind. It has been said that he applied to morality the Darwinian theory of the survival of the fittest.[43] It would be more accurate to say that he agreed with Spinoza, who, rejecting a God made in the image of man, realized the existence of powers beyond man's scope, perceived the limitation of the merely material, and saluted the potency of his fellows. And it would be accurate to say that he envisioned with Plato the possibility that man might be master of his destiny through mastery of himself. He perceived in man, it is already evident, a spiritual being; and once, answering the implicit questioning of Harvard undergraduates in law, he said:

"He will ask, What is all this to my soul? You do not bid me sell my birthright for a mess of pottage; what have you said to show that I can reach my own spiritual possibilities through such a door as this? How can the study of a dry and technical system, the greedy watch for clients and practice of shopkeepers' arts, the mannerless conflicts over often sordid interests, make out a life? Gentlemen, I admit at once that these questions are not futile, that they may prove unanswerable, that they have often seemed to me unanswerable. And yet I believe there is an answer. They are the same questions that meet you in any form of practical life. If a man has the soul of Sancho Panza, the world to him will be Sancho Panza's world; but if he has the soul of an idealist, he will make—I do not say find—his world ideal. Of course, the law is not the place for the artist or the poet. The law is the calling of thinkers. But to those who believe with me that not the least godlike of man's activities is the large survey of causes, that to know is not less than to feel, I say— and I say no longer with any doubt—that a man may live greatly in the law as well as elsewhere; that there as well as elsewhere his thought may find its unity in an infinite perspective; that there as well as elsewhere he may wreak himself upon life, may drink the bitter cup of heroism, may wear his heart out after the unattainable. All that life offers any man from which to start his thinking or his striving is a fact. And if this universe is one universe, if it is so far thinkable that you can pass in reason from one part of it to another, it does not matter very much what that fact is. For every fact leads to every other by the path of the air. . . .

"Perhaps I speak too much the language of intellectual ambition. I cannot but think that the scope for intellectual, as for physical adventure, is narrowing. I look for a future in which the ideal will be content and dignified acceptance of life, rather than aspiration and the passion for achievement. I see already that surveys and railroads have set limits to our intellectual wildernesses—that the lion and the bison are disappearing from them, as from Africa and the no longer boundless West. But that undelightful day which I anticipate has not yet come. . . .

"No man has earned the right to intellectual ambition until he has learned to lay his course by a star which he has never seen—to dig by the divining rod for springs which he may never reach. In saying this, I point to that which will make your study heroic. For I say to you in all sadness of conviction, that to think great thoughts you must be heroes as well as idealists. Only when you have worked alone—when you have felt around you a black gulf of solitude more isolating than that which surrounds the dying man, and in hope and in despair have trusted to your own unshaken will—then only will you have achieved. Thus only can you gain the secret isolated joy of the thinker, who knows that, a hundred years after he is dead and forgotten, men who never heard of him will be moving to the measure of his thought—the subtle rapture of a postponed power, which the world knows not because it has no external trappings, but which to his prophetic vision is more real than that which commands an army. And if this joy should not be yours, still it is only thus that you can know that you have done what it lay in you to do—can say that you have lived, and be ready for the end."[44]

In the solitude of original work, Holmes thought, a man

might turn misgiving into success and thus become master of himself. "One part of the universe," he found, "yields the same teaching as any other if only it is mastered," and he emphasized the difference "between realizing the part as a part of the whole and looking at it in its isolation as if it stood really apart." The consummation of knowledge, he held, lay in applying this to himself. "He may put it in the theological form of justification by faith or in the philosophical one of the continuity of the universe. I care not very much for the form if in some way he has learned that he cannot set himself over against the universe as a rival god, to criticize it, or to shake his fist at the skies, but that his meaning is its meaning, his only worth is as a part of it, as a humble instrument of the universal power. It seems to me that this is the key to intellectual salvation, as the key to happiness is to accept a like faith in one's heart, and to be not merely a necessary but a willing instrument in working out the inscrutable end."[45]

To recognize in one's fellow a separate entity, the Justice once said in conversation, "is an act of faith". It required an act of faith to conclude that he was not dreaming this world, and therefore not dreaming his fellow men. "If the world were my dream," he wrote, "I should be God in the only universe I know. But although I cannot prove that I am awake, I believe that my neighbor exists in the same sense that I do, and if I admit that, it is easy to admit also that I am in the universe, not it in me.

"When I say that a thing is true, I mean that I cannot help believing it. I am stating an experience as to which there is no choice. But as there are many things that I cannot help doing that the universe can, I do not venture to assume that my inabilities in the way of thought are inabilities of the universe. I therefore define the truth as the system of my limitations, and leave absolute truth for those who are better equipped. With absolute truth I leave absolute ideals of conduct equally to one side."[46]

Belief in the truth or in anything else, as well as human wishes, "have a transcendental basis," the Justice wrote on another occasion, "in the sense that their foundation is arbitrary. You cannot help entertaining and feeling them, and there is an end of it."[47] The universe has in it more than we understand, and we have not been told the plan of campaign, or even that there is a plan, but the Justice held that this had no bearing on deportment.

> "We still shall fight—all of us because we want to live, some, at least, because we want to realize our spontaneity and prove our powers, for the joy of it, and we may leave to the unknown the supposed final valuation of that which in any event has value to us. It is enough for us that the universe has produced us, and has within it, as less than it, all that we believe and love. If we think of our existence not as that of a little god outside, but as that of a ganglion within, we have the infinite behind us. It gives us our only but our adequate significance. A grain of sand has the same, but what competent person supposes that he understands a grain of sand? That is as much beyond our grasp as man."[48]

Curiosity about the universe in which we live "is the most human appetite we have," the Justice had observed, in commenting on the fact that somebody had once told him that religion was the only interesting thing in life. He thought the statement true if one included in religion "the passionate curiosity as well as the passionate awe which we feel in the face of the mystery of the universe." Alone of living things, mankind strives "toward the reality of the phantasmagoria which dance before our eyes for three score years and ten." (When the Justice said that, he had not quite turned fifty.) He continued:

> "This endless aerial pursuit is our fate, as truly as to bear offspring or to toil for bread. This passion is as genuine and self-justifying as any other. The satisfaction of it is as truly an end in itself as self-preservation. I do not believe that the justification of science

and philosophy is to be found in improved machinery and good conduct. By producing them, civilization sufficiently accounts for itself, if it were not absurd to call the inevitable to account."[49]

Substituting a nebula for a totem pole, Mr. Justice Holmes thought, did not alter the content of the religious impulse. He vowed he could not swallow transcendentalism, and preferred the word philosophy to metaphysics. Yet no one who reads what he has had to say can doubt that a mystic faith possessed him. Seldom, if ever, has he given more poetic expression to that faith than in a New York speech, more than ten years after he went to the Supreme Court.

"I think it not improbable," he said, "that man, like the grub that prepares a chamber for the winged thing it never has seen but is to be—that man may have cosmic destinies that he does not understand. And so beyond the vision of battling races and an impoverished earth I catch a dreaming glimpse of peace.

"The other day my dream was pictured to my mind. It was evening. I was walking homeward on Pennsylvania Avenue near the Treasury, and as I looked beyond Sherman's statue to the west the sky was aflame with scarlet and crimson from the setting sun. But, like the note of downfall in Wagner's opera, below the skyline there came from little globes the pallid discord of the electric lights. And I thought to myself the Götterdämmerung will end, and from those globes clustered like evil eggs will come the new masters of the sky. It is like the time in which we live. But then I remembered the faith that I partly have expressed, faith in a universe not measured by our fears, a universe that has thought and more than thought inside of it, and as I gazed, after the sunset and above the electric lights there shone the stars."[50]

Inevitably there comes to mind Henry F. Cary's translation of the last line of Dante's *Inferno,* where, after visiting the nether world, "Thence issuing we again beheld the stars."

APPENDIX

Bibliography of Early Writings of Oliver Wendell Holmes*

Articles

Unsigned

"Codes, and Arrangement of the Law" (October, 1870), 5 *American Law Review* 1.

"*Ultra Vires:* How Far are Corporations Liable for Acts not Authorized by their Charters?" (January, 1871), 5 *American Law Review* 272.

"Misunderstandings of the Civil Law" (October, 1871), 6 *American Law Review* 37.

"Grain Elevators: On the Title to Grain in Public Warehouses" (April, 1872), 6 *American Law Review* 450.

"The Arrangement of the Law: Privity" (October, 1872), 7 *American Law Review* 46.

"The Theory of Torts" (July, 1873), 7 *American Law Review* 652.

Signed

"Primitive Notions in Modern Law" (April, 1876), 10 *American Law Review* 422.

"Primitive Notions in Modern Law," Pt. II (July, 1877), 11 *American Law Review* 641.

"Possession" (July, 1878), 12 *American Law Review* 688.

"Common Carriers and Common Law" (July, 1879), 13 *American Law Review* 609.

"Trespass and Negligence" (January, 1880), 1 *American Law Review* [N. S.] 1.

Book Reviews and Comments

Schouler, *A Treatise on the Law of the Domestic Relations* (October, 1870), 5 *American Law Review* 113.

Holland, *Essays upon the Form of the Law* (October, 1870), 5 *American Law Review* 114.

Clark, *The House of Lords Cases* (October, 1870), 5 *American Law Review* 116.

---

*Reprinted from the *Harvard Law Review*, Vol. XLIV, No. 5, pp. 797-8, through the courtesy of that magazine and of Professor Felix Frankfurter.

Bibliography

Addison, *The Law of Torts* (January, 1871), 5 *American Law Review* 340.

Shearman & Redfield, *A Treatise on the Law of Negligence* (January, 1871), 5 *American Law Review* 343.

Clark, *The House of Lords Cases on Appeals and Writs of Error and Claims of Peerage* (January, 1871), 5 *American Law Review* 346.

*Townsend, *The Code of Procedure of the State of New York, as amended to 1870* (January, 1871), 5 *American Law Review* 359 (last paragraph).

Dicey, *A Treatise on the Rules for the Selection of the Parties to an Action* (April, 1871), 5 *American Law Review* 534.

Campbell, *The Law of Negligence* (April, 1871), 5 *American Law Review* 536.

Brightly, *A Digest of the Decisions of the Federal Courts* (April, 1871), 5 *American Law Review* 539.

Langdell, *A Selection of Cases on the Law of Contracts* (April, 1871), 5 *American Law Review* 539.

Bump, *Law and Practice in Bankruptcy* (April, 1871), 5 *American Law Review* 540.

Bump, *The Law Magazine and Law Review* (April, 1871), 5 *American Law Review* 541.

Angell & Ames, *Treatise on the Law of Private Corporations Aggregate* (April, 1871), 5 *American Law Review* 542.

Baldwin, *Digest of Connecticut Cases* (April, 1871), 5 *American Law Review* 542.

May, *A Treatise on the Statutes of Elizabeth* (April, 1871), 5 *American Law Review* 543.

Clark, *The House of Lords Cases on Appeals, etc., 1858-1864* (April, 1871), 5 *American Law Review* 544.

Redfield, *The Law of Wills* (April, 1871), 5 *American Law Review* 546.

Thompson, *The American Reports* (April, 1871), 5 *American Law Review* 549.

‡*Copy before Publication* (April, 1871), 5 *American Law Review* 567.

Bryce, *The Academical Study of the Civil Law* (July, 1871), 5 *American Law Review* 715.

Heard, *Curiosities of the Law Reporters* (July, 1871), 5 *American Law Review* 717.

Redfield & Bigelow, *Leading and Select American Cases in the Law of Bills of Exchange, Promissory Notes, and Checks* (July, 1871), 5 *American Law Review* 720.

Bibliography

Cases Decided in the District and Circuit Courts of the United States for the Pennsylvania District (July, 1871), 5 *American Law Review* 725.

The Journal of Psychological Medicine (July, 1871), 5 *American Law Review* 742 (beginning sentence four, second paragraph).

"Reply to Correspondent on 14th Amendment and Citizenship" (July, 1871), 5 *American Law Review* 780.

Ram, *The Science of Legal Judgment* (October, 1871), 6 *American Law Review* 134.

Bump, *Law and Practice in Bankruptcy* (October, 1870), 6 *American Law Review* 137.

Cooley, *A Treatise on the Constitutional Limitations* (October, 1871), 6 *American Law Review* 140.

Abbott, *A Treatise upon the United States Courts, and Their Practice* (October, 1871), 6 *American Law Review* 149.

"English Chancery Reports" (January, 1872), 6 *American Law Review* 349.

"Massachusetts Reports 103" (January, 1872), 6 *American Law Review* 350.

Langdell, *A Selection of Cases on the Law of Contracts* (January, 1872), 6 *American Law Review* 353.

‡"Short Reply to Correspondence" (January, 1872), 6 *American Law Review* 392.

Williams, *Principles of the Law of Real Property* (April, 1872), 6 *American Law Review* 549.

Hare & Wallace, *American Leading Cases* (April, 1872), 6 *American Law Review* 550.

"American Trade-Mark Cases" (April, 1872), 6 *American Law Review* 553.

"Reports of all the published Life and Accident Insurance Cases" (April, 1872), 6 *American Law Review* 554.

"Massachusetts Reports 104" (April, 1872), 6 *American Law Review* 556.

Hilliard, *The Law of Contracts* (April, 1872), 6 *American Law Review* 558.

The Law Magazine and Review (July, 1872), 6 *American Law Review* 723.

Kerr, *A Treatise on the Law of Fraud and Mistake* (July, 1872), 6 *American Law Review* 729.

Kerr, *A Treatise on the Law and Practice as to Receivers appointed by the Court of Chancery* (July, 1872), 6 *American Law Review* 729.

Bibliography

Bennett, *Fire Insurance Cases* (July, 1872), 6 *American Law Review* 731.

Coppinger, *Index to Precedents in Conveyancing, and to Common and Commercial Forms* (July, 1872), 6 *American Law Review* 732.

Crocker, *Notes on Common Forms* (July, 1872), 6 *American Law Review* 732.

Bennett & Holland, *The Massachusetts Digest* (July, 1872), 6 *American Law Review* 733.

Fisher, *A Digest of the Reported Cases (1756-1870) Relating to Criminal Law, etc.* (July, 1872), 6 *American Law Review* 737.

Lowell, *Judgments delivered in the Courts of United States for the District of Massachusetts* (July, 1872), 6 *American Law Review* 743.

‡"A New Practice Act" (July, 1872), 6 *American Law Review* 748.

"The Legal Tender Cases of 1871" (October, 1872), 7 *American Law Review* 146.

"The Code of Iowa" (January, 1873), 7 *American Law Review* 318.

"Report of Commissioners" (January, 1873), 7 *American Law Review* 318.

Stephens, *Codification in India and England* (January, 1873), 7 *American Law Review* 318.

Greene, *Outlines of Roman Law* (January, 1873), 7 *American Law Review* 320.

Brown, *An Epitome and Analysis of Savigny's Treatise on Obligations in Roman Law* (January, 1873), 7 *American Law Review* 320.

‡*Paragraph beginning "The Journal starts with a good list of subscribers" ending "We believe the weight attached to them is about the best thing in our whole system of law" (April, 1873), 7 *American Law Review* 579.

‡*"The Gas-Stokers' Strike" (April, 1873), 7 *American Law Review* 582.

---

*In part. ‡Other than Book Notices.

Bibliographical Note

In the references which follow, citations are given not only to cases but to those books which have been consulted, yet it is needful that certain special acknowledgments be made. Charles Warren's *The Supreme Court in United States History*, Charles and Mary Beard's *The Rise of American Civilization*, Professor Schlesinger's *New Viewpoints in American History*, the Gray-Ropes *War Letters*, Colonel Bruce's *The Twentieth Regiment of Massachusetts Volunteer Infantry*, Morse's *Life and Letters of Oliver Wendell Holmes* (the elder), Lief's *Dissenting* and *Representative* opinions of Mr. Justice Holmes and *Views* of Mr. Justice Brandeis, all have been of special value. Dr. Dorsey Richardson's survey, for Johns Hopkins University, of the constitutional opinions of the Justice, has been useful because of its comprehensiveness, discernment, and freedom from overstatement. It has seemed unnecessary to cite newspaper clippings.

BOOK I

CHAPTER 1

1—Morse, John T., Jr., *Life and Letters of Oliver Wendell Holmes* (Sr.); II, 82.

2—Quoted by Morris R. Cohen in *Mr. Justice Holmes* (Coward-McCann, 1931), a symposium edited by Felix Frankfurter, p. 24. This may have been said in personal conversation. In an address before the New York State Bar Association, January 17, 1899 (*Harvard Law Review*, XII, 443), Chief Justice Holmes of Massachusetts said: "I think that science, like art, may be pursued for the pleasure of the pursuit and its fruits, as an end in itself." In an address on Nov. 5, 1886, to the Harvard Law School Association, (*Speeches*, p. 39, *Collected Legal Papers*, p. 47) he said "that the ardors of intellectual pursuit should be relieved by the charms of art, should be succeeded by the joy of life become an end in itself." The paragraph is quoted on page 144 of this volume. In another Harvard address, (*Speeches*, p. 63) he observed that "the joy of life is living."

3—Cardozo, Benjamin N.

4—Sergeant, Elizabeth Shepley, *Fire Under the Andes*, p. 315.

5—Richardson, Dorsey, "Constitutional Doctrines of Justice Oliver Wendell Holmes," Johns Hopkins University Studies, pp. 11, 13; 167 Mass. 92, Holmes dissenting; *The Dissenting Opinions of Mr. Justice Holmes*, p. 3; Lochner *v* N. Y., 198 U. S. 45, 74.

6—*Speeches*, pp. 67, 68.

7—250 U. S. 624; *The Dissenting Opinions of Mr. Justice Holmes*, p. 50.

8—*The New Republic*, January 28, 1920, p. 250.

9—*American Law Review* (1872), pp. 723-4.

10—"Natural Law," 32 *Harvard Law Review* 40-1-2; Richardson, Dorsey, *Constitutional Doctrines of Justice Oliver Wendell Holmes*, p. 23; *The Dissenting Opinions of Mr. Justice Holmes*, p. 277; *Collected Legal Papers*, p. 171, "For instance, when we speak of the rights of man in a moral sense."

11—*Massachusetts Law Quarterly*, May, 1923.

12—Southern Pacific Co. *v* Jensen, 244 U. S. 205, 218; *The Dissenting Opinions*, p. 32.

13—Grinnell, Frank W., *Massachusetts Law Quarterly*, May, 1923,

14—Johnston, Forney, *ibid.*

[363]

Reference Notes by Chapters

15—*Speeches,* p. 18.
16—*Ibid.,* p. 22.
17—Hamilton Walton Hale, *Current History,* February, 1931, p. 660.
18—*Speeches,* p. 68.
19—Richardson, Dorsey, *op. cit.,* pp. 10, viii, 28.
20—*Ibid.,* pp. 19, 36-8, 48 ff., 60 ff., 67 ff.
21—*Speeches,* p. 79.
22—*Ibid.,* p. 20.
23—Wister, Owen, *Roosevelt: The Story of a Friendship,* p. 134.
24—*Ibid.,* p. 133.
25—Hand, Learned, *Political Science Quarterly,* XXXVI, 528.
26—Little, Herbert, United Press; and 273 U. S. 536.
27—Warren, Charles, *The Supreme Court in United States History,* II, 742; but de Toqueville thought lawyers and the judiciary constituted our only aristocracy.
28—Gregory, *Samuel Freeman Miller* (1907), Vol. VIII.
29—*The Dissenting Opinions of Mr. Justice Holmes,* pp. ix-x.

CHAPTER 2

1—Morse, John T., Jr., *Life and Letters of Oliver Wendell Holmes,* I, 164-5, 225.
2—*Ibid.,* I, 226, 227.
3—*Ibid.,* I, 322.
4—*Ibid.,* I, 5-7.
5—*Ibid.,* I, 12, 13.
6—Parrington, Vernon Louis, *Main Currents in American Thought,* III, 140-7.
7—*Ibid.,* II, 256; Garrison, Wendell Phillips and F. J., *Life of William Lloyd Garrison* (1885), IV, 248.
8—Morse, *op. cit.,* I, 14.
9—Adams, Henry, *The Education of Henry Adams,* p. 3.
10—Parrington, *op. cit.,* II, 458.
11—*Ibid.,* II, 435-6.
12—Beard, Charles A. and Mary R., *The Rise of American Civilization,* I, 772, 773.
13—*The Guardian Angel* (Riverside Edition, 1891), pp. vii-viii.
14—Morse, *op. cit.,* I, 358.
15—*Ibid.,* I, 241-5; II, 38, 122, 189.

CHAPTER 3

1—Morse, John T., Jr., *Life and Letters of Oliver Wendell Holmes,* I, 15.

2—*Ibid.*, I, 170-71.

3—*Ibid.*, II, 261.

4—*Letters of Theodore Roosevelt and Henry Cabot Lodge*, p. 517.

5—Morse, *op. cit.*, I, 37-8.

6—245 U. S. 418.

7—*Speeches*, pp. 96-7.

8—*The Common Law*, p. 36.

9—Bleistein *v* Donaldson Lithograph Co., 188 U. S. 239, 1903. Laski, Harold J., *Harper's Magazine*, March, 1930, reprinted in *Mr. Justice Holmes*, p. 160.

10—Adams, Henry, *The Education of Henry Adams* (Houghton Mifflin, 1918), pp. 19, 38-9.

11—Morse, *op. cit.*, I, 195.

12—*Ibid.*, p. 196

13—*Ibid.*, p. 197.

14—*Ibid.*, pp. 50-1.

15—*Speeches*, p. 6.

16—*Ibid.*, pp. 20-1.

17—*Harvard Law Review*, April, 1930; *Mr. Justice Holmes*, p. 131.

CHAPTER 4

1—*Seventh Report*, Harvard College Class of 1861 (Fiftieth Anniversary and Final Report), pp. 11-66.

2—"Every year if not every day we have to wager our salvation upon some prophesy based upon imperfect knowledge." Abrams *v* United States, 250 U. S. 623; *The Dissenting Opinions of Mr. Justice Holmes*, p. 50.

3—*The Letters of William James*, edited by his son, Henry James (1920), I, 98-9.

4—*Ibid.*, pp. 101-2-3.

5—*Ibid.*, pp. 124-5.

6—*Ibid.*, p. 155.

7—Gray, John Chipman, and Ropes, John Codman, *War Letters: 1862-1865* (1927), p. 62.

8—The sonnets are in *Poetical Works* (Riverside Edition), III, 77.

9—Morse, John T., Jr., *Life and Letters of Oliver Wendell Holmes*, I, 233, 235, 237-8-9.

10—*Ibid.*, p. 240.

11—Flexner, Abraham, *Universities, American, English, German* (1930).

12—*Speeches*, p. 14.

13—*Ibid.*, pp. 39-40.

14—*The Letters of William James,* II, 9-10.

15—Bode, Boyd H., "Justice Holmes on Natural Law and the Moral Ideal," *International Journal of Ethics,* July, 1919.

16—*The Encyclopaedia of Social Sciences,* I, 162.

17—*Ibid.,* p. 147.

18—Adams, Henry, *The Education of Henry Adams* (1918), pp. 140-1.

19—*Ibid.,* p. 56.

20—*Harvard Graduates' Magazine,* March, 1931, p. 269, told by Arthur Dehon Hill.

21—Adams, *op cit.,* pp. 17, 55.

22—*Ibid.,* pp. 57-8.

23—Harvard College Class of 1861, *Seventh Report,* p. 85.

24—*Ibid.,* pp. 74-5; *Speeches,* pp. 95-6-7.

CHAPTER 5

1—Bruce, Col. George A., *The Twentieth Regiment of Massachusetts Volunteer Infantry* (1906), pp. 43, 48, 53.

2—*Ibid.,* pp. 24-5.

3—Morse, John T., Jr., *Life and Letters of Oliver Wendell Holmes,* II, 158. Letter to John Lothrop Mottley.

(That Col. Lee should so have exposed himself is remarkable, and in the history of the regiment there appears to be no confirmation of this statement by Dr. Holmes.)

4—*Ibid.,* p. 158.

5—Sergeant, Elizabeth Shepley, *Justice Touched With Fire;* reprinted in *Mr. Justice Holmes,* p. 183.

6—Morse, *op cit.,* II, 158-9.

7—Bruce, *op cit.,* pp. vi, 50.

8—*Ibid.,* p. vii.

9—*Ibid.*

10—*Ibid.,* pp. 3, 5.

11—*Ibid.,* pp. vii, 4.

12—*Supra,* n. 5.

13—Bruce, *op cit.,* p. 9.

14—*Ibid.,* p. 13.

15—*Ibid.,* pp. 19, 22.

16—*War Letters,* of John Chipman Gray and John Codman Ropes, pp. 246-7. Gray spoke in a letter received by Ropes, February 19, 1864, of "the preposterously large numbers given the enemy". These fascinating letters, published by the Massachusetts Historical Society, should offer invaluable source material to students of the Civil War.

Major Gray, resigning as Judge Advocate in 1865, practiced law in Boston and lectured with distinction in the Harvard Law School. Mr. Ropes became a notable historian of the war, but his last volume, published in 1898, covered only the campaign of 1862, and death prevented completion of the work.

17—*Speeches,* pp. 1-2.
18—Bruce, *op. cit.,* p. 48.
19—*Ibid.,* pp. 53-4.
20—*Ibid.,* p. 56.
21—*Ibid.,* p. 63.
22—*Ibid.,* pp. 64-5.
23—*Ibid.,* pp. 74-6.

CHAPTER 6

1—*Speeches,* p. 11.
2—Morse, John T., Jr., *Life and Letters of Oliver Wendell Holmes,* p. 173.
3.—Bruce, Col. George A., *The Twentieth Massachusetts,* p. 73.
4—*Ibid.,* p. 79.
5—*Ibid.,* p. 80.
6—*Ibid.,* p. 86.
7—*Ibid.,* p. 91.
8—*Ibid.,* pp. 95-7.
9—*Ibid.,* pp. 102-3.
10—*Ibid.,* p. 109.
11—*Ibid.,* p. 147.
12—*Ibid.,* pp. 149-50.
13—*Ibid.,* pp. 150-1.
14—*Ibid.,* p. 173.
15—Printed in Vol. XIII, *Collected Works;* and in a pamphlet, No. 31, Riverside Literature Series, pp. 9-72.
16—Pages 22-3 of pamphlet, above.
17—*Ibid.,* p. 64.

CHAPTER 7

1—Bruce, Col. George A., *The Twentieth Massachusetts,* p. 202.
2—*Ibid.,* p. 203.
3—*Ibid.,* pp. 182-3, 185-6.
4—Gray, John Chipman, and Ropes, John Codman, *War Letters,* p. 172.
5—Major William A. Obenchain, who, when he died in 1916, was the last surviving member of Robert E. Lee's personal staff, told this story while President of Ogden College, Bowling Green, Kentucky.

John C. Ropes tells a similar anecdote, but about General Hooker, in a letter dated May 9, 1863, *War Letters,* p. 108.

6—Bruce, *op. cit.,* p. 180.

7—*Ibid.,* p. 182.

8—*Ibid.,* pp. 185-6. (This and preceding paragraphs).

9—*Ibid.,* p. 251.

10—*Ibid.,* p. 216.

11—*Ibid.,* p. 196.

12—*Ibid.,* p. 254.

13—Gray and Ropes, *op cit.,* p. 25.

14—*Ibid.,* pp. 108, 118.

15—*Ibid.,* p. 74.

16—*Ibid.,* p. 78.

17—*Ibid.,* p. 49.

18—Bruce, *op. cit.,* p. 182.

19—*Ibid.,* p. 440.

20—*Speeches,* pp. 65-6.

21—*Ibid.,* p. 14.

22—*Ibid.,* excerpts, pp. 4-9.

23—*Ibid.,* p. 58.

24—*Ibid.,* p. 59.

25—*Ibid.,* pp. 62-3.

BOOK II

CHAPTER 8

1—*Collected Legal Papers,* p. 305; introduction to the *General Survey* by European Authors in the Legal Historical Series (1913).

2—*Collected Legal Papers,* pp. 298-9, 300.

3—*Ibid.,* p. 303.

4—*Ibid.,* p. 302.

5—*Ibid.,* pp. 301, 2.

6—*Speeches,* p. 35; *Collected Legal Papers,* p. 43.

7—*Speeches,* p. 29.

8—*Speeches,* p. 31; *Collected Legal Papers,* p. 39.

9—*Speeches,* p. 98; *Collected Legal Papers,* p. 291.

10—*Speeches,* p. 100; *Collected Legal Papers,* p. 293.

11—*Collected Legal Papers,* pp. 164-5.

12—*Ibid.,* p. 247.

13—Morse, John R., Jr., *Life and Letters of Oliver Wendell Holmes,* II, 95-6.

14—*Ibid.,* II, 127.

Reference Notes by Chapters

15—*Speeches*, pp. 70-72.

16—*Ibid.*, pp. 73-4.

17—Speeches at presentation of portrait of Mr. Justice Holmes, March 20, 1930; 32 *Harvard Alumni Bulletin* 741, 747. Quoted, *Harvard Graduates' Magazine*, XXXIX, No. 155, March, 1931, 266.

18—*Letters of William James*, I, 76.

19—*Ibid.*, II, 156-7.

20—*Speeches*, pp. 36-7; *Collected Legal Papers*, pp. 44-5.

21—*Speeches*, pp. 38-9; *Collected Legal Papers*, pp. 46-7.

CHAPTER 9

1—*The Common Law* (1881), p. 2.

2—*Collected Legal Papers*, p. 225.

3—Frankfurter, Felix, *Harvard Law Review*, March, 1931, XLIV, No. 5, 718.

4—*Ibid.*, p. 719.

5—*The Common Law*, p. 35.

6—*Ibid.*, pp. 35-6.

7—*Collected Legal Papers*, p. 224.

8—*Ibid.*, p. 225.

9—*Ibid.*, pp. 186-7.

10—*Ibid.*, pp. 257-8.

11—Spinoza, *Tractatus Politicus*, pp. 5, 9. Mr. Laski suggests comparison with Holmes's *Collected Legal Papers*, pp. 246, 251, 296, 305. To this might be added a passage on p. 167.

12—*Collected Legal Papers*, p. 225.

13—*Ibid.*, p. 170.

14—*Ibid.*, p. 171.

15—*Ibid.*, p. 173.

16—*Ibid.*, pp. 168-9.

17—*Yale Law Review*, March, 1931, XL, No. 5, 729.

18—*The Common Law*, p. 251.

19—222 U. S. 55; *The Dissenting Opinions of Mr. Justice Holmes*, p. 307.

20—*The Common Law*, pp. 2-3; Cf. pp. 4, 5, 7, 8, 34-5.

21—*Ibid.*, p. 18.

22—*Ibid.*, pp. 36-7.

23—*Harvard Law Review*, XLIV, No. 5, 693.

24—*American Law Review* (1873), p. 583; Reprinted in *Harvard Law Review*, March, 1931, p. 796.

25—*Collected Legal Papers*, p. 42.

Reference Notes by Chapters

CHAPTER 10

1—*Speeches,* p. 36.
2—Peirce, Charles S., *The Founding of Pragmatism.*
3—*Speeches,* pp. 36-40.
4—5 *American Law Review* 1 (unsigned).
5—*Ibid.,* p. 3.
6—*The Common Law,* p. 78.
7—*Collected Legal Papers,* pp. 187-8.
8—Morse, John T., Jr., *Life and Letters of Oliver Wendell Holmes,* II, p. 187.
9—Report of speech in Boston *Advertiser,* December 4, 1902; quoted by Arthur Dehon Hill, *Harvard Graduates' Magazine,* March, 1931, p. 39.
10—*Law Quarterly Review,* 1907; *Collected Legal Papers,* p. 283.

CHAPTER 11*

1—Article XXIX, Declaration of Rights.
2—*Speeches,* pp. 87-8.
3—*Ibid.,* pp. 52-3-4.
4—177 Mass. 612-3.
5—167 Mass. 103.
6—*Ibid.,* pp. 104-8.
7—Plant *v* Woods, 196 Mass. 492.
8—*Ibid.,* p. 502.
9—*Ibid.,* pp. 504-5.
10—May *v* Wood, 172 Mass. 14.
11—Moran *v* Dunphy, 177 Mass. 485, Cf. Western *v* Barnicoat, 175 Mass. 454.
12—Commonwealth *v* Perry, 155 Mass. 121.
13—*Ibid.,* pp. 123-4.
14—Heard *v* Sturgis, 146 Mass. 545.
15—Dove *v* Johnson, 141 Mass. 287; Batchellor *v* Commercial Union Co., 143 Mass. 495; Bradford *v* Brinley, 145 Mass. 81.
16—Quoted by Arthur Dehon Hill, *Harvard Graduates' Magazine,* XXXIII, No. 155, 273.
17—Lorenzo *v* Wirth, 170 Mass. 596.
18—Miller *v* Horton, 152 Mass. 546.
19—Nash *v* Minnesota Title Insurance and Trust Co., 163 Mass. 586-7.
20—166 Mass. 595.

---

*The page numbers here refer to passages cited, not to the statement of the case.

21—*Ibid.*, p. 599.
22—Supplement to Vol. 155 Mass. 606.
23—*Ibid.*, p. 607.
24—*Illinois Law Review*, X (May, 1915), 1-3; *Collected Legal Papers*, p. 306.
25—*Speeches*, pp. 101-2; *Collected Legal Papers*, p. 295.
26—*Collected Legal Papers*, p. 252.

CHAPTER 12

1—Introduction to *Mr. Justice Holmes*, pp. 13-14; Judge Cardozo cites "Law in Science and Science in Law," reprinted in *Collected Legal Papers*, p. 210.
2—Attorney General *v* Ayer, 148 Mass. 587.
3—Ryalls *v* Mechanics Mills, 150 Mass. 194.
4—Lombard *v* Willis, 146 Mass. 15.
5—Bradford *v* Brinley, 145 Mass 88.
6—Deming *v* Darling, 148 Mass. 506.
7—Rotch *v* French, 176 Mass. 3.
8—American Waltham Watch Co. *v* U. S. Watch Co., 173 Mass. 87.
9—Loftus *v* Inhabitants of North Adams, 160 Mass. 161.
10—Jefferds *v* Alvard, 151 Mass. 97.
11—Attorney General *v* Walworth Light & Power Co., 157 Mass. 87.
12—Flynn *v* Bourneuf, 143 Mass. 277.
13—Hubbard *v* City of Taunton, 140 Mass. 468.
14—*Harvard Law Review*, XII, 443; *Collected Legal Papers*, p. 230.
15—Bracton, 190a.
16—Cf. Good *v* Riley, 153 Mass. 585, 586.
17—*Harvard Law Review* (1899), XII, 417; *Collected Legal Papers*, pp. 205-6.
18—H. P. Hanson *v* Globe Newspaper Co., 159 Mass. 301, 304, 305.
19—Burt *v* Advertiser, 154 Mass. 243.
20—Cowley *v* Pulsifer, 137 Mass. 393.
21—Fay *v* Harrington, 176 Mass. 275.
22—Brigham *v* Fayerweather, 140 Mass. 413.
23—Commonwealth *v* Keenan, 142 Mass. 473.
24—Bradford *v* Cunard Ship Co., 147 Mass. 57.
25—O'Connell *v* O'Leary, 145 Mass. 312, 313, 314.
26—Commonwealth *v* Hannah Welch, 163 Mass. 273.
27—Olmstead *v* United States (1927), 277 U. S. 438, 469; *The Dissenting Opinions of Mr. Justice Holmes*, pp. 184-5-6.
28—Commonwealth *v* Clifford, 145 Mass. 98.
29—Benjamin *v* Dockham, 134 Mass. 418.

30—Tasker *v* Stanley, 153 Mass. 150.
31—Adams *v* Adams, 154 Mass. 295.
32—Weston *v* Weston, 143 Mass. 278.
33—President of Bates College *v* Sarah C. Bates, 135 Mass. 487.
34—Carpenter *v* Walker, 140 Mass. 419.
35—Attorney General *v* Eq. A. I. Assn., 175 Mass. 198.
36—Commonwealth *v* Sullivan, 146 Mass. 144.
37—Chadwick *v* Covell, 151 Mass. 192-3.
38—Commonwealth *v* Kennedy, 170 Mass. 20.
39—Butler *v* N. Y., N. H. and H. R. R. Co., 177 Mass. 193.
40—Spade *v* Lynn and Boston R. R. Co., 172 Mass. 491.
41—Hamilton *v* West End Street Railway Co., 163 Mass. 200.
42—*Speeches,* pp. 26-7.

CHAPTER 13

1—*The Common Law,* p. 247.
2—White *v* Duggan, 140 Mass. 18.
3—Fort Payne Rolling Mill *v* Hill, 174 Mass. 224.
4—Pound, Roscoe, *Selected Essays on the Law of Torts,* Foreword, p. iii; see also Chapter 13, "Privilege, Malice and Intent," by Oliver Wendell Holmes. This first appeared in the *Harvard Law Review,* Vol. VIII (1894), and was reprinted substantially in *Collected Legal Papers,* p. 117.
5—*Speeches,* p. 83; *Collected Legal Papers,* pp. 245-6.
6—Supplement to 174 Mass. 598; *Speeches,* pp. 75, 77-78.
7—Stack *v* N. Y., N. H. & H. R. R. Co., 177 Mass. 155.
8—160 Mass. 586.
9—*Ibid.,* p. 589.
10—*Ibid.,* p. 593.
11—Vannexein *v* Burr, 151 Mass. 386.
12—Every *v* Burbank, 163 Mass. 326.
13—Walsh *v* N. Y. & N. E. R.R. Co., 160 Mass. 571.
14—Graves *v* Johnson, 156 Mass. 212.
15—Sewall & Day *v* Boston, 147 Mass. 64.
16—Lincoln *v* Street Commissioners, 176 Mass. 213.
17—Beckwith *v* Chesire R.R. Co., 143 Mass. 72.
18—Detrietch *v* N. Hampton, 158 Mass. 14.
19—Flynn *v* Bourneuf, 144 Mass. 352.
20—Grogan *v* Worcester, 140 Mass. 227.
21—Hemenway *v* Hemenway, 134 Mass. 449-50.
22—Kent *v* Todd, 144 Mass. 478.
23—Rosenberg *v* John Doe, 146 Mass. 193.

24—Burns *v* Lane, 138 Mass. 350.

25—Clemens *v* Walton, 173 Mass. 286.

26—Hawkins *v* Graham, 149 Mass. 287, 289.

27—Bourke *v* Callanan, 160 Mass. 198.

28—Smith *v* Dickinson, 140 Mass. 172-3.

29—Commonwealth *v* Pierce, 138 Mass. 175, 176, 179.

30—Reeve *v* Dennett, 145 Mass. 28, 31.

31—Middlesex County *v* McCue, 149 Mass. 104-5.

32—Rideout *v* Knox, 148 Mass. 372-3.

33—Heard *v* Sturges, 146 Mass. 548.

34—Commonwealth *v* Perry, 139 Mass. 201.

35—Boston Ferrule Co. *v* Hills, 159 Mass. 150.

36—Sawyer *v* Davis, 136 Mass. 240, 243.

37—Lincoln *v* City of Boston, 148 Mass. 578.

38—Commonwealth *v* Davis, 162 Mass. 511-12.

39—Moses Perkins *v* City of Lawrence, 138 Mass. 362.

40—City of Newton *v* Perry, 163 Mass. 321.

41—Stanwood *v* City of Malden, 157 Mass. 19.

BOOK III

CHAPTER 14

1—Warren, Charles, *The Supreme Court in United States History*, II, 654; Swisher, Carl Brent, *Stephen J. Field: Craftsman of the Law*, pp. 199-202.

2—*Letters of Theodore Roosevelt and Henry Cabot Lodge*, I, 517-8.

3—*Speeches*, pp. 87, ff.; *Collected Legal Papers*, pp. 266, ff.

4—*Roosevelt Letters, op. cit.*, I, 519.

5—De Toqueville, Alexis, *Democracy in America*, I, 149 (Revised Ed. 1899); Cf. I, 143, 298.

6—Northern Securities Co. *v* United States, 193 U. S. 197, 400; *The Dissenting Opinions of Mr. Justice Holmes*, pp. 163-75.

7—Nicolay, John George, and Hay, John, *Life of Abraham Lincoln* (1890), II, 86; see notes 40, 41, Chapter 19.

8—Beard, Charles A. and Mary R., *The Rise of American Civilization*, II, 194.

9—*Supra*, n. 6.

10—Wister, Owen, *Roosevelt: The Story of a Friendship*, pp. 114, 140.

CHAPTER 15

1—*Speeches*, pp. 92-4.
2—*Collected Legal Papers*, pp. 272-3, 275, 276.
3—Warren, Charles, *The Supreme Court in United States History* (Revised, 1928), II, 718-9.
4—*Ibid.*, II, 320.
5—202 U. S. (supplement).
6—*American Law Review* (1902), XXXVI, *Notes*, 437-8.
7—Frank, Jerome, *Law and the Modern Mind* (1930).
8—Warren, *op. cit.*, II, 718.
9—*Ibid.*, II, 692.
10—*Ibid.*, p. 720.
11—*Ibid.*, p. 718.
12—*Ibid.*, p. 718, and *American Law Review* (*supra* n6), pp. 36, 437.
13—*Ibid.*, pp. 566, 726.
14—*Ibid.*, pp. 718-19, 720.
15—*Ibid.*, p. 720.
16—Reeder, Robert P., *Chief Justice Fuller, American Law Review* (1911), Vol. LIX; Warren, *op. cit.*, II, 721-2.
17—Warren, *op. cit.*, II, 693.
18—Baldwin *v* Missouri, 281 U. S. 586, 595; *Representative Opinions of Mr. Justice Holmes*, pp. 273-4.
19—"Reconstruction—New Style," by Silas Bent, in *Virginia Quarterly Review*, July, 1931, pp. 347, 349-50.
20—*Harvard Law Review*, Vol. XXIII.
21—Chae Chan Ping *v* United States, 130 U. S. 581; Fong Yue Ting *v* United States, 149 U. S. 698.
22—Warren, *op. cit.*, II, 696.
23—Geofroy *v* Riggs, 133 U. S. 258; see also Missouri *v* Holland, 252 U. S. 416.
24—Cunningham *v* Neagle, 135 U. S. 1.
25—Warren, *op. cit.*, II, 697.
26—Corporation of Latter Day Saints *v* United States, 136 U. S. 1.
27—Leisy *v* Hardin, 135 U. S. 100; Chicago, Milwaukee & St. Paul R.R. *v* Minnesota, 134 U. S. 418.
28—Warren, *op. cit.*, II, 698 ff.
29—Beard, Charles A., & Mary R., *The Rise of American Civilization*, II, 570.
30—Warren, *op. cit.*, II, 722.
31—Burley *v* Alabama, 219 U. S. 219.
32—Pacific States Telephone and Telegraph Co. *v* Oregon, 223 U. S. 118.

CHAPTER 16

1—Adkins *v* Children's Hospital, 261 U. S. 525, 567; *The Dissenting Opinions of Mr. Justice Holmes,* pp. 20-1.

2—*Collected Legal Papers,* p. 187.

3—*The Social and Economic Views of Mr. Justice Brandeis,* pp. xx-xxi.

4—Pennsylvania Coal Co. *v* Mahon, et al., 260 U. S. 393; *Representative Opinions of Mr. Justice Holmes,* pp. 62-6; Cf. Wister, Owen, *Roosevelt,* pp. 135-6.

5—Truax *v* Corrigan, 257 U. S. 312, 343, 354.

6—*Supra,* n. 3, pp. 28-9-30.

7—*The Dissenting Opinions of Mr. Justice Holmes,* pp. 11, 12, 13.

8—Towne *v* Eisner, 245 U. S. 418.

9—Eisner *v* MacComber, 252 U. S. 189, 220; *The Social and Economic Views of Mr. Justice Brandeis,* pp. 297-8.

10—*Supra,* n. 6, p. 215.

11—Hammer *v* Dagenhart, 247 U. S. 251, 277; *Dissenting Opinions,* pp. 15, 17-8.

12—Schaefer *v* United States, Vogel *v* Same, Werner *v* Same, Darkow *v* Same, Lemke *v* Same, 251 U. S. 466, 482.

13—Schenck *v* United States, 249 U. S. 47; *The Dissenting Opinions of Mr. Justice Holmes,* p. 231.

14—*Supra,* n. 3, pp. 212, 217.

15—Milwaukee Social Democratic Publishing Co. *v* Burleson, Postmaster, 255 U. S. 407, 437.

16—*Ibid.; Dissenting Opinions of Mr. Justice Holmes,* p. 43.

17—*Supra,* n. 3, pp. 256-7.

18—Whitney *v* California, 274 U. S. 357, 372; *The Social and Economic Views of Mr. Justice Brandeis,* pp. 258 ff.

19—*The Social and Economic Views of Mr. Justice Brandeis,* cited, pp. 260-1.

20—Myers *v* United States, 272 U. S. 52, 177, 240; *The Social and Economic Views of Mr. Justice Brandeis,* pp. 266 ff.

21—*The Dissenting Opinions of Mr. Justice Holmes,* p. 180.

22—*The Social and Economic Views of Mr. Justice Brandeis,* pp. 266-7.

23—*Harvard Law Review,* X, 457; *Collected Legal Papers,* p. 202.

CHAPTER 17

1—Danovitz *v* United States, 281 U. S. 289.

2—Fraenkel, Osmond K., *The Sacco-Vanzetti Case,* pp. 180-1.

3—*Columbia Law Review*, XXXI, No. 3 (March, 1931), 350.

4—*Harvard Law Review*, XLIV, No. 5, 691-2; reprinted in *Mr. Justice Holmes*, pp. 19-20.

CHAPTER 18

1—*Yale Law Journal*, XL, 5, 683-703 inclusive; *Columbia Law Review*, XXXI, 3, 349-367 inclusive; *Harvard Graduates' Magazine*, XXXIX, 155, 265-289 inclusive; *Harvard Law Review*, XLIV, 5, 678-827 inclusive.

2—*Mr. Justice Holmes*.

3—*Journal of the American Bar Association*, September, 1931, pp. 612-3.

4—Warren, Charles, *The Supreme Court in United States History*, II, 726-7.

5—*Speeches*, p. 99; *Collected Legal Papers*, p. 292.

6—*Law Quarterly Review* (1909); a review of *A History of English Law*, by W. S. Holdsworth; *Collected Legal Papers*, pp. 287-90.

7—National Prohibition Cases, 253 U. S. 350; Dillon *v* Gloss, 256 U. S. 368.

8—Village of Euclid *v* Ambler Realty Co., 272 U. S. 365.

9—Evans *v* Gore, 253 U. S. 245.

10—Pennsylvania *v* West Virginia, Ohio *v* West Virginia, 262 U. S. 553, 600; *The Dissenting Opinions of Mr. Justice Holmes*, pp. 124-5.

11—Olmstead *v* United States, Green *v* Same, McInnia *v* Same, 277 U. S. 438, 469; *The Dissenting Opinions of Mr. Justice Holmes*, pp. 184 ff.

12—Southern Pacific Co. *v* Jensen, 244 U. S. 205.

13—Clyde Steamship Co. *v* Walker, 244 U. S. 255.

14—Schlesinger *v* Wisconsin, 270 U. S. 230, 241; *The Dissenting Opinions of Mr. Justice Holmes*, pp. 203-5.

15—St. Louis & O'Fallon Ry. Co. *v* United States, 279 U. S. 261, 488; *The Social and Economic Views of Mr. Justice Brandeis*, pp. 149-182.

16—Adkins *v* Children's Hospital, 261 U. S. 525, 567; *The Dissenting Opinions of Mr. Justice Holmes*, pp. 20-24.

17—Tyson *v* Banton, 273 U. S. 418, 445; *The Dissenting Opinions of Mr. Justice Holmes*, pp. 85-6.

18—Adams *v* Tanner, 244 U. S. 590.

19—Buck *v* Bell, 274 U. S. 200; *Representative Opinions of Mr. Justice Holmes*, pp. 67-70.

20—Gitlow *v* People of New York, 268 U. S. 652, 672; *The Dissenting Opinions of Mr. Justice Holmes*, pp. 52-4.

21—United States *v* Schwimmer, 279 U. S. 644, 653; *The Dissenting Opinions of Mr. Justice Holmes*, pp. 55-7.

CHAPTER 19

1—*Harvard Law Review*, March, 1931, p. 681; *Mr. Justice Holmes*, p. 127.

2—*Harvard Law Review*, March, 1931.

3—*Representative Opinions of Mr. Justice Holmes*, p. ix.

4—Warren, Charles, *The Supreme Court in United States History*, I, 184n.

5—Beard, Charles A. and Mary R., *The Rise of American Civilization*, I, 386.

6—*Ibid.*, I, 360.

7—*Ibid.*, I, 376.

8—Warren, *op. cit.*, II, 232.

9—*Ibid.*, I, 48.

10—*Ibid.*, I, 467, 468.

11—*Ibid.*, I, 139.

12—Beard, *op. cit.*, I, 311.

13—Curtis, George Ticknor, *History of the Constitution*, Vol. II.

14—Schlesinger, Arthur M., *New Viewpoints in American History*, pp. 197-8.

15—Beard, *op. cit.*, I, 652-3.

16—*Ibid.*, I, 341.

17—Wright, Quincy, *The Control of American Foreign Relations*, p. 133.

18—Kawananakoa *v* Polyblank, 205 U. S. 349, 353; *Representative Opinions of Mr. Justice Holmes*, p. 277.

19—Wright, *op. cit.*, pp. 210-11.

20—Canino *v* Insular Government, 212 U. S. 449, 457; *Representative Opinions of Mr. Justice Holmes*, p. 278.

21—4 Dallas 24; Warren, *op. cit.*, I, 813n2.

22—Beard, *op. cit.*, I, 388.

23—*Ibid.*, I, 388-9; Cohens *v* Virginia, 6 Wheat. 264; U. S. *v* Gettysburg Electric Ry. Co., 160 U. S. 668, 681-2; Fletcher *v* Peck, 6 Cranch 87; McCulloch *v* Maryland, 4 Wheat. 316; Dartmouth College *v* Woodward, 4 Wheat. 518.

24—Beard, *op. cit.*, I, 819.

25—*Ibid.*, I, 686 ff.

26—275 U. S. 142; *The Dissenting Opinions of Mr. Justice Holmes*, p. 285.

27—187 U. S. 606; *The Dissenting Opinions of Mr. Justice Holmes,* p. 286.

28—Ware, Adm'r. *v* Hylton, 3 Dallas 199.

29—Warren, *op. cit.,* I, 145.

30—*Ibid.,* I, 146.

31—252 U. S. 416; *The Dissenting Opinions of Mr. Justice Holmes,* p. 287; *Representative Opinions of Mr. Justice Holmes,* pp. 104-5.

32—Beard, *op. cit.,* I, 325.

33—Cohens *v* Virginia, 6 Wheat. 264, *supra* n. 23; quoted by Quincy Wright, *op. cit.,* pp. 7, 133.

34—*American Law Review,* I, 5; reprinted in *Harvard Law Review,* March, 1931.

35—211 U. S. 446; *The Dissenting Opinions of Mr. Justice Holmes,* p. 302.

36—249 U. S. 265; *The Dissenting Opinions of Mr. Justice Holmes,* p. 289.

37—Gompers *v* United States, 233 U. S. 604; *The Dissenting Opinions of Mr. Justice Holmes,* p. 181.

38—State of Washington *v* W. C. Dawson & Co., 264 U. S. 219, 228.

39—Nicolay, John George and Hay, John, *Life of Abraham Lincoln* (1890), II, 162.

40—*Ibid.,* II, 86.

41—Daily press of September 27, 1931; Charles Evans Hughes delivered the address when a bust of Chief Justice Taney was unveiled at Frederick, Maryland.

42—*Collected Legal Papers,* pp. 303, 310; the essay on "Natural Law" is reprinted in *The Dissenting Opinions of Mr. Justice Holmes,* pp. xii-xviii.

43—Bode, Boyd H., *International Journal of Ethics,* July, 1919.

44—*Speeches,* pp. 22 ff.; *Collected Legal Papers,* pp. 29 ff.

45—*Collected Legal Papers,* pp. 165, 166.

46—*Ibid.,* pp. 304-5.

47—*Ibid.,* p. 312; *The Dissenting Opinions of Mr. Justice Holmes,* p. xv.

48—*Collected Legal Papers,* p. 316.

49—*Speeches,* p. 50.

50—*Speeches,* p. 103; *Collected Legal Papers,* pp. 296-7.

INDEX

Abbott, Maj. Henry L., 100, 109, 117
Abolition movement, 26, 31
Adams, Charles Francis, 35, 67, 128
Adams, Henry, 28, 35, 41, 65, 66, 67-68, 69-70, 127, 128, 132-33, 287
Adams, President John, 174, 253, 336, 338, 339
Adams, President John Quincy, 253
Adams, Samuel, 174
Agassiz, Louis, 34, 35, 69
Aldrich, T. B., 35
Allen, Judge Charles, 178-79, 190, 192, 194, 222, 233, 239
Allen, Thomas, 174
Allen, Judge William, 174
Alverstone, Lord, 135
American Law Journal, 139
American Law Review, 142, 146, 156, 160, 267, 346
Ames, Fisher, 170
Ames, James Barr, 170
Ancient Law—Maine, 159
Andrew, Gov. John A., 75, 85
Antietam, 14, 57, 67, 99
Appomattox, surrender at, 115-16
Atkinson, Edward, 250
Atlanta Constitution, 32
Ausonius, 319
Austin's *Jurisprudence*, 6-7, 129, 210, 238, 340
Autocrat of the Breakfast Table, The—Holmes, 23

Baker, Senator (Col.) Edward D., 74, 83
Ballinger-Pinchot investigation, 282
Ball's Bluff, 73, 78, 79, 80, 81, 82
Barker, Justice James M., 178, 192, 195, 205, 226
Bartlett, Major-Gen. Wm. F., 75, 84, 109
Beaman, C. C., 56
Beard, Charles A., 31, 66, 277, 286-87
Beck, James M., 276
Bentham, Jeremy, 61, 203
Berger, Victor, 298
Bigelow, John, 56
Bigelow, Dr. Henry J., 112

Bigelow, Sturgis, 65
Bill of Rights, 339
Blackstone, 311
Bland, Marie Averill, 331, 332
Boston Evening Transcript, 117, 118
Boston in Justice Holmes's Youth, 37, 41, 45-46, 52; censorship today, 63
Boston University School of Law, 167
Bourne, Randolph, 31
Bowditch, H. P., 56
Bowen, Lord, 135, 203, 313
boycott, primary, 183ff.
Bradstreet, Anne, 27, 262
Brandeis, Justice Louis D., 186, 254, 273, 279, 280ff.; background and education, 282; technique, 282, 283-301, 307, 310, 317, 322, 324, 328, 329, 331, 332, 347
Brett, Justice, 160
Brewer, Justice David J., 256, 269, 276, 279
Bright, John, 133
Brown, Justice Henry B., 267, 269, 270
Bruce, Lt.-Col. George A., 75, 79, 92, 93, 115
Bryce, Lord, 135, 348
Buffon, 317
Burke, Edmund, 339
Burleson, Postmaster General A. S., 298
Burnside, Gen. A. E., 106, 108, 109, 114
Butler, Justice Pierce, 324, 327, 329, 330, 331

Cabot, J. Elliot, 35
California "red flag" case, 324, 333
Calverley, Charles Stuart, 320
Cardozo, Judge Benjamin N., 197, 203, 313, 314, 316, 317
Carnegie, Andrew, 255
Cary's translation of Dante's *Inferno*, 354
Cases (*see also* Holmes, opinions)—Southern Pacific Co. v. Jensen, 10
Nash v. Minn. Title Insurance, 204
legal tender case of 1871, 245

Index

Index

Garrison, Wendell P., 56
Garrison, William Lloyd, 27, 29
Gaskell, Charles Milnes, 132
Godwin's *Inquiry Concerning Political Justice*, 66
Goldmark, Alice (Mrs. Brandeis), 282
Gompers, Samuel, 347
Grant, Gen. U. S., 115
Gray, Asa, 35, 65
Gray, John C., Jr., 62, 65, 79, 102, 113, 114, 151
Gray, Justice Horace, 245, 250, 251, 267
Greek Anthology translation, 141
Greeley, Horace, 27
Grinnell, Charles, 65
Grinnell, Frank W., 10, 53
Guardian Angel, The—Holmes, 32

Haeckel, Ernst, 66
Haldane, Lord, 135, 311
Hallowell, Brig.-Gen. E. N., 75, 109
Hallowell, Lt. Norwood P., 57, 84, 109
Hamilton, Alexander, 336
Hammond, Justice John W., 179, 183, 184
Hand, Judge Learned, 18, 55, 335
Hanna, Marcus A., 250
Hardy, Alpheus H., 56
Harlan, Justice John M., 19, 252, 256, 269-70, 275, 279
Harper's Ferry, 89, 98
Harrison, President Benjamin, 266, 269
Harrison, President William Henry, 37
Hart, Henry M., Jr., 316
Harvard College, 27, 52, 56, 61ff., 139, 142, 162ff.
Harvard Class of '29, 51, 56
Harvard Class of '58, 67
Harvard Class of '61, 44, 56, 70, 71
Harvard Club of N. Y., 62
Harvard Graduates' Magazine, The, 315-16
Harvard Law Review, 8, 146, 316, 320
Hawthorne, Nathaniel, 34
Hay, John, 70
Hayes, President, 269
Hayes-Tilden contest, 268
Hays, Arthur Garfield, 311
Hemingway, Ernest, 17
Henry, Patrick, 338, 339-40
Higginson, Henry L., 41, 65

Hill, Arthur Dehon, 308, 316
Hill, James J., 255, 259
Hoar, G. F., 35, 251
Hoar, Judge, 35
Hobbes's *Leviathan*, 77, 228, 238, 340
Hoffenstein, Samuel, quoted, 16
Holmes, Abiel, 25, 26, 27, 32, 50-51
Holmes, Amelia Lee Jackson, 38-39, 140
Holmes, Edward Jackson, 46, 135
Holmes, Fanny Dixwell (Mrs. O. W.), 56, 140, 141, 142, 303, 304, 307
Holmes, Dr. Oliver Wendell, 3, 23-36, 38, 46-47, 51, 62, 63, 100-105, 112, 113, 133-34, 169, 170, 305, 315
Holmes, Justice Oliver Wendell—his characteristics in his old age, 3-4; as a student of jurisprudence, 5-6; conception of the law, 6-8; on "natural rights", 8; criticized, 9-11; character of his liberalism, 11-13; as innovator, 13-14; feeling as an American, 15; as a reader, 16-18; method of reading opinions, 19-20; his last decision, 21

birth, 24; ancestry, 25; fondness for the classics, 35; literary style, how learned, 36; Boston influences on him as a youth, 41-43; Emerson's influence, 43

on thoughts and actions, 43; interest in etching, 44-45; his home and family, 46; country place, 47-48; various boyhood influences, 50-51; on the Puritans, 54

at Harvard, 56ff.; friends, 56-61; member of dinner club, 65-66; Class Poet, 70; poem, 70-71; class speech, 71-72

in the Civil War, 14, 73ff.; commissioned, 77; quoted on attitude toward enemy, 81-82; wounded at Ball's Bluff, 73, 82; at Antietam, 88ff.; captaincy, 89; at Fair Oaks, 91ff.; Malvern Hill, 95; Antietam, 99; wounded, 99-100; Fredericksburg, 110ff.; wounded, 112; Chancellorsville, 112; discharged from army, 113; made aide-de-camp, 115; requiem sonnet on Abbott, 117-118; on dead comrades, 118-124

interest in philosophy, 127-129; studies law, 129; economic beliefs, 130-

Index

statutes, 342-43; on Missouri game-warden case, 344-45

Holmes, Justice, quotations from his writings, 5-6, 7-8, 9-10, 12, 17, 43, 64-65, 70-71, 71-72, 117-18, 118-19, 120-24, 128-29, 131, 136-37, 137-38, 141, 142-43, 144, 147, 148-49, 149, 150, 151, 152-53, 154-55, 157, 160, 161, 163-65, 165-66, 167-68, 170, 173-76, 176-78, 179-83, 184-86, 188-89, 191, 198-99, 200, 202, 203-5, 205-7, 208, 209, 210-11, 212, 213, 214, 215, 216, 217-18, 220, 221-24, 225, 226-29, 229, 230, 231, 233-34, 236-38, 239, 240, 241, 242, 247-48, 256-58, 262-63, 264-66, 273-74, 287, 288-89, 292-93, 294, 295-96, 298, 301, 302, 306, 311-12, 313-14, 318-19, 324, 325-26, 328, 331-32, 333, 341, 342-43, 346, 350

Honorable Society of Lincoln's Inn, 315

Hooker, Gen. Joseph, 112

Hoover, President, 21, 284, 324

Howells, William Dean, 33, 34, 65, 263

Hughes, Chief Justice Charles Evans, 21, 254, 279, 316; on Justice Holmes, 320-22, 322-23, 324, 331, 332-34

Hughes, Thomas, 134

Hunt, Dr. William, 100

Inferno—Dante, 354

Innocents Abroad—Mark Twain, 315

International Mark Twain Society, 315

Interstate Commerce Commission, 259

Jackson, President, 253

Jackson, Gen. Stonewall, 93, 96, 109, 112

James, Henry, 35, 61, 65, 140

James, William, 35, 36, 57-61, 63, 65, 127, 140, 141, 147, 163, 349

Jay, Chief Justice John, 340

Jefferson, President Thomas, 338, 339, 341

Jay Treaty, 338

Johnston, Forney, 10-11

Johnston, Gen. Joseph E., 91

Journal of the American Bar Assn., 316

Jowitt, Sir William A., 316, 335

Keats, John, 314

Kent, Chancellor, 347

Kent's *Commentaries*, 13, 139, 155

King, Clarence, 70

Knowlton, Judge, 187, 188, 189, 192, 194, 205, 226, 233

Knox, Philander C., 255, 256

La Farge, John, 70

LaFayette, Marquis de, 337

Lamar, Justice L. Q. C., 279, 281

Lamb, Charles, 265

Lander, Brig.-Gen., 85

Langdell, Professor, 142

Larcom, Lucy, 305

Laski, Harold J., 151, 307, 315, 335-36

Lathrop, Justice John, 178, 192, 194, 226

law, Justice Holmes's views on—*See* Holmes, Justice

Lawrence, Bishop William, 139

Lee, Fitzhugh, 68

Lee, Gen. Robert E., 91, 93, 95, 96, 98

Lee, Brig.-Gen. Wm. R., 73, 75, 77, 79, 83, 85, 90, 94, 95, 108, 109, 116

Let Freedom Ring—Hayes, 311

Libby Prison, 85

Life and Letters of Oliver Wendell Holmes—Morse, 24, 65, 140

Lincoln, President, 21, 24, 95, 114, 347

Lippmann, Walter, 22

Literary Friends and Acquaintances—Howells, 33

Llewellyn, Karl N., 146, 156-57

Lloyd George's 1909 budget, 252

Lodge, Henry Cabot, 246, 248, 249, 254, 262, 311

Long, Gov. John Davis, 162, 170

Longfellow, H. W., 33, 34, 57

Lord, Justice Otis P., 162

Lowell, Pres. A. Lawrence, 281, 284

Lowell, Brig.-Gen. Charles Russell, 114, 119

Lowell Institute lectures by Holmes, 139, 165, 170

Lowell, James Russell, 26, 33, 34, 63, 134, 162

Lurton, Justice Horace H., 270, 279

Lycidas—Milton, 319

Macintosh, Dr. Douglas Clyde, 331, 332

Macy, Major-Gen. George N., 75, 80, 81, 83, 84

Madison, President, 338, 339

Main Currents in American Thought—Parrington, 29, 30

Index

Maine, Sir Henry J. S., 135, 159
Maitland, Frederick W., 135, 171
Malthusian theory, 17, 66
Malvern Hill, 95
Manitzky, Capt. Gustave, 118-19
Mansfield, Lord, 165
Marshall, Chief Justice John, 22, 247, 248, 249, 253, 254, 267, 290, 304, 335ff.; career, 337ff.; compared with Holmes, 335-54
Marx, Karl, 69
Mason, Capt. Herbert C., 115
Massachusetts Law Quarterly, 10
Mass. Supreme Court—*See* Supreme Judicial Court of Massachusetts
Mather, Increase, 62
McAdoo, Wm. G.—*Reminiscences*, 285
McClellan, Gen. George B., 82, 88, 91, 98, 106, 108, 113, 114
McKenna, Justice Joseph, 269, 270, 296
McKinley, President, 249, 250, 269
McReynolds, Justice, 300, 324, 328, 329
Mediaeval Latin Lyrics, 319
Melville, Herman, 50
Mill, John Stuart, 12, 134
Miller, Justice Samuel Freeman, 21
Milnes, Richard Monckton, 67
Milton, John, 319
Minnesota gag-law case, 348
Moby Dick, 50
Modjeska, Mme., 63
Monopolies and competition, 256-261
Montesquieu, 151, 196, 300
Moody, Justice William H., 270
Morgan, J. P., Sr., 255, 256, 259, 277, 278
Morison, Samuel Eliot, 53
Morse, Miss Frances, 141
Morse, John T., Jr., 24, 25, 65, 140
Morse, Robert M., 135
Morton, Justice Marcus, 178, 192, 194, 205, 226
Motley, John Lothrop, 34, 74, 134
Mr. Justice Holmes—Frankfurter, *Ed.*, 316
Munroe, William A., 136
"My Hunt After the Captain"—Holmes, 100, 119

New England industries, 39-40
Northern Securities Case—*See* cases
Norton, Charles Eliot, 34, 86

Origin of Species, 65
Otis, James, 173, 174
Our Hundred Days in Europe, 134

Paine, Thomas, 337
Palfrey, Brig.-Gen. F. W., 75, 85, 94, 95, 96, 109
Parker, Dean Joel, 130
Parker, Scollay, 57
Parker, Theodore, 27, 28, 41, 42, 45
Parkman, Francis, 35, 65
Parrington, Vernon Louis, 29, 30, 31
Parsons, Theophilus, 174
Pater, Walter, quoted, 4
Patmore, Coventry, 265
Patten, Brig.-Gen. Henry L., 75
Peabody, Robert S., 57
Peckham, Justice Wheeler H., 251, 256, 270, 271, 279
Peirce, Charles S., 34, 163
Peirson, Brig.-Gen. Charles L., 75
Pepys's *Dairy*, 304
Perry, Thomas Sergeant, 65
Phillips, Wendell, 26-27, 29, 33, 162
Pickering, Henry, 56
Pitney, Justice, 290, 292, 293
Plucknett, Theodore F. T., 316
Poe, Edgar Allan, 24
Poet at the Breakfast Table, The, 29
Political Science Quarterly, The, 18
Pollock, Sir Frederick, 134, 135, 159-60, 311, 312, 315, 316
Pollock and Maitland's *History of English Law*, 135
Populist party, 193
Pound, Dean Roscoe, 316
Prescott, William Hickling, 34
Prudentius, 319
Puritanism, 49, 52, 53, 54-55
Putnam, Capt. J. C., 89, 109
Putnam, William Lowell, 85, 86

Rabelais, 18
Randolph, John, 339
Reedy, William Marion, 28
Representative Opinions of Mr. Justice Holmes, 272
Revere, Brig.-Gen. Paul J., 75, 76, 85, 90, 95, 116
Rhodes, James Ford, 65
Ricardo, 12, 146

Index